British Theatre in the Great War

British Theatre in the Great War

A Revaluation

Gordon Williams

Continuum
The Tower Building, 11 York Road, London, SE1 7NX
15 East 26th Street, New York, NY 10010

First published 2003
Paperback edition first published 2005

British Library Cataloguing-in-Publication Data
A catalogue record for this book is available from the British Library.

ISBN 0-8264-5635-9 (hardback)
ISBN 0-8264-7882-4 (paperback)

Library of Congress Cataloging-in-Publication Data
Williams, Gordon, 1935–
British theatre in the Great War: a revaluation / Gordon Williams.
p. cm.
Includes bibliographical references and index.
ISBN 0-8264-5635-9
1. Theater—Great Britain—History—20th century. 2. Performing arts—Great Britain—History—20th century. 3. World War, 1914–1918—Theater and the war. I. Title.

PN2595.W515 2003
792'.0941'09041—dc21

2003055330

Typeset by BookEns Ltd, Royston, Herts.
Printed and bound in Great Britain by Biddles Ltd, King's Lynn, Norfolk

Contents

Prefatory note

Names have been rendered throughout as they existed at the start of the war. Thus Hermann, rather than Herman, Klein; Edward Knoblauch, rather than Knoblock (except in the Select Bibliography); and the hyphenating of Martin Harvey, which coincided with his post-war knighthood, is ignored.

Journal articles in *Era*, *Stage*, and the like, when signed, are cited with just the surnames of the following writers: E. A. Baughan, Henry Belcham, Sydney W. Carroll, Herbert Farjeon, West F. deWend Fenton, James Glover, Arnold Golsworthy ('Jingle'), J. T. Grein, John Francis Hope, Mabel Koopman, Samuel Langford, S. R. Littlewood ('Agravaine'), H. Bernard Marks ('Tristram'), H. W. Massingham, H. Chance Newton ('Carados'), Fred Russell, Walter Terry ('Pilgrim').

London is omitted from details of books published there, and where theatre names have no place appended they are in central London. The abbreviations 'p.p.' and 'n.d.' are used in bibliographical sources that are privately published and have no date, respectively, whilst references with dates in square brackets mean that they were originally undated but the dates have been verified.

'Met' and 'Rep' are used for the Metropolitan Opera and repertory theatres habitually referred to in that shorthand form; BNOC, WNOC (respectively British and Welsh National Opera Company); DORA (Defence of the Realm Act). Some abbreviations are obvious: WW2 (World War Two); MP (Member of Parliament). Others are military commonplaces: Lt (Lieutenant), DCM (Distinguished Conduct Medal), DSO (Distinguished Service Order), MC, VC (Military/Victoria Cross), RAMC (Royal Army Medical Corps), RFC (Royal Flying Corps), VAD (Voluntary Aid Detachment personnel), POW (prisoner of war). There are professional organizations and publications: AMU (Amalgamated Musicians' Union), NOA (National Orchestras' Association), VAF (Variety Artistes' Federation); *SYB* (*'Stage' Year Book*).

The reference LC, followed by numbers, alludes to playscripts submitted to the Lord Chamberlain, and now housed in the British Library Department of

Manuscripts. Although an extensive sampling has been taken of these scripts, my interest in them is primarily for what they reveal of theatrical conditions and practice. Quite as revealing of these things are contemporary reviews, which have been drawn upon heavily. The critics' response, of course, is not identical with public response, and an interventionist rôle is frequently adopted. The critic's position between theatrical product and its public is as much dialectical as mediatory.

In memory of 67514
Dvr G. W., RFA,
who had little enough time for theatre-going in 1914–18

1

Introduction

A character in a 1917 comedy jokes that 12 August 1914, the day that Britain declared war on Austria-Hungary, was also the start of the grouse-shooting season.[1] Declaration of war on Germany had its coincidences, too: Marie Lloyd returned triumphant to the London stage after an American tour; and Sarah Bernhardt, at the Coliseum, was improbably singing 'Everybody's Doing It', an unconscious parody of *Entente Cordiale*.[2] One mock attempt to explain the war reads like Swiftian caustic irony: 'The Germans are trying to capture Gaby Deslys and we're trying not to let them.'[3] Gaby being revue's highest-paid star, this points to the ferocious trade rivalry which was damaging both theatre and nations, as well as acknowledging the primacy of revue in Britain's wartime theatre. The war began with the tango and ended with the shimmy, a dance with similar ethnic roots. The tango found its way from the brothels of Buenos Aires to the absinthe dens of the European capitals. At one such den in Ball and Leybold's 'Ein und Kein Frühlingsgedicht' a tango-tart is knifed, while from every bottle scream nightmare biplanes: alcoholic delirium or *in vino veritas*, placing this amongst the many Expressionist poems foretelling holocaust.[4] Meanwhile '1914 – the wild tango year' (so called by the Prime Minister's daughter[5]) found London's fashionable young simulating spasmodic lust at their tango teas. They appear 'frivolling and dancing the tango' at the start of Knoblauch and Hicks's sketch 'England Expects' before news of Louvain's desecration arrives to give their primal urges another focus: another, less ambiguous, dance of death.[6]

Even here there is a hint that the customary dismissal of wartime theatre as merely frivolous is too facile. This view has been encouraged by the dominance of revue, the stage image of the war's febrile excitements. It is supremely the theatre of that machine age which the war so garishly advertised. Not being strongly text-based, it suffers extremely from that assessment on the basis of unsuitable literary criteria which bedevils a good deal of theatrical criticism. Another factor which has helped to mask the extent to which 'serious' theatre throve in the war years is the tendency to treat opera as something outside theatre proper. For, as Newton observed towards the end of the war, 'stimulating, original, and memorable things' had been happening not on the legitimate stage but in 'opera, in the variety theatre, and in revue'.[7]

In some ways the war years represent one of the most exciting half-decades in British twentieth-century theatre. One striking development was noted by Henry Belcham when he claimed, with pardonable exaggeration, that the war had seen practically everyone becoming a playgoer.[8] Theatre cannot be evaluated properly apart from audiences, and in the sense that playgoing had 'become an integral part of national life',[9] this was a theatrical golden age. Factors which threatened to jeopardize the industry in fact produced a boom, and disposed of much anti-theatrical prejudice. Theatres filled as unemployment vanished, and many lower-class people had their spending power boosted by current labour needs.[10] Nor were the gainers only the established providers of artisan entertainment. Distinctions were blurring as the regular theatre's adoption of revue 'was countered ... by the presentation of full-length plays in music-halls', and notable figures of both variety and legitimate stage moved ever more freely between the two.[11] But such change drew a testy retrospect from Huntly Carter, who remembered wartime theatre stagnating on 'revues, musical comedies and other bare flesh stuff' provided 'for the edification of the vast new audience of war-workers'.[12]

His anxiety is as much social as aesthetic. 'Up in the North,' cooed one society columnist, 'there's such prosperity that at the theatres it's the best seats that are filled and the cheapest left empty, while the young women of the working-classes who now "conduct" the trams and 'buses take stalls and boxes [casually] asking officers of the New Army they'd never seen before to come along as their guests!'[13] That working girls should become theatre-goers, flirting with officers in some of the better seats, was viewed with tolerant amusement by those who accepted things outside nature for 'the duration', like the socialism which had become necessary to the war effort but would be repudiated with the Armistice. Besides, aberrations were to be expected the further one moved from the metropolis. London set the standards, not least in the theatre. Even artists like Florrie Forde, who were based elsewhere, found it desirable to venture occasionally to the capital. And Jewish-American entertainer Myron Gilday, who considered the London practice of rushing from hall to hall too frantic, especially since in London he and his partner received 'less than half the salary we can get in the provinces', was still seen there quite often.[14]

Likewise, most of what was significant originated in London, 'The ring of West-End theatres [being] still – despite various provincial emulants – the producing centre.'[15] The West End effectively dictated the dominance of light fare throughout the provinces, only the stronger centres of repertory theatre having the power of resistance. Although many people accepted that this dominance was a result of the war, the assumption was persuasively challenged by 'Lancelot': 'public desire for bright entertainments, with intensity, significance, and humour [and] distaste for the ponderous, the dull, and the artificial' had been growing for years. The war simply meant that 'appreciation of the light side of sentiment is no longer apologised for; its cleverness is realised'. If too much of the mindless variety appeared, that was because managements frequently underrated their audiences.[16]

William Archer took a sourer view of audiences, finding the spectacle of officers taking wives or sweethearts, 'on the last evening they may ever spend together, to a piece of garish and cynical inanity, humiliating alike to our national and to our personal self-respect'.[17] Amongst other things, Archer fails to acknowledge that the play, however important, is but one part in the totality of that social event of going to the theatre. His inability to put himself in the young soldier's place is remedied by Milton Hayes, himself an officer as well as only begetter of 'The Green Eye of the Little Yellow God'. According to Hayes, what 'may sound silly to a man when he's by himself sounds very different when he's with his best girl [which] is why a play like *Romance* seems so bad to the critic. He's gone there by himself, when he should have gone there with a girl.'[18] The couples he envisages may have their experience shaped by a private and intimate relationship. But they also contribute to and participate in that overall atmosphere which belongs to the theatre. If pre-war audiences had their attention divided, especially on first nights, by such pastimes as 'lorgnetting the nobs'[19] (by no means extinct in the wartime theatre), now there was a khaki as well as a society presence to provide a distraction. And this, like the other, proved an asset to managements even at concessionary rates of admission. For four years Britain was 'a sort of clearing house for armies on their way to and from the Continent', a good proportion finding its way into the theatres.[20] The scale of this khaki presence even generated the hypocrisy 'that the chief reason, nowadays, for keeping open our places of amusement is to provide some relaxation for our sailors and soldiers'. 'We have kept going for them,' declares George Robey, 'because they taught us that amusements taught them, for a few hours, to forget.'[21] The real story is told by the squalid controversy over camp theatres, introduced belatedly in 1917 and immediately resented for diverting some of the khaki trade from the commercial theatre.

Even while servicemen were indispensable not only to fill the house but to instil the right spirit or atmosphere, they demonstrated that the so-called levelling effect of war is yet another myth. Shows specifically provided for troops, sometimes wounded, all too often had 'well-dressed and apparently prosperous civilians occupying the front seats, and the Tommies relegated to the rear'. The latter, it was insisted 'should have the best seats – indeed, *all* the seats'.[22] But Mabel Koopman, noting that special matinées had been 'the big thing' of 1915, offers a different gloss on seating arrangements for the wounded. 'At first they were accorded the seats of honour – the front rows of the stalls or the dress circle – but it soon became manifest that they were not at home in the "seats of the mighty" and although they ate the teas and pocketed the cigarettes and chocolates showered on them by the well-meaning, they did so silently, almost morosely, and attempts at conversation met with no success.'[23] Just how crass these attempts might be is suggested by Landon Ronald's account of a 'great lady' at Wandsworth Hospital telling 'a Tommy, she hoped he'd soon be better, as he must be just longing to get back to the front'.[24] It was doubtless in relief at escaping such attention, rather than because they knew their place, that the wounded were happiest in the pit or gallery, laughing and making 'direct comments, to the huge delight of the rest of the house'. Evidently they were part of the entertainment for fashionable matinée audiences, Koopman remembering 'the laughter and applause that greeted the remark of a soldier, with much bandaged head' at a charity performance of Jerome K. Jerome's *Three Patriots*: 'Two old friends, one English, the other German, have met, both wounded, in a cowshed "somewhere in France," and the Englishman, chipping his old pal, tells him, "You beggars can't shoot straight." From the pit came a voice full of simple, deep feeling, "Don't you believe it." He had had some, poor dear, he *knew*.'[25]

As a significant economic factor, servicemen had their impact on the structure of shows. Camp curfews, making early performances desirable, helped to spread the twice-nightly system to the playhouse from the halls.[26] Whether they had much impact on the content of shows is more doubtful. They were frequently credited with a good deal: 'How often had we heard the remark from a man on leave, "Take us to something to make us laugh, but for heaven's sake don't take us to a war play".'[27] This kind of hearsay encouraged the critics to use the soldier as stalking horse for their own pet dislikes. Allegedly he had 'no time for experimental drama', for problem or war plays, and certainly not for 'the pornographic revue'. Thus does an *Era* leader (22 March 1916, p. 15) endorse prevailing practice in the commercial theatre, where it was the stall occupant, not the bob-a-day soldier, who paid the piper and therefore called the tune. Another page (11) signals the futility of generalizing about the millions in this citizen army with an RAMC lieutenant's claim that 'the higher class the concert or show, the more it is appreciated by Mr. Tommy Atkins'. Lena Ashwell, with more experience than most, corroborates this. Those participating in her 'Concerts at the Front' programme were speedily rid of preconceptions that soldiers' artistic horizons were limited to ragtime and 'trivial comedies',[28] discovering with Thomas Beecham that wartime tastes, when escaping commercial pressures, became 'graver, simpler, and more concentrated'. And Beecham, like Harrison Frewin, emphasizes the importance of the khaki element in wartime opera audiences.[29] If in Britain's cities it was opera which principally catered for a taste in serious theatre this was not, as might have been urged in pre-war days, because opera audiences were a breed apart from ordinary playgoers. Rather it was because those supplying it were not dominated by considerations of profit. They were thus able to give opera a broad appeal, demonstrating that there was an extensive market for serious theatre, and that it was not dependent on stars.

Neither point caught the attention of commercial managements. H. W. Massingham lamented the dominance of an 'empty form' of theatre which reduced the play to a frame for its star.[30] When Massingham's opponents claimed that he and his fellows improperly enmeshed art with politics, their politics are equally transparent: John Francis Hope hailed 'the revival of the "star"' because it marked 'the supercession of the repertory theatre movement' along with 'dramatic reformers' like Granville Barker. Their reform, he complains, 'was not dramatic, but democratic; its inspiration was political, not artistic; and the denial of the artistic value of the "star" was only a perverted expression of the denial of the real existence of great men'.[31] He proceeds to invoke the war, which is not especially intelligent since it reminds where 'great men' are apt to lead us; as Massingham puts it, 'the State and the Stage are equally in the hands of the Philistines'. But it was not the war which generated this new phase in star-besottedness and the accompanying manic rise in salaries. America was the main driving force, especially in the cinema industry once player anonymity had been breached. The figure itself was an advertising ploy when it was leaked that 15-year-old Mary Miles Minter was receiving £20,000 a year; though Robey shrugged it off by claiming to get considerably more.[32] The situation was particularly bad in the halls, where cut-throat competition for the likes of Robey perpetuated a system generally acknowledged to be deeply damaging. The boosting of a limited number of artists was a useful marketing gambit; one which led to exaggerated effects on takings, as an action against Little Tich for alleged breach of contract made clear. Receipts averaging £300 or £400 a week were pushed to £509 by Wilkie Bard, £520 by Vesta Tilley and £718 by Marie Lloyd.[33]

Marks deplored the fierce bidding 'for the half-dozen (or less) stars who are worth more than a hundred pounds a week' in terms of their drawing power, but failed to recognize that often the drawing power was based less on art than on marketing.[34] As dramatist Frank Stayton said of the regular theatre, 'Success is boomed and merit ignored.'[35] Yet whereas Marks saw the explosion of revue giving many variety artists the opportunities for which they had hungered, only to find them wanting,[36] 'Extra Turn' frequently championed the 'talent to be found in the less "swanky" London halls', which the 'big managers' ignored. For him, 'The critic who takes his key from the salary list is not worth his salt'; and of Austin Rudd he wrote impatiently, 'One of these days I shall drag de Courville and Cochran, and Butt and Rolls and Charlot by the scruffs of their necks to some hall where Rudd is scoring his ruddy success – and then I shall watch them all scrambling with contracts.' His talent-spotting was evidently sharp enough: Little Mary was elevated to the Coliseum soon after his protest that if she 'had descended upon London with her wonderful globe-trotting and drapery-manipulating in a Russian ballet, all London, including the most elevated high-brow, would have gone crazy over her'.[37]

The star system was only one factor in soaring production costs: big business, which now controlled theatrical output, was 'sky-rocketing theatre-rents and squeezing out the "small man"'.[38] By the Armistice, the Strand and the Duke of York's were fetching £360 a week, when the former had cost just £30 a few years before; and it was rumoured that the producers of *Charley's Aunt* were to pay £400 for the Garrick.[39] Independent operation became hardly feasible in the West End, and with the disappearance of the old-style actor-manager went his specializing tendencies. That the sombre '*Damaged Goods* should have immediately succeeded the revue *Houp-la* at the St. Martin's' typified the 'lack of direction and continuity' which followed from money-chasing.

The war had accelerated rather than initiated the process. Mrs Herbert Cohen's complaint while presiding at the Lyceum Club's Dramatic Section dinner, that it was a theatre 'enslaved by commercialism, which was responsible for the plays of a fluffy nature, played by fluffy casts', echoed pre-war controversy over the purpose of the theatre. Against this commercialism, wartime restrictions had scant effect: fuel-saving regulations still saw the theatre better lit than it had been for the previous generation, and 10.30 p.m. closing was not imposed until 2 April 1918. Most controversial of all was the imposition of an entertainment tax which came into force on 15 May 1916. The original surcharges ranged from ½d. to 1s., and it was complained that whereas twopenny seats carried a tax burden of 25 per cent, for a 12s. 6d. stall it was only 8 per cent and for a £1 box a mere 6 per cent.[40] The concern was not with the unfairness – governments regularly discriminate against the poor in their systems of taxation[41] – but because it was likely to exclude a section of the public from theatre-going. On the other hand, some called for a flat rate: 'The expensive seat is in itself a tax upon class.'[42]

Amidst all the bickering, the only real casualty of wartime singlemindedness, a theatre which challenges conventional ideas or social iniquities, passed virtually unremarked. There seems to have been little need of DORA, section 27, to discourage questioning of the government's war policies. Yet here again, mainstream endorsement of current orthodoxies was nothing new. The point is made in *Era* leaders, along with promotion of wartime theatre 'as a diverting and distracting agency', a favourite idea now that it had become less awkward to declare what people must be distracted from. One leader treats the arts as 'an end in themselves', troublesomely close to seeing life as one thing and art as another. Now that priorities had shifted from 'increasing the enjoyment of life' to extinguishing it, the arts had 'to take a back seat ... Their function is not to render life more intense, but to make it tolerable.'[43] This is not only a terrible indictment of war, but a depressingly reductive view of art. Nothing may be expected of it: 'Both playwrights and actors must be merely "marking time" and waiting for better days.' The prospect of art coming into its own again after the war would do nothing for the millions of Europe's dead; and probably not too much for the millions more left to grieve. But an earlier leader uses Tree's remark 'that the drama had replaced vodka in the economy of Russian life' to warn that closing Britain's theatres would produce a nation of drunkards, since people in these trying times need 'respite from the torture of thought'. This time there is no contrasting of pre-war and present theatrical possibilities. Evidently the play as sedative rather than stimulant is not just a wartime phenomenon: 'All that the theatre asks is to be allowed to go on its way, performing the functions it has always performed, of soothing tired brains and resting hearts from their aches awhile.' Certainly this is no 'time for "war-plays." The reality is too near us; the actual facts are so close as to make a mimic representation border dangerously on caricature. The playgoer goes to the theatre not to be reminded of current events, but to be helped to forget them for a few hours.'[44]

But there is a good deal of wavering about war plays, too. That soldiers were supposed not to like them merely concealed unease that to represent war on a legitimate stage dominated by naturalistic convention risked jeopardizing official policy and public morale. War implies death; and at a time which was reeking with it, death was thought inappropriate theatrical fare. Jesse and Harwood's lightweight and witty *Billeted* earned censure through its heroine's feigning to be a widow: 'I do not think that at the moment the general public is in the mood to listen to jokes on the subject of death, real or pretended; and it is a little surprising to find the astute management of the Royalty Theatre overlooking such a cardinal condition of the time.'[45] As Phyllis Bottome wrote, for 'complacent audiences', death was the 'only uncertainty', requiring to be 'hidden behind the baffling insincerities of doctors and nurses'.[46] When Maud Allan performed Ase's Death from Grieg's *Peer Gynt* Suite at the Pavilion, one reviewer, while admiring her 'beauty and grace', doubted 'whether a dance which is intended to suggest the emotions of a dying woman is quite the most appropriate for a popular audience'.[47] Contrariwise, when Tree adapted *Trilby* for the halls, that he allowed Trilby to recover at the end showed 'correct appreciation of what is most effective on the variety stage'.[48] That just pre-war Hollywood had helped to keep the normal patterns of death at bay by imposing the happy ending hints at a dialectical relationship between Tinsel Town's mass culture and the mass slaughter on the Western Front: explosive conjunction of new markets and new technology. With death on the battlefield sublimated by ideas of honour and glory, not even the Indian Mutiny or the American Civil War sufficiently distanced cinema's representations of the grim reality: witness reactions to the Broadway film *The Campbells Are Coming* and to Griffith's *Birth of a Nation*, the latter 'certainly a sermon against the fearful horrors of war. Whether Europe can stand its awful details is another matter.'[49] As for direct representation of the Western Front, one interned officer protested that no 'real man' would 'describe the revolting details of life out there', and attempts 'to lay before the public a true, unvarnished account of modern warfare are an offence against D.O.R.A.'[50] However, when the Liverpool police acted against the exhibition of *A Patriot of France* for showing 'the morbid side of the war, … independent witnesses said the picture would stimulate recruiting' and the summons was dismissed.[51] The live theatre, too, seizing opportunities for vilifying the Hun, gestured towards the theatre of cruelty in progress across the Channel. At the Rotherham Hippodrome scenes of German atrocity were transferred to England, and one fat lady became so incensed by a German officer's brutalizing of women that it took three attendants to restrain her 'from rushing up on the stage and assaulting the villain'.[52] Marks 'frequently warned managers against inflicting such things upon the public. It is never wise to harrow the feelings of audiences at a time when so many have such deep cause for anxiety and sorrow.' So it was with a certain grim satisfaction that he related how a war play at a provincial variety theatre 'aroused such a feeling of revulsion that some of the women present shrieked in protest. One woman went into hysterics and fainted.' When assistance was summoned, the 'strain and excitement' was too much for one ambulance man, who 'dropped dead'.[53]

Split-mindedness also showed in the Lord Chamberlain's rulings; but inconsistencies were resolved by an overriding concern with patriotism. The *New Statesman* (27 June 1914, p. 359) had taken the view that by maintaining 'an anomalous, stupid, and quite arbitrary censorship, the State implicitly declares that the drama does not really matter'. It declares just the opposite. That flurry of colourful epithets obscures a censorship clearly alive to theatre's power to affect thought and behaviour, and determined to use it in an interested way. And beyond the Lord Chamberlain was a second line manned by critics and local authorities.[54] Not only the stage but its personnel fell under scrutiny. In many cases the LCC's Theatres and Music Halls Committee 'recommended that applications for licences should be refused because the applicant was of military age'.[55] In pre-conscription days actors were bribed, cajoled and above all coerced (the simplest means being to refuse them engagements) into joining the colours. Companies were formed consisting entirely of members of the profession, like that of the 19th London Regiment: 'DON'T HESITATE – the quickest way of filling your date-book for some months. The Spring is coming, and with it fine weather – when soldiering is a pleasure. You can really play The Man on the greatest stage in the world in the *greatest* theatre in the world.'[56] However, John Warr, in an astonishingly frank article, indicates that managements would have been less co-operative in pushing eligible men from the stage if replacements had not been to hand.[57] Those disliking the chorus against shirkers, he says, keep quiet 'lest they be branded as "traitors" to their country'. But if accusations of cowardice have foundation, he asks, 'where could there exist a better reason for not going?' Naturally the legitimacy of the fear motive was not allowed; and it is difficult to gauge the extent to which conscience money came into play. The music-hall artist Apollo (W. Bankier), claiming home responsibilities, sought this route: while managers continued to book him, he would live on the equivalent of a private's pay, distributing his £100 a week amongst the dependants of 100 men willing to enlist.[58] (It is not the attempt at evasion but the implicit social tiering which renders such moves repugnant.) Godfrey Tearle, receiving the white feather treatment, asserted both the actor's unsuitability for fighting and his New York birth before being harried into a gunner cadetship.[59] Others were subjected to persistent attack in the popular press as well as on stage.[60] Disclaimers about liability in theatre programmes were treated cynically; and abuse was directed indiscriminately at dischargees and rejects. It was groups of subalterns who interrupted the turns of a musician who wore DSO and MC ribbons under his lapel and of Clarkson Rose, rejected with defective lungs.[61] Allegedly touring players took advantage of having no fixed address, and Nottingham's chief recruiting officer complained about 'a lot of trouble with music hall people'.[62] Thus raids on theatres following conscription were directed at shirkers on stage as well as in the audience. In the later phase of the war audiences showed resentment when performers appeared in a uniform which they had never worn in earnest, just as earlier they had expressed displeasure at seeing on stage anyone they thought should be in uniform. It was said of *The Lads of the Village* at the Oxford: 'It is something of an achievement at this stage to make khaki in the stalls laugh heartily at the jollity of khaki behind the footlights.' But most of those on stage had been at the front, several of them wearing the DCM ribbon on their tunics.[63]

Times were sensitive, then, and the profession had good reason for publicizing the extent to which it was doing its bit in and out of uniform.[64] Nevertheless, the endless self-congratulation could prove nauseating, one weekly including an example in its column of 'current cant': 'Eight of our favourite actresses tell us how the stage is helping the war along.'[65] A better instance would have been Lena Ashwell's claim that no other profession (apparently not even the military or medical) 'has done so much in the present war'.[66] But on the whole the industry's formidable publicity machine worked well, despite controversial moments such as 'wounded soldiers "booing" a band that was not present' at Reading Barracks. After devoting many Saturday afternoons to free concerts at the barracks, members of the Palace Theatre orchestra raised the question of remuneration with the AMU, which forbade them to perform without pay. *Era* (29 December 1915, p. 16) deplored this withholding of pleasure from the wounded warriors without acknowledging that while it was no hardship for the indefatigable Robey (soon to be hitting £500 a week) to be generous, for musicians earning £2 or less it was another matter. Besides, *Era*'s viewpoint shifts with circumstance. Earlier (21 October 1914, p. 9), when there was a danger of amateurs providing for the Tommy, a leader endorsed the principle of all entertainment being paid for.

At this distance we may find irony in the way that artists who so wholeheartedly helped to cheer up the Great War Tommy were a few years later entertaining troops used to break the General Strike.[67] The Kaiser's army or British workers had become indistinguishably the enemy, just as the worker who dons khaki is transformed from potential dissident to protector of wealth and property. During the war it was aptly said that 'members of the profession very rightly rank themselves with the privileged classes in their untiring exertions on behalf of every conceivable war fund'.[68] But there were other interests at work besides commitment to the cause. For one thing, glamorous charity matinées gave ample scope to indulge that strange propensity for being patronized by the great.[69] A typical example at the St James's was obviously a good self-advertising bet: 'The audience will include many distinguished people, and as ... all the foremost actors and actresses are giving their services, it will undoubtedly be *the* thing to go to.'[70] Above all, performers were impelled by anxiety about mounting pressure for theatres to be closed. Those who felt that entertainment was inappropriate in those dark days gave a new credibility to surviving prejudices against all manner of theatrical activity. But although there were no lasting effects such as wartime conditions allowed the anti-drink bigots to achieve, the dangers were real enough; bigotry could easily translate into wartime emergency measures.[71]

But the government was far too conscious of what it was gaining from the theatres ever to contemplate closing them. Even if they served as no more than a national recuperative force, their contribution would have been substantial.[72] But that was only their starting point. The halls had the greatest reputation for jingoistic activity; and their very style of performance contributed. What distinguished this style from that of the regular theatre was 'exuberance of action, breadth and unlimited assurance'. This 'Elizabethan robustness' was thought to demonstrate 'how simple and honest a people we are, and how much we dislike subtlety'.[73] Things could be less happy when indirection yielded to abstract pageantry. An early instance at the Alhambra found Britannia and her allied counterparts receiving customary homage from 'shapely ladies in uniform. Now, if our music halls had any sense of symbolism, which is, after all, their real business, something very dramatic might have appeared to stir every heart in the house.' Alas, instead of 'Belgium, stained and stricken and unconquered, stagger[ing] on the stage with a broken shield', she appeared 'spotless, neat, and smiling'.[74]

The regular theatre, too, supplied fulsome rhetoric. On the fourth anniversary of the declaration of war, the Prime Minister chose to use every theatre for the promulgation of his message to 'Hold fast!' At the Queen's it was leading man Percy Hutchison, a naval officer here playing a naval officer, who in the interval adopted the statesman's mantle and received hearty cheers for his 'inspiriting message'.[75] For Newton, Lloyd George's move supplied 'a charter of the theatre's liberties, dignity, and usefulness. It meant that the theatre is no longer "out of bounds." It recognised the theatre as a vantage-ground upon which, since the people cannot all go to the Premier, the Premier can go to all the people.'[76] It set the seal on the theatre's wartime agitational rôle. Governments will not normally encourage mobs to take to the streets; but in the early stages of the war this was approximately what was required. If hitherto the theatre had contributed little enough towards producing a juster society, it now played a conspicuous part in creating a warmongering one; and in the most direct way it turned many young men from civilians into soldiers. As so often, people were led by a thick-textured orchestration of propaganda completely against their own interests. Every devious trick was used to secure recruits; and at the same time Martin Harvey spent time on his theatrical tours to proclaim that voluntarism demonstrated Britain's moral superiority over Germany.[77] At a recruiting concert in Lambeth an appeal was made for women to release their men, a pretty girl earning 'tremendous applause' when she 'ungrudgingly' handed over her boyfriend like a sacrificial goat.[78] One woman recalled the callousness of those flapper days: 'I expect the men we knew were often terribly frightened, but of course they never said so, and we didn't think about it very much.'[79] Both on stage and in the street, actors used their powerful 'persuasive eloquence and personality' for the purpose of 'gathering in men'.[80] As they made their impassioned pleas, it is idle to speculate where performance ended. Some, in spite of themselves, must have been carried away by their own rhetoric, while others would have been like that Parisian performer whose ardent patriotism was said to be assumed like any other rôle as a means of earning a living.[81] There is a revealing passage in a piece of pulp fiction dating from before the war and set in Yucatan. The hero is coached in the way to deliver a full-blooded recruiting speech: 'Pitch it in strong! Shedding de blood for de country; facing fire and sword for de children's sakes.' The voice must be raised, then lowered 'to a thrilling whisper', aided by a discreet sob.[82] The hero successfully follows this advice; and since he is an honourable, not to say an Oxford, man, the reader is not invited to have reservations. That actor-recruiters worked in the war with similar calculation is evident from Leo Dryden's account of a meeting wrecked by the obtrusion of reality: he adopted his customary 'cheerful tone', whereas a fellow-speaker's 'continual references to the "horrors of modern warfare", "young wives being widowed", "widows losing their only support", "children being orphaned", &c., drove the people from the building long before the recruiting sergeant could get to work'.[83]

The theatre itself provided the ideal environment, a place where audiences felt comfortable and relaxed. New décor contributed. George Sackman's act-drop for the Victoria Palace depicted the celebrated Stirrup Charge of Greys and Gordons, and another house was still more blatant: 'This is the safety curtain of this theatre. The men of England are the safety curtain that shields our country from death and worse than death. Are you part of that khaki safety curtain? If not, why not?'[84] A placard at each entrance to the Pavilion thanked patrons for past favour, but urged those of suitable age 'to go and enlist before coming in'.[85] But it was more convenient to collapse distinctions, so that while Knoblauch and Hicks's *England Expects* was playing there, the London Opera House became 'a recruiting office', the War Office arranging for the daily attendance of recruiting officers and doctors.[86] Reality and performance merged: audiences were assigned a rôle in the action, and no marginal one. But for all this spillage over the footlights, authority remained on stage; young men were provoked into participating in an action which promised danger, though it was represented in exhilarating guise, the realities masked by images of glory and adventure. In this way theatrical illusion and illusions of war as heroic endeavour fed on each other.

Thus, while contributing to the early hysteria, the theatre maintained a festive view of war. However morally deplorable, the results could be theatrically exciting. As lines of demarcation, of fatal import in the war zone, became blurred in the theatre, this was not just a matter of formal or conventional change; the distinction between actors and audience was dissolving as both categories were cast in a great patriotic pageant called the people's war. Theatres became concerned not just to entertain but to mobilize; and theatre-goers were invited to drop their inhibitions and submit to the great swelling mood of national solidarity. They were coached and cued into a script of pride and heroic imperatives which could easily turn to one of terror and futility. But it was projected as a great collaborative venture: popular theatre with a vengeance. Volunteers scrambling up onto the stage were soon transformed into khaki-clad performers parading through the town. This was just one of the ways in which theatre was spilling on to the streets: street theatre as history in the making.[87] It explained the poor business done by Aldershot's theatres during the early days of war, 'The crowds of soldiers and civilians [being] content in finding amusement from the scenes which take place in the streets'.[88] Soon these street players would find their ultimate theatre in the mutilated land of Flanders, a soil which many of them would ensure should become for ever England. As spectacle, the very Zeppelin raids held all the piquancy, all the sublimity of terror, of a high-wire act with the added adrenalin-producer of personal danger. They were perfect support for the contention that drama was not dead, merely 'transferred from the stage'.[89]

Notes

1. F. Tennyson Jesse and H. M. Harwood, *Billeted* (French, 1920), p. 60.
2. *Era* 12.8.14, 10.
3. *Era* 21.11.17, 15.
4. *Aktion* 28.3.14, col. 267.
5. Cynthia Asquith, *Diaries 1915–18* (Century, 1968), p. 34.
6. *Era* 23.9.14, 10.
7. *Referee* 15.9.18, 2.
8. *Era* 22.3.16, 15.
9. Farjeon, *'Era' Annual 1918*, p. 43.
10. Typically, Yorkshire 'village lads of 15 and 16 were bringing in £2 weekly, men over 60 were earning between £5 and £6, whilst men paid by scale were getting their £10 and £12 ... Whatever falling off in patronage there may be when the wages question is readjusted, it is certain that the necessity for an antidote for the depressing influences of the times has created a play-going public that in pre-war days would not even have contemplated the theatre as a means of relaxation' (*Era* 18.9.18, 11).
11. Farjeon, *'Era' Annual 1918*, p. 39.
12. Huntley Carter, 'The German Theatre in War-time and After', *Fortnightly Review* 110 (February 1921), 284–94 (287).

13. *Bystander* 5.1.16, 11.
14. *Era* 24.10.17, 5.
15. Newton, *Referee* 6.2.16, 3.
16. *Referee* 23.1.16, 5.
17. William Archer, 'The Music-Hall, Past and Future', *Fortnightly Review* 100 (July–December 1916), 261.
18. Alec Waugh, *The Prisoners of Mainz* (Chapman and Hall, 1919), pp. 44–5.
19. 'Criticus', *Era* 20.2.18, 13.
20. Arthur Armstrong, *SYB 1919*, p. 31.
21. Marks, *Referee* 23.9.17, 5; *Era* 15.11.16, 15. The myth was perpetuated even post-WW2 by Irene Vanbrugh, who claims that 'theatres kept open, even at a very big financial loss', to boost morale and provide 'entertainment for the boys when they came home on leave' (*To Tell My Story* (Hutchinson, 1948), p. 112).
22. Russell, *Performer* 18.7.18, 15.
23. *Era* 22.12.15, 17.
24. Landon Russell, *Myself and Others* (Sampson Low, Marston, 1931), pp. 107–9. Annie Rooney turned it into a music-hall joke ('Extra Turn', *Era* 24.7.18, 12). The anonymous *WAAC* (Laurie, 1930), p. 78, describes the tactlessness with which a London theatre entertainment for the wounded included a play 'with a realistic dressing-station scene' in which the heroine declaimed: 'No man who has been in the trenches does not long to get back there again!' Cf. *Encore* 25.3.15, 10, on a professional singer regaling the wounded with 'We Don't Want To Lose You, But We Think You Ought To Go'; J. B. Priestley, *Margin Released* (Heinemann, 1962), p. 110, when hospitalized, being frequently subjected to 'that drivelling refrain'.
25. *Era* 22.12.15, 17. But such intrusions were not necessarily welcome. At Harrogate a soldier's vigorous expostulations when a comedian slandered the Germans as cowards 'who did nothing but hold up their hands and shout for mercy' earned him prompt ejection (Wilfred Saint-Mandé, *War, Wine and Women* (Cassell, 1931), p. 441).
26. At Ipswich the system was introduced following representations from the military. But other factors such as blackout regulations, the innovation of putting the clocks forward in May 1916 and even rationing played a part, and unstable social conditions caused fluctuations in the relative popularity of early and late performances (*Era* 18.8.15, 8; Marks, *Referee* 23.6.18, 5).
27. J. B. Fagan, *Era* 6.11.18, 8.
28. *Sunday Times* 10.11.18, 4.
29. Thomas Beecham, *A Mingled Chime* (Hutchinson, 1944), p. 152.

30. *Nation* 12.1.18, 486.
31. *New Age* 20.4.15, 588.
32. *Performer* 20.12.17, 16.
33. *Stage* 11.3.15, 19. H. G. Hibbert, *Fifty Years of a Londoner's Life* (Richards, 1916), p. 213, mentions Tich's '£250 a week', while Tilley 'reached £350'.
34. *Referee* 16.7.16, 7.
35. *Weekly Dispatch* 3.2.18, 3.
36. *Referee* 7.11.15, 4.
37. *Era* 14.11.17, 17; *Era* 17.4.18, 14; *Era* 3.4.18, 12; *Era* 9.10.18, 16.
38. Farjeon, *'Era' Annual 1918*, p. 39. H. G. Hibbert, *A Playgoer's Memories* (Richards, 1920), p. 220, concurs, blaming the 'wealthy syndicate' rather than the leaseholder, who did no 'more than take a shrewd advantage of the market'. But some theatres had several sub-lessees, all taking a cut and putting nothing into the theatre.
39. *Era* 11.12.18, 8; *Performer* 14.11.18, 11.
40. *Era* 30.5.17, 8.
41. Cf. *New Statesman* 28.11.14, 188: 'Even with all the fiscal changes of the past decade, the wage-earner still pays to the State a much heavier tax in proportion to his income than does the wealthy property-owner, or even the middle-class professional'.
42. Newton, *Referee* 6.2.16, 3. *Stage* 24.2.16, 18, advocated a uniform 1d. a seat impost, a subsequent leader (9.3.16, 16) noting that Canada had just imposed '½d. per head'.
43. *Era* 6.10.15, 15.
44. *Era* 23.6.15, 13. On the same page Robey advocates 'no reference whatever to the war in any performance'.
45. Arnold Golsworthy, *Bystander* 12.9.17, 502.
46. Phyllis Bottome, *A Certain Star* (Hodder & Stoughton, 1917), p. 22.
47. *Era* 8.5.18, 7.
48. *Era* 7.7.15, 7.
49. *Era* 4.10.16, 19; *Era* 29.9.15, 7.
50. E. L. S., 'A Deprecation of Realism in War Literature', *British Empire Fortnightly* (The Hague) I(16) (25 October 1918), 9.
51. *Encore* 8.7.15, 12.
52. *Performer* 1.10.14, 11.
53. *Referee* 25.4.15, 4.
54. Newton, *Referee* 8.9.18, 3, boasted that 'whenever I come across anything objectionable I say so – and, I am glad to believe, by no means always in vain'.
55. *Referee* 19.11.16, 4.

56. *Encore* 11.2.15, 4. Various professional battalions had been formed to reassure men that they would be grouped with others of their own class (*Daily Sketch* 31.8.14, 5).
57. *Performer* 18.3.15, 31.
58. *Era* 20.1.15, 14.
59. *Era* 13.1.15, 15; *Era* 24.5.16, 8; *Passing Show* 10.4.15, 18.
60. *Performer* 2.12.15, 25.
61. *Era* 8.8.17, 12; Clarkson Rose, *With a Twinkle in My Eye* (Museum Press, 1951), pp. 70–1. 'Derbyite' wrote to *Era* 26.1.16, 11, complaining that one management had forbidden those enrolled under the Derby Scheme to wear their armlets on stage; a prohibition supported by Arthur Bourchier (2.2.16, 10) not only on the grounds of 'inartistic incongruities' but because the public did not 'go to the theatre to be reminded of the war'. But the practice was common enough (*Era* 29.12.15, 16; *Stage* 3.2.16, 21). An actor playing a slacker in a touring play anomalously wore his silver dischargee badge in his lapel: 'Excusable, if not artistic' (*Era* 5.12.17, 14).
62. *John Bull* 11.12.15, 4; *Era* 6.6.17, 22.
63. *The Times* 13.6.17, 9.
64. In 1911 the number of men on stage, including variety, was estimated at upwards of 9000; by mid-1915 at least 1000 had enlisted (*Era* 30.6.15, 13).
65. *New Age* 9.12.15, 141.
66. *Era* 25.7.17, 8.
67. Maisie Gay, *Laughing through Life* (Hurst and Blackett, 1931), p. 198.
68. *Era* 27.12.16, 11.
69. Things could go too far, 'a certain popular comedian' finding himself ordered about like a footman's flunkey, and finally approached by an elevated lady to 'take up a collection among the other artistes, as the financial results of the matinée had fallen considerably short of her expectations' (*Performer* 12.7.17, 15).
70. 'Olivia', *Sphere* 24.2.17, iv.
71. *Era* 10.1.17, 13; *Era* 7.3.17, 8.
72. Neville Chamberlain, as director of national service, declared (3.3.17): 'The amusement of the people is an *essential* part of national work.'
73. Carroll, *Sunday Times* 25.8.18, 2.
74. *Manchester Guardian* 24.8.14, 4.
75. *The Times* 6.8.18, 7.
76. *Referee* 11.8.18, 2.
77. *Era* 16.6.15, 8. Cf. Benson's blatantly propagandist production of *Henry V*, during which he declared that, although believing in conscription, he was throwing his weight behind 'the voluntary principle, so that we

could not give gratification to our enemies by letting them see we had to adopt their methods to gain our ends' (*Daily Graphic* 12.1.15, 7).

78. *Vivid War Weekly* 20.3.15, 100.
79. C. S. Peel, *How We Lived Then 1914–1918* (Lane, 1929), p. 68.
80. Lewis Waller's efforts in South Wales earned him a gold medal from the recruiting officers of Glamorgan and Monmouthshire (*Era* 30.6.15, 13).
81. *Crapouillot* 7.17, 7.
82. S. Clarke Hook, *The Last Stand* (Amalgamated Press, Boys' Friend Library No. 142, c. 1910–11).
83. *Era* 14.7.15, 13.
84. *Era* 4.11.14, 10; *Era* 2.6.15, 8.
85. *Referee* 20.9.14, 3.
86. *Daily Sketch* 15.9.14, 5; *Era* 16.9.14, 9.
87. 'London under arms' provided 'various side-shows unknown in calmer days', though security sometimes prevented the sight of Highlanders marching to 'the pipes, or a squadron of Lancers trotting past with pennons flickering' (*The Times* 17.1.16, 11; *Daily Sketch* 31.8.14, 5).
88. *Stage* 13.8.14, 4.
89. Arthur Thorn, *New Age* 15.4.15, 644.

2

Musical comedy and musical anarchy

The two biggest hits of the war years were musicals; or at least one, *Maid of the Mountains,* was clearly in that category. The other, *Chu Chin Chow* (His Majesty's), which broke all records, was described by its producer, Oscar Asche, as an 'Eastern Revue'.[1] That was at the first night, which left *Athenæum*'s reviewer (September 1916, p. 445) bemused that a 'nation engaged in fighting heroically, and financing less heroically, the greatest struggle of all the ages' should pack a theatre to see 'a jumble which had neither the merits of a fairy tale, a play, a pageant, a musical comedy, or a music-hall show'. But Lily Brayton (Asche's wife and co-star) held 'the audience breathless with her dramatic intensity';[2] and if the wartime allies filling London were not always competent enough in English to handle sophisticated verbal wit, they could appreciate the 'crowds of beautiful slave girls',[3] whose bare midriffs prompted Tree's sally 'more Navel than Millinery'.[4]

The inclusive cost of mounting this spectacular production had been only £5,356 17s. 9d.[5] It proved unstoppable, running for 2235 performances despite sundry calamities such as air raids and the death of a camel. (The latter occurred during the meat shortage and the carcase was sold to a Soho restaurant.[6]) Frederick Norton's music was not only 'light and graceful and haunting, [but] a most joyous holiday from ragtime'.[7] More innovative was the staging, by Joseph Harker: 'The little tableaux, in place of front scenes, slowly revealed in a sort of camera with cross-shutters half-way up a black frame, proved a most effective and serviceable notion – especially for songs. Again, the one ray of light falling on a pile of jewels in the darkened cave was more to the purpose than much candle-power.'[8] Old Baghdad came alive with camel, donkey, 'palm trees and riparian residences', 'women bearing pitchers from the well, dancers, and a potter actually at work upon a wheel of primitive pattern [turning] out three very presentable pots during the progress of the action'. Ancient Persian xylophone and dumbshow contributed, the latter cleverly burlesquing 'the style and movement of a Chaplin film'.[9] As occasional intrusions, Baghdad's capture was celebrated by a party of Tommies entering an Arab street singing 'Tipperary';[10] while on Armistice night, Lily Brayton as Britannia 'released a peace dove into the auditorium, and robber chief Asche was transmogrified into John Bull'.[11]

Asche had also produced *The Maid of the Mountains*, which was a bid (successful beyond all hope) to get the George Edwardes estate out of the red. Its star, José Collins, began the engagement at £50 a week, and for the entire run 'wore the same dresses, merely renewing the gauze scarves from time to time'.[12] The brigands' lair was set against moonlit peaks, their striking exit made by descending the rocks and disappearing into 'a yawning chasm about 12 feet wide' designed by Asche to prevent the artists from hugging the footlights.[13] Collins dominated the show, with the thrilling intensity of her voice and those high 'sweet pianissimi'.[14] However, that she was a touch limited in dramatic intelligence is suggested when, finding 'the ending ... far too unhappy', she forced author Frederick Lonsdale to alter it by 'that old feminine artifice of tears'.[15] The show could have run for a great deal longer than its 1353 performances had Collins not tired of it. Her only break had been during the 1917–18 Christmas season at Manchester's Prince's Theatre singing in *A Southern Maid*, a show expressly designed for her, though the protracted stay of *The Maid* at Daly's delayed its arrival there until 1920.

Wartime audiences had to wait a while for *The Maid* and *Chu Chin Chow*. As in the non-lyric theatre, revivals of musical comedy successes were 'accepted as one of the cost-effective ways of "carrying on"'.[16] *Miss Hook of Holland* and *Floradora* were updated with patriotic numbers, Evie Greene repeating one of her greatest successes as Dolores in the latter. When, two years later, she died of Bright's disease, she was remembered for her definitive performance in this rôle, and for 'the rare gift of tears in her voice'.[17] Within ten weeks of Greene's death, one of her contemporaries, Lily Elsie (London's original Merry Widow) emerged from premature retirement to appear in *Pamela* (Palace) opposite Owen Nares. Nares played a young man about town journeying 'to St. Imaginario, the only place in Europe untouched by the War', in old-fashioned pursuit of heiress Elsie.[18]

The Merry Widow had established a fashion for Viennese musicals which the war seemed destined to end. But trading with the enemy continued on many fronts, the musical being one of the more amiable. The technique was to leave 'Viennese names out of the programmes' or to engage in considerable rewriting. In the case of *Mam'selle Tralala* at the Garrick, masquerading as *Oh, Be Careful*, book by Wimperis and Carrick, with music by Melville Gideon, 'remnants ... of the tuneful Viennese' original (by Jean Gilbert, alias Max Winterfeld of Hamburg) were easy to hear.[19] Another Gilbert work, *The Girl in the Taxi*, was revived without subterfuge at the Garrick (23 January 1915), and after several changes of West End home aggregated 165 performances. But (a sign of things to come when favoured continental sources ostensibly closed) a revival of *The Belle of New York* was running at the Lyceum when war broke out. This American show, following failure in New York, had brought to London's musical stage in 1898 a new vivacity and attack; thus far none of its successors had achieved the same West End impact.[20] But the circumstances of war, although by no means Americanizing the British stage in the manner of the British cinema, certainly prepared the way. At the Armistice, E. A. Baughan thought musical comedy had been 'never more alive', with *The Maid, Chu Chin Chow, The Boy* and *Yes, Uncle* completely sold out. But he spoke of several more as highly promising, two of which (*Soldier Boy* and Hirsch's *Going Up*) were American, the latter heading for a run of 573 performances at the Gaiety. And although Jerome Kern's *Very Good, Eddie* had received a cool reception at the Palace some months earlier, the 1920s would see London's total capitulation to this New Yorker.[21]

Robert Courtneidge was unlucky with some good musicals, *My Lady Frayle*, despite a clever female Faust story and delightful music, barely paying its way.[22] It was replaced at the Shaftesbury by *The Light Blues*, which had 'played for thirty weeks in the provinces to most satisfactory business', but now managed just twenty performances. Perhaps Courtneidge would have had more success a year on, since in 1917 musicals scored 'the highest percentage of successes'.[23] That year the only West End failure was Seymour Hicks's *Cash on Delivery*, which collapsed at the Palace after 49 performances. But there were some outstanding successes to compensate. Amongst them were two shows which helped to establish Leslie Henson in the West End. He describes how, when he obtained the part of Pony Twitchin in *Theodore and Co.*, he found the script 'a mere skeleton' and got Clifford Grey to help him flesh it out.[24] For his next show, *Yes, Uncle*, he never saw a script at all: 'So far as I was concerned, a lot of it grew out of the first night, when by good luck the audience was on top of its form. After all, it is the audience that really "plays" the show.' *Theodore and Co.* began its run at the Gaiety in September 1916, and managed 503 performances by December of the next year. *Yes, Uncle*, beginning at the Prince of Wales's and ending at the Shaftesbury, did still better with a tally of 626. A huge success was *The Boy*, a musical version of Pinero's *The Magistrate*, which filled the Adelphi for 803 performances and amused officers home on leave with a song about importunate 'daughters of Eve' who made them wish 'to be "somewhere in France" '.[25]

Good shows like *The Boy* used war references as a *sauce piquante*, while poorer ones seized on them in a bid for survival. In *Where's the Chicken?*, a musical farce varying an old theme by stuffing a chicken with an inheritance, a tableau was introduced, based on F. O. Salisbury's picture of Jack Cornwell, VC, on board HMS *Chester*.[26] Such a static painting, with no hint that it was a scene of blood and death, hardly translated to the stage, despite the participation of Cornwell's brother, who had been the painter's model.[27] *Violette* (Lyric), John Ansell's 'uncommonly fluent and melodious' comic opera, had George Barrett working in topical wheezes: a prisoner bribing a sentry with four meat coupons, and a comic chancellor lamenting 'the eight months which separate him from the age of 51' (and ineligibility for call-up).[28]

It was observed in *Era*'s Music Supplement (17 July 1918, p. 1) that the public was turning from 'ordinary musical comedy' towards light opera. *Carminetta*, with a sparkling and humorous score by Offenbach's disciple Emile Lassailly, is a kind of sequel to Bizet's opera. Alice Delysia, in the title-rôle, did wonders with an untrained voice, 'and her acting was a revelation'. She had Carmen's impudence and 'boiling passion', and provided a lesson for José Collins at the end, holding the stage all alone with a 'heart-broken, heroic song of farewell'.[29] In the same category is *Arlette*, with a score by Guy le Feuvre and additions by Novello. Its opening at the Shaftesbury coincided with the worst of the London air raids, causing Laurillard to consult the company about 'closing up at night' but there was total support for continuing and the opera ran successfully for 257 performances.[30] The lyrics were by Clifford Grey, and Stanley Lupino tells how the management tried to jettison one of his songs, 'I'm On The Staff', because 'it was a skit on the Brass Hats': 'I'll dive in Scotch-and-soda and simply swim in cham/But all I'll give the Army is plum-and-apple jam.'[31] The argument went on for several days, but the song was left in and proved a hit. Yet another light opera, Isidor Witmark's *Shanghai*, was Drury Lane's over-ambitious response to *Chu Chin Chow*. American variety artists Ray Kay and Betty Bush were imported to add a crook play element to exotic scenes at a Shanghai temple and on the deck of a Chinese junk.[32]

Asche's labelling of *Chu Chin Chow* as a revue is symptomatic of the way that the revue was colouring all theatrical forms. Dissonance and illogic had already invaded the European theatre; and in Britain innovators like Poel and Barker had done much to overthrow 'the once rigid laws of acts and intervals'. They had rejected the dominance of the proscenium in favour of fluidity, continuity and closer links between stage and audience. But it was revue which forced these things into the conservative heartland of the West End, stealing the avant-garde's thunder with a dramaturgy whose only rule seemed to be 'the more revolutionary the better'.[33] At a time when Donne's poetry was coming into its own, revue's abrupt transitions and broken rhythms had obvious appeal. If revue had imaged pre-war urban tensions, the outbreak of war found it reflecting the paroxysms of a continent. In Britain, its increasing centrality shows between March 1914, when *Era* was running articles asking 'Has the Revue come to stay?', and the end of the next year when Edgar White found revue sharing 'with Charlie Chaplin and the war the chief attention of the British public'; while another critic saw that it was destined 'to be the form of entertainment associated in theatrical history with the great war'.[34] The war had found its theatre of disintegration, part of that fragmented modernist consciousness which found grisly expression in those fragments shipped endlessly back from France.

The folly of associating order and reason with normality, something which found ample corroboration in the trenches, had been proclaimed by various art forms besides revue. What set revue apart from other modernist modes was its commercial value, its majority appeal. Stravinsky and Joyce never achieved wide popularity, but the disjunctions of revue were completely accessible. Not that its arbitrary yokings were universally appreciated. De Courville stressed the 'tremendous prejudice' faced by Britain's newest form of entertainment.[35] It was revue's self-reflexive tendencies which aroused particular opposition, so it is apt that the anti-revue lobby should provide the core of Fred Thompson's *Lady-Birds*.[36] But its disjunctions caused alarm too. Arthur Armstrong saw revue as a 'theatrical blight', an incoherent nonsense where a song on 'the joys of Tokio' is prompted by a sudden rain of Japanese lanterns 'from the summer-blue skies off Brighton front', or where a beauty chorus prostrates itself 'upon the floor of an old English mansion' to be 'jumped over ... by a band of yelping, roaring, whip-cracking cowboys' while someone croons a prairie ditty.[37] Even the likes of 'Philistine', contesting the idea of revue as 'an empty appeal to empty minds', its audiences 'largely composed of unfledged subalterns gaping at a sophisticated chorus', failed to see that dramatic unity represents only one of several options. So long as his eyes were dazzled and his ears tickled he could '*put up with* general incoherence, and the violation of every canon that Aristotle laid down'.[38]

Despite these violations, Cochran emphasized the importance of 'running order'.[39] Revue might dispense with 'plot or connected theme, [but] must have rhythm'. It was in pursuit of 'the necessary contrast, cumulative effect, and climax' that, at the dress rehearsal of *Watch Your Step*, he switched the order of first and second acts; and, story being of scant consequence, little doctoring was needed to render it as plausible as before.[40] Nimbleness was a prime requisite in its writers, who had to accommodate frequent last-minute changes.[41] Amongst the best were Bovill and Harry Grattan. Charles Bovill was remembered as 'perhaps the neatest and most polished' of revue writers when, in early 1918, aged 39, he died of wounds while serving in the Coldstream Guards.[42] Delysia compared Grattan favourably with her countryman Rip (Georges Thénon), who only wrote whereas Grattan engaged in production and choreography. Like her peers, she thought that revue had come to stay, since it could be enjoyed 'from the commencement or the middle . . . as there is no plot to worry about'.[43] On the other hand, Nelson Keys found that revue actually encouraged early attendance: with 'musical comedy many don't turn up till the second act, because they know there is nothing doing. In revue, the interest starts the moment the curtain goes up.'[44]

Farjeon candidly declared that 'Revues should not have plots'; and when *Bits and Pieces* was seen at the Euston Palace, its lack of plot seemed a virtue, investing 'the show with an agreeableness peculiarly its own'.[45] *Chutney* claimed novelty: 'A Revue, for a change, with a Plot.'[46] It was the producer's job to select and shape, Gus Sohlke (one of the best) indicating how plot was just a pretext for 'rapid and startling changes of scene and dresses', something on which to string music or comedians' gags.[47] Charlot's *5064 Gerrard* typifies the high-speed process of creation, taking 'about seven weeks' for writing and production: 'There is an idea suggested for a bit of business. Everything is arranged, and then the tunes are put in last.'[48] Rehearsals were the period in which creativity and practicality conjoined. Changes were wholesale, hence much money could be saved by commissioning expensive sets and costumes late in the day.[49]

There was much probing into revue's nature and origins. Cochran points to a new, 'a younger audience, without preconceived ideas as to what a theatrical production should be', but favouring 'irresponsible, amusing entertainment of the lightest kind'. Revue became any 'jumble of more or less amusing and pretty things'.[50] It seldom reviewed, unless, as *Most* put it, it was a site for reviewing 'old jokes'.[51] In *Rosy Rapture*, manager and authors struggle to prevent the collapse of 'a great unwieldy sack of a thing which has "Revue" written on it'; but along with the nonsense there is a hint of revolutionary possibility in the suggestion that 'when the *real* revue comes to be written all the performances will take place in the stalls and the audience will sit on the stage'.[52] Elsewhere, Cochran discovered Shakespeare and Jonson amongst revue's antecedents, as well as Aristophanes, the latter also cited by Findon.[53]

Revue, declared André Charlot in 1915, had 'been around about half a century in Paris'.[54] But Delysia, who thought its elasticity and powers of hospitality made it Paris's 'most popular form of light entertainment', pointed to a profound difference between the French and British modes, not only because there was little reviewing of the latter but because its topical comment lacked the strong local flavour found in Paris.[55] Cochran saw no prospect of developing 'revue in its purely Parisian style and circumstance; on the other hand, it has unmistakably shown signs of revolt from the leggy and lewd compositions which are no more than a variant on the American "girl act"'.[56]

But if American performers Jack Norworth and Beth Tate overstated in claiming British revue as a purely 'American importation',[57] Newton could still grumble about 'those transatlantic "gang-plank" displays of half-dressed damsels hopping in and around the auditorium'.[58] Indeed, a song in *Bric-à-Brac* recommended: 'Pinch from America all you can, Hot stuff . . . Plenty of rag-time and very little clo'es.'[59] Undoubtedly wartime conditions favoured this. When, in 1913, Glover had carped that 'every "revue" has its Eastern scene, its licensed licentiousness, and its parade through the audience of semi-naked figurantes, whose "shapes" are their only claims for public acceptance', he blamed Reinhardt's wordless Arabian Nights production, *Sumurun*, for introducing to London in 1911 not only the gang plank but the 'fleshy, flabby pornography' of 'the German beerhouse'.[60] Now it became politic to borrow such things at second hand from America, along with the latter's one direct gift of quick continuity. It was said that theatrical pace arrived on 'the day the first automobile did the mile in sixty flat';[61] and Sohlke recognized its contribution to the success of *The Bing Boys Are Here*, 'a striking contrast to the long black-outs to which the Alhambra had been accustomed'.[62]

Revue was described as 'really and truly a connected vaudeville entertainment, proceeding at break-neck speed'.[63] And just as, pre-war, Mair had seen vaudeville answering the commercial theatre's loss of 'artistic vitality',[64] so Farjeon detected wartime revue attracting the 'high-brows' as 'the living dramatic art-form of the day'.[65] But if revue broke away from the rigidities of the well-made play, with its fraudulent implications of an ordered world, by 1917 Farjeon saw formula reasserting itself through the obsessive demand for newness.[66] The idea that revue was ailing had already become a commonplace; though it was pointed out in the *Evening News* (11 January 1916, p. 3) that the 'revue craze' would hardly abate with so many vested interests at stake. Six of the nine West End vaudeville houses were playing revue, as well as five legitimate theatres. In addition there were 80 revue companies on the road. Figures were little lower 15 months on, but mounting pessimism[67] reflected the war mood, affirming the symbiosis between war and revue. Revue itself mocked this pessimism, Grattan's *Tabs* beginning with Revue on his sick-bed, surrounded by doctors: 'Poor little Revue. Why you were almost epidemic a little while ago, and now there's only four cases in London. – And they're all pretty serious.'[68] In the intensely competitive world of West End revue the ceaseless demand for novelty itself became subject of wry comment. In the Ambassadors' revue *More (Odds and Ends)*, the principals 'go on strike, not for more money, but for fresh material'.[69] But by the time that Cochran presented *£150* at the same theatre, Farjeon was complaining of 'the now thread-bare "wheeze" which shows us the author of the revue at his wits' end for a new "stunt" . . . Revues that "take off" revues have been done to death.'[70] Even so, the changes were rung by opening not with the usual chorus but with a spy about to be shot. A lieutenant has him released 'on condition that he provides a new kind of revue for the British to enjoy on their return to London'. However, when the episode is resumed later in the show, the disgruntled lieutenant cries out from the stalls, 'We wanted something new; you have given us only the old stuff.' Whereupon 'the spy-compère is hauled off ... and we hear, only too plainly for the purposes of such an entertainment, that the Lieutenant's order, "Take him away and shoot him" has been staged with startling promptness' (a conclusion thought in need of 'toning down').[71]

If producers had 'exhausted their store of ... invention', one answer lay in finding new comedians with the personality to attract full houses.[72] Cochran, emphasizing the difficulty of getting comedians with the necessary breadth for a big house, also recognizes that 'even your finest comedian needs good situations' when faced not with 'a 20 minutes' turn [but] a three hours' entertainment'. Herein lay the secret of Robey and Lesters' success in *The Bing Boys*.[73] But managers paid for big names rather than clever situations, booking them 'three or four years ahead', special arrangements being made to enable 'Harry Tate to appear twice nightly at the Palladium and every evening in "Joy-Land!" at the Hippodrome', while George Formby was moving between the Victoria Palace and *Razzle-Dazzle* at Drury Lane.[74] As a parallel to larger events, 'a fight for existence' was imminent amongst 'rival managers ... out-bidding each other for the services of established favourites, because not one of them appears capable of discovering young talent'.[75] Typical was Stoll's paying '£450 a week' to pry Ethel Levey away from Butt; and she showed herself well aware of how the game was played by having refused 'to bind herself to the Empire directorate more securely than at 14 days' notice'.[76]

This largely demolishes T. S. Eliot's claim that 'Our best revue comedienne ... has seldom had the revue, and never the appreciation, that she deserves'.[77] Besides, seven years earlier,[78] Desmond MacCarthy had celebrated that 'peculiar spice' of irony which attracted Eliot. Irony certainly loomed large in *Follow the Crowd*, where Levey made 'her first appearance by stepping out of the chorus ranks, singing a good song called "Why don't they give us a chance?"'[79] It emphasized the huge economic gulf between star and chorus girl, who had seen little advance on pre-war pay (£2 a week in the West End and on first-class tours)[80] despite the steep rise in the cost of living. Other classes of theatrical employee fared still worse;[81] but exploitation of such a key element as the chorus seemed particularly flagrant. Soldiers on leave were known to 'make a bee line for the show [with] the comeliest chorus'.[82] One 'Professional' deplored the pretence that salaries ranging between 25s. and 45s. a week were commensurate with the professional skills required, adding that a girl requesting a rise for her chorus was summarily dismissed, as was an acting manager who gave 'subs' to a chorus which the previous week received 13s. 9d. apiece for 'two houses a night and a matinée'.[83]

In late 1918 top salaries were said to be those recently announced by Alfred Butt, '£3 for West-End work and £2.10s. on tour'. In fact, Nevill Graham had been paying £3 since Christmas 1917 for chorus girls touring in *Carminetta*.[84] He recognized that it was 'impossible for a girl to tour upon a salary of £2'; with lodgings at 15s. and food taking the rest, there was no surplus for insurance, laundry, dress and the likelihood of having to 'repay debts incurred during the vacation'. Propagandists had been working for years to draw girls away from a grudging theatre into war work. Hall Caine relates how the chorus of 'a rather foolish revue' found itself in lodgings with a munition girl. Why be content, asked the latter, with 'kicking your legs over the footlights when you might be earning more money in our shop, and doing something for your country ... and on the Friday night following the whole chorus presented themselves at the factory and were engaged'.[85] This was a parable of 1916, by which time the revue craze had already created a shortage of good quality chorus girls. The result, reported G. H. F. Nicholls, was that 'many of the girls are secured by contract' and Stoll was making some remuneration for rehearsals and finding their 'practice clothes and shoes'.[86] De Courville felt constrained to make a statement when Drury Lane girls complained about lack of pay for rehearsals:

> The greater number ... were not ordinary professional chorus people, but better class suburban girls, who ... could not expect to be paid while they were learning their business ... a batch of girls had been dismissed after rehearsing for about ten days, ... because they proved entirely unsuitable.[87]

This is disingenuous: there would have been no question of payment whatever the status of the girls; and someone of his experience would hardly need 10 days to discover professional ineptitude. He knew how much they contributed to success, claiming to have selected his 52 girls for *Smile* 'out of 2,000 candidates' to form 'the most wonderful chorus ever seen in any of my shows'.[88] For his 1917 pantomime at the London Theatre of Varieties Charles Gulliver found it necessary, in conjunction with the VAF, to draw up a contract which gave the chorus half-pay for two weeks' rehearsals.[89] There is no mention of the same arrangement applying in his other theatres, though he complained 'that eighteen of the girls who signed the contract failed to fulfil their engagements'. The VAF accepted uncritically, assuming that many of these girls viewed their stage work 'as of a temporary nature', thereby vitiating 'strenuous efforts to protect their interests'.[90] But by late 1918, even VAF's cautious chairman, Fred Russell, acknowledged that unpaid rehearsals were 'a very grave hardship', especially when the long slog entailed no guarantee of eventual employment.[91]

Courtneidge's pre-war example of 'paying his chorus half their wages throughout the rehearsal period'[92] found few managements ready to follow it even in late 1918. Butt thought four weeks of unpaid rehearsal entirely reasonable, though he would support (not initiate) 'a movement to pay the chorus for rehearsals where the engagement did not last eight weeks'.[93] It was the accident sustained by Hilda Duff (stage name Hilda Hayward) which brought the situation to the public eye. She had been seriously injured during rehearsals ('nearly two months') for *Razzle-Dazzle* at Drury Lane, and sued Moss' Empires for compensation. The company pointed out that it followed normal practice by running unpaid rehearsals with no guarantee of employment; the judge remarked that this 'raised an interesting question whether the plaintiff was "in the employ" of Moss' Empires' when the accident occurred.[94] The company was unwise to appeal against the damages award (£367. 6s.) since this put the whole system under the spotlight. The *Weekly Dispatch* (5 August 1917, p. 5) pointed out that rehearsals were 'long and exhausting', with girls sometimes fainting because they could not afford to buy a meal. Revue producers 'have boasted of the large sums – £20,000 or so – that they have lavished on the staging of one show. But they could not spare £600 for the six weeks' rehearsal by the chorus girls!' Further, what supplied material for a joke in Parsons and Kelsie's *It* (a '£2 a week' dancer managing to acquire sables and diamonds as perquisites, since her lissom body allows her to make 'both ends meet')[95] is here seen as a tragic consequence of exploitation. Yet six months before (21 January 1917, p. 4) this same paper, concerned with boosting sales not correcting abuses, had carried a paragraph on nightclub-haunting chorus girls, who 'would be much safer taking home their £2 10s. or £3 a week salaries to their mothers than in wearing white fox and pearls after midnight'.

Men were subject to a different kind of abuse; and being in acutely short supply they tended to earn more (Graham's tour rates show a differential of £3 to £3 10s., and Butt's of £2 10s. to £2 15s.) – though this in itself was a disincentive to their employment. During *Business as Usual*, a deputation of extras approached de Courville, refusing to go on without a pay increase to the level enjoyed by chorus men: '"Very well, gentlemen," he said with the utmost charm, "if that's how you want it – *don't* go on. I can run my show very well without you."'[96] This was all too true, and the likes of de Courville took full advantage of the fact. The war saw male theatrical staff in most categories being laid off. The arrival of conscription had little appreciable effect on revues, 'male members of the chorus [being already] the exception'.[97] Frederick Sandy, Karno's general manager, found men touring in revues were liable to abuse, despite announcements about their ineligibility.[98] A letter to the *Weekly*

Dispatch (31 January 1915, p. 6) from A. H. C., 'prominent' in London's 'commercial circles', took a harsh view of 'Shirkers in the Revue Chorus'. Most of them were bachelors, whose job kept them fit and inculcated a sense of rhythm, making them ideal subjects for military induction. It was clear 'that they could be dispensed with without the slightest injury or inconvenience being inflicted on the shows', while their involvement in 'patriotic songs and flag-waving in Jingo scenes constitutes as gross a travesty on patriotic fervour as could be imagined'. Drury Lane's manager Arthur Collins followed this up (28 February 1915, p. 6), advocating that his policy of turning down 'able-bodied men' be adopted by 'patriotic agents'. Theatrical author Harry Vernon, declaring that those under attack were silenced by dependence on managers' goodwill, wondered how many of these patriotic agents ('or any other kind') were 'shouldering a gun'.[99] Under the circumstances, it is remarkable that, in 1917, a super-revue, *The Silver Lining* (Theatre Royal, Leeds), should be considered unusual in having 'no chorus gentlemen, only ladies'. (It also dispensed with a 'juvenile man' in favour of a pantomime-style principal boy.[100]) Besides turning to older men, managers sometimes looked in the opposite direction 'by engaging a male chorus below the military age'.[101] They might also look to Ireland, which was free from conscription. But this could backfire, three Irishmen appearing in Joe O'Gorman's revue *As Irish as Ever* being 'charged with failing to report for military service'.[102]

Whatever the means, revue continued to give good value in song and dance, veteran actress Madge Kendal noting wryly that it needed about twenty girls on stage 'while the artiste sings a song'.[103] Nineteen-year-old American Hilda Glyder made a hit with her 'Horse Dance', 'backed by a full chorus', when she joined *Razzle-Dazzle*.[104] Before that, two years of success had been bought for *Le Petit Cabaret* by this 'Parisian Pony Trot', with two women in glossy black and white costumes and flowing head-plumes prancing mettlesomely, 'while the gentleman, holding the white ribbons and the whip, steps it briskly in the rear'.[105] Equally camp was Delysia in *Pell Mell*, as the sultan's slave performing 'a weird dance in chains',[106] while the Persian scene of *Here and There* presented 'an up-to-date sultana with a male harem', the gender reversal requiring her favourite, George Clarke, to perform a 'sensuous dance'.[107] Specialities included the serpentine dance in *Flying Colours*, with which Little Tich had been burlesquing Loïe Fuller since the 1890s, and Stanley Lupino in *Hullo, America!* imitating Nijinsky's 'famous flying spins' before reaching a spectacular finish in which he would run up 14 steps to smash the face of a temple idol and 'fall backwards down the steps – dead'.[108] Phyllis Monkman, whose emergence from a carpet in *See-Saw* (Comedy) made Mark Antony signal 'that he would like that little lot for his very own',[109] relished the scope given by revue 'for displaying one's versatility'.[110] On the opening night, her gyrations displaced one of her breastplates, releasing its contents. Of this scene, fellow-performer Beatrice Lillie comments, 'Audiences weren't used to such treats in 1915';[111] and the *Times* reviewer (15 December 1916, p. 11) felt 'disinclined to say more at present than that it is what is commonly known as sensational'.

Gertie Millar, 'greatest of all musical comedy actresses', adapted wonderfully to revue in *Bric-à-Brac.*[112] Again, in *Airs and Graces,* she sang and danced 'with the sure and irresistible touch of one who has all the technique of irresponsibility at her command'.[113] Good voices like Millar's were scarce, but plenty of artists knew how to substitute technique for voice. In *Some (More Samples),* Billie Carleton made 'effective use, mainly *parlando,* of her small voice', singing demurely a 'rather risky song' about the effect on the fellows of 'a little bit of lace, And a little bit of silk that clings'.[114] Basil Hallam, with no voice but perfect rhythm, phrasing and articulation,[115] became a matinée idol in *The Passing Show* with Finck's 'Gilbert The Filbert'. And the song's composer was bitter about the way that, although unfit for military service, Hallam was goaded into joining up, dying when he jumped from a drifting observation balloon and his parachute failed to open.[116]

Perhaps the French term for ragtime, *le temps du chiffon,* prompted a remark in *Era*'s Music Supplement (17 July 1918, p. 2) that revue music was 'as durable as white chiffon in a thunderstorm'. It was supposedly all rhythm, 'flowing motion and a regular succession of light and heavy accents'. One soldier's reminiscences suggest otherwise:

> The song writers knew their business. Harmony, and above all the rhythm of marching feet, possessed, informed and inspired their work. When Robey gazed at Violet Loraine and for the first time sang in his most effective unmusical voice, 'If you were the only girl in the world,' he gave impetus to a buoyant wave of song that flowed across the battlegrounds and lightened the load of a million marching men.[117]

And this was only the most memorable of a clutch of fine songs composed by Nat Ayer for *The Bing Boys,* a show visited five times during a fortnight's leave by an officer in the Royal Irish Rifles, who concluded that Robey and Loraine were 'one of our greatest war assets'.[118] In fact, plenty of shows offered far more variety and sophistication than *Era*'s specialist could discover. A more discerning critic, 'Lancelot', recognized Darewski as 'one of the greatest masters of modern rhythms and accentuation among our present composers', getting 'his effects by putting the stress of the music on the accentuated syllable of the word' and being 'keenly alive to the value of shifting the strong accent in succeeding bars'.[119] This is apropos of his work in *Joy-Land,* where he showed a subtle grasp of ragtime's 'syncopated effects on the scale'.

But it was with the arrival of Irving Berlin's two revues that ragtime's pulse-quickening connection with the war fully asserted itself.[120] Berlin has been dismissed by the ragtime purists; but unauthenticity has more to do with context than style. Meaning could hardly remain constant in the shift from some mid-West bordello parlour to the world of Tin Pan Alley; from the self-expression of an underclass to a new thrill for the socially successful. But it is the latter who were parodied in the first-act finale to *Watch Your Step*, as they sat in stage boxes at the New York Met, wearing 'tiaras and diamond necklaces, which in reality were studded with tiny electric bulbs'. At the burlesque climax these 'lit up and the whole stage was a blaze of light', a short circuit at one performance resulting in the lit-up showgirls receiving electric shocks.[121] The scene opened with 'a singer vainly trying to make 'On with the Motley' heard above the din from the boxes, as New York's elite talked 'scandal through telephones' or had their nails manicured. They were oblivious to the clever ragging of operatic favourites, ending 'with the whole company singing a "rag" version of the quartette from *Rigoletto*. At this point a crash of cymbals and a green spotlight heralded the appearance of Verdi's ghost in one of the boxes, where he sang the real melody, begging us not to "rag" his opera.' But even he slipped 'unconsciously into syncopation'.[122] *Stop! Look! Listen!* (1915), retitled *Follow the Crowd* for British audiences, proved less of a draw at the Empire than on Broadway. But it had two striking musical episodes. The final scene was 'nothing less than an entire "tabloid" melodrama, done from beginning to end in ragtime, ... a kind of ragtime Russian ballet'. The other was a patriotic piece, pushing that trick of quotation from an alien mode to near-burlesque proportions. From 'a little dot-and-dash ragtime ditty' sung on board ship by versatile American Joseph Coyne, who had partnered Elsie in the British première of *The Merry Widow*, it gradually expanded 'as team after team of sailors and passengers join in, until in the end the whole thing merges into a tremendous chorus of "God Save the King," with the ragtime still frolicking round it'.[123]

Patriotic song loomed large. Amongst the best was Finck's 'I'll Make A Man Of You' from *The Passing Show*, sung originally by Clara Beck and in the new edition, by which time recruiting songs were all the rage, by Gwendoline Brogden. In her 1915 recording, the latter sings with great verve and a due sense of that latent bawdry which was released when the song was appropriated by the troops. Since Shirley Kellogg's 'outstanding asset was robust loveliness',[124] she was well equipped to deliver that 'trumpetty-toned American War song called "Over There!"', dressed as a Sammy 'with a US regiment aboard a transport, all over Stars and Stripes'. This was in *Zig-Zag*, de Courville having bought the performing rights 'at a high figure'.[125] He thus trumped Clay Smith's 'America Answers The Call', composed in anticipation of

America's entry so that his wife Lee White could sing it 'in her strong contralto' on the great night.[126] First heard in *Some,* this dire song ('Blood is thicker than water, John Bull, America's in with you') was carried over into the next show, *Cheep,*[127] which Robert Graves, experiencing revue for the first time, saw while on leave.[128]

Ina Garvey describes a more spontaneous seizing of opportunities in *Quite All Right,* when a Zeppelin raid interrupted just as she was about to start 'Oh, Dear, What Can The Matter Be?' She changed to 'Where can the Zeppies be?', and continued to improvise: 'How you cheered me when I snapped my fingers at "*That* for their frightfulness!" And how you made me sing the verses again and again till you knew them and could join in.' Afterwards a cabinet minister came backstage and told her that she had performed a national service.[129] But topicality had its problems. Farjeon thought 'Beautiful Girl, Good-bye', in *Smile* (Garrick), 'must be almost unbearable to any sensitive soldier in the audience who is about to leave his sweetheart for France'. But absurdity may have saved it; 'for after the singer has proclaimed that he sees his girl's face in every flame in the fire, we are suddenly treated to the spectacle of a perfectly enormous fire at the back of the stage, with the girl's face in every flame, just as if she had been consigned to a very expansive Hell'.[130] One Canadian soldier's sensibilities were offended by a London show with a prancing 'vulgar-faced comic' backed by 'about fifty girls dressed in gauzy khaki'. Their breasts bobbed to the rhythms of 'Oh! It's a Lovely War', and he resented the audience's laughter at this parodic view of the conflict.[131] There may be a degree of hindsight in this recollection; but Sassoon and Stone both expressed similar sentiments during the war. When the latter saw *Follow the Crowd* he 'was a bit shocked by the frivolous atmosphere ... It's unfair to say that they don't realize that there's a war on, but still such a scene would be impossible in France or, I expect, Germany.'[132] Likewise, when a young lieutenant, recovering from a wound, saw his first revue, 'the patriotic songs and allusions made him sit very still and draw his young brows together in a disapproving frown'. This was 'as bad as seeing men in khaki on the stage'; and his companion wondered how many soldiers shared his resentment of 'music-hall patriotism'.[133]

But Canadian subaltern John Brophy relished *Joy-Land* (Hippodrome) with its 'amazing flag scene' in which chorus girls ingeniously combined their banners into one great Union Jack which filled the stage, while simultaneously an even larger specimen was gradually unfurled from the back of the gallery to cover 'the whole of the auditorium, amid a scene of wild enthusiasm'. In the words of the song, players and audience were 'all under the same old flag'.[134]

Women on stage enjoyed a special khaki dispensation, though it became bad form for men who had not seen service to appear in uniform: perhaps because of the extent to which reality and rôle-playing had become entangled, preventing patriots from detaching actor from performance, or enjoying both the fiction and its contrivance. But exceptions were made. In *See-Saw*, Jack Humphries, rehearsing for subsequent appearances as Bairnsfather's Old Bill, made a hit with a khaki number about 'the lack of space or opportunity for personal expression afforded by the regulation Army field postcards'.[135] Koopman misses the point in describing these cards as 'the refuge of the dilatory and the illiterate'. Others do not. Newton rejoiced at Humphries's cockney lament that 'the Service Postcard has no space for writing in anything that really matters' – such as 'his *real* opinion of his sergeant-major'; and 'the omission of such an essential line as "For Gawd's sake send some fags"' made Golsworthy think that the War Office had still not realized 'the far-reaching effects of Armageddon'.[136] A *Times* reviewer (4 January 1917, p. 11), reflecting that usually 'patriotic songs sung by actors in khaki are detestable', saw Harry Lauder in *Three Cheers* (Shaftesbury) differently. This was not only because he had, during the course of this show, lost his son in action, but because in his intensity he seemed to be 'the very voice of all those' enduring life at the front. 'The Laddies Who Fought And Won' was his own composition, its recruiting potency acknowledged in the War Office's supply of Scots Guards to embellish the scene.[137] But a sour note intruded on the opening night, after the brilliant dancing of Ivy Shilling and Fred Leslie. Lauder and Levey, following, refused to give way for an encore,

> and for several minutes the play stopped, the audience still shouting and the two distinguished principals still holding their ground. Ultimately Miss Levey saved the situation by coming forward and saying that Miss Shilling was 'doing a quick change'. Something was undoubtedly wrong about this ... the sporting thing would have been for Mr. Lauder to have taken the lead in bringing his younger comrades back.[138]

Despite the likes of Lauder doing their stuff, 'First Player' still wondered why revue 'isn't more widely used for purposes of propaganda' (*Sunday Pictorial* 22 July 1917, p. 11). After all, it caters for 'the most thoughtless public in the world, and, if you give them enough legs and laughter, they will swallow anything'. Still later, in *Performer* (16 May 1918, p. 15), it was urged that revue should ridicule 'pessimists, pacifists and rumorists' or depict some 'tragedy in miniature, enough to stimulate a thought which would be carried away from amid the camouflage of mirth and song'. But both that trio of undesirables and tragedy in miniature had featured in revue from the outset. Cuthbert, a slacker in perpetual 'terror of the recruiting officer',[139] appeared first in the second edition of *More*, and again in *Cheerio!*, by which time the name had been popularized by 'Poy' (Percy Hutton Fearon) in a series of

Evening Post cartoons.[140] *Cheerio!* finds him working 'tranquilly in his Whitehall Funk-Hole while his father and grandfather are in khaki, loyally doing their bit'. And they sing a trio on 'the fatuity of allowing the older men to join up while there are so many youthful shirkers around'.[141]

But it is the pacifist who receives the most lively attention. *Follow the Crowd* has a particularly ugly song against 'canting cranks/Who refuse to join the ranks,/The Simple Simon clique/Who turn the other cheek' (not even the Christian gesture being immune from sneer); 'All the rubbish should be shot/ To stop the rot'.[142] The wartime stage enacted its brutal rituals, drawing audiences into a complicity of vicarious bloodletting, a regular target being Keir Hardie, MP for Merthyr, who had resumed the Independent Labour Party chairmanship in 1913. The war was prefaced by the assassination of Jaurés in Paris, and had its epilogue in Berlin with the murders of Liebknecht and Luxembourg (Wall Street providing its own ironic tenth anniversary celebration of the latter deaths). But whereas in other countries the alternative voices were silenced by a bullet, in Britain the hounds of Fleet Street and the West End theatre were enough, and Hardie was harried to his death in 1915. 'Kur' Hardie, as Bottomley liked to call him,[143] was stigmatized as a traitor, so revue 'humour' looks forward to his hanging. *The Passing Show*'s 'When The Clock Strikes 13' expresses the hope that he 'Will get plenty of rope'. And mock news in *By Jingo If We Do –!* elaborates: 'The Kaiser's got pinched/And Keir Hardie's been lynched.' A cable from the Kaiser reads: 'Triumphal entry into London unavoidably postponed – cancel my double turn with Keir Hardie at the Empire ... I and my brave troops are making awful examples of all babies found in arms. Kiss me Hardie.' This Nelson appropriation triggers: '"Terrible outbreak of swine fever among the German Troops" ... By Jove; then Hardie *has* kissed him!'[144] Newspaper placards in *Business as Usual* read 'Keir Hardie practices Goose Step ... embraces Bernhardi' and 'Ramsay Macdonald joins Crown Prince's Army'; and the pair figure again in song: 'Though old Ramsay Macdonald may whine/We'll remember Louvain ... Then Keir Hardie no doubt will repine,/But his life will be grand Out in Hel-igoland,/When we've wound up the watch on the Rhine.'[145] In *Rosy Rapture*, Norworth used another pairing: 'China for the Chinese, America for the Americans, and the rest of the world for the Kaiser, by kind permission of Bernard Shaw and Keir Hardie.'[146]

Fun was also had with Ford's Peace Conference, and in *The Pedlar of Dreams* the car magnate is made to threaten that if he doesn't get peace 'there'll be a fresh name on somebody's family tombstone', banging the table with his revolver for emphasis.[147] In *Half-Past Eight* the subject was linked with Lysistrata, who invites women of the allies to discuss peace, trying to sell them an 'old Ford car'. Greece, as the model for European democracy, has been replaced by France, which has no word for 'Conscientious Objector' (that 'quivering mass of unwholesome fat' being unknown there).[148] But *The Times*'s reviewer (2 May 1916, p. 11) was unseduced by such laboured gibes and unfortunate reflections on Greece and America. However, in *Any Old Thing*, John Humphries 'was accorded a splendid reception' for submitting 'conchies' to a false medical examination and passing them for overseas service. '"The blokes what make bad language a pleasure" are the butt of many a good line, such as "Are you English, or do you live at Brighton?"',[149] deriding the influx of Jewish refugees from London air raids

As for the proposal for mini-tragedy, there are examples in two of the better-known 1914 revues, *Business as Usual* and *By Jingo*. But the patriotic appeal of the latter was inevitably tainted with jingoism, about which there was acute sensitivity, especially with its original target now 'giving such splendid help in the fight against the Blonde Beast and his Kultur'.[150] But representation of the 'blonde beast', too, caused trouble, Newton considering it 'a mistake to introduce such a gruesome Prussian "atrocities" episode'.[151] The censor's office, however, lent support: 'The principle of allowing attacks on the Kaiser, references to German atrocities and so forth has been conceded, in the case of seriously intended plays, melodramatic sketches and the like. I do not think it can be taken away in the case of more or less comic productions ... chaff of the Kaiser's use of the name of the Almighty ... can hardly [be forbidden] to a stage production any more than to "Punch".' Thus G. S. Street, who allows that 'no country can be denied the satisfaction of vilifying its enemies in war time', but continues troubled by 'an attack on the brutality of German officers to women': 'Well, we've taught that little village a lesson. Lord, how those women squealed when the boys routed 'em out.'[152] There is disquieting reminiscence of German officers cutting cards for the women when a British war correspondent saves the heroine while her maid is 'flung to the soldiery'. However, since response was mixed, Butt contented himself 'with slight modifications',[153] though deferring 'to public opinion' by eliminating 'the tragic ending to the coffee stall episode'.[154] Critics appreciated the comic dialogue of Fred Groves as the proprietor of this Embankment stall, along with some 'smart satire on war scaremongers'.[155] But it was deemed 'an error of judgement' for a poor little wife, rouged up and holding the wages of sin, to be confronted by her out-of-work husband who, reading the signs, stabs her; an episode 'so finely ... acted that the memory of it is likely to haunt one in the darkened street'. That Cochran was right in ascribing *By Jingo*'s comparative failure not to these controversial episodes, but to the difficulty of making a big house like the Empire pay,[156] finds confirmation in Groves's speedy reappearance in the coffee-stall sketch at the Coliseum. Later still it was incorporated in *Airs and Graces* (again drawing comment about 'the unwisely retained finish').[157]

Fenton offered a minority view on *Business as Usual*: 'Instead of the incessant war topics, a series of irresponsible American stunts would be far more appreciated.'[158] But most critics relished the opening scene, so violently disrupted as grey uniforms and huge guns appear amidst the golden harvest sheaves to 'work havoc among the hitherto happy villagers'. If the phoney picture of a carefree peasantry aroused doubts, they were obliterated like the kneeling harvesters' rendering of the hit song, 'When The Angelus Is Ringing', by the brutal roaring of the guns.[159] However, doubts were expressed over both the presence of wounded soldiers and the 'machine-made' galloping in a subsequent scene:[160] 'A ruined city with soldiers, red cross nurse, Kaiser. At the end of this scene the curtain rises suddenly on a cavalry charge, in which real horses and real people are blended with painted ones to make half-minute's tableau.'[161]

Yet even in this hyper-critical atmosphere mockery intruded. In *More*, the 'red-nosed comedian, suddenly and without preparation, says to the caricature of a wife: "Why is the moon like the Union Jack?" She replies: "I don't know! Why *is* the moon like the Union Jack?" "Because it will never come down!" And patriots without a sense of humour shrieked their applause.'[162] Black humour was left little room for exaggeration: the Army Council's 'order that wounded soldiers must salute all officers on every occasion and in every possible circumstance no matter whether the physical exertion retards their convalescence or not'[163] might have inspired a sequence like that in William Naud's 1972 film, *God Bless the Bomb*, where a colonel demands a salute from a crippled soldier and leaves him a tangle of shattered limbs and crutches on the ground. But one on the medical board was equally sour, causing Newton to remonstrate that *Hullo, America!* might be taken for 'a pacifist patchwork'.[164] When a sergeant wheels in a corpse-like sufferer from heart disease, the doctor, assuming he is 'swinging the lead', has him tipped from his chair, commenting: 'H'm pity – genuine case – we've killed him. Never mind. Served his country.'[165] The cult of the wounded was treated to lighter irony. A scene in *Cheerio!*, 'one of the funniest things in the revue' according to one critic,[166] shows a wounded soldier bored by those offering to take him on a cultural jamboree. Street would get rid of it, though conceding that it 'will be popular with real wounded soldiers who have suffered in the same way'. However, a lady's proposal to spend a solitary afternoon with him ('I'll stroke your forehead and teach you to read poetry.– I don't think I'm strong enough yet, lady, for that sort of thing') had to go, being an 'allusion to the notorious Cornwallis West case'.[167] It would have been hard to delete from *More* satire of 'would be War nurses from Society' who have 'a profound disinclination for nursing anything "below" a captain – a true, but now, fortunately rarer type!';[168] though Street discouraged a song in *The Passing Show*, considered a 'gross affront to people ... caring for wounded officers', where one such opens her house 'As a Home of Recreation/For disabled officers' in return for cuddles and diamonds.[169] In *Follow the Crowd* Lady Diana Customs [Manners] is late because she has 'been so frightfully busy kissing wounded subalterns'.[170]

Stalls chatter at big society matinées was all 'about flag days and programme-selling'.[171] Esmond's *The Law Divine* pictures the rivalry for the best places in selling theatre programmes, and the ill-feeling provoked in those assigned to pit or gallery.[172] E. F. Benson thought 'it would be simpler and fairer to add a penny to the income-tax' rather than be subjected to the 'pillaging propensities' of 'elegant young females' selling flags.[173] And Logan, in *Vanity Fair*, believes 'no decent woman ought to lend herself to such a system of piracy', but ends up buying an entire trayful of flags.[174] One revue, *Shell Out* (Comedy), takes its title from the flag-sellers' importunities; and Fred Emney, slower than his companions in disappearing 'when the flag girls enter ... is a wreck when he finally escapes'. One act of retaliation is noted by Newton: 'a workman' snatching a collecting tin from one of the girls during the chorus.[175] 'I'll tell your wife just where you've been, unless you buy a little flag', runs a Paul Rubens number from *Half-Past Eight*;[176] and Graves, in *We're All in It*, is accosted by a flag-seller in Leicester Square whom he mistakes for a prostitute.[177] In *Bubbly*, Phyllis Monkman as a flag-seller catalogues its rewards, not the least of which is the opportunity afforded to 'quite nice' girls for entering into conversation with delightful officers to whom they haven't been introduced.[178] Seeking more direct benefits, some of these gentle flag-sellers were convicted in the courts, 'damsels who in no sense belonged to the criminal classes, but who, in their extreme unwisdom, appropriated certain excess profits while doing, as they no doubt thought, a work of charity'.[179] There is high comedy in the idea of 'excess profits', a phrase popularized by the government to justify its own larceny.

On the whole society's upper echelons are seen as war's victims. *Cheerio!* provides a typical picture of titled folk impoverished by taxation and patronized by newly affluent munitioners and coal heavers, who go 'to see how the erristocracy enjoy theirselves on a Bank Holiday'.[180] In *Vanity Fair*, a 'foreman in the Howitzer Department' keeps beer in the grand piano, and his son declares of Lady Hyacinth, the parlour-maid: 'I love this girl. Wot if she 'as got nothink but a title to her name, she's flesh and blood same as you and me.'[181] An impoverished gentleman in *£150* runs a pawnshop, fearing that he won't survive until the post-war boom with 'all the munition workers pawning their diamonds and pianos and Corots and Rembrandts and Ford cars'. Beneath the comic exaggeration lurks real anxiety about the consequences of exposing the underclass to relative affluence; but to show it as grotesquely ill-equipped to handle its new fortune made the situation appear reassuringly just a wartime aberration. Contrariwise, it was important to show the privileged suffering from wartime restrictions. In *Cheep*, a marchioness wheeling a perambulator loaded with tins of sardines (bought in order to qualify for 'half a pound of sugar')[182] meets a duke carrying a bagful of coal, obtained with a coal ticket won at his club the night before (rather like playing bridge for cutlets in Cochran's *£150*). The man he beat had no need to shoot himself in traditional style since, being 'a munition maker's valet', he could well afford to lose. The marchioness gossips that her husband is housebound until she can mend his only pair of trousers, and they are loath to walk to their place in Scotland with a crop of potatoes coming up in the Park Lane window-boxes. So they have let the shooting 'at six eggs a week'.

The marchioness discards a diamond in order to use its wrapping for a lump of coal, and in de Courville's *Happy Go Lucky* the new significance attaching to such commodities shows in chorus girls dressed as 'tasty lumps of sugar, precious pieces of coal'.[183] Coal was in limited supply for domestic use because it was fuelling the fleet and heavy industry. As a result, 'pacifism, anti-nationalism, cowardice, and greed, to say nothing of German gold' were alleged to lie behind any attempt by the miners to secure reasonable conditions.[184] Newton reports that one of *Bric-à-Brac*'s 'most popular wheezes was that on the Welsh miners, who used to be "getting coal" but had since been "getting slack"'. No reviewer notices that blame is apportioned to both sides, a three-round contest being used to satirize not only striking miners but their enemy the chiselling Marquis of Cardiff (i.e. fourth Marquis of Bute), 'famous short-weight champion'. John Bull eventually settles both parties after absorbing a good deal of punishment.[185]

Petrol was another fuel in short supply; and revue, reflecting the inconveniences endured by the privileged, adverts repeatedly to the taxi situation. With demand exceeding supply, the supplier achieved a certain undesirable independence, the blackout scene outside the theatre in *Some* depicting a scramble for the services of 'a lordly taxi-driver'.[186] An addition to *Pell Mell* finds a taxi-driver booking a table for four at the Savoy and 'four stalls at the Ambassadors'. His party would scorn circle seats: 'they're making munitions.'[187] But an important part of the problem was identified by Philip Page, who complained: 'A taxi-man wouldn't drive me from Bedford-street to the Palace Theatre last night for half-a-crown [or even] for a pound ... the fact is that millionaires who have had to lay up their Rolls Royces are "taming", at enormous cost, more and more of the alleged public cabs.'[188]

Sectional interest is usually at work on 'the food problem', *The Bing Girls* smearing those who would 'dictate to their neighbours what they should and should not eat':[189] the privileged were as adroit then as now at persuading people against their best interests. *Tails Up* (Comedy) mocks War Office red tape through a young man who grows old searching for the right department. That this worked as a safety valve showed in the hearty applause from 'many sympathetic sufferers in the house'.[190] Big anxieties become manageable through laughter: the child-husband and superannuated lover in *The Passing Show* recycle broadside humour of the mid-seventeenth century when the Civil War took all the able-bodied men.[191] Archie Pitt's *It's a Bargain*, in which Gracie Fields first made her mark, represents 'a naturalised German and his wife after having their pork business wrecked by a misguided and Yellow-Press-incited section of the English public'. These East End riots involved one of those deft negotiations between official ideology and unofficial, even illegal, action. Here difficulties are evaded by having the victims revealed as saboteurs, who open another shop in the guise of 'Scotchmen'.[192] Fun could be had from the daylight saving bill, with people in *Half-Past Eight* hardly aware 'whether they are breakfasting or supping'.[193] But Nat Ayer's song on the subject for *Pell Mell*, representing it as Asquith's sleight of hand ('Soon 'e'll be ... shoving the clock on a couple of years/And saying there isn't a war'), was 'cut out at the dress rehearsal'.[194]

As Nelson Keys said: 'You cannot make fun of politicians; you cannot have a comic soldier; you cannot, for instance, use such wheezes as "Celluloid George". The Minister of Munitions is now popular with all.'[195] Keys himself suffered from being construed as mocking the uniform. *Era* (29 November 1916, p. 14) reported that his '"imitation" of Mr. George Grossmith in naval uniform has been taken out of the Palace revue, "Vanity Fair", by order of the Admiralty. It should never have got in.' The smugness is hardly appropriate considering that just three weeks earlier the same paper found Keys's antic 'the finest bit of all'.[196]

Notably, however, *Half-Past Eight* defied the comfortable convention that 'the revue cannot lampoon Cabinet Ministers',[197] representing McKenna, Lloyd George and Asquith as incompetent bookies, backing a hopeless horse ridden by fat American jockey 'Mr. Woodgrow'.[198] What was described as legitimate and ingenious fun in *The Times* (2 May 1916, p. 11), and in the *Graphic* (6 May 1916, p. 622) as 'rather silly conventional chaff about the Government, which, significantly, got no great response from the over-fed audience' (a revealing phrase in the light of food shortages and resistance to rationing), brought a demand for 'wholesale cuts' from the trade papers. That 'a not over-scrupulous American jockey' imparted to the British leaders 'an apparently needed lesson in honesty' was repudiated along with such 'Gutter Press gibes as "This is a Government horse; it will swallow anything but the truth".'[199] In the censor's office it was deemed 'undesirable, but ... not malicious', though Lloyd George's nobbling the horse with whisky was blue-pencilled. What ruled this out was not only an anti-drink minister resorting to alcohol for political ends but (another section of the ruling class to be protected) the crack that 'All the best racehorse owners nobble their horses'.[200] Hastings Turner's *Hullo, America!* produced a similar reaction: 'The cheap and ill-chosen gibes at "those who are set in authority over us", military, political, and paternal, are unworthy of the brilliant reputation of the author, nor did they meet with the approval of the audience' (*Era*, 2 October 1918, p. 11). Despite subsequent claims (16 October 1918, p. 12) that this had been eliminated, 'Après la Guerre', where much of it occurs, became 'a big hit number': 'Some on the Staff now it's safe and sound/ Will venture a trip to the battle-ground.' And, as a change from satirizing munition workers, there are cynical comments about members of the governing classes whose profiteering will bring signal recognition at the end of the war.[201]

Revue was a prime target for the moralists. The *Weekly Dispatch*'s leader-writer (17 October 1915, p. 6) was incensed to find the Alhambra crowded for Charlot's *Now's the Time*: 'Men stand at the back and at the sides in scores. Who would think there is a war on?' Particularly offensive was 'A Garden Somewhere in Asia', parodying the fall of Adam, the snake being 'a man's arm pushed through the scenery', while Adam resembled Robey's Prehistoric Man and Eve Lady Godiva in the Coventry pageant. Any glancing at biblical themes on stage was courting trouble. But here, at a time of such terrible disorder, it was felt particularly that witty cynicism was not the required response to man's fallen condition. It is harder to see why Cochran's *As You Were* upset so many of the critical fraternity. Although adapted from Rip's *Plus ça change,* Wimperis had taken off its Parisian edge. The basic situation concerns Sir Bilyon Boost, anxious to escape his French wife's infidelity and the war, taking 'transit pills' which whisk him back in time to ancient Athens and beyond as well as to the court of Louis XVI (a stopping place which allows Delysia her lovely line: 'Are you married, single, or in Paris on leave?'). It was his medieval sojourn at the court of the Hunzollern, where the king, 'in appearance and entourage, bore an amazing likeness to a certain All-Highest',[202] which caused the bother. One reviewer protested about the court ladies' stoutness: 'This may have been meant as satire on German grossness, but the giggles of the audience proved that a different interpretation could be put, and was, on this unsightly and indelicate joke.' Delysia as Lucifer attracted particular abuse and censorial intervention,[203] though Carroll was fascinated by her close-fitting 'black maillot', which showed 'her figure and talent to equal advantage'.[204]

But professedly Cochran avoided 'scantily-dressed shows', claiming that the public would not tolerate 'bad taste'.[205] Butt, in an adjoining piece, agreed, blaming everything disagreeable on the provinces and that 'host of people previously not connected with the profession', who had jumped on the revue bandwagon. But the provinces had no monopoly of 'high kickers in short knickers'.[206] An elaborate *pas de trois* was danced between manager, critic and censor's office, the critic often angling for the latter's intervention while managers courted moral protest as deliberate marketing strategy. As songs in Butt's *Passing Show* acknowledge, 'legs and lingerie', or indeed anything 'risky', fill seats.[207] Some of the breezy papers were very relaxed about stage disclosure: 'Autolycus' found a lady in *All Scotch* 'entrancing, perhaps because her bathing-cloak revealed more than it concealed' (including a recent vaccination mark).[208] But officialdom decreed: 'Dresses appropriate for the sea or baths are *not* suitable for the stage',[209] with the qualification that a girl might appear 'in regulation swimming costume, providing she actually gave a bona-fide exhibition of swimming, and donned a cloak when emerging from the tank'.[210] However, *Encore* (27 May 1915, p. 6) established that not only were 'extremely tight and abbreviated bathing costumes ... to be checked' but chorus girls were 'to be clothed down to their knees'. The latter spelt trouble for Vincent Erne's *The Beauty Spots*,[211] which turns on identifying an heiress by a mark on her right knee. Consequently, Street marked for excision a parade of mannequins, 'since it is obvious that the women's knees are exposed'. This receives an interesting gloss from Second Lieutenant Harold Price, of Methodist stock and the Canadian Flying Corps, after a visit to *Vanity Fair* (27 December 1916): 'Parts are good, but parts are as sensual as ever. I like the music, I like pretty flowers, I like pretty girls, but I hate legs above the knee.'[212]

Complaints about Frank Rubens's *Mind the Step* brought a visit from one of the Lord Chamberlain's minions to the Islington Empire where, seated in the front row, he checked the performance against the submitted script. He raised objections to 'some of the patter', to 'bathing costumes, cut low and very tight at the back', and to 'disrobing behind a gauze curtain'.[213] The gauze curtain evidently derived from 'certain recent French revues seen in London', Newton grumbling that in *S'Nice* (Coronet), it enabled girls to pose 'as though they were quite nude'.[214] But the Moulin Rouge company, in London following the disastrous fire at its home theatre, pointed a contrast between British and French styles: 'in the lingerie scene, these Parisians take off their petticoats as if no male eye was upon them', the effect being delicious, and even proper. 'Our English girls, ... behave as if their best boys were at the back of the circle, and they hoped they were not looking.'[215]

Ed Pelton, specialist in erotic bathing, induced a certain split-mindedness in one reviewer with *Now We Know*: 'one lifts the eyebrows as well as the opera glasses at the sight of some of the prettiest of girls wearing the lightest and filmiest of costumes.'[216] But the lingerie shop allowed a leavening of humour. Oswald, in *The Bing Girls,* who mustn't kiss a girl until he is wed, experiments with wax models; but the second one is alive and runs off screaming.[217] The store in *Bric-à-Brac* is decorated with a series of framed drawings, ranging from the fully clad woman to the nude, 'all very well on paper but they never materialise'. This is the cue for the fully clad woman to burst through the paper, and so on until only the nude is left. After a dramatic pause, out of this frame comes Nelson Keys, made up like comedian Fred Emney in his famous dame costume.[218]

Humour, however, was no safeguard for a scene in *Flying Colours* where Little Tich as a tailor measured a fat lady. This was assailed in sections of the press, which in turn brought the Hippodrome's licence into jeopardy. It was only evidence that demands for cutting had been speedily met that placated the LCC.[219] But despite this, the episode was closely imitated in Bantock and Simpson's one-act *Physical Culture*, where a fat lady's gym costume caused censorial unease. As she raises her arms to be measured about the bust, the inevitable 'Kamerad' joke is followed by: 'This way to the mountain railway.' Request for 'a plaquet hole' and the response, 'this is a gymnasium costume. You're making a bloomer', had to go; though no notice was taken when the lady is instructed to 'retire to your bunk: leave the door ajar, and in order to create a draught, open wide the port hole'.[220]

According to Stone, her family was 'rather distressed by Fay Compton's undressing song' in *Follow the Crowd*.[221] General Smith-Dorrien found it distasteful.[222] The clean-up campaigns waged by him and the Bishop of London are discussed in Chapter 4. Stage response is necessarily mild. *Cheerio!* quibbles on reviews, which 'Generals have – where men present arms', and revues, which 'Generals don't want to have – where girls present legs'; and *Vanity Fair* mocks 'that General bloke' who visited 'the Gaiety larst week and didn't like the sermon'. But the censor's reader thought it perhaps 'depreciatory of him as a soldier' to follow up a remark that he 'saved the British Army at Mons' with the exchange: 'Why didn't 'e stay there then? – Modesty. The Germans had both flanks exposed.'[223] The Bishop also got a mention. The Cant and Humbug Purity Crusade would 'close the Palace, close the Hippodrome' and 'put the kibosh on the soldier's joy'. It is led by a Dickensian pair, Stiggins and Chadband, though behind them is *l'Éminence grise*: 'Have you *no* bit of scandal we can dish up? – Well, nothing worth retailing to the Bishop.' When a revue girl in *Wait and See* anticipates that 'Those funny old Bishops will cuss/As she bounds here and there/With her legs in the air',[224] she alludes primarily to the Bishops of London and Kensington. In 'a somewhat sensational sermon at St Martin's, Charing Cross', the latter warned that revue promoted 'all kinds of indecency. It seems that those artistes who are most successful in their performances pass through various stages of undress until they suggest nudity.' And he added darkly that theatres staging such things were apt to accommodate even worse goings-on amongst the audience.[225]

The moral guardians were equally upset by verbal indiscretion. *Look Who's Here* earned displeasure when talk about lots of men having 'gone back to live with their wives for economy's sake and the duration of the war' drew the retort from Levey: 'Adversity makes us acquainted with strange bedfellows.'[226] 'Drastic excisions' were urged, too, on the Turkish de Light Bath scene in *Half-Past Eight*, where 'gossiping masseuses ... talk some very unpleasant scandal about the personal peculiarities of their lady clients'. According to the script most of the gossip is inaudible, though one genteel client is said to have a 'season-ticket to the Divorce Court'.[227] Either Cochran's claim that his comics generally followed the script is unreliable,[228] or this reviewer was hypersensitive about any chit-chat by menials concerning their betters. However, on a revisit he was gratified to discover that his censure had caused the offensive bits to be dropped.[229]

It was a Turkish bath attendant in a performance of *Hot and Cold*[230] who upset one of the censor's scouts by describing how the lights went out and he 'had hold of the lady's foot and my other hand on the accumulator'. Similar innuendo was suspected of an 'unintelligible phrase' in Stiles and Carrick's *Mustard and Cress*,[231] where a man puts his arm about a woman, and she advises: 'Higher up – nearer the Abbey.' (Evidently the allusion is to the double towers fronting Westminster Abbey.) Ernest Bendall, Street's colleague, chopped the laundry scene in Parsons and Kelsie's *It* vigorously.[232] He disliked a joke about 'young ladies nowadays [having] their undies stamped with the crest of the regiment that their lovers belong to': 'judging by the number of crests on this one the girl what owns it must have been in a Mess or two.' Another troublesome moment occurs when one of the washerwomen delves into the pocket of a pair of flannel trousers: 'Look, a toothbrush and a wedding ring. – Looks as if the gent has been away for a weekend.' He marked for deletion several mock-adverts in Chapman's *Dusky Revel*, including one asking for window cleaners: 'Females only. By gent whose business is *looking up*'; and 'Wanted to sell, a light Wardrobe. By a lady – Making a shift.' But unaccountably he ignored: 'To those about to get married. A chat with a doctor. In plain sealed envelope.'[233] This is Marie Stopes territory: allusions to family planning could hardly be countenanced when any joking about the generative process was likely to be excised. In *Vanity Fair* girls cluster about a baby singing to their absent soldier-boys: 'Won't you please come back? Here's a job you can do after all'; and Street blue-pencils because 'it is the sort of thing some people think improper'.[234] He is similarly wary of Alec Daimler's *Got 'Em* when a commercial traveller, told by a potential customer that she has no children, declares: 'I can supply you with almost anything.'[235] In *By Jingo* there are bureaux supplying 'free servants, free houses, free holidays, free meals, and our special Lloyd George bounty for free births at any time', and the allusion to the maternity grant is marked for deletion.[236] The comic postcard abounds in such humour,[237] and the double standard is acknowledged in *Flying Colours*: 'a joke about a soldier being hit "not anywhere that really matters" – reminiscent of my Uncle Toby' being thought 'too suggestive'.[238] What is all very well in Sterne is not allowable in revue; and indeed an exchange which Street finds acceptable in Conal O'Riordan's cynical and 'in a way daring' play, *His Majesty's Pleasure*, 'would be cut out of a revue', since it appeals 'to quite a different sort of audience' at the Birmingham Rep: 'Would anyone take me for 55? – No, . . . a wench might be deceived by candlelight and yet suspect all in the dark.'[239]

One revue lost 'the whole of the dialogue . . . while recently in town the last act of a revue was forbidden on the opening night, and the entertainment closed soon after eight o'clock'.[240] Street was so incensed at *Nurses* that he would have spun it and consigned its authors, Sydney Blow and Douglas Hoare (its composer Philip Braham evidently escapes), to 'a term of hard labour'.[241] It is set in a New York hospital above a fashionable restaurant, the hospital manager seeking to poison those frequenting the restaurant in order to improve his business. Street detested the way it made 'hospitals and nurses the theme of stupid innuendo', subverting that wartime Angel of Mercy image. But he had to content himself with blue-pencilling references to stays and 'non-skid corsets', the stage direction 'Enter Ellery very limp, Mrs. Longacre and Mrs. Washington follow him' seeming 'conclusive as to the intention of all this'. Despite his efforts, enough 'boisterous fun' survived to ensure a good reception at the Wood Green Empire; though one critic noted the problem of assessing a piece where 'very little of the original script is to be found after the first few performances', another found 'some decidedly risky stage business and dialogue, which seemed to ignore the recent circular of the Lord Chamberlain'.[242]

Era's discussion of this circular (12 May 1915, p. 13) identifies revue as the chief offender, most of the mischief lying 'with the licentious gagger'. But improvisation was the essence of revue, creating problems for regular actors: 'In playing an ordinary part you know exactly what you are going to do, but in revue you don't have anything until you start rehearsing.' Thus newcomer Beth Tate, and Ethel Levey assented: 'You are handed a few lines on a large sheet of paper', and have to hunt out your own 'scenes and songs'.[243] In checking the script of *We're All in It*, Street worried about the input of George Graves with his 'reputation for suggestiveness'. Graves's presence in *Houp-La!* meant that no one could guess what would happen before the week was out'.[244] *Era*'s critic (19 July 1916, p. 16) thought some of his jokes in doubtful taste, but added, 'surely there is no need to be squeamish at the Empire'.[245] Others were less genial, especially about Graves's dance with Levey in which he 'removed a bunch of keys from one pocket to the other'.[246] Complaints brought Lord Chamberlain Sandhurst himself to the show, though he found nothing to concern him. But Henry Maltby deplored Graves's readiness to sacrifice anything for a laugh. He surprised the hero of one play into affirming that he was going to the South Pole, requesting him to bring back 'a broody penguin' for Graves to cross 'with a Buff Orpington'.[247] Clearly the quip to which Street took exception in *We're All in It*, following the emergence of a pig from a dovecot ('Evidently the outcome of an unnatural flirtation'), was introduced as a springboard for Graves's fertile invention.[248]

Officialdom sought to regulate revue financially as well as morally. When, in 1917, Neville Chamberlain (Director of National Service) urged the patriotic need to curb theatrical extravagance, John Dunbar, *Performer*'s editor, identified this as one of the two most significant wartime developments for revue.[249] Chamberlain was unspecific, but de Courville had no doubt that it was his kind of show which was particularly under attack. Taking issue, he claimed that 75 per cent of his audience was in khaki, and that he would hardly spend £16,000 if £5000 offered equal return.[250] According to his autobiography, he exaggerated costs as a selling point,[251] though overspending was rife to evade the government's excess profits tax. Whatever the truth, de Courville had no part in that amazing managerial somersault in 1917,

> when the economy campaign, which had been waged with but mediocre success in the country ever since the beginning of the war, now made such headway with public opinion that some of our theatres ... actually took to advertising the unprecedentedly small sums of money which were being expended on forthcoming productions.[252]

Cochran boasted that he had 'spared no economy' in the production of *Odds and Ends* and *£150*;[253] and gowns for *Cheep* and an economy scene added to *The New Bing Boys* cost 9s. or so.[254] Managements were doubtless making a virtue of necessity. Although Sohlke found 'wood and canvas, ironwork and such like ... far from easy to obtain', he saw how this brought a healthy shift of focus from gymnastics and spectacle back to comedy and 'artistic ensemble'.[255] Charlot, whose *Now's the Time* had been 'amazingly lavish' considering wartime limitations, turned in the other direction.[256] Simple staging, ingeniously lit, allowed for easy and effective transitions. Thus in *Samples* a 'seaside curtain was raised, discovering a darkened setting in which masses of tropical foliage were dimly seen. Then, as the lights were gradually raised, dazzling colours flashed out', providing a 'hot background [for] cool figures in white and neutral tones singing and dancing in harmony with the rhythm and atmosphere of the scene'.[257]

Cochran needed no conversion to economy, having long seen the danger of managements vying through ever more expensive productions. He contended that revue rested on a 'wealthy West End coterie', perhaps 4000 stalls patrons for whom managements competed every night. Unless they could be drawn to a show some half a dozen times, it would fail. The vast public for cheap amusements was irrelevant since most of the big houses had little cheap accommodation: 'The cheap part of the house is not worth £20 a night to the Empire.'[258] The impetus behind changes whereby 'pit and gallery have literally to take a back seat' (famous clown Whimsical Walker's disapproving phrase)[259] was American: by 1914 New York theatres were no longer built with a gallery.[260] And Cochran followed their logic by opening the St Martin's as a luxury house with orchestra stalls at a guinea and balcony stalls at half a guinea.[261] At the Ambassadors, holding about 500, 'stalls' patronage [represented] considerably more than half the total receipts'.[262] His first production there cost £200, the highest salary being £20. He kept outlay down in succeeding shows, though salaries increased as his principals became sought after.

Cochran rightly boasted that his Ambassadors shows 'gave London a new form of theatrical art'.[263] It was at such shows that people 'interested in the advance of stagecraft' watched 'for things to flash out' as they seldom did in the regular theatre. The freshness and excitement came from a blend of music hall talent and a stimulating 'influx of refugee designers and players from the continent'.[264] *Odds and Ends* derived a double benefit, being partly inspired by the factual adventures of eight English dancing girls, the Grecian Maids, making their way home from Germany at the outbreak of war. It began in a theatre deserted since its manager had joined the army. Through the actual stage door porters brought all the 'paraphernalia of a travelling troupe', a largely French company headed by Max Dearly. But the promising conjunction of empty theatre and refugee players seemed doomed with 'no dresses, no scenery, nothing'. Then Dearly (playing himself) 'got a laugh' by pointing out that with no dresses to speak of and 'eight English dancers – which is the most necessary thing in a French revue', that was what they must undertake. A burglar would enter Delysia's bedroom ('you must have one bedroom scene nowadays');[265] and Delysia being unknown in London, fun was had by confusing her with Deslys.[266] The premise of both show and show-within-the-show called for economy, black curtains sufficing for scenery; but this and other novelties proved too much for critics and first-night audience. One reviewer considered it 'naïve in its obvious lack of preparation and disregard of scenery'.[267] Eventually, with resounding irony, it was allowed to be 'the more enjoyable because it never underrates the intelligence of its audiences'.[268]

Huntley Carter was much taken with the show's sequel, *More*, in which stage design as well as playing relied on intimacy:

> Take the quite wonderful Noah's Arky backcloth of the 'Bathing Scene' with its blue pier and white pavilion and pink tipping seats and brown ships and pot-bellied sea-gulls stamped on the delirious curves of the green waves. Or the intoxicated backcloth of the New York Scene, with its big masses of skyscraper and whorling spots and lines.[269]

It was George de Feure who brought this 'intimate French humour' to the Ambassadors. Wartime shortages and continental theory fed into a new economy of stagecraft, and it is intriguing that Hanako, coming from a Japanese tradition of symbolic simplicity, was also drawn there. Another of *More*'s scenes which caught attention was the Command Performance 'played upon an entirely blacked-out stage, only the illuminated words, "Stage Door" being visible'.[270] Mimicry brought into 'this pitch-black chaos' such celebrities as Tree, Bernhardt, Marie Lloyd, G. P. Huntley, Cyril Maude and even Caruso, 'heard in a regular battle royal' with Lewis Waller. Grattan, who wrote this, created other dark scenes. One in *Cheep* (Vaudeville) harps continually on 'Chamberlain's plea for economy'. This is characteristic of revue, where not only is economy achieved but it is 'gaily laughed at', the audience's nose rubbed in it by way of title and episode: 'Spectacular revue must wait/Till Germany's rubbed off the slate.' 'Here's economy in dressing for you', declared Lee White as she came on clad in copies of the *Evening News* and *Daily Mail*. One read her 'agony column' and another asked for the 'wanteds'; but was told that it was all 'wanted'. After news about stripping 'the American back' was torn off, a joker behind her ripped a huge piece from his own newspaper, so that in mock-embarrassment she asked the audience 'to get up and turn your back while I walk off'.[271] The dark scene also contributes to the economy theme with a three-minute melodrama. Imagination is called for, and the audience is asked to 'regard it as if you went to a picture show and closed your eyes' since it will be played chiefly in darkness, 'thus saving the cost of scenery – also without a company – as although actors and actresses are cheap, we don't want them, and who knows but that this may be the entertainment of the future' (a dig at Gordon Craig's anti-humanist theories). It summarizes: 'Lamp flashes. Breaking Glass. Muffled Voices. Ah! silence. Voices in alarm. Knocking at door, then Crash. Pause, then Moonbeam on Body, then on open safe that has been rifled, then on bowler hat.' Again, in *Some*, Grattan wrote a scene in a blacked-out street as the audience leaves the theatre. There sounds in the 'pitch darkness, a din of whistles, shouts, recriminations, adverse comments on the play': 'Well, what did you think of it? – Rotten ... Positively indecent, that what's-her-name woman.' The commissionaire, asked to call a cab, advises that there is a strike on: 'Oh, this war is really becoming quite a nuisance. I shall welcome peace, for one.' Then a speaker with a German accent is heard: 'I, too, am mit you as a British subject. Beace at any Brice. You agree mit me, don't it? – Oh, I could stand any sort of peace except one like we saw to-night.'[272] Intimate revue clearly benefited from a lit auditorium; but these dark scenes needed the body of the theatre to be dark as well as the stage. Darkened auditoria were not unknown in the later nineteenth century; but at the start of the war Asche noted how development in stage lighting was hastening their spread.[273] The house was lit during the 1914 Russian opera season; but the next year a devotee declared himself so incensed by the new practice, which prevented him following the score, that he was shunning the theatre.[274]

By mid-war, the success of *revues intimes* and the failure of some of the big spectaculars to justify outlay demonstrated 'that extensive staging is unnecessary'.[275] But revue had its different publics: spareness and wit might satisfy those at the Ambassadors, but de Courville's confidence that 'the Hippodrome public likes something spectacular and mechanical'[276] prompted a burlesque in *Cheerio!* where he planned a 'new Super-Economical Revue': 'Cochran's put up a revue which has only cost £150. Charlot has produced one that's *Cheap* – well, ... My new Revue at the old Hippo will cost me nothing at all ... I'm going to have no scenery: no costumes to speak of – That sounds like *Chu Chin Chow* – No book – But you never do have a book'; and the usual hundred-strong beauty chorus will reduce to 'just one girl'.[277] *Joy-Land* (1915), de Courville's third Hippodrome revue of the war, had opened with a great liner about to leave Liverpool Docks. The stern of the huge vessel was in view along with a motley crowd on the landing stage. The last arrival, by way of a gangplank through the stalls, was Harry Tate, hauled aboard just as the ship began to move.[278] But the spectaculars must always compete with themselves, and *Razzle-Dazzle* (Drury Lane, 1916) was the biggest production de Courville 'had ever undertaken'. For a St Moritz ice scene champion skaters had been recruited from the Americas, Russia, Sweden and Switzerland.[279] A special electric plant was imported from America to freeze the water, de Courville evading the question raised by Colonel Norton-Griffiths about whether the equipment had taken up urgently needed cargo space by referring lightly to 'a few packages'.[280] But 'Scotland For Ever', climaxing the first half, was still more extravagant. The various tartans worn by 300 chorus girls pouring down the glen in response to a chieftain's summons had taken several months to weave. After them came marching pipers, completing a feast of cultural imagery.[281] The fiery cross romanticized conscription, the grimness of technological warfare dissembled through a riot of tartans emphasizing group loyalties and responsibilities, and affirming the process by which an old feudal enemy had been claimed for the cause through those ever-popular Highland regiments. It became a declaration of moral values and common causes, evocative ceremonial bespeaking unity, ardour and warrior culture.

Pantomime elbowed the show from Drury Lane to the Empire. There it acquired yet another spectacle, the Ladder of Roses, brought from New York by Alfred Butt for his Empire production, *We're All in It*.[282] This 'daintily beautiful scene' had a never-ending procession of Empire beauties facing the audience in their rose-tinted dresses as they climbed ladders to the rhythm of a good swinging tune by Raymond Hubbell, eventually being lost to view in a blue haze at the top. The backdrop was 'painted with strings of pink roses, hanging straight down after the fashion of a bedroom wallpaper', while similar strings disguised the outlines of the ladders, glowing with light as hundreds of bulbs lit up. 'It was a kind of climbing ballet,' thought Newton; but Carter considered it mixoscopic.[283] The effect was retained in de Courville's next show, *Zig-Zag* (Hippodrome, 1917), its Chinese Lacquer scene warm with 'yellows and reds and blacks and every other gleaming oriental tint, and a gorgeous glowing background of lattice ladders' where chorus girls trotted 'nimbly up and down' to give an 'impression that there must be some thousands of beautiful (and shapely) creatures hovering about the stage'.[284] Another triumph of subtle colouring was the Autumn scene, for which de Courville got McCleery, 'the best scenic artist for landscape painting in this country'. But it was a straight crib of those 'soft brown tints and tree-stumps' from which emerged 'a number of pretty girls' while Molly Drew sang 'Autumn Leaves', which had already done service in Wylie and Tate's *1914*.[285] The one new element was Marie Spink's virtuoso whistling solo as a nightingale (she settled in Chicago after the war, having met and married an American officer when the show visited Paris).[286] In complete contrast were Robey's celebrated Prehistoric scene, and another which held real promise but failed to survive into the second edition. In this he played a tipsy North Countryman who mistook a box at the Savoy Theatre for his Savoy Hotel bedroom, encouraged by a plant in the audience advising him to continue 'Straight on, sir'. His getting into pyjamas and settling down for the night was counterpointed with the chatter of the theatre crowd, excitedly anticipating 'the Bed Scene'.[287] The show's dark scenes, by the American Ned Wayburn, were altogether different from Grattan's. 'Spooks' gave 'a weird impression of faint, luminous figures dancing against a black background in a perfectly dark house', while the only light in 'Sparkings' was achieved 'by the steel-tipped shoes of the dancers striking an "electric" carpet'.[288]

For Barrie's *Rosy Rapture*, using a good deal of film, the auditorium was kept dark throughout. But this was exceptional enough to draw comment.[289] In general, revue avoided imposing that psychological barrier, reversing the trend which had changed audiences from participants into voyeurs. It deliberately fostered drastic rethinking of the boundaries between the real and the imaginary. Plants, derived from the music hall, helped. *Joy-Land* had critical but unconstructive comments from Harry Tate as a deadhead in the stalls during a dramatic scene: 'Is anyone listening? – No. – (*From audience:* Liar!) – Ebenezer, have pity on me, remember the love you bore me. – (*From audience:* And you bore me.) – What a terrible situation for a man to be in. But what can I do? – (*From audience*: Work for your living.)' When an attendant came to eject the interrupter, he snapped: 'Don't be a fool, I'm engaged to do this'; but at the urgings to 'Put him out' from those on stage, he was removed struggling.[290] What Street called 'a silly and pointless interruption' occurs in *The Passing Show*, when a woman rushes on to the stage complaining that her husband is in the theatre with another woman. A man protesting against the interruption comes to suspect that his wife is the other woman and mounts the stage seeking confirmation. The manager appeals for 'any lady answering the description ... to leave the Theatre. Half a dozen couples in stalls and circle rise to go out' and the interrupted performance is resumed 'from the start'. (A supposedly factual analogue appeared in a German Catholic magazine eager to demonstrate mid-1915 decadence.[291]) Altogether more flat-footed was the patriotic interruption in *By Jingo*, with Julien Henry in khaki shouting agreement when a character announced 'We are a hopeless lot of wasters', and ascending the stage. Asked who authorized him, he replied: 'the King', singing 'Everybody's Got To Do His Bit'.[292]

Various of revue's techniques were anticipated by Shakespeare, who absorbed much of the 'hotchpotch' (a word used by Lyly in the late sixteenth century, but frequently applied to revue in the early twentieth) which he found occupying the London stage. His theatre, too, saw the containments of the stage world continually being violated. Affinities were obvious to Newton when he wrote of the tercentenary production of *The Taming of the Shrew* at His Majesty's, where an apron effect was achieved: 'Once, at any rate, [Harvey's] Petruchio comes boldly out upon the platform and renews for a moment the relations between actor and audience that link modern revue with Shakespeare's stage.'[293] Here was another means whereby de Courville's colossal Hippodrome shows broke out of the stage frame. As Mistinguett well knew, 'These sorties into the auditorium need careful timing and a good deal of agility.'[294] Indeed, at the Fémina Theatre in wartime Paris, Carter had seen her 'partly undressed by a soldier spectator'.[295] That Hippodrome favourite Shirley Kellogg, a great user of the gangplank, experienced a more prosaic mishap during a performance of *Push and Go* when 'she overbalanced, and turned a complete somersault into the stalls'.[296] Many besides de Courville adopted the gangplank; indeed, in Barrie's *Rosy Rapture* it is disputed whether the show in progress can be a revue when it lacks that 'gangway over the stalls'.[297] But it became so much his trademark that he emphasized its omission from *Razzle-Dazzle* as a novelty.[298] It was used for 'Watch On The Rhine' in *Business as*

Usual, which Newton would have dropped as 'unduly bragful'. But Darewski describes how a first-night failure was turned into a hit for Harry Tate, Morris Harvey, Violet Loraine and Ambrose Thorne. Divided into pairs, perambulating 'the plank midways through the audience', they induced one half to vie with the other in the chorus.[299] Gangplank interludes kept audiences amused during a big scene change.[300] In *Zig-Zag*, with 'one of those audacious flirting with the audience songs that she has made peculiarly her own', Kellogg led a group of dancing anglers on to the gangplank. They playfully tempted stalls patrons to reach for the fish dangling from their lines, 'laughing merrily' as they were no sooner grasped than dropped when a button in the handle of the rod communicated a mild electric shock.[301]

Pyjama choruses were popular, *5064 Gerrard*'s gangplank version 'so cunningly revealing', despite the dazzle of the dancers' torches, as to be 'worth the price of a stall close-up'.[302] In *See-Saw*, cream pyjamas were complemented by richly coloured cushions which flew in from the wings during one number. The girls reclined on them, finally gathering at the footlights to 'chuck little cushions of the same brilliant shades at the audience'.[303] Here was another ploy for breaking down the spatial separation of performer and public; and again it became so strongly associated with Hippodrome revues that in *Cheerio!*'s burlesque the notoriously extravagant 'de Courville' sought to economize by engaging a pair of unknowns, who seldom lasted beyond the first night and eked out by selling quack medicine. Since balloons, snowballs and pom-poms had been thrown into the audience in previous productions, they would throw sample bottles of their embrocation; and whereas Kellogg went 'down the gang-plank into the audience' the audience would now come up it on to the stage and be cured of their ailments.[304] It was in *Push and Go*, its title deriving from Lloyd George's need of a 'man with some push and go',[305] that de Courville first used the throwing gambit. It was introduced at the very last minute when he asked Darewski for an 'audience' song.[306] It meant that Kellogg not only sang 'On The Road To Dublin Town' from a 'portable gangway, held up by a small army of stalwarts in military tunics of Muscovite sort',[307] but also hurled dozens of coloured rubber balls into the auditorium while rendering 'Won't You Come And Play With Me'. This started a craze in 1915 for throwing things, one columnist saying of 'the famous "flight of toys" ... thrown to the audience at the finale' of *Oh La La* (Queen's), that 'their one fault is their lightness'. It was Kellogg's balls which proved the 'most "carrying"', even reaching the gods.[308] There was no discouragement of audience retaliation: Darewski mentions one instance, and another saw a party of officers begin a bombardment of their own from the royal box – 'To this Miss Kellogg responded with such energy that the officers hung out a white flag.'[309]

The missiles were often carried off as trophies: one officer took one thrown by Kellogg back to Flanders, returning it to her three weeks later punctured by bullets where he had 'held it above the parapet on the end of a bayonet, singing "Won't You Come And Play With Me?"' Darewski's story of a bombing party assailing an enemy trench while singing his song has numerous anologues, many of them probably true. Such was the relationship in which theatre stood to this war that horror was continually becoming enmeshed with stage frivolity. Many officers planned their leave around London shows: when Major Leslie Faber was reported missing in action it was recalled that on his last 14 days' leave he aimed at 12 shows whilst in town.[310] Harold Alexander, the World War II general who at this time was a captain in the Irish Guards, was infatuated with Laurette Taylor, star of *Peg O' My Heart*, who supplied him with a gramophone at the front. It was a great success, he wrote, but was also somewhat disorientating: 'When I go to a music hall or revue now I know all the songs by heart and they remind me of my dugout and people out here. It seems all round the wrong way – the tunes ought to remind me of London.'[311]

This offers oblique confirmation of the French *fin-de-siècle* idea of comedy being rooted in diabolism. Macabre humour associates easily with the Dance of Death: 'Just as our soldiers laugh at death, so our helpless stay-at-homes laugh at the low comedian.'[312] The dancing with corpses is also a sexual dance, and Robey's creation of Lucifer Bing represents convergence of diabolism and sex, a cartoon by Bert Thomas reducing *The Bing Boys* to 'two good turns – One Robey and the other Dis-robey'.[313] A tank commander asked Robey for *Bing Boys* posters to decorate his tank 'next time we go into action'; and Stoll received hundreds of requests from 'France, Salonika, and Mesopotamia' for the one representing Robey and Lester 'each with a girl on their knees'.[314] The show was alleged to 'put a new vitality into trench-tired boys',[315] which received an unconsidered twist in Wyndham Lewis's short story 'The War Baby' where a subaltern and his girl, going to the Alhambra fed on war-wine and kisses, found that 'Robey, with his primitive genius, flattered the mood of the evening'. Afterwards, a taxi witnessed 'the ultimate convulsions of love ... The corpses of the battlefield had perhaps cheapened flesh? Anyway, realities were infectious; and all women seemed to feel that they should have their luxurious battles, too; only they were playing at dying, and their war was fruitful.'[316]

The heady incongruity with which horror and humour commixed points to the way that revue's erosion of theatre convention went beyond throwing things or clutching at performers intruding on what was ordinarily considered to be the spectators' domain. In insinuating doubt about whether the world of Robey and Loraine or that of the Western Front represented reality, it went well beyond H. E.'s worry that in ridiculing stage illusion, it was reducing audience capacity 'for being illusionized'.[317] Revue is a form which, intent on money-making rather than subversion, strangely anticipated Dada. Yet, a product of the commercial theatre, not a challenge to it, its freedoms are illusory. By asserting that things are as they are, it aligns with a good deal of modernist poetry in putting an innovative form at the disposal of conservatism. But paradox clings: it implies the proximity of stage absurdity and that of the Western Front, where the revue of revues was translating fantasies of destruction into needs: the endless need for more shells was consumerism run mad, with humanity paying the price. Revue, thought Farjeon, 'satisfies our restless clamour';[318] and for Sydney Carroll it was 'as much a part of modern life as the cinema, the motor-car, the aeroplane, or wireless telegraphy'[319] (during the war he might have said the 4.5 howitzer or Vickers machine gun), possessing 'the same celerity, variety and efficiency'.

Some detected in it the maddening whorls 'of a "Futurist" painting';[320] and few could overlook the demands it made for renegotiating spatial or fictional relationships. The war play sought to attach to its subject some of the assumptions about the well-made play: beginning, middle and end, with unseen but competent manipulators guaranteeing a satisfactory conclusion. Revue seemed to travel a less certain path, its catastrophes (performers on strike, or costumes failing to arrive) threatening not just some fictional protagonist but the audience with a curtailing of its entertainment. That this should give more than a general sense of life's mishaps, glancing at those belonging to the war itself, was inevitable when war-generated interruptions were far from unusual. One simulated and one actual instance will suffice to make the point. In *The Bing Girls*, Loraine's hit song, 'Let The Great Big World Keep Turning', was interrupted by an 'official' announcement: 'the theatre has been taken over by the War Office.' The audience was asked not to leave as 'public co-operation and volunteers' were required.[321] But the stab of anxiety produced by revue pranks soon passed. Reality intruded on Harry Roxbury's revue, *Fine Feathers*, during a stint at a naval port, a mass exodus following an Admiralty order to rejoin ships. Thus Jutland made its mark on the theatre before a shot was fired.[322] Under these conditions the subversive potential of revue might have reverberated far beyond the aesthetic sphere. Instead, that favourite ploy of the revue about making a revue became almost a paradigm of those various fictional elements fed to the civilian population out of which it was encouraged to construct an unproblematic version of the war.

Even so, during its earlier phase at least, revue engaged in some exhilarating theatrical experiment, sometimes barely skirting political danger. Grattan's revues have their moments, through 'the union that they establish between the players and the audience. One has the delightfully comfortable sensation that those generally detached great personages of the stage are really only human beings after all, and are just as much dependent on us as we are on them.'[323]

The political implications would have alarmed some. And although a new dimension had come into view since leading players now enjoyed power through startling advances in salary and status, this recalls that theatrical preoccupation with power and the powerful, explored through the intricacies of rôle-playing, which had caused so much commotion some 300 years before. Grattan's method takes us right to the heart of intimate revue. He was said to have abolished 'the footlights except for illumination purposes', his

> recipe for putting players and public on the friendliest of terms [being] to show exactly how author-manager and players conspire together to concoct a revue. In 'Cheep!' we are present at a rehearsal, see the principals arrive, hear them greeted by their Christian or pet names, and listen with delight to the slang of the stage.[324]

The ubiquitous rehearsal scene perhaps served as a special kind of purging after the tension and nervous wear and tear of a hectic and uncertain preparation period. As unconsidered vehicle for the democratizing impulse, the most obvious alternative which it offered to Grattan's approach was through the exposure of star temperament. De Courville's *Good-bye-ee*[325] typically contains a rehearsal without the cast having 'had the decency to turn up'. The usual result is that stage-hands, stage-struck groupies, or just anyone within reach get roped in to substitute. Although at first cutting ludicrous figures in ill-fitting costumes, the deputies soon demonstrate their capability. At the dress rehearsal in Roxbury's *Fine Feathers*, the leading lady makes a temperamental disappearance, and the theatre cleaner is prevailed upon to replace her. (These charladies – cf. Dorothy Summers's Mrs Mopp in *ITMA* – were stock figures of revue like the waiter.) In Rubens and Bovill's *Half-Past Eight*, a revue management seized an opportunistic solution to imminent disaster, enrolling country bumpkin Will Evans and his 16 pretty daughters as comedian and chorus.[326] But Mabel Russell's co-option into the show, 'understudying herself in the part of a dresser who impersonates the absent actress', revealed the full labyrinthine possibilities of revue.[327]

Follow the Crowd (Empire) includes 'an amusing squabble between the principals about who is to star in the production'.[328] This recalls Bernini's *I due covelli* (1637), with its dispute between these two blusterers from the *commedia dell'arte* as to which is the genuine article. Such internal arguments are a feature of wartime revue. The comics in *Half-Past Eight* (Will Evans and Rube Welch) have a similar quarrel; and an insertion into *£150*, 'The Four Commères', finds competition for the rôle mounting as each claimant invokes a member of the theatre's hierarchy as sponsor, the fourth routing her rivals by announcing that she has been backed by Cochran himself.[329] In *See-Saw*,[330] Gaw is about to begin conjuring when Ruby Miller enters as a special constable, 'advances to footlights and nods to Braham – as if she was ready for her song'. Neither being ready to give way, the stage manager finally blacks out the stage.

But a feature of Bernini's play was that its fashionable audience was nonplussed to find itself mirrored on the other side of the curtain.[331] Thus the idea in *Razzle-Dazzle* of two audiences facing each other was not quite so novel as the *Telegraph*'s critic (8 June 1916, p. 4) supposed:

> The actual audience will witness the ascent of the curtain, the actors going through the business of the scene with their backs to the auditorium. In front of them are the footlights, and beyond them the audience [quite substantial with a cast of 350], not figures painted on canvas but real live spectators, evincing their interest in the proceedings by frequent outbursts of applause.

But further liberty was taken with staider notions of reality when, at one performance, a group of critics was tempted out of the real stalls to play a part in mimic stalls on stage.[332] The audience of *Bubbly* was inveigled into playing an audience, taking directions. Thus since the rehearsal scene required the audience to imagine the performers as 'village amateurs', it was further invited to imagine itself 'the village audience'; and 'a village audience laughs very heartily and applauds very freely'.[333]

But it was the buttonholing approach which could achieve the most remarkable results. Grattan was said to have 'set the fashion for the free-and-easy *revue*, which professed to be an impromptu or a rehearsal and took the audience into the confidences of behind the scenes'. But in his *Some*, structural self-exposure turns into an elaborate game with mirrors: 'We begin with the finale, and then follow the comedian to his dressing-room and the leading lady to hers and the chorus to theirs, and hear what the kind friends in front and the manager and other people have to say about the performance.'[334] The confidential manner is there from the outset, with Gene Gerrard as compère deciding to cut out the amenities: 'I don't know if you *are* ladies and gentlemen.' He is confident that 'none of you know what a revue is, or you wouldn't be here'. So he explains: 'Revue commences, but has no beginning. It finishes, but has no end. It has bits in the middle which can be part of the whole or not, just as they like ... very few of you ever come in to see the beginning. Still fewer see the end.' So they may as well start with 'the Finale. The beginning of the end will be the end of the beginning.'[335] (Churchill, who had a taste for revue, may have recalled this in his 1943 speech on the fall of Tripoli.[336]) The 'Finale' is given, flowers are handed up and confusions multiply as the 'Conductor about to play "King"' is stopped since there is more to come.

Vertiginous shifts from one dimension to another, and the way that conventionally invisible theatre personnel step in and out of the frame, became so commonplace that it is hard to trace lines of indebtedness. But some suggestions may have been picked up from the stage-door scene in *Shell Out*, where, 'after a first night which the author ventures to think has been particularly successful, [he] learns from all concerned, including the scenic artist, the costumier and even a "dresser", that from their point of view the show has been a miserable failure'.[337] There are certainly points of similarity in the near-contemporary *Pell Mell* (Ambassadors). This has a 'saucily effective "spoof" opening' supposedly taking place ten minutes after the scheduled starting time, with 'an independent and back-answering painter ... still busily engaged touching up one side of the proscenium, and successfully defying both real manager and Mr. J. M. Campbell, who represents the stage manager in the revue'. As a result, Cochran 'has to make an appearance in the stalls' to settle the dispute; and confusion reaches lunatic proportions when he informs Campbell, who has been remonstrating with the painter 'for interrupting a rehearsal', that this is no rehearsal 'but a first-night'. So 'Campbell, adapting himself to circumstances, decides to let things go as they like, and begin at the end, and prophesies correctly that nobody will notice any difference'.[338] This last point is reaffirmed in *See-Saw*, where, during an interlude, the night watchman enters, 'sweeping the stage with a broom'. Uncertainty is expressed about whether the show is over, and when he indicates the lowered curtain and the fact that 'the lights are out in the auditorium', he is reminded that 'you can never tell when these revues begin or end'.[339]

Any kind of internal arrangement was grist for revue's mill. Casting and costuming both provided humour; the censor proving squeamish over a snatch of telephone conversation in *The Passing Show*: 'We can rehearse here. What? No, I haven't got anything on. What? That'll be all right – we can use the sofa.'[340] Costuming gags were less tired, and their very ubiquity reflects abiding managerial anxiety. Experience had taught Sohlke that it was 'good policy to entrust the dresses for one scene to one dressmaker, those of another scene to another dressmaker, and so on. When it is remembered that in "Hullo, America!" there are 355 dresses, or, including principals, 415, it will be conceived what part this question plays in the production.' Likewise, there are '700 pairs of shoes, too much to be handed out to one firm'.[341] *The Bing Girls*[342] finds a theatrical manager, made up like Butt, worrying that his revue is due to start the next night and 'the Hawaiian costumes aren't ready yet'. But in *Flying Colours* Little Tich can respond more positively on hearing that only the girls' underwear is ready for the night's performance, promptly departing 'to book a seat'.[343] In Herbert Sargent's *Love Birds*, it is the dress cleaners who have proved remiss, and the stage manager interrupts the overture to beg the audience's indulgence. But just then a porter arrives at the 'back of the auditorium, carrying a pile of dress boxes'. Porter and boxes are hauled 'on to the stage, and pushed through the tabs. The curtain is raised leaving the cinema screen down. On this is shown the reflection of the girls getting into their frocks. There is a blackout and the revue proper starts.' Those reflections were marked by the censor for cutting, but survived at the Middlesex: 'The cinematic cloth is lowered, and the ladies of the chorus are revealed scrambling into their clothes. In another moment all is brightness, and the spectators behold a score or more of scintillating sirens.'[344]

Revues had this amiable trait of laughing at themselves. 'Certain things in the hotch-potch are positively funny', allowed a *Times* critic (25 August 1915, p. 9) of *Shell Out*; 'among them the domestic scene in which the quarrelling husband and wife and the reconciling child are so used to *revue* and to a chorus that they cannot conduct their dispute without each his row of imitators in dumb show'.[345] But they were equally unsparing of the regular theatre. Genres were despoiled and conventions gleefully ripped apart, demolition the more effective because it was done by people who understood these things from the inside. A series of skits in *Bubbly* (Comedy) won unanimous approval. The hoary subject 'of the headstrong youth who has fallen in love with the wrong woman' was handled first in the epigrammatic style of the St James's; then in 'slick and slangy O. Henry fashion'; as a Stage Society piece 'full of Lancashire gloom'; and finally 'as a bold and dashing "Rule, Britannia" drama by Walter Melville at the Lyceum', enacted on the deck of a battleship. This latter had Arthur Playfair 'as a hearty old Admiral' and 'Jack Hulbert as the heroic young lieutenant determined to marry a forbidden young thing in book-muslin', who turns out to be the admiral's daughter.[346] Randal Charlton considered Playfair 'our greatest revue actor', who 'as a satirist ... had no equal on the English stage'. His performance as George Alexander in the St James's episode 'was perhaps the most remarkable piece of dramatic criticism that has ever appeared on the stage. It was so faithful to life that certain people called it cruel.'[347]

Vanity Fair (Palace) included an economy play, *Without the Walls*, the title indicating that not only the fourth wall but the remaining three as well are dispensed with. So at the start Harry is both seen and heard ('swearing at dresser') before his entry. Rejected by his girl, he 'tears up her letters and throws them into the fire place', whereupon a stage-hand enters with dust-pan and brush. When Harry draws a revolver and rushes off-stage to commit suicide, he can be seen with his fingers in his ears. After the bang he 'lights cigarette and stands chatting with Props'. When the heroine supposedly arrives on a galloping horse, she is revealed being dusted with fuller's earth while a property man appears 'working clams' to resemble hoofbeats.[348] This was one of the techniques demonstrated by Philip Rodway, manager of the Theatre Royal, Birmingham, when he lectured to the wounded on the tricks of the trade in 1918.[349] That Rodway should do this, and find an eager audience, suggests that fears about revue's demystifying tendency infecting the regular stage were well grounded.

Fusing of stage illusion and 'audience reality' aroused critical disapproval in *5064 Gerrard* (the title borrowing the Alhambra's stage-door telephone number and exchange). Before Gaby Deslys joined the show she was being impersonated by Robert Hale, in her association with James Barrie (Jack Morrison): 'All the little stage tricks of the Parisian comedienne are hit off neatly, while the foibles of Sir James and his popular fiction characters also come in for treatment.' Barrie 'in abbreviated kilt and prominent knees is perhaps not in the best of taste', but anyone entering 'the revue ring ... must expect a crack or two in the process'. The concluding 'dance in which Barrie turns into Pilcer is a wonderful imitation of Gaby's cuddle'.[350] When the real Gaby arrived, she could meet the imitation face to face, raising intricate problems of identity. However, it was the blurring of private and stage personae when she reunited with her old dancing partner Harry Pilcer which Marks denounced as 'an error of taste': 'The public is not concerned or in any way interested in the fact that the appearance of Mlle Deslys and Mr. Pilcer at the Alhambra marks the patching up of a recent quarrel between the artists.'[351] But this is entirely characteristic of revue's hit-and-run approach to convention, already seen in the way that known relationships between Hallam and Deslys or Hallam and Elsie Janis became interwoven with the show in which they were appearing. The personal intruded readily because revue made everything intensely visible. The result was to create audience uncertainty about how much was stage business and how much belonged to its own world. Refusal to accept any footlight demarcation forced reconsideration of the relation of stage action to both backstage and front-of-house realities. It called attention to audience implication in the constructing of fictions enacted on stage and elsewhere. The theatre customarily invites audiences to respond to the stage character simultaneously as both real and fictitious. But revue audiences were forced to relinquish their hold on such distinctions and to acknowledge that there was no knowing where the real ended and simulation began. Characters (or performers) veered beyond the creativity or mediation of author or actor; and in achieving self-definition they were often redefined. This theatre had that habit of assailing identity which characterized the theatre of war. So Edwin Turner, who worked on music for the revue, *Pretty Darlings*, 'whilst in his billet at the front', is referred to as 'Mr .. or to give him his proper title, Private Edwin Turner, of the 8 Royal Scots'.[352] Ernest Thesiger, when he moved from one kind of theatre to the other, experienced the same shimmering uncertainty: 'I seemed entirely to have forgotten my real identity, but at the same time I never could quite forget that it was only a character part that I was playing – with the help of an ill-fitting uniform ... and a closely-cropped head.'[353] He had joined what that fine revue artist Elsie Janis called *The Big Show*.[354] As an American, Janis felt the war's narcotic tug in 1917, abandoning lucrative London leads for a bit part in those long-running Follies playing in France.

Notes

1. *Era* 6.9.16, 1.
2. A. B., *Era* 5.9.17, 1.
3. *Era* 26.7.16, 8.
4. Chance Newton, *Cues and Curtain Calls* (Lane, 1927), p. 151.
5. Oscar Asche, *Oscar Asche: His Life* (Hurst and Blackett, 1929), p. 162. H. G. Hibbert, *A Playgoer's Memories* (Richards, 1920), p. 152, calculated that income was at least double the 'outlay of £200 on each performance', without counting that from music and recording rights. A request to send *Chu Chin Chow* recordings to her son on the Western Front was received in May 1917 by Mrs Patrick Campbell, *My Life and Some Letters* (Hutchinson, 1922), p. 320.
6. Asche, *Oscar Asche*, p. 165.
7. Newton, *Referee* 28.2.17, 3.
8. Newton, *Referee* 8.9.16, 3.
9. Newton, *Referee* 28.2.17, 3.
10. *Era* 14.3.17, 8.
11. *Graphic* 21.12.18, 734; Asche, *Oscar Asche*, p. 165.
12. José Collins, *The Maid of the Mountains, Her Story* (Hutchinson, 1932), p. 165.
13. *Era* 14.2.17, 1; Asche, *Oscar Asche*, pp. 169–70.
14. *Referee* 17.2.18, 3; *Era* 14.2.17, 1.
15. Collins, *Maid*, pp. 119, 153.
16. *The Times* 24.5.15, 9.
17. J. S., *World* 3.11.14, 79; *Stage* 25.2.15, 22; *Era* 19.9.17, 14.
18. *Graphic* 15.12.17, 796.
19. *The Times* 21.6.15, 11.
20. W. J. Macqueen-Pope, *Ghosts and Greasepaint* (Hale, 1951), p. 194.
21. *SYB 1919*, p. 5.
22. B. W. Findon, *Play Pictorial* 28(167), 18; Robert Courtneidge, *'I Was an Actor Once'* (Hutchinson, 1930), pp. 222–3.
23. *Era* 18.4.17, 11.
24. Leslie Henson, *Yours Faithfully, an Autobiography* (Long, 1948), pp. 57, 61.
25. Fred Thompson, *The Boy* (Chappell, 1918), No. 23.
26. *Era* 31.10.17, 1.

27. Charles Graves, *The Cochran Story*, p. 68, notes that Cornwell's brother was similarly employed in Hicks and Shirley's musical play, *Jolly Jack Tar*, which had 67 performances at the Prince's at the end of 1918.
28. *Era* 15.5.18, 13; *The Times* 14.5.18, 9.
29. Charles Cochran, *The Secrets of a Showman* (Heinemann, 1929), p. 227; Robert Keable, *Simon Called Peter* (Constable, 1921), pp. 324–5.
30. *Referee* 17.10.17, 3.
31. Stanley Lupino, *From the Stocks to the Stars* (Hutchinson, 1934), pp. 104–5.
32. *Era* 4.9.18, 13; *Era* 21.8.18, 8.
33. *Referee* 9.6.18, 2.
34. *Era* 22.12.15, 21; *The Times* 1.12.15, 11.
35. *Era* 7.3.17, 14.
36. Its composer was James Glover, and it was premièred at his Theatre Royal, Plymouth (*Era* 11.8.15, 18).
37. *SYB 1916*, p. 31; *Stage* 7.10.15, 18.
38. *Sunday Review* 15.9.17, 203 (my italics).
39. Charles Cochran, *Cock-a-Doodle-Do* (Dent, 1941), p. 308.
40. Cochran, *Secrets*, p. 207.
41. Jack Norworth, *Era* 5.1.16, 9.
42. *Referee* 31.3.18, 3.
43. *Era* 29.12.15, 25.
44. *Era* 22.12.15, 21.
45. *Era* 25.7.17, 1; *Era* 29.9.15, 20.
46. LC 1915: 28/3797.
47. *Performer* 26.9.18, 15.
48. *Evening News* 9.4.15, 7.
49. Cochran, *Cock-a-Doodle-Do*, p. 308.
50. *Daily Express* 28.11.17, 2.
51. LC 1916: 3/63.
52. LC 1915: 5/3226.
53. *Sunday Times* 3.11.18, 4; *Play Pictorial* 33(199), 49.
54. *Evening News* 9.4.15, 7.
55. *Era* 29.12.15, 25.
56. *Era* 24.1.17, 13.
57. *Era* 5.1.16, 9. America's first unmistakable revue was *The Passing Show* of 1894.
58. *Era* 3.11.15, 15.
59. LC 1915: 25/3719.
60. James M. Glover, *Jimmy Glover and His Friends* (Chatto, 1913), p. 284.
61. Brett Page, *Writing for Vaudeville* (Springfield, Mass.: Home Correspondence School, 1915), p. 258.

62. *Era* 10.5.16, 13. Cf. the 'slickness' of *Watch Your Step* (Empire), which provided 'a striking lesson in the stage methods of our American cousins' (*Era* 12.5.15, 12).
63. *Era* 8.4.14, 15.
64. G. H. Mair, 'The Music-Hall', *English Review* 9 (1911), 123.
65. *Cartoon* 4.3.15, 142, and *Era* 8.11.16, 13.
66. *Era* 25.7.17, 1.
67. *Era* 4.4.17, 12.
68. LC 1918: 8/1553.
69. *Era* 23.6.15, 9.
70. *Era* 2.5.17, 1.
71. *Stage* 3.5.17, 15.
72. Alfred Barnard, *Era* 2.8.16, 13.
73. *Weekly Dispatch* 23.7.16, 5.
74. Marks, *Referee* 16.7.16, 7.
75. *Weekly Dispatch* 28.5.16, 6.
76. *Sunday Chronicle* 11.6.16, 3.
77. *Dial* 70 (January–June 1921), 686–91 (688).
78. *New Statesman* 1.8.14, 533.
79. *Stage* 24.2.16, 14.
80. *Era* 5.8.14, 11, citing a fantasy minimum of 35s.
81. Programme-sellers at one West End variety theatre which had for years paid dividends varying between 15 and 25 per cent, received 'commission only', often barely '10s. a week'. Assuming they lived with relatives for as little as 15s. a week this still meant that 'those relatives were subscribing 5s. per week towards the profits of the theatre' (*Era* 5.7.16, 20).
82. Arnold Golsworthy, *Bystander* 15.3.16, 488. Reviewing *Bric-à-Brac,* Fenton (*World* 21.9.15, 287) typically assigns 'pride of place ... to the Sixteen Palace Girls'.
83. *Era* 25.9.18, 12; *Era* 7.3.17, 8.
84. *Era* 2.10.18, 6; *Era* 18.9.18, 8.
85. Hall Caine, *Our Girls* (Hutchinson, 1916), p. 41.
86. *Evening News* 27.3.16, 2.
87. *Performer* 15.6.16, 21.
88. *Era* 23.5.17, 14; *Referee* 3.6.17, 3. It certainly impressed Newton, *Referee* 10.6.17, 3: 'One thing which must be cut out bodily is the leg-waving of the said "Beauty Chorus" while lying on their backs all over the stage, after one of the soubrettes has sung an unveracious song asserting that "Legs Only Matter in Revue".'
89. *Performer* 9.8.17, 13.

90. *Performer* 21.2.18, 17.
91. *Era* 4.9.18, 15.
92. *Weekly Dispatch* 5.8.17, 5.
93. *Era* 18.9.18, 8.
94. *Era* 28.3.17, 7.
95. LC 1917: 8/907.
96. Henry Kendall, *I Remember Romano's* (Macdonald, 1960), p. 31.
97. *Evening News* 12.6.16, 3; *Era* 17.11.15, 16. Typically, a revue at the Kilburn Empire was prefaced by a screened announcement that all those eligible had joined up and were appearing 'by permission of their commanding officer' (*Era* 9.6.15, 7); while in most Christmas pantomimes 'the male chorus [would] be dispensed with altogether' (*Star* 12.10.15, 5).
98. *Star* 8.10.15, 3.
99. *Era* 3.3.15, 9. For Warr's particularly telling reply to Collins, see p. 9 above.
100. *Era* 25.7.17, 8. Interestingly, Gertie Millar's 1917 recording of 'Pretty Baby' from *Houp-La* is backed by the St Martin's Theatre Orchestra and male chorus.
101. *Era* 11.8.15, 12. This worked very successfully for *Some Glee*.
102. *The Times* 21.4.17, 3. The case was dismissed (*The Times* 23.4.17, 5).
103. *Era* 23.5.17, 7.
104. LC 1915: 15/3480; *Era* 28.6.16, 8.
105. *Era* 3.11.15, 21.
106. *Era* 24.5.16, 8.
107. Farjeon, *Era* 5.12.17, 1.
108. Lupino, *From the Stocks*, pp. 105–7.
109. Golsworthy, *Bystander* 3.1.17, 26.
110. *Era* 29.12.15, 25.
111. Beatrice Lillie, *Every Other Inch a Lady* (1972, rept. New York: Dell, 1974), p. 90.
112. Cochran, *Weekly Dispatch* 23.7.16, 5.
113. Grein, *Era* 27.6.17, 1.
114. *Stage* 20.9.17, 16; *Era* 5.7.16, 12; lyrics by Valentine, music by Tate (Francis, Day & Hunter, 1916).
115. Macqueen-Pope, *Ghosts and Greasepaint*, p. 182.
116. *Weekly Dispatch* 27.8.16, 4.
117. Anthony French, *Gone for a Soldier* (Kineton: Roundwood Press, 1972), p. 40.
118. F. P. Crozier, *A Brass Hat in No Man's Land* (Cape, 1930), p. 174.
119. *Referee* 23.1.16, 5.
120. Lena Ashwell, *Modern Troubadours* (Gyldendal, 1922), p. 27.

121. Kendall, *I Remember Romano's*, pp. 31–2; W. J. Macqueen-Pope, *Gaiety: Theatre of Enchantment* (Allen, 1949), p. 211, records Nellie Farren, in Reece's *Our Cinderella* (1883), as the first to wear electric lights on stage.
122. *Stage* 6.5.15, 16; *Era* 12.5.15, 12.
123. *Referee* 20.2.16, 3.
124. Ernest Short and Arthur Compton-Rickett, *Ring Up the Curtain* (Jenkins, 1938), p. 129.
125. Marks, *Referee* 11.11.17, 5; *Era* 7.11.17, 17.
126. Lillie, *Every Other Inch*, pp. 89, 95–6.
127. As indicated by the song-sheet (Francis, Day and Hunter, 1917).
128. He recalls White singing of black-eyed Susans, and how 'Girls must all be Farmers' Boys, off with skirts, wear corduroys' (Robert Graves, *Good-bye to All That* (Cape, 1929), p. 332).
129. *Passing Show* 11.12.15, 20.
130. *Era* 13.6.17, 1.
131. Charles Harrison, *Generals Die in Bed* (Douglas, 1931), pp. 152–4. The song was not always played for laughs. When George Heston sang it in *Jack-in-the-Box* 'he imparted just a touch of bitterness' ('Extra Turn', *Era* 16.10.18, 12).
132. Christopher Stone, *From Vimy Ridge to the Rhine: The Great War Letters*, ed. G. D. Sheffield and G. I. S. Inglis (Ramsbury, Marlborough, Wilts.), p. 49.
133. *Era* 30.8.16, 12.
134. [Don Brophy and Harold Price], *A Rattle of Pebbles: The First World War Diaries of Two Canadian Airmen*, ed. Brereton Greenhous (Ottawa: Canadian Government Publishing Centre, 1987), p. 31; *Era* 29.12.15, 15; *Stage* 30.12.15, 16.
135. *Stage* 21.12.16, 18.
136. *Referee* 11.3.17, 3; *Era* 16.5.17, 1; *Era* 17.12.16, 3; *Bystander* 3.1.17, 26.
137. Harry Lauder, *A Minstrel in France* (Melrose, 1918), p. 89.
138. Newton, *Referee* 24.12.16, 3. Lauder, probably the highest-paid British artist, enjoyed exercising his power. It was 'woe betide any ... employee who mar[red] in any way the master's performance' (W. H. Boardman, *Vaudeville Days*, ed. David Whitelaw (Jarrolds, 1935), p. 277).
139. *Stage* 4.11.15, 22.
140. One cartoon (31.3.17, 1) shows Cuthbert presenting Haig with the curate's egg, labelled '45 years old', a solution to the manpower problem by raising the age limit which would have brought Poy (born in Shanghai 6 September 1874) into the danger zone.
141. Marks, *Referee* 20.5.17, 7.
142. LC 1916: 3/59.

143. *John Bull* 12.9.14, 2 and *passim.*
144. LC 1915: 5/3221; LC 1914: 31/2981. 'The German's Hymn Of Love', in *Good Evening* (LC 1915: 17/3543), playing off Ernst Lissauer's notorious 'Hymn Of Hate', claims a mutual love between Hardie and the Germans.
145. LC 1914: 14/3014. Heligoland, ceded to Germany for its strategic position commanding the western end of the Kiel Canal, also glances at current squeamishness.
146. *Era* 24.3.15, 8; 'Which Switch Is The Switch, Miss, For Ipswich?' (Francis, Day and Hunter, 1915).
147. LC 1915: 34/3923.
148. LC 1916: 9/203.
149. Barnard, *Era* 12.12.17, 1.
150. *Era* 21.10.14, 10. The paper kept up pressure (28.10.14, 10): 'Mr. Butt does not inform me what patriotic purpose is served by the retention of the clumsy title, which only typifies the anti-Russian feeling so prevalent in this country during the Russo-Turkish war of 1877–78. During the present crisis the word Jingo should be banished from the vocabulary of every Briton.'
151. *Referee* 25.10.14, 3.
152. LC 1914: 31/2981.
153. Newton, *Referee* 25.10.14, 3; Glover, *Era* 17.3.15, 12.
154. *Era* 28.10.14, 10.
155. Newton, *Referee* 25.10.14, 3; *Era* 21.10.14, 10.
156. *Weekly Dispatch* 23.7.16, 5.
157. *Stage* 15.4.15, 14; Marks, *Referee* 2.9.17, 5.
158. *World* 24.11.14, 146.
159. Newton, *Referee* 22.11.14, 3; *Era* 18.11.14, 14.
160. Newton, *Referee* 10.6.17, 3.
161. LC 1915: 14/3014.
162. 'Autolycus', *Passing Show* 4.9.15, 19. In another scene, 'Morton is being measured for a suit of clothes by a couple of tailors who are discussing war strategy, and who demonstrate their sartorial theories by drawing chalk diagrams all over him and sticking flags on his tenderest spots.'
163. *Weekly Dispatch* 9.9.17, 4.
164. *Referee* 29.9.18, 3.
165. LC 1918: 17/179.
166. *Era* 28.2.17, 14.
167. West, wife of Colonel Cornwallis West of Ruthin Castle, Denbighshire, was very well connected; her eldest daughter, Princess Pless, had married into the German aristocracy, while another was Duchess of Westminster. Her son's first wife, displaced by Mrs Patrick Campbell, was Churchill's

half-sister. Hence she had little trouble in securing the transfer of an unresponsive junior officer. When the affair became public, Lt-Colonel Delmé-Radcliffe was relieved of his command, but Lt-General Sir J. Cowans, her man at the War Office, was evidently too important to suffer more than the temporary 'displeasure of the Government' (LC 1917: 4/793; *The Times* 4.1.17, 9).

168. Newton, *Referee* 31.10.15, 3; *Stage* 4.11.15, 22.
169. LC 1915: 5/3221. In the same show a German woman claims that her work for the 'Faterland' is singing 'to der Briddish vounded'.
170. LC 1916: 3/59. Manners, daughter of the Duke of Rutland, seems to have complained (cf. Street on *Vanity Fair*, LC 1916: 27/554).
171. *Manchester Guardian* 17.5.16, 4.
172. H. V. Esmond, *The Law Divine* (French, 1922), p. 41.
173. E. F. Benson, *Up and Down* (Hutchinson, 1918), p. 155.
174. LC 1916: 27/554.
175. *Stage* 26.8.15, 22; LC 1915: 22/3664; *Referee* 29.8.15, 3.
176. LC 1916: 9/203.
177. LC 1917: 18/329.
178. Farjeon, *Era* 21.11.17, 1.
179. *Sketch*, 11.10.16, 28.
180. LC 1917: 4/793. Farjeon, *Era* 21.11.17, 1, says of Margaret Campbell's munitionette song in *Bubbly* (where she 'explains how, what with spare gramophones and things, she is doing so well for herself that she would like the war to go on for ever'): 'I am glad for the peace of the evening that there were no munition workers in the auditorium.'
181. LC 1916: 27/554; *Era* 8.11.16, 1.
182. LC 1917: 8/905.
183. *Era* 28.8.18, 12.
184. *Daily Dispatch* 23.10.17, 4. Such attacks on the South Wales miners were more or less continuous, a whole crop of such slanders being gathered in *New Age*'s 'Current Cant' column (22.7.15, 290).
185. *Referee* 19.9.15, 3; LC 1915: 25/3719.
186. W. P., *To-day* 15.7.16, 338.
187. LC 1917: 12/761.
188. *Daily Sketch* 27.9.18, 7.
189. *Era* 7.2.17, 14.
190. *Era* 5.6.18, 11.
191. LC 1915 :12/3417.
192. *Stage* 10.2.16, 15; LC 1916: 2/48.
193. Newton, *Referee* 23.7.16, 3.
194. *Era* 28.6.16, 14; LC 1916: 13/272.

195. *Era* 22.12.15, 21. This Cellu-Lloyd gibe reminds that Lloyd George's cultivation of newsreel cameramen began before the war. Nicholas Hiley, 'Lloyd George on the Newsreels', in David Berry and Simon Horrocks (eds), *David Lloyd George: The Movie Mystery* (Cardiff: University of Wales Press, 1998), pp. 121–37, shows him to have been unrivalled amongst political contemporaries in his exploitation of the medium.
196. *Era* 8.11.16, 1. It was all harmless nonsense, confusing dog watch with watchdog, and chicken coop with poop, from whence Keys scanned 'the neighbouring meadow for the hostile periscope' (LC 1916: 27/554).
197. *Era* 28.6.16, 13.
198. Woodrow Wilson was a regular target, though Grattan's 'Will-soon' crack in *Cheep* was overtaken by events (LC 1917: 8/905).
199. *Stage* 4.5.16, 15; *Era* 3.5.16, 13. *Stage* (27.7.16, 18) rejoiced that the scene was 'knocked out' of the second edition.
200. LC 1916: 9/203.
201. LC 1918: 17/179; Macqueen-Pope, *Gaiety*, p. 185.
202. Findon, *Play Pictorial* 33(199), 52.
203. Cochran, *Secrets*, pp. 246–7; Charles Cochran, *I Had Almost Forgotten* (Hutchinson, 1932), p. 233.
204. *Sunday Times* 4.8.18, 4.
205. *Weekly Dispatch* 3.9.16, 5.
206. Horace Wyndham, *Nights in London* (Lane, 1926), p. 36.
207. LC 1915: 5/3221.
208. *Passing Show* 7.8.15, 19.
209. *Water Birds*, LC 1916: 26/5588.
210. *Performer* 20.5.15, 21.
211. LC 1918: 8/1559.
212. [Brophy and Price], *Rattle of Pebbles*, p. 168. Harold Price concluded (p. 184) that British audiences could 'stand rawer stuff than the average Canadian crowd'.
213. *Era* 5.5.15, 20; *Era* 19.5.15, 14. The next week the revue was given at the Hammersmith Palace 'with the omission of the business and scenes to which exception was taken'.
214. *Referee* 11.4.15, 3.
215. 'Autolycus', *Passing Show* 21.8.15, 19.
216. *Era* 25.11.14, 14.
217. LC 1917: 4/794.
218. LC 1915: 25/3719; 'Autolycus', *Passing Show* 23.10.15, 18.
219. *Era* 20.9.16, 13; *Referee* 17.9.16, 3; *Referee* 19.11.16, 4.
220. LC 1917: 9/913. But placket holes are always out: cf. *Love Birds*, where a supposed detective hides under a petticoat and secures 'a lovely view

through the placket hole'; and *A Suitor to Suit 'Er,* where Mrs May puts on a pair of trousers backwards, mistaking the flies 'for a plaquet hole' (LC 1915: 28/3791; LC 1917: 9/914).

221. Stone, *From Vimy Ridge,* p. 46.
222. *Weekly Dispatch* 3.9.16, 5.
223. LC 1917: 4/793; LC 1916: 27/554.
224. LC 1915: 28/3800.
225. *Era* 5.4.16, 14. Kensington had already created a stir in 1913 over the supposed immorality of a Deslys vehicle, *A La Carte* (Palace); and this is recalled by a *World* columnist (14.7.14, 1202), who, remarking Gaby's 'fondness for changing her beautiful frocks and lingerie in sight of the audience', hopes that her arrival to star in *The Passing Show* 'will not invoke the thunders of the bench of bishops'. The entry into the fray of another episcopal combatant left a *London Life* columnist (2.9.16, 8) wondering how many shows had 'the Bishop of Northampton seen that appeal to the "leering beast within us that is always hungering for the obscene"?'
226. *Era* 20.9.16, 14.
227. *Stage* 4.5.16, 15; LC 1916: 9/203.
228. Cochran, *I Had Almost Forgotten,* p. 118.
229. *Stage* 27.7.16, 18.
230. LC 1915: 9/3335.
231. LC 1915: 28/3796.
232. LC 1917: 8/907.
233. LC 1916: 17/370. Easy means of contraception threatened to boost pre-marital activity, anxiety about which is evident in *See-Saw!,* where a railway station boasts an 'Automatic Wedding Machine' supplying marriage lines, 'ring, and so on, ... It seems that the novelty is designed for young couples who have ... missed the last train home' (*Era* 20.12.16, 1; Golsworthy, *Bystander* 3.1.17, 26). A song in *Business as Usual* (LC 1915: 14/3014) anticipates the motorist's problem of an 'all night' breakdown with 'a marriage licence in the tool box'.
234. LC 1916: 27/554.
235. LC 1915: 20/3616.
236. LC 1914: 31/2981.
237. One drawn by A. E. shows a man wearing a Derby Scheme armband and pushing a pram, who, noticing a news placard, 'Another great battle – enormous casualties', says: 'What a life! Lloyd George gives the kid thirty bob to come into the world, and Lord Derby gives the father two and nine to get out of it!'
238. LC 1916: 22/457.
239. LC 1915: 28/3808.

240. *Stage* 13.5.15, 15.
241. LC 1915: 12/3398.
242. *Stage* 20.5.15, 14; *Era* 19.5.15, 17.
243. *Era* 5.1.16, 9; *Era* 22.12.15, 21.
244. *The Times* 24.11.16, 11.
245. But a new squeamishness was just a few weeks away, as the theatre's famous promenade faced abolition. This had been 'its great attraction', that 'wonderful array' of courtesans walking 'slowly backwards and forwards, in the most orderly manner' (W. J. Macqueen-Pope, *Nights of Gladness* (Hutchinson, 1956), p. 205).
246. Cochran, *Secrets*, p. 220.
247. H. F. Maltby, *Ring Up the Curtain* (Hutchinson, 1950), p. 169.
248. LC 1917: 18/329.
249. *Star* 29.3.17, 2. The other was the touring boom, which he ascribed to the emergency co-operative scheme.
250. *Era* 7.3.17, 14.
251. Farjeon, *'Era' Annual 1918*, pp. 41–2.
252. Albert de Courville, *I Tell You* (Chapman & Hall, 1928), p. 149.
253. *Era* 18.4.17, 11.
254. *Performer* 29.3.17, 19; *Evening News* 4.4.17, 3.
255. *Performer* 26.9.18, 15.
256. Lillie, *Every Other Inch*, pp. 86–8.
257. Huntly Carter, *The New Spirit in the European Theatre 1914–1924* (Benn, 1925), pp. 81–2.
258. *Weekly Dispatch* 23.7.16, 5.
259. Walker (called 'Whimsical Walker'), *From Sawdust to Windsor Castle* (Stanley Paul, 1922), p. 223.
260. Felix Isman, *Weber and Fields* (New York: Boni and Liveright, 1924), p. 22.
261. *Era* 19.7.16, 10. This failing, he moved less radically with the refurbished Pavilion, its floor space being 'arranged to include more stalls' (*Daily Sketch* 31.7.18, 7).
262. *Weekly Dispatch* 23.7.16, 5.
263. Cochran, *Secrets*, p. 218.
264. Carter, *New Spirit*, p. 82, and 'Vues and Revues', *Colour* 3 (January 1916), 222–7 (222).
265. Fenton, *World* 20.10.14, 42, enjoyed this 'daring skit on the prevailing craze for disrobing on the stage'.
266. At this time Cochran was paying Delysia £6 a week, as against Deslys's £550.
267. Fenton, *World* 20.10.14, 42.
268. *Stage* 29.4.15, 20.

269. Carter, 'Vues and Revues', p. 225. 'Leon Morton's extraordinary facial play' and 'Delysia's swift and intimate note of suggestion could only be seized at close quarters' ('Vues and Revues', p. 224). G. M. Ellwood, *Drawing* 4(21) (January 1917), 52, admired her 'understanding and complete surrender of personality to the requirements of every moment in the play'; and Tree considered Morton 'the best comic actor he ha[d] ever seen' (*Weekly Dispatch* 23.7.16, 5).
270. *Stage* 24.6.15, 21.
271. LC 1917: 8/905; *Era* 2.5.17, 9. In *Topsy Turvy* (Empire) Robert Hale impersonated White in her newspaper frock. The germ of the idea may have been found in *Le Petit Cabaret*, where Billy Douat sang that he would rather not go to a fancy-dress ball 'as the "Daily Mail," in case somebody might want to cut his advertisements out' (*Era* 3.11.15, 21).
272. LC 1916: 15/315. Jerrold's 'peace at any price' strictures had acquired new vitality.
273. *Referee* 13.9.14, 2.
274. Phyllis Bottome, *A Certain Star* (Hodder & Stoughton, 1917), p. 20; *Proceedings of the Musical Association* (Novello, 1915), p. 157.
275. *Era* 9.8.16, 11.
276. *Graphic* 1.1.16, 30.
277. LC 1917: 4/793.
278. *Stage* 30.12.15, 16 ; *Era* 29.12.15, 15.
279. *Evening News* 13.6.16, 2.
280. *Referee* 28.5.16, 3; *Era* 14.6.16, 13.
281. de Courville, *I Tell You*, pp. 152–3; *Referee* 11.6.16, 2; *Era* 21.6.16, 8.
282. *Era* 31.5.16, 14; Marks, *Referee* 6.8.16, 7.
283. *Referee* 16.7.16, 3; Carter, *New Spirit*, p. 41.
284. Golsworthy, *Bystander* 28.2.17, 399.
285. *Era* 24.2.15, 10.
286. de Courville, *I Tell You*, pp. 119–23; *Era* 7.2.17, 1.
287. LC 1917: 2/763; *Stage* 8.2.17, 12; *Era* 14.11.17, 1.
288. *Era* 7.2.17, 1.
289. Owen Seaman, *Punch* 31.3.15, 258.
290. LC 1915: 34/3935; *Era* 29.12.15, 15. A curious music-hall analogue occurred in a suburban hall where Tom Waters and Eddie Morris were playing their 'Father and Son' sketch, with Waters as the father interrupting Morris's performance from the auditorium: 'At the usual interruption a stalwart attendant marched down to the stalls and threatened ejectment if he (Tom) did not sit down quietly and behave himself. Mr. Waters eventually persuaded him, sotto voce, that it was part of the act' (Terry, *Era* 21.11.17, 17).

291. LC 1915: 3221; Magnus Hirschfeld and Andreas Gaspar (eds), *Sittengeschichte des Weltkrieges*, (Leipzig/Vienna: Verlag für Sexualwissenschaft, Schneider, 1930), vol. I, p. 100.
292. *Performer* 22.10.14, 18.
293. *Referee* 21.5.16, 3.
294. Mistinguett, *Mistinguett: Queen of the Paris Night*, trans. Lucienne Hill (Elek, 1954), p. 226.
295. Carter, *New Spirit*, p. 138.
296. *Era* 26.5.15, 12.
297. LC 1915: 5/3226.
298. *Referee* 14.5.16, 2.
299. *Referee* 22.11.14, 3; Darewski, *Everywoman's Weekly* 29.1.16, 586–7; Grein, *Sunday Times* 11.4.15, 4.
300. In the gangplankless *Razzle-Dazzle*, George Formby appeared in a frontcloth scene candidly called 'Killing Time', while the frozen lake was being readied (*Stage* 6.7.16, 18).
301. *Era* 7.2.17, 1; de Courville, *I Tell You*, pp. 120–1.
302. *Passing Show* 24.7.15, 19.
303. *Era* 20.12.16, 1.
304. LC 1917: 4/793; Marks, *Referee* 20.5.17, 7.
305. *The Times* 10.3.15, 14.
306. *Everywoman's Weekly* 12.2.16, 649.
307. *Era* 12.5.15, 14.
308. *Evening News* 11.1.16, 5.
309. *Era* 2.6.15, 14. A similar engagement with cotton-wool snowballs at a performance of *Honi Soit* (Pavilion) is illustrated by Norman Morrow in *Bystander* 2.2.16, 208. Evelyn Laye, *Boo, to My Friends* (Hurst & Blackett, 1958), p. 23, took over Zoe Gordon's part on tour, and when she sang 'I Want You To Snowball Me' 'at various ports and garrison towns, ... they *did* – with oranges, apples, and anything else they had handy'. This would have been more appropriate to *Ducks and Quacks* where Agnes Fraser sang 'Oranges', and the audience returned the 'imitation fruit with which they [were] pelted by the chorus ladies' (*Era* 15.12.15, 24).
310. *Era* 17.4.18, 13.
311. Marguerite Courtney, *Laurette* (New York: Limelight, 1984), p. 145. W. A. Chislett, 'Sixty Years of Records', *Gramophone* (September 1966), p. 147, 'arrived in France late in 1915 with a new Decca portable ... and two boxes of records'. The officers 'were kept up to date with the shows ... for it was a point of honour for anyone going on leave to bring back records from the latest productions'.
312. *Era* 23.12.14, 13.

313. *Bystander* 29.3.16, 568.
314. *Era* 15.11.16, 15; *Star* 27.1.17, 3. See the illustration of the Robey-embellished tank in *Stand To!* 55 (April 1999) 37, and my gloss in 56 (September 1999), 28. Naturally other shows received this treatment. Ruby Miller records that she had many requests for her picture, as it appeared on Barribal's poster for *A Little Bit of Fluff*. One was returned to her after it had been retrieved from German hands bearing the legend in German 'This is the girl we shall make for when we reach London', and a rejoinder: 'NOT BLOODY LIKELY!' (Ruby Miller, *Champagne from My Slipper* (Jenkins, 1962), p. 63).
315. Short and Compton-Rickett, *Ring Up the Curtain*, p. 65.
316. *Art and Letters* II(i) (1918–19), 14–41 (32).
317. *Athenæum* 6.17, 283.
318. *Era* 8.11.16, 13.
319. Sydney W. Carroll, *Some Dramatic Opinions* (White, 1923), p. 84.
320. Raymond Blathwayt, *Play Pictorial* 27(165), 100.
321. LC 1917: 4/794.
322. When, several days later, the survivors were back in port, a special bluejacket performance of the revue was arranged (*Era* 14.6.16, 14).
323. *Era* 5.7.16, 12.
324. *Era* 2.5.17, 9.
325. LC 1917: 11/971.
326. *Era* 3.5.16, 13.
327. *Era* 26.7.16, 13.
328. *Stage* 24.2.16, 14.
329. LC 1917: 9/924.
330. LC 1917: 4/809.
331. Filippo Baldinucci, *Vita di Gian Lorenzo Bernini*, ed. Sergio S. Ludovici (Milan: Edizioni del Milione, 1948), p. 151.
332. White, *Era* 5.7.16, 8.
333. LC 1917: 9/923.
334. *The Times* 30.6.16, 11.
335. LC 1916: 15/315.
336. He was observed enjoying himself in a box at *The Passing Show* (*Era* 13.1.15, 16).
337. 'Autolycus', *Passing Show* 11.9.15, 19.
338. *Stage* 8.6.16, 18; *Era* 7.6.16, 13.
339. LC 1917: 4/809.
340. LC 1915: 3221. The realities of the casting couch had been exposed as early as 1897 in his novel, *Miss Tudor*, by T. Murray Ford, *Memoirs of a Poor Devil* (Philpot, 1926), p. 89.

341. *Performer* 26.9.18, 15.
342. LC 1917: 4/794.
343. LC 1916: 22/457.
344. LC 1915: 28/3791; *Era* 20.10.15, 22.
345. Cf. *Half-Past Eight* (LC 1916: 9/203), where the transparently named Mary Chickford, has been a cinema star so long that she has almost lost the power of speech, communicating through cinematic gesture.
346. *Stage* 10.5.17, 14; *Referee*, 29.4.17, 3.
347. *Weekly Dispatch* 1.9.18, 4. Playfair (died 29 August 1918) was the one-time husband of Lena Ashwell and son of Major-General A. L. Playfair. Fenton (*World* 16.3.15, 498) describes him as 'a modern edition of Arthur Roberts, toned down to suit present-day requirements'. Cochran (*Secrets*, p. 202) mentions how at the opening night of a revue, Playfair spotted in the audience a person of distinction in government food control whose 'friendship with a French actress was well known. Playfair alluded to his presence, and added he had heard that his activities had been extended to the control of French pastry'.
348. LC 1918: 1/1326. This is obviously indebted to *Fun and Beauty* (Palladium), with its 'skit upon a romantic drama, in which spectators see both stage and wings, and can compare utterances "on" with the actions "off"' (*Stage* 4.5.16, 13).
349. Phyllis Philip Rodway and Lois Rodway Slingsby, *Philip Rodway and a Tale of Two Theatres* (Birmingham: Cornish, 1934), p. 243.
350. *Stage* 4.11.15, 22; *Era* 24.3.15, 12; Fenton, *World* 23.2.15, 525.
351. *Referee* 6.6.15, 4.
352. *Era* 29.12.15, 24. The revue was premièred at the Palace Theatre, Gloucester.
353. Ernest Thesiger, *Practically True* (Heinemann, 1927), p. 112.
354. New York: Cosmopolitan, 1919. Janis, following her British debut in *The Passing Show*, received a rave notice in *Stage* 23.4.14, 14: 'Delightful as she is as comedienne, dancer, mimic, or vocalist, there would appear to be no limit to her versatility, and she does all with a lack of effort and a girlish joyousness which go straight to the good graces of the audience.'

3

Pantomime and tradition

The relationship between revue and pantomime is subtle and intricate. Pantomime, too, is paradox: at once the most hospitable of forms and one supposedly fixed in tradition. The recognized centre of pantomime was none other than Britain's 'national theatre', Drury Lane, where it continued to flourish throughout the war years. But pantomime throve as importantly in the provinces as in the capital; and although contracts no longer specified 'ten weeks certain and the run',[1] wartime seasons continued to dominate a substantial proportion of the theatrical year.[2] Pantomime's rôle as a national institution, usually regarded as the one peculiarly British theatrical form, gave it particular wartime significance. Hence rumours that pantomime might be an early victim of the war caused special disquiet. One writer placed it alongside Christmas pudding as 'a British institution'; and it was recommended as both balm and inspiration.[3] By 1915 it was marvelled that, while 'some national institutions' had succumbed, Drury Lane pantomime continued as joyous, beautiful and delightfully flippant as 'in the hardly-to-be-remembered days before the war'.[4] But its pleasures were evidently outside the pre-war experience of many of the wounded soldiers invited to the dress rehearsal; hence 'they were almost overawed by the wonder of the production', by the 'marvel of the Butterfly ballet, exquisite, living, human butterflies of gold and green and blue and rose flittering and pirouetting and swaying' against a 'background of fountains gleaming and plashing'.

But these beauties are shadowed in irony. The soldiers had won access to them at a heavy cost; and the suffering of these dainty dancers would have been hardly less intense had war produced a pantomimeless Christmas. It would have brought 'ruin to thousands – stark, staring poverty'. The words are those of a popular principal girl writing in the *Graphic* (2 January 1915, p. 26), the initials 'M. C.' probably concealing the identity of Madge Crichton. For the stars, whose 'weekly salary would keep a ballet-girl for a year', cancellation would have meant a holiday 'or dates on the halls'. But 'they couldn't earn that salary, in pantomime, unless the girls who change their clothes half a dozen times in each performance needed work so badly that they were thankful to take starvation wages'. Had Sassoon read this article and realized 'the way life looks when a guinea a week represents the difference between Heaven and Hell', we might have been spared that ill-considered moment in *Blighters* where 'prancing ranks/Of harlots shrill the chorus'. Responsibility for trivializing and falsifying the war lay elsewhere, but chorus girls were a soft target. A woman who had tended wounded officers in the war recalls the latter talking coarsely to nurses 'as though we were chorus girls'; yet the facile comparison brings sudden recognition that these girls are no more legitimate targets for incivility than nurses.[5] It was all too easy to confuse private persons with those sensual delights which so excited the reviewer of a Liverpool *Babes in the Wood*; if he had thrilled to the gorgeous sets, his raptures over the chorus read like cut-rate D. H. Lawrence: 'And to give a throb and pulse to all these are the well-drilled troupe of pretty, gracefully-figured girls, full of animation and life, which seem to transmit their influence to, and quicken into life also, every inanimate materialism around them.'[6]

But at the heart of pantomime is a more ambiguous sexuality. It was after the Grimaldi era, as the Harlequinade went into decline, that the principal boy rôle developed. There was sexual tension in her snugly revealing attire, Deuteronomic prohibitions adding piquancy. Like ballet costume, it provided conventional justification for a leg show in an era of floor length dresses. Even when the impersonation was taken seriously, the effect came from an obtrusive femininity. Thus two children visiting the Lyceum *Jack and the Beanstalk* in 1914 recognized that Jack 'wasn't a boy really ... because he was too fat behind; a boy never bulges out like that'.[7] But 1915's Nan Hearne as Crusoe, 'burly enough ... to frighten Friday', handled her gun with a practised air that would have recommended her to 'the most exacting boy [as] a man after his own heart'.[8] This new-style 'boy' was encouraged by cinema fashions: just as Theda Bara had created the new woman as vamp, so Mary Pickford reconstructed her as flapper, starting a vogue which would eventually oust the heavyweight.[9] It is in part this change of taste which is reflected in the praise lavished on Cressie Leonard for her Robin Hood in the 1915 Aldwych *Babes in the Wood*. One advertising clip saw this Robin, 'tall, lissom, and active', as 'a great improvement on the protuberant principal boy not yet entirely superseded'.[10] Indeed not. Victorian proportions were amply represented by the 'fine, strapping' Dora Sephton, a Glasgow Crusoe in 1914; or Louie Beckman in the same part at Manchester the next year, who made 'a magnificent return to the majestic type of principal boy'.[11] As late as 1917, Farjeon still complained that 'Prince Charming is apt to run to thighs and size'.[12] He preferred 'a gait and a swagger', the logic of which might have been to give the rôle to a man; but pantomime has little truck with logic. Light-comedian Randolph Sutton, taking the part in Burton-on-Trent's 1916 *Babes in the Wood*, was said to be 'the only "male" principal boy in the provinces',[13] though there was one at the Wimbledon that year. In 1915 it was tried at the Croydon Hippodrome, *Stage*'s reviewer (30 December 1915, p. 29) suggesting guardedly that there was virtue in both approaches. But it remained an anomaly even though there had been a few essays just before the war, including a Drury Lane experiment in successive editions of *The Sleeping Beauty*. Manager Arthur Collins was premature in pronouncing 'the female "Principal Boy" ... dead as far as the West-End of London is concerned'; and when Bertram Wallis took over in the 1914 edition, he was effectively guyed by Robert Hale in the Alhambra revue, *Anything New? Not Likely*, where an hour-long pantomime burlesque was introduced.[14] Farjeon applauded: 'It is not easy for a man to pretend to be a girl pretending to be a man.'[15] This added a fresh turn to that sexual ambiguity which he looked for in pantomime. Two years on (17 January 1917, p. 13), he was telling *Era* readers: 'Dick Whittington played by a man loses as much savour with the public as would his cat played by a real feline. Pantomime should have no commerce with the craze for realism.'[16] On the other hand, his preference for the new woman as principal boy registers not only a shift away from Victorian taste but the different meaning which the war had attached to the rôle. As women increasingly took over jobs traditionally assigned to men, along with a more masculine style of dress to facilitate the work, the principal boy might reasonably symbolize that social reality. The move was not away from femininity but from the fripperies conventionally associated with it. Hence it is no accident that the most remarkable assumption of the war years was that of Madge Titheradge at Drury Lane in 1916 and 1917. 'She is like no other pantomime boy. She dances little and sings not at all. But she is both gamesome and poetic, sparkling with smiles and vibrating with feeling.' She was a gifted and wide-ranging actress, realizing 'The loneliness, fear, and exaltation of Aladdin in the cave scene' with uncustomary power.[17] She made Farjeon wonder what Terry or Bernhardt might have made of a principal boy rôle. But withal, her performance was 'somehow well-thumbed – nothing new – just a confirmation of our dreams'. And this, too, is important; for he insists that tradition is more than half of pantomime's charm.

The dame is another traditional cross-dresser,[18] and further evidence of how people value as unchanging traditions which are in the highest degree fluid. In earlier decades, the dame gave scope for coarse humour; but wartime reviews settle into a groove of reassurance that 'the Dame part never for a moment deviates into vulgarity'.[19] It was often undertaken by prominent music-hall comedians. Amongst the best was Fred Emney, who in the Birmingham Royal's 1914 *Sinbad* played Sinbad's mother to George Robey's father. Years later it was recalled how they complemented each other perfectly: 'Emney gave a consistent study of an old woman from the mean streets of London, preserving her peculiarities, racial and personal, in a strange land.' Robey, in contrast, ran through a succession of guises – as tailor, suburban photographer, bus conductor and 'bearded denizen of Baghdad speaking in a strange Oriental tongue'. Where Emney preserved illusion, Robey 'ignored the "fourth wall," and incorporated the audience in his company'. In a striking domestic scene Emney nagged while Robey 'sat perfectly still, saying never a word, just biting his lip and staring at his nails'. When they made up, Robey 'brought the house down', pushing Emney 'off his knee with an agonised expression and the words "You're sitting on my keys"'. [20] But contemporary reviews had reservations about Robey's approach. When he played Will Atkins in Manchester's 1915 *Crusoe*, it was complained that the story was 'little more than a peg upon which to hang the varied and inconsequent entertainments of what is practically a revue de luxe'. Robey's 'richly humorous' delineation soon reverted to a music hall vein of 'eccentric character-comedy' with a 'complete neglect of the traditional proprieties'. [21] This neglect was troublesome on more than conservative grounds. Until the wartime explosion of touring revues pantomime had quietly absorbed elements from the big shows. But now, when 'Every big revue success in London ha[d] been sent on tour',[22] it was more than ever important to assert a separate identity.

Not that it is easy to find much that is enduring in pantomime, despite all the insistence on tradition. It is probably this spurious sense of tradition coupled with a real capacity for adapting, which has ensured its survival. Modern-style pantomime, abandoning verse for prose, came with the advent of the music-hall performers who brought their own rhythms, and the decades leading to the war saw a process of continual modification. In such circumstances, tradition became a telescoped concept, and those writing of pantomime tradition never reached back beyond their own childhood memories. The rigidity with which they discuss this most plastic of genres is quaint. Although comic aggression became inseparable from the Victorian Harlequinade, the inclusion of burlesque melodrama in Bradford's 1916 *Whittington* was deemed 'scarcely the thing in a children's pantomime', despite the admission 'that it was received uproariously'.[23] Reviewers are frequently at odds with audiences in this way. Even speciality acts, for which pantomime has always found room, and which became staple as theatre managers sought to steal some of the thunder of the emergent halls, were often treated like a new and doubtful innovation obscuring the story. Only the most perceptive recognized that 'a heavy precipitate of music hall' could make its appeal to one cohort without disturbing that other which responded strongly to, say, a re-enactment of the *Aladdin* story, without realizing that it was anything else.[24]

According to a review of the 1916 Palladium pantomime, its 'attention to topical humour' makes it more of a revue than many shows advertised as such; but withal pantomime excels revue because it only departs from the story under artistic compulsion.[25] The importance attached to pantomime story results in part from the need to maintain a distance between these disquietingly similar forms. Both are hospitable in the highest degree; both are a theatre of unreason and incongruity, playful counterpart of the theatre of war. But in 1914 pantomime represented tradition whereas revue derided it in the accents of modernism. Not many viewed the blurring of boundaries so genially as the reviewer of Hartlepool's 1915 *Red Riding Hood*: 'There is very little in it dealing with the nursery tale as it *was* known; in fact, it may almost be classed as a revue or vehicle for stringing up a merry mixture of capital singing, smart dancing, and amusing comicalities.'[26] On the other hand, pantomime could play legitimately with the idea of revue. *Robinson Crusoe* at Manchester's Osborne Theatre in 1918 incorporated a Revueland scene, 'forming a good background for the specialities, instead of the usual palace formula'.[27] But distinctions were necessary since revue stood for the future and pantomime for the past. Britain's century had been the nineteenth, and she was fighting a war to preserve the order and values represented by that century against the perceived irresponsibility of Germany's emergent power. Conservative and progressive were locked in terrible conflict, obscurely mirrored in the opposition between the two theatrical modes. To have admitted that these rival modes were at bottom strangely similar was as out of the question as to concede as much about the opposing political ideologies.

The knowingness of revue, which pantomime was intent on keeping at bay, was attacked by actor-dramatist Weedon Grossmith. But what he condemns as a new disillusionizing trend is a feature of the earliest English secular drama that we have. Medwall's *Fulgens and Lucres*, apparently a Christmas entertainment as pantomime was to become, demonstrates that confusing different dimensions of reality was no newfangledness but part of an ancient tradition. That pantomime producers had chosen to abandon it meant that revue could inherit the old 'carnival spirit' and 'battles royal with balls of wool between audiences and choruses'.[28] However, the very satisfaction expressed by *The Times* reviewer (26 December 1914, p. 3), that the 1914 Lyceum *Jack and the Beanstalk* showed 'no trace of Reinhardt influence', suggests that exceptions did occur. There was one example at the Birmingham Royal's 1915 *House That Jack Built*, where Clarice Mayne in parti-coloured dress duetted with a 'mammoth Jingle Johnnie, second cousin to a Billikin', which sang 'by a clever arrangement of synchronised telephone and microphone amplification'. The duet was backed by a troupe of

Jingle Johnnies, and replicas were thrown into the house each night', some finding 'their way into the front line trenches'.[29] And there were other kinds of discreet boundary crossing. In the 1914 Stoke-on-Trent *Whittington*, as Dick sang 'Wonderful Rose Of Love', the last verse was tellingly 'taken up from one of the boxes ... by the Emperor'; and at Bradford in 1918, Prince Charming's 'Everybody Loves A Big Brass Band' brought a local band from 'unexpected places among the audience'.[30] Whereas, in a 1915 *Old King Cole* at the Leeds Grand, Shaun Glanville's 'repartee to a well-known local Irish sportsman in the upper circle' proved 'one of the drollest bits in the show', the joy plank was thought better left to revue.[31]

Grossmith would probably have deplored the joy plank; he would surely have detested the scene introduced into Drury Lane's 1914 revamping of its two-year-old *Sleeping Beauty*. This so-called 'Missing Scene' was devised for funsters George Graves and Will Evans.[32] They were provided with no scenery. Their 'loud and persistent demands' for the appearance of set designer Bruce Smith finally produced him. But he explained that he was not to blame: 'So many of the staff of the theatre had gone to the front that he was unable to paint the scene in time.'[33] Although the upshot was that the comedians elected to paint the scenery themselves, with 'much daubing of silent suffering supers', there was obviously more than horseplay involved here. The realities of wartime conditions appeared on stage seemingly unmediated, and the disclosure of the mechanics of stage illusion is obviously indebted to the self-referential habit of revue.

Grossmith had a soul-mate writing to the editor of *The Stage* a few months earlier (6 April 1916, p. 25). In fact, the two complaints bracket the Somme battle in 1916, a year when fine discriminations must have been in short supply. Even so, it is remarkable that both writers should blatantly lump together examples of what they decry as bad practice with others of sheerly slack performance. *The Stage* correspondent inculpates pantomime as well as revue, both for its 'slipshod construction and that art of "playing down," mostly by comedians who imagine it far funnier to amuse themselves than the audience'. It is irresponsible to comment on a colleague's greasepaint: 'Hullo! You haven't got enough two and a half on', since this is supposedly gagging which 'only the artists themselves understand'. But the demystifying intent is unmistakable when an actress asks a juvenile lead: 'Why so frisky? – and at a *matinée* too.' Nor is it reasonable to assume that another of his experiences was the result of unprofessionalism rather than calculated illusion-breaking: 'I have seen six chorus girls eating chewing-gum, and the rest screaming with laughter at their audacity, and not one attempting to sing.' Although he advocates 'instant dismissal' for offenders whether they be salaried at £2 or £200 a week, the former would be too readily dispensable for them to risk their livelihood in the way described. In one show, 'The clocklike regularity with which the chorus move is a delight to the eye.'[34] Regimentation was the current trend with chorus lines – whether in London or Flanders: it expressed the all-conquering technology of those 'Modern Times'. Like Chaplin's film, those gum-chewers were surely designed to subvert a tendency that led to the Nuremberg Rallies as well as Busby Berkeley.

This clash of ideologies in the theatrical world has a more familiar counterpart in that of fine arts. With the indignity of the 1911 Post-Impressionist exhibition at the Grafton Street Galleries still chafing, Burne-Jones told a gathering at the Authors' Club that the modernists 'offered the untutored scribbles of the nursery enlivened by the delirium of the madhouse'. Their work was evidently part of a larger decline: 'Even in the nursery, with golliwogs, billikins, and gazeekas, we trained the eyes of children in monstrosities that they might one day learn to appreciate the full significance of a Van Gogh.'[35] Or was it that these monstrosities shadowed the dark mysteries of the child's psychological world just as the brutality or happy ending of fairy tales helped to acknowledge the anxieties and clarify the confusions of nursery existence? And, although the bowdlerizers had been at work throughout the nineteenth century, folklore showed itself remarkably resilient. This was in part because a lore which was no longer meaningful to an adult world, where the sense of wonder had been lost to widespread literacy, could retain its secrets. Its sophistications and subtleties, and in particular its widespread sexual symbolism, survived because they became invisible to those force-fed on print. Thus sexual and other dubieties were smuggled onto the stage in some of the favourite pantomime embodiments. Onset of puberty is to be descried in both Jack's beanstalk and Aladdin's lamp, while Cinderella's hopes are centred on her furred slipper (glass being an elegant but transparent shift from *vair* to *verre*). The familiar vaginal symbolism operates again with that fecund old woman who lived in a shoe, who (with perhaps more aptness than was realized) secured a place in the Kilburn Empire *Goody Two Shoes* of 1915.[36] The following year her distinctive mode of dwelling was given to Dame Trot in *Mother Goose* at the Lyceum. This was said to be 'amongst the least hackneyed of pantomime subjects', giving the writer scope 'to follow his own devices'.[37] But from early in the nineteenth century it had assimilated the story of the goose laying golden eggs, the scatological point of which is underscored in the version of Giambattista Basile (died 1632). In fact, that separate featuring of *The Goose with the Golden Eggs* at Southport in 1915[38] was a rare bird.

Pantomimes, in the early nineteenth century, were adult fare. By the later decades they had become an extension of the nursery world, a Christmas treat for children. They had been so when Max Beerbohm was a child; but some twenty years on, when reviewing the 1898 pantomime season, he reflects that since the conditions of childhood are now much altered, pantomime too will have changed accordingly. 'The children of my day loved to follow the plot', he recalls, whereas now it serves 'merely as a thread to connect the turns of an infinite variety show'.[39] He refers to youngsters of his own class, formerly circumscribed by the nursery world but now welcome in 'drawing-room or dining-room – wherever their elders may be', and thus inclined to put away childish things. Their taste, or that of a small sample observed by Beerbohm, is not for story, skin-parts or Harlequinade, but for the dancing and topical elements.

For Beerbohm, children have lost their sense of wonder; and Barnard agrees (*Era*, 5 January 1916, p. 15): in this practical age children have become less 'impressed by fairies' and are 'likely to become restless at the pantomime while the comedians are off'. But wartime reviewers generally paint things differently, perhaps using children as cover for their own predilections. Thus at Glasgow in 1918, *Jack and the Beanstalk*'s story was prominent, giving 'the pantomime an interest for children which a string of variety turns never can give'.[40] The Birmingham Rep's 1914 *Cinderella* was supposedly exceptional in keeping 'strictly to the familiar story ... children like a real story they can follow, although they do not often find it in the Christmas entertainments supposed to be prepared for them.'[41] But wartime reviews offer scant evidence for lack of story. The intrusion of Chaplin into Woolwich's *Cinderella* was one of 'few departures from the orthodox story'; and since this was 1915, year of the Chaplin craze, 'doubtless even the children – most conservative of audiences – will forgive'.[42] Whether or not children were most comfortable when the story was adhered to, reviewers clearly were. For them, an important factor in *Cinderella*'s popularity is that it 'is well defined and cannot be altered to any considerable extent'.[43] It is as if fidelity to the original story signals that all's well with the world, an allied victory assured. Departures might be deemed unpatriotic; so on the comparatively few occasions when they are found, reviewers seem impelled to excuse or explain away. *Babes in the Wood*, highly popular during the war years, will serve for demonstration purposes. A reviewer of the Middlesbrough production in 1916 is happy with a story 'on the old familiar lines', albeit 'enhanced with up-to-date quips and drolleries'. But a coeval version at Liverpool's Court Theatre prompts awkward rationalization: 'There is no story to tell, or at most there is not one needful to be told; the traditional history of the famous Babes is a mere figment, and Robin Hood only there in name.'[44] Ironically, this story has a better chance of having historical basis than most of the pantomime favourites. The 1595 ballad version is perhaps a journalistic account of an actual Norfolk murder; and in pre-Victorian pantomime the story ended tragically. It merged with a respectably ancient folk source, which already in Basile's version uses the happy ending favoured in more recent pantomimes. A 1917 version at the Lyric, Hammersmith, offers oblique comment on preoccupation with what is customary: 'While the story runs on familiar lines, the impersonation of the Babes by child actresses of rare promise, and the engagement of a lady to play the Dame, make an acceptable wrench from pantomime tradition.'[45] A key scene in a 1915 Sheffield *Babes* was that in which Baron Stonehenge watched a conjuring performance from a false box, the conjurer opening his cabinet to reveal the missing babes.[46] But it is the Aldwych version of that year which showed real innovation. Here, too, 'Nursery-orthodoxy [was] flouted by an omission of the time-honoured scene of the desolate and weary babes covered with leaves by the robins.' And that gifted theatrical writer Fred Bowyer introduced still more drastic departures. He began not with the conventional quarrel between demon and fairy but with the babes hanging up their stockings on Christmas eve: 'A big grandfather clock suddenly opens, and a dainty little fairy announces the coming of Father Christmas, ... The Babes in their dreams converse with him and the fairy' and in what follows they 'only dream of their undoing'.[47]

On this question of innovation, *The Stage* (27 December 1917, p. 18) provides an instructive account of Drury Lane's *Aladdin* of that year. The hero's 'adventures are foreshadowed by means of fleeting pictures coming and going iris-wise, for a kind of contractile diaphragm is used, as in "Chu Chin Chow"'.[48] It was frustrating that nothing more was borrowed; but *Chu Chin Chow* belonged to a different genre precisely because it availed itself of freedoms which pantomime was expected to shun. Despite innovations, 'pantomime is pantomime, ... and Mr. Collins no doubt hesitated to go as far in consistency to period and relevancy of matter as Mr. Asche had done'. In this 'least progressive of the dramatic forms' it would have been too risky to abandon those 'familiar incongruities of Drury Lane pantomime'.

Even this reviewer, a progressive amongst reactionaries, seriously underestimates pantomime's innovative capacity. He responds to tradition as part of the meaning with which pantomime was invested. It mattered little that most of what were now regarded as staple ingredients became so only in the later nineteenth century. Emphasis on spectacle, for instance, is pantomime's hyperbolic version of a Victorian theatrical taste. All the possibilities made available by the Industrial Revolution came into play. The process generated its own apt symbolism. Whereas formerly the folk-tale characters were transformed by magical intervention into those of the Harlequinade, now the transformation was one of scenery. That older transformation had been facilitated by the wearing of huge carnival heads in the preliminary part of the show which concealed the costumes of the Harlequinade. Like the Harlequinade itself, these big heads occasionally survived in wartime pantomime, though quite divorced from their original place and function.[49] One such throwback occurred in the Drury Lane *Sleeping Beauty* already mentioned, where 'Arthur Conquest appears as a Big Head of terrifying aspect in the Pine Forest'.[50] In the 1917 *Red Riding Hood* at Liverpool's Court Theatre, 'Giant Head and Giant Fowl' emphasized their new ('mechanical and electrical') rationale. That 'Great Electrical Chicken', which showed effectively in its mechanical movement about 'the darkened stage', had been accompanied by electric airships and glow-worms when the pantomime was given at Newcastle upon Tyne in 1915.[51] Productions of *Miss Muffet* provided another electrical and mechanical feast with their Spiderland scenes, full of 'creeping and flying things'.[52]

Although every theatre of consequence had long been fully equipped with electricity, turns utilizing it continued to be a novelty since domestic electricity had made only patchy progress since its introduction in the 1880s. It was the war which supplied the impetus for it to spread, though it was only after the establishment of the Central Electricity Board in 1926 that this was undertaken on a systematic basis. Cinderella's coach of light continued to impress thirty years on, but its effect on wartime audiences must have been startling. Although not a wartime innovation, it must have been as much a source of wonderment as electrical gadgetry. Features like 'the vacuum cleaner that draws everything in its wake' in the 1915 *Little Boy Blue* at Edinburgh would have made an impact requiring an effort for us to appreciate.[53] Electricity was a thematic aid, too. Pantomime had been assimilated to that ancient seasonal pattern of light triumphing over darkness, of which *Cinderella* is exemplary. The Palladium production in 1915 opened 'with the customary dark scene', Killjoy, demon of pessimism, opposing weather's inclemencies to the fairy Sunshine.[54] At the Kennington the same year, the process was elaborated when the fairy godmother disguised herself as a beggarwoman to prove that goodness of heart still survives in the world. Cinderella's act of charity changed 'the forest from a wintry and frost-bound scene to one of summer sunshine', complete with live, frolicking rabbits. That there would have been no overlooking of wartime nuance is clear from a review of the 1915 *Crusoe* at Windsor: 'The choruses are breezy, clean, and full of life; the staging is good, with plenty of light, all essential in these gloomy days.'[55] That clean lyrics are associated with light, of a piece with insistence on purified dames, implies that obscenity resides with the Hun.

But electricity was just the latest trick in pantomime's repertoire. In Sheffield's 1915 *Babes in the Wood*, the Fairy Wood was enlivened with a huge, resplendently coloured, electrical butterfly; but still more of 'a triumph of art' was the Palace of Chess, with 'living "pieces"'. Both this and Toyland continued to be popular from Victorian times,[56] though the latter was updated in a 1917 *Babes* at Manchester where Meccano Land made 'a striking conception'.[57] Futurism was only played with, though often prettily. Rainbowland, in the 1917 *Sleeping Beauty* at Croydon, offered 'an up-to-date scene with its black and white pillars and masses of futuristic flowers', the dancers 'in black Punchinello hats' and skirts unfolding in a variety of shades. This may have found some inspiration in Drury Lane's *Puss in New Boots* of the previous year, where the first half ended in a riot of colour and 'Futurist Fantasy' as dancers performed against 'densely populated spiral staircases which seem[ed] to hang high in the air'.[58] George Kirby's flying ballet, popular throughout Edwardian times, survived the war. It graced the Highgate Hill scene in Croydon's 1914 *Whittington*; and Wimbledon's *Sinbad* of the same year saw 'charming ladies make daring and graceful flights, some of which come right out into the house'.[59] The Wylie-Tate *Cinderella*, which first 'made a hit at the Palladium in 1915', resorted to the well-tried and the new. Cinderella's kitchen was the scene for 'old-time pantomime trap-door and wall disappearances', the frantic comedy which these allow being splendidly preserved in several Lupino Lane films.[60] But it was the quasi-Venetian garden-setting, complete with gondola, which most caught the attention. Crossing the Bridge of Sighs, the prince dropped the glass slipper, several of the fairy queen's attendants diving after it. Strikingly, only the fairy bearing the slipper re-emerged from the water, necessitating reassurance in the programme 'that this feat is accomplished by means of a diving apparatus invented by Julian Wylie'.[61] Fire and water effects were always winners; and it was in another *Cinderella*, at the London Opera House in 1916, that fire played a conspicuous part: 'Instead of the usual method of transforming pumpkins and the etceteras into coach and equipment', the raw materials were thrown into flames which reached a height of 20 feet.[62]

The pageant of the nations, with an appropriately be-flagged and costumed chorus, was one pre-war spectacle which translated easily to the new mood.[63] In Newport Lyceum's 1914 *Beauty and the Beast* it boomed a message of solidarity as allied troops 'pass through the mist in scenes of battle, the wounded attended by Boy Scouts and Red Cross nurses, and then in the blaze of day group themselves around Britannia as, with great guns pointed seaward, she guards the white cliffs of Old England'.[64] Placed at the service of patriotism, spectacle was as indispensable as ever. Even without overt flag-waving it exuded that 'Business as usual' spirit of 1914. Despite maintenance of low prices, the wood scene in Bowyer's *Cinderella* at the Aldwych included 'real deer ... drinking at a brook of real running water'.[65] At the Prince of Wales, Birmingham, *Aladdin* was evidently thought to be within bounds, running for 'exactly four hours – from 7.30 until 11.30'.[66] In the London Opera House version, which interwove the story of the Forty Thieves, the 'Feast of

Lanterns' utilized 'practically the whole company of about 400 performers'. In the 'Babyland' ballet, 100 girls aged from 8 to 14 fluttered 'with the lightness of sylphs'; and the cave scene was advertised as 'the largest of its kind ever produced'. Now under Stoll direction, the theatre sought to revive in its first pantomime all the old-time glories 'including the grand transformation scene and the harlequinade'.[67] The Palladium *Whittington* revived the old-style Harlequinade and elaborate star-traps and introduced a Louis Wain-style cat circus.[68] Drury Lane's *Sleeping Beauty*, with a thrilling forest fire, maintained the Augustus Harris tradition and competed in length with *Die Walküre*. Indeed, 'Harris's description of Wagner's Das Rheingold as "a damned pantomime"', won approval from Shaw. Had 'the Hare-Bancroft style' prevailed utterly, it would have become impossible to stage *Rheingold* with its transformations and swimming Rhine maidens.[69]

Clearly the impact of stage naturalism had even modified pantomime performance, though not to the extent where old modes could not be reinstated. Paradoxically, the war seems to have conduced to their return, despite such exigencies as the twice-nightly system, and the growing practice of sending pantomimes on tour.[70] A heightened sense of tradition ensured that scaling down was not especially noticeable during the war years; even a two-hour twice-nightly could be spectacular. One such, Derby's *Dick Whittington*, was hailed as a triumph of stage design, the most astounding of its twelve scenes (six of them full sets) representing 'the deck of H.M.S. Queen Elizabeth, with monster guns firing and searchlights playing', while Dick (Edna Latonne) in admiral's rig sang 'The Silent Navy' surrounded by midshipmen.[71] That was in 1918, when most pantomimes preferred celebrations of peace. In *Robinson Crusoe* at Bognor, Lilian Phillips, 'a sweet and dainty Fairy Peace', delighted audiences with her singing of 'When The Great Red Dawn Is Shining', written in anticipation the previous year by Lockton and Sharpe.[72] The first half of Drury Lane's *Babes in the Wood* concluded with a Pageant of Peace at once riveting and hieratic, the goddess standing serene amongst her nymphs, while the rest of the huge stage filled 'with whirling masses of serpentine convolutions, of advancing and retreating ranks of dancers in mad joy'. Wild shouts greeted the allies; but the cheers were deafening when the symbols of Britain and her empire finally appeared. The scene was dominantly white: white robes and wings of dancers and angels, white classical columns forming 'the simple architectural background'. In effective contrast, the defiant Spirit of Evil, black-clad and red-haired, 'with black eagle on her shield', is forced to surrender her sword 'to Lord Fairplay, who breaks it across his knee (no undue emphasis being laid upon this act of submission)'; the politicians would be less nice at Versailles six months on. Finally, the singing of 'The Bells Of St Mary's' was a cue for the peace bells to chime as the curtains closed.[73]

This was the victorious peace which the government had brainwashed people into seeing as the only acceptable kind. Pantomime patriotism assisted this belief, and at least once it found direct spectacular expression. That was at Edinburgh in 1915, when the highlight of *Little Boy Blue* was a derisory tableau, 'the rocking cabin of "Ford's Peace Ship"'.[74] Since the automobile manufacturer's mission to bring peace to Europe only set sail for Norway on 4 December, the devisers of the scene had wasted no time in preparing its mechanics. That year, Glasgow Pavilion's *Mother Goose* was more orthodox with its sea scene, borrowing a warship's great guns and dazzling searchlights from the 1914 pantomime seen at the neighbouring Princess's Theatre.[75] In 1916 the Princess's acknowledged that here was the great shipbuilding centre by climaxing with the 'Launch of a Dreadnought'.[76] A pantomime antecedent can be found as early as 1810,[77] when it would have helped to assuage a real anxiety: Britain possessed the world's most powerful navy but lacked Napoleon's capacity for shipbuilding. Although eventually Waterloo was celebrated on the pantomime stage in terms somewhat like those of the 1918 victory,[78] the army during the Napoleonic Wars was held in nothing like the esteem that khaki was in 1914–18. It was the King's Navee which gripped the popular imagination in song and on stage.[79] Britannia still ruled the waves in 1914, and a torrent of songs appeared to keep people mindful of the fact (a number of them by McGlennon the song-publisher and author of 'Sons Of The Sea'). Now, although Tommy's appeal had overtaken that of Jack, naval tableaux were apt to be more effective than scenes of trench warfare. An 'old-fashioned style of pantomime', *Tom, the Piper*, another spectacular at Glasgow's Princess's Theatre, simulated the 'deck of a ship' while, by means of 'a fine piece of mechanical work', in the distance could be seen a 'German warship being pursued by a British Dreadnought. The British boat fires on the German, and, to the delight of the house, the German ship explodes and sinks.'[80] Destruction of the forces of evil is an expected feature of pantomime. The previous year, *Dick Whittington* at Lowestoft showed the Saucy Sally in port, threatened by 'some very Germ-hun sailors,[81] and the open sea, where the Kaiser's fleet comes to grief'.

Nearly eight months on, the shock of the *Lusitania* sinking was still keenly felt; but 1916 was to bring a fresh crop of outrages, torpedoing of hospital ships and the passenger steamer *Sussex* confirming the popular view that German U-boat commanders were outright pirates. Hence the villain of *Robinson Crusoe*, Will Atkins, became a 'piratical Hun of the deepest dye' at Huddersfield, while at Hammersmith he was a German spy plotting to have Crusoe's ship torpedoed. The latter sought to dispose of Crusoe by means of the Press Gang,[82] eerily reminiscent of those frequent raids made on theatres since the introduction of conscription. Typical was a 'round-up' conducted by police and military at the Star Music Hall, Bermondsey. Doors were closed 'and everybody of military age ... called upon to produce his documents'. Ten men were arrested.[83] Performers were caught in the same net, and were also subject to denunciations: an informant brought a bewildered Doddy Hurl, the Scottish comedian, before Bristol's chief of police as a supposed deserter, and even Teddie Le Roy had to convince Edinburgh detectives that she was indeed a male impersonator and not an ingenious draft-dodger.[84]

Although there was no shortage of khaki on the pantomime stage, it took several years before the war in France could compete with that at sea in these Christmas annuals. To begin with it might be refracted through the antics of the ever-popular children's chorus, manoeuvring 'upon a miniature battlefield' (Leeds, 1915), or strutting 'in paper helmets, after the manner of the urchins who perambulate our streets' (Aldwych, 1914).[85] But these were mild delights. What turned the fighting in France into spectacle was the introduction of the tank to the battlefield (15 September 1916). That Christmas, principal boys and dames up and down the country were singing 'The Tanks That Broke The Ranks Out In Picardy',[86] and many a pantomime introduced a tank episode. The hugely popular films of tanks in action were not released until 15 January 1917, so had no influence on the fantasies of pantomime designers. It was Heath Robinson improvisation at the London Opera House *Cinderella*. The Brothers Egbert gained entry to the ball by means of a tank fabricated from a coffee stall, which took 'the Palace gates in its stride'.[87] Similarly, in Drury Lane's *Puss in New Boots*, 'the Baron and his helpmeet, after trouble with the domestics, attempt with qualified success to cook a war-time dinner on a practicable stove which is convertible into a "tank"'.[88] In Glasgow's *Tommy Trotter* there was uproar at the labour exchange when comedians Hellier and Haynes formed their own military tribunal to 'grant each other conditional exemption for 25 years'; but it was 'cut short by the entrance of a Tank spitting gunfire right and left', the curtain falling 'with the Tank triumphant amid the ruins'.[89] By Christmas 1917, hopes that the tank would prove the war-winner had subsided. However, in the King's (Hammersmith) *Red Riding Hood*, Robin Hood employed a tank in the defeat of evil, one of its embodiments being Baron Bolo. Baron Bolo also figured as the wicked uncle of the *Babes in the Wood* at the nearby Lyric Theatre, the original being a German agent, a French notary's son, arrested in America in September 1917.[90]

The endowing of pantomime's villains with a Teutonic identity became a commonplace.[91] Croydon's 1915 *Cinderella* boasted both the fantastical 'Baron Blighter-bad-skunkenschwein' and Espinosa's punning appearance as the 'Wehr Wolf'.[92] Although in 1914, when producers were still being urged to avoid the cheap gibes and crudity of German shows,[93] matters hardly got beyond a crop of Demon Kulturs,[94] Drury Lane's revival of *Sleeping Beauty* registers the shift in preoccupation with wicked spirit Anarchista becoming Spyreena.[95]

Pantomime was quick to declare its loyalty: and when Beauty herself, Connecticut-born Ferne Rogers, aired 'views on the war which gave strong offence to her British colleagues', she was packed off home on the next boat.[96]

Notes

1. *Era* 7.8.09, 24.
2. *Tommy Trotter* 'attained a run of 91 nights and 37 matinées' at the Princess's, Glasgow, in 1916–17, and was succeeded by two weeks of Harry M'Kelvie's *Tom the Piper*, which was set to break 'the record for touring pantos, being already booked into May' (*Era* 11.4.17, 7).
3. *Era* 23.12.14, 13; *Stage* 24.12.14, 18.
4. *Era* 29.12.15, 8.
5. [Anonymous], *WAAC* (Laurie, 1930), p. 31.
6. *Stage* 28.12.16, 27.
7. *World* 29.12.14, 248.
8. *Era* 5.1.16, 11.
9. Cf. Langford Reed, *Era* 21.2.17, 13: 'The kinematograph has set up a new standard of beauty, altogether foreign to the "fleshly school", and there are signs that it will not be long before the stage and music hall veer round to the same opinion.'
10. *Era* 29.12.15, 11.
11. *Stage* 17.12.14, 25; W. H. M., *Manchester Guardian* 27.12.15, 8.
12. *Era* 17.1.17, 13.
13. *Era* 14.2.17, 20.
14. *Referee* 13.12.14, 2. Wallis succeeded Wilfrid Douthitt, who had played the prince in 1912 and 1913.
15. *Cartoon* 4.3.15, 142.
16. Women taking over skin parts caused no commotion. The innovator was Pauline Prim, playing a cat in the Aldwych's *Cinderella* (*Era* 23.12.14, 16; *Era* 20.1.15, 13, records her as 'wonderfully realistic', spending the interval 'collecting for the Belgian Fund'). This now became the norm, with Renée Mayer as Puss in Boots at Drury Lane; cf. *London Life* cartoon (15.1.16, 19) where she appears as a curvaceous young woman in high-heeled boots spilling out of a cat-skin. A Tommy enters her dressing room determined not to rub her up the wrong way.
17. *Stage* 27.12.17, 18. This was the only West End pantomime of 1917, and Collins preferred to call even this a 'fairy musical comedy'. Following British Museum prints, he carefully set it in pre-pigtail days (*Era* 19.12.17, 8).

18. Even the splendid Nellie Wallace was 'a woman dressed as a man who is dressed as a woman – a duplication of reversal's mirth' (M. Wilson Disher, *Clowns and Pantomimes* (Constable, 1925), p. 49).
19. *Stage* 27.12.18, 20.
20. Phyllis Philip Rodway and Lois Rodway Slingsby, *Philip Rodway and a Tale of Two Theatres* (Birmingham: Cornish, 1934), pp. 200–1.
21. *Era* 29.12.15, 24.
22. *Star* 12.10.15, 5.
23. *Stage* 28.12.16, 15.
24. W. H. M., *Manchester Guardian* 27.12.15, 8.
25. *Stage* 28.12.16, 21. Attendance figures given by Terry, *Era* 24.1.17, 14, have been garbled, but the proportions add up: 61 per cent women, 8 per cent children, and 31 per cent men, '46 per cent of the latter being in uniform'.
26. *Stage* 30.12.15, 10.
27. *Stage* 12.12.18, 16.
28. Disher, *Clowns and Pantomimes*, p. 49.
29. Rodway and Slingsby, *Philip Rodway*, p. 210.
30. *Stage* 31.12.14, 21; *Stage* 27.12.18, 7.
31. *Stage* 30.12.15, 10. The device had been used there two years earlier, *The Stage*'s use of 'joy plank' (1.1.14, 19) predating *OED*'s earliest citation by a decade.
32. The scene was copied in a Glasgow *Sinbad* (*Stage* 28.12.16, 26).
33. *Stage* 31.12.14, 26. This was a real problem, especially after the introduction of conscription. Drury Lane scenic artist R. C. McCleery, speaking at the Southwark Tribunal on behalf of 'the only two expert assistants he had left out of eight', secured them 'two months' exemption each' (*Era* 18.4.17, 8).
34. *The Million Dollar Girl* (*Stage* 22.4.15, 15). The innovation was due to American dance instructors, who reminded de Courville of their army equivalent, the girls being 'trained like soldiers' (*I Tell You* (Chapman & Hall, 1928), p. 118).
35. *Daily Mail* 20.2.12, 5.
36. It was the celebrated Hickory Wood's version of *Jack and Jill* which 'blended the familiar legend of that eventful journey up the hill with the equally well-known story of the old woman who lived in a shoe'. This was played at Her Majesty's, Dundee, in 1914, the year after Wood's death (*Era* 13.1.15, 13).
37. *Stage* 28.12.16, 20.
38. *Stage* 30.12.15, 20.
39. Sir Max Beerbohm, *More Theatres 1898–1903* (Hart-Davis, 1969), p. 95.
40. *Stage* 19.12.18, 11.

41. *Stage* 31.12.14, 14.
42. *Stage* 30.12.15, 29.
43. *Stage* 28.12.16, 25.
44. *Stage* 28.12.16, 27. A. E. Wilson, *The Story of Pantomime* (Home and Van Thal, 1949), p. 76, believes Robin first intruded into the babes' story at Covent Garden, 1857.
45. *Stage* 27.12.17, 18.
46. LC 1915: 34/3928.
47. *Stage* 30.12.15, 26; *Stage* 27.12.17, 6. Inspiration may have come from Hickory Wood, whose 1910 *Jack and the Beanstalk* at Drury Lane made the central figure 'a Boy Scout who went to sleep on Leith Hill and dreamed that he was Jack' (A. E. Wilson, *Christmas Pantomime* (Allen & Unwin, 1934), p. 215).
48. The *Chu Chin Chow*-style sliding shutters had been used in *Puss in New Boots* the previous year, one of the tableaux represented thereby being 'a recruiting meeting in Trafalgar-square' (Newton, *Referee* 31.12.16, 2).
49. Whimsical Walker, last of the old-time Harlequinade clowns, figured continuously from the mid-1890s to the end of the war in Drury Lane Harlequinades.
50. *Stage* 31.12.14, 26.
51. *Stage* 30.12.15, 18. It was essentially Fred Carr's music hall turn, involving 'monstrous and mirth-provoking illuminated animal apparitions – dogs, beetles, fishes – culminating in the giant electric chicken, which lays eggs of the most prodigious size' (*Era* 12.6.18, 14).
52. *Stage* 24.12.14, 20, reviewing a Glasgow production. A Liverpool *Red Riding Hood* and a Birmingham Royal *Babes in the Wood* both had their Spiderland (*Era* 2.1.18, 10; *Stage* 27.12.18, 6).
53. *Stage* 30.12.15, 9.
54. *Era* 29.12.15, 16. Pantomime's 'dark scene' runs back to January 1725, though Disher, *Clowns and Pantomimes*, p. 246, hints that it may have derived from Italian Harlequinade.
55. *Stage* 30.12.15, 20.
56. *Stage* 30.12.15, 18. The Surrey Theatre's 1865 pantomime had included a chess scene (Wilson, *Christmas Pantomime*, facing p. 232), while Toyland seems to date from 1853, when Blanchard produced *Harlequin King Humming-Top and the Land of Toys* at Drury Lane (Disher, *Clowns and Pantomimes*, p. 311).
57. *Stage* 30.12.15, 29; *Stage* 27.12.17, 8. This reappeared at Birmingham Royal the next year where 'the climax of the Babes' flight in a Meccano aeroplane invariably "brought the house down"' (*Stage* 27.12.18, 6; Rodway and Slingsby, *Philip Rodway*, p. 280).

58. *Stage* 27.12.17, 20; *Stage* 28.12.16, 20. The Drury Lane scene, designed by McCleery, was judged 'a masterpiece both in the colour-scheme of the Comelli costumes of green and primrose-yellow and grey and rose and in the ingenious device of those two spiral staircases (reminding one curiously of the Crystal Palace water-towers), with the flag-waving coryphées marching up to Fairyland above the "flies" – and down therefrom – like an endless army' (Newton, *Referee* 31.12.16, 2). *Graphic* 27.1.17, 102, illustrates the scene, with its fairies tripping down 'from the ceiling, their movement downwards, guided by the overhanging banners, creating the illusion that the column is revolving'.
59. *Stage* 31.12.14, 29. Flying ballet was first introduced at the Gaiety in 1873, being taken up by pantomime at the Grecian soon afterwards (A. E. Wilson, *Pantomime Pageant* (Stanley Paul, 1946), p. 120).
60. *Stage* 21.12.16, 23. Lane's skill at trap-work is best demonstrated in *Joyland* (1929).
61. This 'Enchanted Lake', with 'real ducks', made a hit at the Birmingham Royal in 1917, though during a rehearsal 'the huge tarpaulins burst under the strain, and the orchestra was submerged in four feet of water' (Rodway and Slingsby, *Philip Rodway*, p. 240).
62. *Stage* 28.12.16, 21; *Stage* 4.1.17, 8.
63. It had its first full expression in the grand pageant of Drury Lane's 1891 *Humpty Dumpty*, to celebrate the wedding of Princess Allfair (Marie Lloyd), who gave her rendering of 'Ta-ra-ra Boom-de-ay', complete with high kicks (Wilson, *Christmas Pantomime*, p. 184).
64. *Stage* 31.12.14, 21. This was based on a divertissement, *Europe*, produced at the London Lyceum in the early weeks of the war, the work of C. Wilhelm, a Kentishman despite his professional name (*Era* 9.9.14, 10). He had designed pantomimes for Druriolanus and those of Oscar Barrett at the Lyceum and elsewhere.
65. *Era* 11.11.14, 9.
66. *Stage* 31.12.14, 14.
67. *The Times* 26.12.14, 3; *Era* 25.11.14, 8; 'Candida', *Graphic* 8.1.16, 68.
68. *Era* 9.12.14, 8. The star trap, a star-shaped opening in the stage which springs shut as soon as performers shoot through, had not been used in London for many years. Wain's cat drawings had grown immensely popular since their first appearance in 1883.
69. George Bernard Shaw, *Our Theatres in the Nineties* (Constable, 1932), vol. III, p. 22.
70. *Stage* 18.11.15, 18, records increasing dependence on touring pantomimes in this second year of war. The growing refinement of the halls had been 'the doom of 75 per cent of resident pantomimes. Everyone

visits music halls now, whereas the majority of the public used to wait till Christmas to see the stars' (*Era* 7.8.09, 24). Cf. *Era* 25.12.18, 6: Charles Austin 'especially tickles the better parts of the house, the frequenters of which are not supposed to have seen the renowned comedian in the halls'.

71. *Stage* 27.12.18, 9.
72. *Stage* 27.12.18, 6.
73. *Stage* 27.12.18, 19; *The Times* 27.12.18, 9. Dennis Castle, *'Sensation' Smith of Drury Lane* (Skilton, 1984), p. 206, claims that celebrated scenic artist Bruce Smith found distasteful what he dubbed 'the "Victory Vomit" set'.
74. *Stage* 30.12.15, 9.
75. *Stage* 24.12.14, 20.
76. *Era* 20.12.16, 21.
77. David Mayer, *Harlequin in His Element: The English Pantomime 1806–1936* (Cambridge, Mass.: Harvard University Press, 1969), p. 274.
78. *Ibid.*, p. 292.
79. *Ibid.*, p. 271.
80. *Stage* 23.12.15, 26.
81. Bottomley (*John Bull* 12.9.14, 22) popularized the feeble pun borrowed here by *Era* 6.1.15, 19.
82. *Era* 27.12.16, 21 and 10.
83. *Era* 13.9.16, 21.
84. *Era* 7.8.16, 18; *Era* 28.6.16, 14.
85. *Stage* 30.12.15, 10; *Era* 20.1.15, 13. Cf., too, *Stage* 31.12.14, 29, for a production of *Whittington* at the Grand, Croydon: 'A chorus of small boys dressed as street arabs with paper helmets and wooden swords gives some piquancy to the "Tipperary" song.'
86. When this was sung by George Gregory in Reeve's *Hula Girl* at the Manchester Hippodrome, a tank designed by stage manager J. P. Jones, one-time engineer with Vickers and Maxim, dashed 'across the stage, twisting and twirling in the most realistic fashion' (*Performer* 28.12.16, 21).
87. *Stage* 28.12.16, 21; *Era* 27.12.16, 9.
88. *Era* 27.12.16, 9; cf. the cast-iron bath utilized as a tank in the Harold Lloyd comedy *Next Aisle Over*, filmed at the end of 1918.
89. *Stage* 21.12.16, 23.
90. *Stage* 27.12.17, 18. A mock-pantomime, 'The Forty Thieves of 1918', in *Any Old Thing* (London Pavilion) included Food Hog Baron Bolo, who tried to steal from Red Riding Hood 'a pound of real butter lent by the Maypole Dairy Co. (by kind permission of the Food-Controller)' (*Era* 12.12.17, 1).

91. War-inspired names were naturally not exclusively Teutonic. The good fairy Searchlight in a Lyceum *Jack and the Beanstalk* (*Stage* 31.12.14, 26) reflects the novelty of the dozen searchlights so far installed for London's protection. A Newcastle *Babes in the Wood* included both Nurse Rosy Rapture and Baron Blighty (*Stage* 27.12.17, 8). The Wimbledon *Crusoe* had Jack the Slacker and King Na Poo the 19th (*Stage* 27.12.18, 21), the latter anticipated by 'King Na-Poo, the civilised cannibal' in Hammersmith's *Crusoe* two years before (*Era* 27.12.16, 10). The ugly sisters in the Summerdown Convalescent Military Hospital *Cinderella* were called Nahpoo and Finee (*Stage* 28.12.16, 26). E. Fraser and J. Gibbons, *Soldier and Sailor Words and Phrases* (Routledge, 1925), list *napoo* (also *napoo finee*): 'ex French *Il n'y a pas de* – + *fini* (there is no – + finished).'
92. *Stage* 27.12.18, 19; *Stage* 30.12.15, 29.
93. *Era* 23.12.14, 13.
94. *Stage* 17.2.14, 25; *Era* 6.1.15, 19; *Era* 13.1.15, 13.
95. *Stage* 31.12.14, 26.
96. *Daily Graphic* 6.1.15, 7. True to form, *John Bull* 16.1.15, 2, decides that 'denunciation of her by her fellow-artistes' was delayed because she regularly 'joined in the "National Anthem"', though doubtless substituting 'Heil Dir Im Siegeskranz', which shares the same tune. Rogers, who had been seen in London for several years, though it was her success in *By Jingo* which earned her the panto part, told her landlady 'that she was the victim of newspapers' (*Daily Chronicle* 7.1.15, 3). Her 'pro-German sentiments' were unsurprising since she was engaged to Detmold Robert, a German merchant whom she would marry on 14 December 1915 (*Era* 26.1.16, 11; *Era* 2.2.16, 10).

4
Variety on the halls

The war years saw not only the last great phase of the music hall, but an accelerated closing of the gap between legitimate and illegitimate stages which had begun in the 1870s, when the halls adopted the proscenium and segregated seating. By mid-war the AMU recognized three classes of variety theatre for salary purposes.[1] Besides the respectable suburban or provincial houses and the flea-pits there were the West End's palaces of variety. It was opulence rather than size which set those central palaces apart: some of the outlying theatres had stage facilities and a seating capacity which could accommodate big West End shows, though pit as well as gallery occupants were still apt to be seated on wooden benches.[2] What were already styled 'old-time' music halls[3] co-existed with those up-to-date houses which imitated the regular theatre in moving to a quieter mode. Wilkie Bard characterizes this stylistic shift, attuning himself to middle-class respectability with 'rigid spareness and economy' made up of 'hints, and half-spoken confidences, rather than of complete statement'.[4] Although Bard's use of a plant retained some of the old-style link between stage and audience, the broad tendency was one of separation: action pushed from an already shrunken forestage behind that proscenium of respectability. The lifting of the curtain gave a sense of privileged entry into a private world; and the halls frequently borrowed picture-frame illusionism for their sketches. It was a theatre of illusion in more senses than one, its cosiness of outlook reflecting that optimistic belief in an expanding industrial economy which, undeterred by war and recession, had continued blithely until 1914.

Defining the target for this illusion is none too easy. The proportion of working-class to middle-class attendance is not only a variable in terms of period and locale, but the working class offers no easy subject for generalization. Communities, even in the same town, could vary quite considerably in terms of atmosphere, outlook and standards of behaviour. The growth of music-hall circuits over large parts of the country helped to flatten out these variations, imposing external ideas of identity in place of those emerging from shared experience.[5] But Newton, in an apocryphal account of how he warned Marie Lloyd against taking those 'blue' songs with which she had regaled West End audiences to Hoxton, Whitechapel or Mile End, both obscures and reflects the tendency by reducing distinctions to a crude one of supposed sophistication.[6] The houses accommodated all age groups, even to babes in arms. At the Oxford, Bertram Banks, child mimic, improvised a duet with a baby crying violently in the stalls; and 'Extra Turn' advocated prohibition on health grounds after seeing a baby enduring 'the smoke-laden atmosphere' of the Shoreditch Empire.[7]

Moss-Thornton's 1899 ban on babies was based on class rather than health considerations.[8] This was part of a continuing effort to woo the middle class, which found fullest expression in the supply of increasingly high-toned fare: a double gain in reducing harassment from the authorities and increasing profit. With war just weeks away Oswald Stoll, one of the great forces in variety management, had bemused Coliseum audiences with Marinetti's Futurist music, where raspings and grindings joined a cacophony of seeming 'factory hooters, train whistles, and ship sirens'.[9] The war saw 'music of the best class ... invading all our best halls',[10] Stoll drew Genée out of retirement in 1915, engaged Loïe Fuller, with her *Jugendstil* swirls of drapery aided by light and colour, in 1916, and (his greatest feat) brought the Ballets Russes from Spain across war-torn Europe in 1918.[11] The outstanding contralto Louise Kirkby Lunn made her variety debut at his Coliseum in 1915, enchanting audiences with Eboli's aria from *Don Carlos*, an opera which had never secured a hold in this country;[12] and Mark Hambourg was another whose visits there demonstrated that it was unnecessary to popularize for variety audiences.[13] Elgar came, too, conducting both his *Carillon* and *Fringes of the Fleet*, the latter with baritone Charles Mott, who was killed in France a twelvemonth later.[14]

However, it was less this increase in high art than the sentimental songs of performers like Gertie Gitana which explained for Ivor Brown the expanding popularity of the halls. Sentimental appeal was 'a child of Capitalism', attracting the bourgeoisie just as much as workers seeking respite from the ugly industrial grind.[15] For some, music hall's classlessness seemed won at the cost of its 'chiefest glory', sturdy 'Anglo-Saxon vulgarity and individualism'; for others, the move to 'internationalism, respectability, and syndicated halls' was sheer gain, achieving for variety 'a popularity that has no parallel in the history of amusements'.[16] But this ignores the shadow cast by cinema, transforming the whole popular entertainment scene. Cinema taught people that 'there was no more advantage in trying to amuse themselves than there would be in making their own boots or clothes'. Thus the AMU's London organizer,[17] who anticipated something of this momentum feeding back into the halls. Then there was revue, seen by 1915 as 'the staple attraction' of the halls;[18] and an astute manager would take advantage of fluctuations in demand by means of the double licence. This existed from 1912, 'a practical if unwieldy working compromise' pending a more rational amendment of the law.[19] The theatre licence for music halls required 'six separate items' to appear on the programme, the first five often raced through before the main attraction began, and for the curtain to be lowered after each item.[20]

Marie Lloyd deplored this development, advocating 'The Single Turn's Return' in an *Era* article (21 March 1917, p. 13): in pre-revue days, it was widely acknowledged 'that for real talent and for real vitality the variety houses were far ahead of the theatres. The highest of the highbrows declared their opinion that a night at the Tivoli was intellectually more stimulating than a night at almost any West End theatre.' At that time 'the work of the artiste was everything and the setting a mere conventional street-scene drop or full-set marble hall which nobody troubled to look at twice'. Robey recalls the ludicrous incongruity of backcloths in the early 1890s, when he might sing 'You Can Tell Her By The Pimple On Her Nose' before a representation of 'Melrose Abbey by moonlight'.[21] But that it was not always so Lloyd well knew. Shaw, visiting the Empire in 1892, commented on the 'brilliancy and grace of effect' of the stage design, finding it odd that at an entertainment where 'half the audience have come to hear Marie Lloyd sing Twiggy voo', there is 'real stage art', whereas at the opera 'all the art' is left to the singers.[22] Her concern was that revue would push the halls in the same direction as Shakespeare, wit becoming subsidiary to setting. She hoped that government calls for economy would reverse the trend; and so it did up to a point, *Performer* (29 March 1917, p. 19) noting that the Oxford had dropped revue 'and reverted to the ordinary variety programme'. But many agreed with Robb Wilton that, in the long run, big productions would take over: 'The empty stage will seem very drear after the full stage that audiences have become used to, and the front-cloth turn will be spoilt.'[23]

Single turn, sketch and revue had been jostling for some time; indeed, it was the halls' powers of hospitality, making them a microcosm of wartime entertainment, which ensured their prosperity during those years, often at the expense of a less flexible straight theatre. Naturally music hall had its casualties like most other lines of business, the Isle of Man being a conspicuous example. Its entertainments industry was virtually wiped out by sailing restrictions imposed by the Admiralty,[24] which also forced the closure of Portsmouth's Coliseum, with a 9 o'clock curfew on 'all licensed premises in the great naval centre'.[25] But usually it was areas experiencing the loss of young adult males without the compensation of nearby army camps or factories converted to war needs which suffered. Travel restrictions created a problem in the first weeks, especially for those touring with scenery and props; they forced G. M. Polini, who had been managing tours for decades, to suspend activities, and hastened his death.[26] Artists who had been working in Germany when war broke out sometimes abandoned everything in their bid to evade internment. E. G. Bale, due to spend the winter performing at Leipzig, and the following summer at Hamburg, lost horses worth £800, and accoutrements worth another £300, reaching Copenhagen to find it 'full of artistes nearly starving'.[27] Escaping artists created a problem in Britain, too, though Avrigny, a well-known juggler, butted against managerial vested interests in advocating that turn working (obverse of the controversial barring clause) be abandoned. He considered it unjust that some 'should be working a number of halls, while others [we]re suffering from unemployment', advocating a union approach to the problem.[28]

On the whole, however, the war proved variety's salvation, arriving when 'Many halls [had] paid no dividends for several years'.[29] Although the directors of Moss' Empires decided to postpone payment of the declared interim dividend on the company's ordinary shares in view of the crisis,[30] this proved an unnecessary precaution. The end of 1914 saw a profit increase, and a year on the company's chairman was ecstatic, ascribing the 1915 boom 'to the general absence of unemployment,[31] the great activity in all production centres', and chiefly to the need for relaxation in these tense times, especially amongst the working class upon whose support their business 'depended greatly'.[32] The next year proved still rosier, despite the impact of conscription, the major operators issuing 'statements of sound business, increased reserves, and general financial improvement'.[33] The war, summarized the *Financier* (13 March 1918, p. 2), had brought widespread prosperity, pessimism about the impact of rising costs and imposition of an entertainment tax proving 'completely unjustified'.

In late 1914, Henry Tozer, chairman of the Variety Theatres Consolidated, Ltd., claimed that, with a drop in attendance of 25 per cent or more, his halls were losing money and few 'were making any profit'. But Tozer's politic pessimism was a response to the way that emergency financial arrangements were under heavy attack for favouring manager over performer. The reality was that at worst the big combines found things balancing out. It was only the small-timer who risked ruin through local circumstances; but most of these had already been squeezed out between the pincer-jaws of industrial giants and licensing authorities. Stoll, although aware that nine houses in the London area had 'been injured seriously', found the war benefiting 'as many places as it has injured'. A military presence could have a startling effect: one theatre where almost immediately on the outbreak of war takings dropped 'as low as £3 a performance' was now 'doing better business than it has ever done in its career'.[34] Stoll was chairman of the London Theatres of Variety, embracing 19 houses in London and the suburbs and including the Palladium. Charles Gulliver was managing director of this group; but Stoll was managing director as well as chairman of the Coliseum and the 12 London and suburban halls allied thereto. His principal rival was Alfred Butt, with important West End and Parisian interests. He also operated a dozen provincial halls as joint managing director of the Variety Controlling Company. He and Stoll were not in open conflict until August 1915, when Butt's 'tentative agreement' to take over the Alhambra, chief competitor to his Empire, was trumped by Stoll. Commentators saw the Alhambra becoming associated for the first time with circuit management as 'an important step in the gradual splitting-up of the British variety industry into two great combines'.[35]

Given his importance in the industry, Butt's statement within days of the outbreak of war is especially instructive: already things were proving 'disastrous' for the industry generally, though, with the uncertainty over, things should 'become more normal'. Meanwhile, the halls must be kept open: since many in 'humble positions [he discreetly forgets others in far from humble positions] are directly or indirectly dependent upon this big industry for a living'; and further there is the rôle of the halls as both sop and (correctly administered) stimulant. To shut off this source of 'harmless amusement' would depress public morale just when it needed boosting. So, and here he gets to the heart of the matter, it was the patriotic duty of artists, particularly the highly paid, 'to bear some part of the loss' which the halls must suffer (an assumption which is never challenged).[36]

Thus Butt finesses his way between a disaster scenario, to justify emergency measures, and a concern for the low-paid employee, who would be unmercifully skinned by those measures. Evidently this co-operative (or 50–50) scheme had already been floated amongst the industry's hierarchy: de Frece circulated managers on 9 August 'suggesting that all companies booked should play on a sharing basis of fifty–fifty until things again became normal'.[37] The proposal was placed before the VAF on 13 August; but even before that West End artists had been peremptorily told that their salaries would be cut by 50 per cent.[38] The 50–50 scheme was presented as the only way of keeping the halls open, and threat of closure was sufficient to force agreement from a Federation which had long lost the militancy shown in the 1907 strike. The suggestion that stars earning 'more than £50 a week should be asked to contribute towards a special fund for their less well-paid brethren'[39] was ignored, as was Butt's hint that protection of the low-paid was negotiable. It would later be asserted that the VAF was concerned to fight strenuously only 'in the interests of the biggest salaries'.[40] Consequently, it was agreed that for

12 weeks starting on 17 August a theatre's takings would be split 'evenly between the management and the artistes, the amount in the latter case to be sub-divided pro-rata'. Should the amount apportioned to the artists' salaries exceed the amount of the full salary list, the surplus would go not to the artists but half to the management and half to the VAF to aid those hard hit by the scheme (the West End halls withheld this VAF contribution). But subject to a few such variations, most halls adopted the scheme.[41]

Even had 50–50 operated honestly (and one victim reported packed houses and a 20 per cent salary cut)[42] it would have had a punishing effect on the low-paid. But one provincial managing director reported much bad faith on both sides: 'the unscrupulous overloading of bills on the part of some proprietors, and the unscrupulous demands by artistes for increased salary'. Both abuses squeezed the low-paid.[43] Overloading was rife, extra turns being engaged to boost door receipts though managers' liabilities could not extend beyond the 50 per cent agreed. 'A Small Turn', forced to disband his sketch-act as a result of this malpractice, complained through *Era* (7 October 1914, p. 10): 'If you have a salary list of about £250 to £275 you may get your money, but you are not going to get it in a hall where they have put a £300 turn on top, and the takings amount to £600 – in some cases just about as much as they can take. They ... can inflate their bills, put on a very powerful company, and make £300', quite apart from 'doing a roaring trade at the bars'. This correspondent was in no doubt that, in the big towns, proprietors were doing better than ever, thus reinforcing the view expressed in another letter (9 September 1914, p. 10), which advocated a 60–40 split in favour of the artists, pointing out that the last salary 'bill at the Alhambra, Glasgow, ... was about £450, and you cannot get me to believe that the manager's out-goings for rent, &c., was that amount'. The celebrated dancer Lydia Kyasht was evidently unimpressed by the Alhambra manager's arithmetic (it was ultimately under Butt's control) and declined to appear.[44]

But it was only major stars who could afford to opt out of the scheme. Some declared that 'they "could do with a rest," [and] wouldn't agree to any diminution of pay'. Others chose to abuse the system; so many 'swollen-salaried' stars feigned indisposition that the complaint 'became known as "The Co-op Sore Throat"', while others, seeking to skirt possible litigation for breaking their contracts, 'came along unwillingly and in "Weary Willy" fashion gave off one song and fled'.[45] Caught between this waywardness of the overpaid and the increasingly transparent misery being inflicted on the underpaid, the managerial hierarchy met to repeat their threat of closure if the scheme was not adhered to.[46] Nevertheless, under mounting pressure, some profit was diverted towards alleviating the hardship of the small turns, it being agreed that this revised scheme would run until 30 January 1915.[47] By that time it had cost artists an estimated £100,000.[48]

There were two lasting consequences of the 50–50 scheme after it had run its course. One was that managers were reluctant to relinquish its very substantial advantages. This was a major factor in the explosion of revues in 1915. John Dunbar describes how revues, unlike single turns, could be engaged 'on sharing terms, whereby the salary risk of the artistes previously engaged was taken over, and the proprietors of the halls paid their share of the gross takings – usually 50 per cent.'[49] The second consequence was that inflated salaries became a highly controversial issue; indeed it was confidently expected in some quarters that the expiry of 50–50 would see some 'rearrangement of music hall salaries in general'.[50] Fierce international competition inflated pay, though artists were often 'pushed up to big salaries, not by any extraordinary talent, but by the cuteness of some agent'.[51] The AMU and NOA were in no doubt about that: 'a small section of variety artistes are using the present conditions to extort salaries that are much above their real value and drawing power' at the expense of the low-paid.[52] Both were opposed to conditions which had not only created an ever-widening salary gap, but had forced the independent halls out of business. It was asked whether 'even the "star" artistes [would] be better off with all the principal halls under one management'.[53] But the trend was all in the direction of a monolithic structure; Stoll could even reflect equably on the way that an entertainment tax would contribute: 'Moderate rates … might be quite easily borne by strong houses when weak ones had been crushed out.'[54]

The AMU's three objectives were: 'A minimum of 50s. per week, with £5 for conductors', protection for oboe, bassoon and horn players, and a closed shop in the orchestra pit.[55] It would be a long while before those rates were achieved, but more modest increases were negotiated widely. Stoll held out, even reneging on his agreement to match at the Coliseum any increases obtained at the Hippodrome. But *Era* (18 October 1916, p. 15) strongly supported Stoll, rejecting the idea that he was paying 'less than other managements'. Much weight was given to Stoll's willingness to allow Sir George Askwith, chief industrial commissioner, to arbitrate; but no mention was made of Stoll's refusal to meet with union representatives, a necessary prerequisite according to Askwith's own arbitration procedures. He was thus effectively blocking the very process that he was supposedly favouring. Eventually, it was gloatingly recorded that Stoll had now settled the matter by replacing the militants with non-union women. The only failure was to find bassoonists; and, in view of the union's desire to protect that species, there is a touch of malice in his remark that they could be replaced easily by cellists. Then he levelled a combined sexist and patriotic charge: the AMU rejected women while admitting aliens, despite the policy statement made months earlier by J. B. Williams, joint secretary of AMU and NOA, that they much preferred 'to put British women players in before aliens'.[56] The next week saw an attempt to weasel out of the charge when Williams pointed to substantial support from women members.

Another telling point was made by Williams: although Stoll had actually given the pay increase to musicians at the London Opera House, following the crisis at the other theatres he first fired them, then invited them to stay on at the old salaries. This offer was properly refused, so their places were filled with more low-paid women musicians. Later, however, Williams blundered by opposing renewal of the licence for Stoll's Middlesex on the grounds that the entertainment offered there was highly improper for a theatre with an all-women orchestra.[57] But the response of *Era*'s editor-in-chief, Alfred Barnard, who wished that Williams would fall victim of the blackout 'by getting under a motor omnibus', seems out of all proportion even for an inveterate union-basher.[58] It is notable that, although the LCC had refused to renew the licence, the Middlesex's programme of suggestive revues continued unchanged under the Lord Chamberlain's permit, and despite LCC protest.[59]

Double licensing allowed this playing of one licensing authority off against the other. Anomalies could be removed by establishing free trade in entertainment.[60] But its advocates often hypocritically excluded film, and continual vigilance was maintained to limit the spread of variety acts at the cinema.[61] The LCC's Theatres and Music Halls Committee was effectively policed by the Entertainments Protection Association, a union of halls managers; and when for once the LCC ignored its recommendation not to allow vocal turns at the Majestic cinema, Clapham Road, there was a great outcry from interested parties. (The Association, which exerted an unhealthy influence over the LCC, had successfully opposed all such applications since 1911.) *Era* (16 December 1914, p. 13) insisted that the effect would be to create 'a number of music halls of a lower grade than is desirable'; but desirable for whom? This was a replay of the hostility shown by the regular theatre towards the increasing presence of sketches or playlets on music hall bills. Double licensing was the big breakthrough, bringing a stream of prominent thespians into the halls, led by Tree. An enthusiastic interview in *Referee* (3 October 1915, p. 2) suggests that he found his music hall tour of *Trilby* more than just 'a great financial success'. Interestingly, Lillah McCarthy was said to have blundered by making her début on the halls in such a trivial piece as Macdonald Hastings's *The Fourth Act*, 'for music-hall audiences expect something unusually good from the leading people of the legitimate stage when they enter vaudeville'.[62] But this influx apart, the halls had their own excellent sketch artists. During the war two of the best were Joe Elvin and Alfred Lester, the one boisterous and the other lugubrious. But the most notable names in the field were linked in a version of a popular soldier-song:

'We Are Fred Karno's Army, And Lew Lake's Cavalry.' Karno's *Mumming Birds*, a springboard to success for Charlie and Syd Chaplin amongst others and credited with starting 'the furore for the comedy pictures', came off during the war after playing for over 12 years, to release resources for new shows. These included the topical *Rations* by Lee and Weston, where Robb Wilton was abused first by spooning couples for rationing kisses,[63] and then, as a butcher, by women in a meat queue. But he was more popular in exposing Lady Hoardley's vast stores of sugar.[64]

Lew Lake (1874–1939) was a busy man during the war, adding to his theatrical activities as performer, proprietor and producer that of agent in 1916. He was also King Rat for two years besides serving on the VAF executive committee. By the end of the war he had decided to give up stage work to concentrate on his other interests.[65] He played Nobbler in the famed Nobbler and Jerry farces, which started well before the war with Arthur Rose's *The Bloomsbury Burglars*.[66] This enriched the language with the expression 'Stick it, Jerry', giving a humorous cast to that endless exhortation to the lower orders, both before and during the war, to endure their lot rather than seek to improve it.

However, while congratulating the halls on their raised standards, Belcham dismisses such sketches as 'primitive, broadly splashed caricature or extravagant burlesque', designed 'not to show life, but to make the spectators forget life. And the great music hall public – the millions of toilers, "dreary dwellers in little drab brick boxes" – are content that it should be so. Their mental horizon is restricted by the pettiness of their daily life; they are content with forms of humour that demand no thought.'[67] The double-think is patent: he would have the quality of fare improved, but not the toilers' political awareness. Contrariwise, Archer credited this 'unpretending' dramatic element with counteracting 'the gibberish song' to achieve variety's 'marked improvement over the past ten years'.[68] Furthermore, an official demand for wartime topicals resulted in leading dramatists writing expressly for the variety theatres. Various parables produced at the behest of the National War Savings Committee arrived at the Coliseum, including Pinero's *Mr. Livermore's Dream* and Alfred Sutro's *Great Redding Street Burglary*.[69] Walter de Frece, husband of Vesta Tilley and future Tory MP, whose extensive music-hall holdings had been failing, was rescued by the wartime demand for entertainment and the increased spending power of the workers. But in his view they were 'spending their earnings far too freely', causing apprehension that they, and consequently *he*, would 'feel the pinch' after the war.[70] That the workers were unable to handle their new affluence was a constant plaint.[71] Chancellor of the Exchequer Reginald McKenna, addressing a conference of organized labour at the Central Hall, Westminster, saw 'very big wages' producing 'a great demand for pianos' rather than any inclination to save.[72] But denouncing the excesses of the poor is a common reactionary mode, and he was rebuked in one paper: 'Will Mr. McKenna remember the next time he speaks about the unexampled prosperity of the working classes that there are over a quarter of a million women and girl munition workers working for sums ranging between one penny farthing and three pence per hour.'[73]

Sutro's piece, the first to appear, amplified McKenna's point in portraying a £7-a-week munition worker sampling the good life. (It is conveniently overlooked that such a wage would entail working probably more than 100 hours a week, allowing the recipient scant time for anything but working and sleeping.) Symbol of the good life is a piano, but the £20 Thomas has put aside for its purchase has disappeared,[74] and it is eventually revealed that a relative helping about the home has converted the cash into war-saving certificates in his name. The help has been persuaded that those who don't 'make sacrifices ... with their pore lives and bodies' must do so 'by lendin' their money to the Government'. But this propaganda of economy ladies 'wot drives up in their automobiles' has left Thomas unmoved. When it is objected that 'This one warn't in no automobilly', there is the immediate retort that 'she'll 'ave left it round the corner'. Working-class members of the audience would recognize the ruse (the Hippodrome revue *Flying Colours* mocks 'those dear people who went to the Guildhall in Rolls Royces to encourage the lower orders to economise'[75]). Indeed, the best speech was thought to be that where Thomas denounces the high-living 'upper classes, who tell him to economise', and those present on the first night indicated 'by their applause that their sympathies [were] with him'.[76] It is certain that if the help dealt thus cavalierly with money belonging to one of those high-livers, it would not be represented so approvingly.

Michael Morton's *My Superior Officer* is more canny in attacking those who take 'high war-wages' without 'lending some of it to the Chancellor of the Exchequer' through the mouth of a wounded soldier.[77] It shows munition workers destroyed by indulgence 'in taxis, gramophones, expensive cigars, whisky, and other things supposed to belong exclusively to ... their social superiors'.[78] The prototype for this sort of thing is Walter Ellis's *Too Late*, which establishes the gamut of extravagances, including whisky and 'shilling cigars', though wartime austerity offers no reason for denying these to any but the workers.[79] But Morton's piece also stands in relation to *War Mates*, by Herbert de Hamel, whose active service with the London Scottish was perfect qualification for rebuking munition workers according to Marks (*Referee* 21 November 1915, p. 4). The play launches an attack on trade-union attempts to force better working conditions by the threat of disrupting shell production. A soldier on leave, nephew of the strike-leader, attacks this in 'a speech of red-hot eloquence and passion', telling how his uncle's boy was one of those left behind wounded after an assault which failed through inadequate artillery support. When condemned for not attempting to save his cousin, he retorts that 'he gets a bob a day for fighting; for rescuing Tom he should have had to stick out for another fourpence for overtime. Further, Tom was a Territorial – a non-union man; he himself was a Regular, and to consent to fight in line with amateurs was already going back on the rights and principles of the Regular Army.'[80] The reality, of course, is that he has gained the VC for rescuing his cousin. And just as he scores a secondary success in taking a girl from a rival who has been supporting the strike, so does this plea for unity between labour and the army perform the equally useful function of fostering the soldier's dislike for those at home earning good wages.[81]

There is perhaps concord between the heavy targeting of workers and the way that William Moore's sketch-title 'The Supreme Sacrifice' alludes not to a glorious death but, with no sense of irony, to exchanging a lucrative partnership for khaki.[82] At least Pinero's 'lesson in thrift' points a finger at the well-to-do, and even avoids making the culprit pro-German rather than simply pro-money, a feature vitiating not a few of these stage clashes between profit and patriotism, including Beresford and Richmond's *Howard and Son*.[83] George Alexander played Sir Anthony Howard, ready to consign copper to the Germans to save the firm for his homecoming son. Treachery is averted when he learns that he won't be seeing his son, who has succumbed to wounds. A child's death is again the redemptive force in Walter Ellis's *Profiteer*. Against a background of bread riots, the entrepreneur is busily 'cornering the people's food and making huge profits' while expectantly awaiting a knighthood. But then comes the death of his estranged daughter, unable to fight off sickness because of the high cost of food which he has brought about.[84] Fred Moule's *Jim Jam Jim* represents the capitalist with a conscience, though it comes into play only after Jim has 'gone the way of many contractors, and ... made illicit profit out of the Government'.[85]

This type of story, often adapted to recruiting purposes, though using a more interesting gambit, the octogenarian hero, had been thoroughly anticipated in the mid-seventeenth century.[86] At that time, with the whole country up in arms, the oldster could actually find opportunities to fight; now, he can only regret that his age prevents his sailing for France. Marguerite Oldfield's *Veteran's Farewell* 'was received with great enthusiasm' at the Battersea Palace as a notable recruit-raiser. The old man is roused by the sound of a military band and spots his son-in-law in the ranks. His excitement produces a heart attack and he imagines himself back on the field of valour before falling down dead. George Bealby's *In the Blood* centres on a veteran with a son at the front who is given a portrait of General French for his 82nd birthday. As his grandson rummages amongst his trophies, including the inevitable VC, the excitement proves too much for the old man, who dies in his chair. The child assumes he is sleeping and strikes a military attitude on the table with the old man's sword, 'a pathetic and fitting tableau in the presence of the dead soldier'.[87] Robert Bedford, who appeared in this, had a namesake, Henry Bedford, playing a similar rôle in Malcolm Lisle's *The Empty Sleeve*.[88] Here, the old man had lost his arm saving the life of his general, who had promised 'to repay him for his noble act'. The old man's grandson has deserted and is tracked down by an officer who proves to be the son of that general, whose promise is redeemed by hushing up the desertion when the grandson returns to his regiment.[89] Desertion was an uncomfortable topic since, regardless of circumstances, it led often enough to the firing squad. As far as the theatre was concerned, if lapses from military virtue were to be ascribed to the allies, it was safer to make the offenders foreigners: a Frenchman in Barry Shell's *The Deserter*; and, in Norman Lee's *The Eve of Liège*, a Belgian officer whose cowardice is atoned for when his colonel-father enters the Uhlan death-trap in his place.[90]

Officialdom was slow to acknowledge the part played by shell-shock in military failure. But the therapeutic effect of music hall on sufferers was well attested, the first instance noted in *Era* (1 December 1915, p. 16) taking place 'at a hall in the North [when] a soldier in the audience, who had been wounded and gassed at Hill 70, . . . was so highly amused at one of the comedians that he recovered' both speech and hearing. A similar case occurred during a performance of *Sheba* at the Camberwell Empire, and conjurer Patric Playfair also worked the trick. So did George Formby and the energetic blackface comedienne May Henderson.[91] It became the basis for a sketch, Thelma Antony's *Coppernob*, where 'a young actress and dancer' performs for the wounded, effects the cure of a shell-shock victim, and discovers that he is her sweetheart.[92]

A more immediate way in which the sketch blurred fiction and actuality was in the all-women productions which demonstrated how women were filling the gaps left by men. One by Karno, actually called *All Women*, both offered a concrete example and showcased women in other capacities 'as munition workers, policemen, dustmen, carpenters, gardeners, &c.'[93] Inevitably, the raised profile of women prompted both farcical response and conservative reaction. *In the Year 9999* forecasts a world of female dominance where women are both seducers and protectors of the 'poor, weak-minded, effeminate creature' man.[94] And in Denton Spencer's *Ruling the Roost*, a newly married man congratulates himself that his wife has severed connection with the Knickerbocker Club, 'a sort of suffragette or "new woman" organisation', only for her to dress in knickerbockers and Norfolk jacket for a visit to his rich maiden aunt. He brings her to her senses by assuming some of her clothes, though 'put on in such a manner as to suggest that he has had at least one too many whiskies'. Another of Spencer's sketches, *Settling Day*, represents a discharged Tommy with a DCM discovering that his munition-worker wife has acquired a taste for the gay life in his absence: powder, paint, false hair and even a lover. His first instinct is to shoot the lover, but instead he persuades her to change her ways for the sake of the children. Yet another expression of anxiety about munition-workers' new affluence, it was deemed 'excellent propaganda'. Indeed Albert Brasque, who had been running a couple of Spencer's playlets for over 2½ years, considered that his efforts should fall within the government's definition of 'Work of National Importance'.[95]

Women are also shown as key figures in the dynamics of class. In drama critic Louis Cowan's farcelet, *One of the Family*, an intellectual socialist who tries to introduce equality into the home is effectively cured by his wife's friend who, masquerading as a servant, 'demands beer, addresses her master as "old dear", and displays a shocking disregard of table manners'.[96] War's social shuffling fuels Henry Seton's duologue, *The Link*, where a wife's advertisement for a lady companion during her husband's absence at the Front is answered by a woman with an unsuitable cockney accent. But the tables are turned by the discovery that the cockney's husband is a major in the very unit where the lady's husband serves as private.[97] A major instrument of social levelling supposedly fostered by the war was unequal marriage. Wylie and Parker's musical sketch, *Kiss Me, Sergeant*, finds a pickle millionaire failing to prevent his son's wedding to a Belgian refugee.[98] Possibly Belgian refugees or self-made men were in a special category, since the usual denouement was rather different. Seton's *Hon. Gertrude* starred Esmé Beringer as a VAD nursing a shell-shocked VC. He becomes smitten and she promises marriage as a restorative ploy. But the 'social inequality knot' is conveniently cut when the recovered Tommy, having fallen out of love, realizes that there is no obligation to honour the engagement.[99] It is Sutro, however, who gives this most intriguing shape with *The Marriage … Will Not Take Place*, premièred at the Coliseum in 1917. A baronet seeks to prevent his soldier son from being trapped into marriage by a minor musical-comedy actress. The baronet recruits his brother-in-law, a celebrated barrister, to buy her off with a thousand or two or even five if necessary. But she is no gold-digger, and only accepts a cheque for £2000 when assured by the genial barrister that she may do so 'with the clearest conscience and the profoundest self-respect'. And even he, on being shown her wedding ring, 'looks at it with an expression something like that on Lady Macbeth's face during one of her bad nights'. Thus Alfred Barnard, who considers it 'a bit hard on musical comedy artistes as a class' that the woman, happily married with children, makes no attempt to return the cheque. Had she done so, he opines, these 'perfect gentlemen' might well have responded to her playing the game by handing over the full £5000. (A more plausible speculation might be that the baronet would now stop the cheque.) Barnard compounds the familiar confusion of moral and social status with another myth: that the rich recognize a material responsibility towards the worthy poor. The barrister, having no such illusion about his boorish brother-in-law, facilitates some modest redistribution of wealth. This was doubtless one more problem for Barnard, and he exerted his very considerable power as boss of *Era* to have the ending changed.[100] In subsequent performances, as well as in the printed text,[101] the heroine tore up the cheque before leaving. Women share the heroics with men in the war playlets. Many are set along what is vaguely called the Belgian frontier, others in that territory of the mind dubbed the Western Front: regions where lines inscribed on maps by politicians, and for the most part invisible on the ground, yet mean the difference between freedom and captivity, life and death. That censor's evasion, 'Somewhere in France', takes no account of the Franco-Belgian frontier; and heavy bombardment will obliterate all but the most durable landmarks. Hence those serving at the Front seldom have any clearer idea of locale than the civilian who has never ventured overseas. It is sufficient to recognize that they defend a frontier marking the limits of civilization, a bulwark against barbarism. And characteristically into this world strays a woman, a Red Cross nurse who somehow, amidst shot and shell, discovers her officer-sweetheart in need of aid. Or it may be a French woman who selflessly furthers the escape of stranded Tommies. Piquancy is added to the situation by threatened rape, with common sense warped into accepting this as a peculiarly Hunnish activity. Prussian officers resort indifferently to brute force or blackmail: a lapse in virtue being the common price demanded for the life of parent, lover or some small child who has offended military sensibilities. Honour is preserved through the woman's own resources or the timely arrival of British troops: the desperate measure of a Tosca or a burly Highlander's precipitate entry through a window serve equally well.[102]

Rape is a key factor in A. J. Waldron's *The Wages of Hell*. The war, claimed one reviewer, was putting Christianity to 'the severest test of its existence' over the question of loving our enemies; and he reprimanded Eton's headmaster, Lyttelton, for speaking out against humiliating the German 'when hundreds of Eton's own have suffered the horrors of the Hun'. Since Lyttelton's views had been expressed more than a year before, he had clearly made a deep impression by swimming against the tide of clerical opinion. But now the former vicar of Brixton staged the more commonplace view that the 'German must never be forgiven; the barbarity of his warfare never forgotten'. The scene is the German entry into Louvain, one girl remaining in the school dormitory when a 'wine-sodden German officer' bursts in. The curtain falls discreetly and rises 17 years on, with the rapist recognized and, after his victim hesitates, properly despatched by her brother.[103] The undisclosed economic motive for post-war maintenance of hate propaganda emerges in Gertrude Wiskin and Martin Lewis's playlet, *And Afterwards*; a City merchant tearing up a contract with a Dresden firm following protests from the young people in his home, who had both experienced Hun atrocities.[104]

This reiterated the official government line as disseminated in the Ministry of Information film, *Once a German* (March 1918), though at the outset the authorities were slow to maximize on the propagandist possibilities of cinema. Technically there was no problem about providing hot news: in 1899, film of Buller's embarkation for South Africa was shown at a music hall just a few hours after the event.[105] And as usual, in 1915, the directors of the Empire secured exclusive filming rights at the Grand National, the results being shown at the theatre the same evening.[106] But it was 1916 before 'some real War pictures [we]re beginning to find their way past the Censor'.[107] The military had been coy about releasing action footage, though war events were shown at the halls from the outset, when both Butt and Moss' Empires arranged for 'leading film producers to give a constant supply of war pictures'.[108]

But film also played an integral part in variety performances. The world's champion box-makers and orange-packers contextualized their amazing demonstration with film of the California orange-picking and packing industry;[109] and a dramatic sketch, *The Revenge of the Lions*, included a bioscope account of the live lions' origins and capture.[110] 'The Movie Girl' utilized a reflexive mode, Irene Hammond appearing first on screen and then, in response to a serenading fan in the stalls (her partner Arthur Swanstone), as an image come to life when she burst through the tissue-paper screen. More elaborately, *Charlie Chaplin Mad*, where a millionairess's suitors all disguised themselves as Chaplin, introduced a Chaplin film and ended in the Los Angeles Cinema Park where bogus and 'real' Chaplins confronted each other. Author Leonard Durell claimed to have rehearsed Chaplin when he first joined Fred Karno.[111] American comedian Will Armstrong offered a pale imitation of something which Max Linder had done at the Paris Olympia. It began 'with a cinema picture representing the horse and van which conveys a large box to the residence of an actress. The man in charge carries the big box inside the house and here the film gives place to a real interior, with the baggage man entering, shouldering his heavy load, and preceded by the lady whose property it is.'[112] More topically, in a late 1914 playlet, *Under the Flag*, a character's heroic ride through enemy lines was allegedly shot 'in France in the actual war zone'.[113]

But this piece relied chiefly on the staging of aerial and aquatic sequences: a Zeppelin 'blown up in mid air', and the heroine, a Red Cross nurse, diving 'from a great height into a huge tank of water' simulating the Atroy Falls, to escape a German's unwelcome attentions. Such spectacle was common, the growing importance of war in the air generating a variety of responses. It doubtless added spice when Captain de Villiers released his wireless airship in the auditorium of the Camberwell Empire, just as it prompted ventriloquist Gerald Cyril to appear in an aeroplane suspended above the stage with his doll Nutta as observer.[114] Hicks claims that 'the first time an aeroplane was ever seen on the stage' was in Paul Rubens's musical one-acter, *The Fly by Night* (Palace, 14 December 1908), in which he and his wife initiated migration 'from the theatres to the halls'.[115] But during the war aeroplanes became a regular site for cross-talk though not without some risk. One used at the Coliseum by the Kenna Brothers crashed to the stage, and they were lucky to escape with a few bruises.[116] Their act was a clever blend of fun and acrobatics; but it is a comment on the effect of the war on aviation and people's perceptions of it that when Conn Kenna asked a provincial tobacconist if he intended seeing their show, the man 'replied that he didn't care to pay and see an aeroplane in a music hall: you could see them for nothing in the sky'.[117] *In the Clouds,* story and production by Leslie Stiles and Henry de Vries respectively, offered the spectacle of 'searchlight and anti-aircraft gun operations against a Taube', and a climactic struggle 'in the clouds' between two soldiers in 'an almost unrivalled exhibition of sensational staging'.[118]

Water spectacle provides a useful lead into the censorship issue. The acknowledged master of such spectacle was Albert Hengler, whose *Kultur* at Manchester's Hippodrome, beginning with the inhabitants of a Flanders town crushed by 'a gigantic mailed fist', ended with the opening of the sluice gates which washed 'the Germans ... to their doom'.[119] He produced *The Cossack* at Glasgow, a picture of the Eastern Front with an icy ending anticipating that of *Alexander Nevsky.*[120] This required special facilities; but more modest provision was available at many of the leading theatres. During a bad spell of Zeppelin raids Alfred Butt boasted that his Palace Theatre was as safe as anywhere, 'because many thousands of gallons of water were stored in the roof'.[121] This would certainly supply a glass tank of the kind described in 1890, in which a young woman not only sewed and wrote under water but smoked a cigar;[122] a trick still being performed after World War II, with a mouthful of milk expelled in bursts to simulate tobacco smoke.[123] During the war Daphne and her two Diving Belles performed clever feats under water; though, following an opening 'tableau of mermaids awaking in delicately illuminated seashells', emphasis was on graceful diving and trick swimming.[124] The Human Submarines attached topicality to their underwater tricks. The curtain rose on 'a submarine with its conning tower and its silent watchers'. After a blackout, their tank became the interior of the submarine, which eventually exploded.[125]

In 1915 Daphne's Diving Belles were augmented by Nellie Smith, who had been appearing with Lily Smith and Sisters on the halls from mid-1913. Lily was a well-known Channel swimmer and high diver, who, with her sisters, joined William Fowell's *The Lovely Limit*, hailed as the finest of water revues, which included 30 chorus and swimming girls, as well as 'the largest tank ever put on a music-hall stage'.[126] But it was the Ray Brothers who were responsible for most of these water shows. Their *Beauty Baths* struck a patriotic note with a naval review, where a smart crew of chorus girls supported officer Jack Dowley on the deck of HMS *Lion*.[127] Another Ray creation, *Have a Plunge*, included a scene 'at breezy Brighton', with a 20,000-gallon tank. Unhappily, at the Burnley Empire, this witnessed a fatal accident when 29-year-old Jessamine Lucy Sharp attempted a back dive. Variety artist Jack Alert, who witnessed it from the stalls, considered that to have attempted the dive in four feet rather than 'at least seven or eight feet of water' was asking for trouble.[128]

This was not the only disaster overtaking the Rays, whose strip shows ran foul of official and unofficial censorship. The Lord Chamberlain's demands in respect of *The Beauty Baths* resulted in a loss of £2000 and must have produced a still more costly nervousness in managers, so that George Marks (professional name George Ray) ended up in the bankruptcy court.[129] Belcham acknowledged the attractions of bathing dress:

> But some producers, with pornographic intent, pander to the lowest tastes, put a premium on nakedness, and do their utmost therefore to degrade the poor girls of the chorus by their insistence on scanty clothes, generally accompanied by cunningly arranged business of an indecorous character.[130]

Thus he welcomed the Lord Chamberlain's circular (4 May 1915), directed against 'a tendency towards suggestiveness and impropriety of language as well as scantiness of dress'. This was soon followed by another, redefining as stage play dialogue or song-patter 'with more than one character engaged'. VAF chairman Fred Russell advised readers that 'the law must be complied with'; but, since performers who had given the same routine for years were now losing work, he succeeded in obtaining a concession excluding 'inconsequent and disjointed patter' (*Performer* 8 June 1916, p. 23; 17 August 1916, p. 19; 14 December 1916, p. 23). *Encore*'s editor (15 April 1915, p. 6), complaining that 'French dialogues and songs' received far more latitude than English, declined 'to make a stand for bare legs' or suggestiveness, since they appealed to 'the threepenny gallery' rather than the more profitable parts of the house. But there was uncertainty on this point. Belcham, dismayed at hearing 'a line uttered by a comedian' as bad as anything to be 'heard in a Continental bagnio', was confident that the Lord Chamberlain would have co-operation from proprietors intent on attracting 'the toiling millions who want clean and bright entertainment'. Had not 'the grosser forms of humour [reduced] the popular appeal of the variety stage during the last twelve months'? But he subsequently piled up the contradictions, asserting that with 'The toiler uncultured, ... coarseness would pass unnoticed'. At one point banishing 'the offensive gagger' is represented as 'a sound commercial proposition'; and at another there is an attack on unscrupulous managers who, in pursuit of profit, 'largely create and unquestionably foster the degraded appetite to which they minister and seriously imperil the good name of the halls and menace the advance of the entertainment therein to higher ideals'.[131] Eventually, applauding the Lord Chamberlain's sharp check on an 'intolerable scandal', Belcham exploded the whole case:

> It would be ridiculous to contend, as some of the runners of pornographic productions did, that the success of a blatantly salacious production gives it a certificate of character; if such were the case, we should not want any censorship at all.[132]

General Smith-Dorrien understood that censorship's primary function was not to reflect prevailing attitudes but to buttress official policy. He and Winnington-Ingram (Bishop of London) were dubbed 'The Heavenly Twins', the title of the comedy duo Fyne and Hurley, following their attacks on the theatre.[133] The General was quite prepared to be disingenuous in insisting that servicemen would prefer 'cheerful and inspiriting' performances to 'exhibitions of scantily-dressed girls and songs of doubtful character'.[134] Meanwhile, one correspondent reasonably suggested that he might first set his own house in order by curbing the brutal obscenity customarily used by drill sergeants: 'The language they use would not be tolerated on any stage.'[135] And, challenging the idea of virtuous young officers for whom the General claimed to speak against 'demoralising shows', the manager of a child troupe asked if he could not 'prevent officers of all ages and ranks from waiting outside stage doors and stopping little girls in socks in the street'.[136] But the kitbagful of private mail received by Smith-Dorrien must have been largely supportive, turning the pragmatic general, intent primarily on a theatrical clean-up to reduce venereal infection amongst young men who were thereby 'lost to the fighting ranks',[137] into a confused moralist. In looking beyond a supply of manpower for the trenches to the idea of imperial mission he began to sound like the Bishop.[138] Even so, as Belcham acknowledged, his approach was rather more honest. Challenged to be specific, he responded as the wily Bishop would not; and his complaint about scanty dress and Robey's suggestiveness in *The Bing Boys,* the most popular show in town, resulted in a libel writ from Stoll.[139] Thereafter he confined himself to soft targets and imprecision, having 'gathered' that provincial cinema and music halls 'were considerably worse than they were in London'.[140]

It was said of the Bishop: 'nobody seems to be taking him very seriously'; and when the general declared that a scene in Vernon's *Mr. Wu* was 'absolutely immoral', the author chose not to respond, saying: 'Why should I be the only person in England to pay any attention to an old gentleman with a bee in his bonnet' (*Era* 27 September 1916, p. 13; *Era* 1 November 1916, p. 8). But Newton had indicated early on that the stakes were high; it was folly to provide further ammunition for those already using the war as a pretext for closing the theatres.[141] And derision barely disguised recognition that the twins had both impressed the censor and generated considerable nervousness in the industry. Unlike Smith-Dorrien, the Bishop began by subjecting the entertainment trade to comprehensive attack. Wearing khaki and carrying his crozier, he mounted the pulpit outside St James's Church, Piccadilly, to attack writers of 'lecherous and ... slimy plays' who had 'the insolence to make money out of the weaknesses of our boys' with their 'filthy innuendoes'.[142] He evaded a challenge from the Incorporated Society of Authors, claiming that his target was certain objectionable music-hall sketches and revues. Although Newton denounced this 'shiftiness and temporisation',[143] displacement onto the halls appeased the Society, which was unworried that the Bishop had mentioned leading a deputation to the Lord Chamberlain on the strength of a handful of unverified newspaper comments.[144] And not many months had passed before he resumed wholesale assault against 'indecent plays [being] acted and applauded'.[145]

The Bishop was a dangerously unscrupulous publicist. Addressing a large gathering in Victoria Park, he claimed: 'The war had saved us from a [still] worse ordeal', an imminent 'industrial strike which would have been the worst ever known in our time'. 'Our boys' would have died in vain if there was a post-war return to that 'old struggle between capital and labour'. He was impudent enough to suggest that in waging war against the music-hall promenades he was fighting the battle of the working man, saving 'the working-class daughter' from vice. He sought to persuade the LCC that the promenades were populated nightly by whores who posed 'a constant danger and temptation to the young men who naturally wish to have some amusement after a hard time in the trenches'.[146] At the London Diocesan Conference he urged members to coerce their LCC representatives into voting his way on this 'great moral question',[147] since 'a tremendous percentage of [venereal] disease had been traced to certain music halls in London'.[148] In the event, however, the chairman of the Theatres and Music Halls Committee pointed out 'that they could not absolutely prohibit promenades, for this could affect places like Queen's Hall', then home of promenade concerts.[149] Besides, as one parent recognized, soldiers frequented far more dubious haunts than the theatre 'with little sluts whom they had picked up in the Strand, or the Euston Road', intent on compressing sexual experience into what was apt to be a very short life.[150] Possibly amongst the Bishop's tangle of motives may have been a desire to protect the khaki element from destructive women as some atonement for making them confront far more destructive men. But a warped sense of mission seems to have been the mainspring of his activities. The *Daily News* (13 September 1916, p. 3) reported his speech on Tower Hill when, in characteristic vein, he sorrowed at Britain, 'the chosen instrument for the freedom of the world', spending 181 millions on drink, and countenancing '150 bad women at every music hall every night'. Equally characteristic, once his inflammatory rhetoric was controverted, was his attempt to claim misrepresentation.[151]

The demise of theatrical promenades only stimulated the Bishops' Council to more strenuous efforts: 'The music-halls are being watched to see that the promenade habitués ... are not tolerated in other parts of the houses.'[152] The manager of the Pavilion was fined for allowing prostitutes to operate in the grand circle. He pointed out that women were not allowed to book seats there, and that both police and military authorities visited the house nightly without finding cause for complaint. But no amount of discretion could deceive the zealot.[153] Even in those two or three houses habituated by prostitutes the women were orderly, venturing no more than a smile, asserted the Rev. Stewart Headlam (LCC), in what *London Life* (21 October 1916, p. 4) described as a 'dignified rebuke' of the Bishop. Headlam, who had founded the Church and Stage Guild in 1879 as an attempt to reduce religious bigotry towards the theatre, made a further point of interest: 'Our stage reformers talk far too much as if our Australian soldiers, say, were innocents' having their first brush with vice in the theatre. Since many of them came from large cities he found it inconceivable that they were encountering anything new. (This recalls a remark made by the woman who laundered the costumes for the 'great ladies' exhibited at Madame Tussaud's, that no one knew about their lack of underclothes 'except me and a few Australian soldiers'.)[154]

This matter of innocence is a vexed one. Gilbert Frankau remembered that 'in the so-called "naughty nineties" unnatural practices were at least deemed filthy, kept secret, and tolerably rare'. There would have been no cheap laughs for comedians who 'put on high voices and waggled their hips', since (and here Ervine, agrees[155]) most of their audience would have been oblivious to what was being conveyed.[156] This hardly squares with the fact that both the Boulton and Park case of 1871 and that of Wilde had generated popular jokes; while the stereotype of limp-wristed effeminacy, used in Alfred Lester's wartime rendering of *The Conscientious Objector,* runs back to Chaucer. Nostalgic distortions obliterate ambiguity, Larkin's *MCMXIV* supplying not only a title for Martin Stephen's anthology of Great War verse, *Never Such Innocence* (1988), but throwing Paul Fussell badly off-track. Areas of verbal sensitivity, sexual or otherwise, are ceaselessly changing, consequent triggers and filters being developed and modified. It shows scant grasp of semantic processes for Fussell to argue innocence because people in 1914 'could use with security words which a few years later, ... would constitute obvious *double entendres*'.[157] Nor does respectability mean inability to understand implication and innuendo, simply a dislike of being invited to do so in public. So-called loss of innocence is better understood as a process whereby sex gave ground to more pressing sources of guilt and anxiety:

> Mothers laughed publicly at jokes with their sons, which under peace conditions they would not have tolerated for an instant. What did anything matter so long as the dear boy was amused? They might very soon be informed officially that they were never to hear him laugh again.[158]

The subject of dubious gagging provoked much discussion, and the effect of atmosphere was noted: one night the comedian 'may be responsible for a bit of business that has the quality of raciness or piquancy; on another night the piquancy may sink into suggestiveness'. Yet at the LCC meeting when the Middlesex lost its licence, it was recognized that 'whether a gag is suggestive or not is a matter people may differ about'.[159] One extreme was represented at the preceding meeting of the Theatres and Music Halls Committee, when the Rev. W. T. A. Barber, Headmaster of the Leys School, Cambridge, brought a complaint against the Euston which he had entered in mistake for a cinema: 'Several songs were of a very suggestive character, including one, "I am glad I took my mother's advice." The girl who sang it said that when she went to Brighton her mother told her to take care she did not come back too late at night. "I am glad I took my mother's advice," she added, "for when I went with my boy to Brighton I did not come back till next morning."' Complaining to a commissionaire that this was a police matter, Barber was told that the police were already present.[160] Indeed this is the song which one reviewer thought 'a pleasant little ditty with many pointed references', the singer being Maidie Scott, who specialized in demure charm.[161]

There were better singers and finer dancers than Scott, but 'no one else who ... could master the gentle art of being innocent so completely and inimitably'. As such she was the antithesis of Marie Lloyd, whose art was that 'of pretending not to be innocent'.[162] For Cochran, Lloyd's 'supreme talent of timing' underpinned the exquisite 'delicacy of her indelicacies';[163] and Fergusson believes that 'of sauciness her genius consisted'.[164] Yet perhaps

Lloyd is undervalued by too much stress on this sauciness. There is an endlessly repeated anecdote about her suggestive peering under the bed during a production of *Cinderella*, and a disregard for Ford's memory that this was 'one of the best pantomimes ever seen at Drury Lane' and one in which 'Marie proved that her art could be effective without coarseness'.[165] There seems no reason to doubt her magisterial status in the latter; but she clearly had various strings to her artistic bow. And by the war years she had turned substantially to character songs, revealing herself as 'a comic actress of outstanding ability'. This was the period of some of her greatest successes despite having suffered a brief breakdown in 1916.[166] By the war, introducing a new song brought hitherto unknown bouts of anxiety.[167] A 1915 number was Collins and Leigh's sprightly 'Now You've Got Yer Khaki On', adding to the abundant testimony of the uniform's sexual fetishism; though, as Naomi Jacob points out, it is also 'a bit of East End life – a real character study.'[168] She sang it in coster costume, 'her "bloke" John', in khaki, joining her in the final chorus and dance.[169] But unlike many in the profession, Lloyd was little engaged in patriotism of the triter kind.

More memorable still was her introduction of two new numbers at the Pavilion in late 1917. Her new Paris dresses also caused a stir, one of them

> a real breath-snatcher – a sort of rising sun Constantinople-in-Bond-street confection .... Her first song is called 'You Like What I Like – A Little Love Now and Then,' and she gives it with all that half-simulated huskiness, all that larky, daring flashing of the eyes whenever 'the boys' are mentioned, which has endeared her to the heart of the public.

The second new item was 'a gem', Collins and Leigh's unforgettable 'Cock Linnet Song'[170] in which she is recalled by Fergusson: 'Her shawl well round her, a birdcage clasped tightly in her hand, Marie Lloyd stepped a trifle unsteadily on to the stage – a bewildered, almost pathetic figure.'[171] Between the two verses 'Marie Lloyd talked, and in that wonderful monologue told us all there is to be known about the souls of charwomen, of a life where a little too much beer is drunk, where husbands are hasty, where "shooting the moon" is a constant preoccupation, and where a black eye may be either a corrective or a compliment'.[172] A few months after its introduction the song was 'already a classic', though Lloyd continued to add depth to the characterization. But more than that, she offered 'new readings every night' so there was always 'freshness and spontaneity'.[173]

Lloyd is one of the artists who came to mind in the *New Statesman*'s response to Smith-Dorrien's indictment (18 November 1916, p. 154). Mrs Grundy, it is claimed, is no longer shocked by music-hall performances: 'She will forgive almost anyone who can make her laugh.' While twenty years ago she would have considered Lloyd and Robey 'decidedly vulgar', she now accepts their 'genius'. But opposition to 'universal tolerance' on the ground that 'genius is one thing, and the pimp disguised as a music-hall artist is another' produces unease since it took a good many years for Lloyd's genius to be widely recognized. That she was still not to everyone's taste is indicated by a young clerk who frequented the wartime halls in the Hastings area. She thought Marie Kendall 'very much after the style of Marie Lloyd, who I don't think much of'.[174] But there is scant merit in Colin MacInnes's claim[175] that Lloyd 'was never loved outside London'. Her first extended tour included the main South Wales halls, and I have heard those whose memories of the Newport Empire extended back to pre-Great War days recall her visits with keen enjoyment. Authority, however, continued to view her with suspicion, perhaps more for off-stage reasons than on account of her act. Boardman mentions how during the Boer War she 'was willing to throw up contracts and engagements and sail at short notice' for South Africa to entertain the troops.[176] But War Office response was discouraging; just as in 1914, when a projected visit to France led by Marie foundered while another led by true-blue Seymour Hicks won Kitchener's approval.[177] There are several possible reasons. Although in the 1907 music-hall dispute Marie was only one of a number of stars who participated, she did make her home a kind of strike headquarters.[178] This, her risqué and unpredictable style of performance, and marital irregularities all probably combined to make her seem undesirable, just as they had for the 1912 Royal Command Performance.[179] It was certainly the fact that she had boyfriend Bernard Dillon in tow when she crossed the Atlantic in 1913 which caused her detention on Ellis Island, prompting one of her most memorable *bon mots* as she gestured towards the Statue of Liberty: 'I love your sense of humour.'[180] But although American officialdom continued to be tiresome, the public and critics frequently warmed to her and she was able to advertise her return with a whole pageful of favourable reviews from North American newspapers.[181] Returning in a rather susceptible state, she was distressed to find the Charing Cross Cinematograph in the Strand, where she was appearing on film, adorning an almost life-size poster of her with the title of another film on show, *White Slave Traffic*. Since Dillon had been threatened with America's White Slave Act, she found this beyond a joke, and in the resulting libel action she won an apology and £250 damages.[182] But she suffered another snub during the war, by which time her marital situation had been regularized. At the OP Club's dinner held in recognition of entertainers' contributions to the war effort, *Era*'s Walter Terry (20 March 1918, p. 12) thought it a serious 'oversight' that as a leader of her profession she was not included amongst the many speakers.

Lloyd may have had some kind of symbolic status as a thorn in the flesh of moral watchdogs; she certainly opened up vistas of sexual fun not easily fettered by bourgeois respectability, and hence a source of concern. Trite lyrics were a mere vehicle for telling intonation and body language: 'Watch the play of the hands, the eyes, the controlled and perfect gesture.' For 'Paris On The Seine' her dress 'was graced with a bustle which was almost a crinoline, and, when Marie walked up-stage, "every little movement had a meaning of its own"'.[183] But it is doubtful if these motions offered any serious disturbance of established values, or if her songs went beyond subverting the Victorian drawing-room ballad. T. S. Eliot apparently saw something more, wondering (in 1922) 'why that directness, frankness, and ferocious humour which survive in her, and in Nellie Wallace and George Robey and a few others, should be extinct, should be odious to the British public, in precisely those forms of art in which they are most needed, and in which, in fact, they used to flourish'.[184] But does that ferocity represent anything seriously oppositional? Certainly Robey's suggestiveness incorporated its own elitism, it being claimed that he was given more leeway than lesser artists: 'Neither Mr. Robey nor the management is to be complimented on the words or patter of the new "Mormon" song which he is singing at the Palladium.' Surely he noticed 'that the humours of his "That's That" song' went down far better 'than those of the Mormon number'.[185] However, whether absence of sexual innuendo is a more certain guarantee of popularity (and hence of profit) is highly speculative: hence the web of contradictions which we have noticed ensnaring Belcham. A leading article in the *Weekly Dispatch* (28 May 1916, p. 5) concedes that managers had lost £150 a week through the abolition of promenades, but suggests that this would be more than recouped by their having thus rendered the halls fit for family attendance. Stoll, for all his reputation as moralist and leader in refining the halls, solved the problem in his own way: if the Coliseum guaranteed immaculacy, he was also controller of the Middlesex, which catered for a less nice audience.[186]

Nonsense, like sex, is another potential destabilizer with its exposure of life's absurdities, its logical or semantic dislocations. At a time when rational discourse had yielded to battlefield brutality, it offered particularly fruitful possibilities. But these were explored in neutral Switzerland rather than Britain, where its major exponents, performers like Dunville, far from undermining, reaffirmed conventional logic to which their performance was a counterpoint. Singers and comics all conspired to one end: to underscore the recognized values and standards, not to question them. Speciality acts, too, served as reinforcements of order, poise, balance. There was in reality no escape: everything confirmed the rightness of their world, the need to accept. The real potency of the halls lay in the fact that they created the illusion of representing an alternative, while all the time reaffirming the values and interests of a minority. They were a place of delight and wonder, where amazing feats were performed and where the major singers and comics were so full of bounce and energy that they filled the stage single-handedly. Dealing with working-class life, they helped to develop the myth that this was truly a people's theatre, its songs 'the real songs of the people, the folk-songs of to-day'.[187] But, rooted in reality as these performances were, they were socially static, providing no hint of any alternative system. Like the camaraderie of the trenches or the factory floor, the halls contrived to make a harsh existence bearable, but not to ameliorate the harshness itself. They were a painkiller, not a remedy, and insofar as they conspired to make the intolerable tolerable they are to be deplored.

That the idea of music hall as a site of Gramscian resistance should have gathered strength during the high point of Thatcherism and Reaganism seems, as Gruneau has it, uncomfortably like a compensation reflex.[188] Not that control could ever be complete, but serious challenge was rare and fundamental opposition non-existent. The technique then, as now, was to turn the capacity for resistance against itself. People during the war were, like ourselves, susceptible to the massed forces of commercial and political advertising. Many of those attending music hall would have been gratified to find in this art-form an acknowledgment of their existence, even the means of defining and redefining that existence. That the terms were being supplied by sources with quite different interests would hardly have weighed against the spurious sense of a world turned upside-down as patrons in the gods gazed at those below in dress circle and stalls. The mythology of the halls as manifestation of lower-class culture is so convenient that it might be supposed to have been deliberately constructed. But in this fiercely competitive industry the driving force was profit: allow that free rein and the politics look after themselves. The halls certainly reinforced the convention that politics and religion were inappropriate as topics for either stage or pub-conversation. In reality politics formed a strong presence; what was excluded was political debate. Without that, political progress is hardly possible. The trick was to ingrain the idea of taboo, so that people employed self-censorship. This effectively disempowered people and helped to ensure that a message of uncontested uniformity was coming from virtually every source, not least that of the music-hall stage. Distrust of argument continued as strong as in one of Herbert Campbell's old songs, 'They Ain't No Class', in which he impersonated a Shoreditch oyster-seller: 'I've heard 'em running down the House o' Lords, ... When they comes a talking in that sort o' way to me, "Well," I sez, "we've allers 'ad our Nobilitee".'[189] Clearly the protagonist lacked Mill's conviction that 'The despotism of custom is everywhere the standing hindrance to human advancement.' *The Ragged Trousered Philanthropists* (Ch. 44), written by Robert

Tressell in the first decade of the century, sums up music-hall's effect on working-class politics when the workers are induced to interrupt a discourse on the merits of socialism with a chorus of 'Down At The Old Bull and Bush'. Also sung is 'Work, Boys, Work, And Be Contented', which had been performed on stage with right-wing zeal by Harry Clifton (died 1872, aged 40), and revived during the war by the rumbustious Harry Champion when industrial action could be denounced as treachery.[190]

Neville Cardus, expressing distaste for television's mass entertainment as compared with the old music hall, fails to acknowledge that the key thing is not that everyone is watching the same programme at 8 o'clock but whether that programme is any good. Why should the placebo of live entertainment be thought more worthy than a broadcast (pipe-dream under present controls) exploring ways of remedying economic injustice? Cardus gives the example of George Formby, who, though troubled by the tuberculosis which eventually killed him, was at the height of his powers during the war years. With his played-out lungs, Formby was the perfect paradigm for endurance (or 'sticking it' in the wartime cliché). Formby is used by Cardus to rebut highbrow charges of escapism: he 'brought to the music-hall stage the very aspects of life that people would normally want to get away from'. So why did they flock to see him 'mirroring their own lives, with all its struggles ...? Because his genius revealed a vein of acceptance and humour beneath the troubles of everyday life.'[191] And there we have it: acceptance, whether of the economic deprivation imposed on these people during peacetime or those still worse deprivations during more than four years of European war. If, as Cardus contends, these entertainers persuaded people that, despite hardship, they were not 'nonentities', this lasted only while they were in the warmth and glitter of the halls. Outside they were once again just so many 'hands' – assuming that they had a job; or, during time of war, so many 'bayonets', having been cajoled and coerced from these self-same stages into surrendering identity to a khaki sameness.

But besides acceptance, Cardus also mentions humour. This was the sugaring on the pill, though a fine-quality sugar since, as one commentator insists, 'ordinary people are not cultural dopes'. Indeed those in the halls' cheaper seats were often neither dopes nor ordinary. The latter term is not only disagreeable but inaccurate: lack of money and power does not of itself make people ordinary any more than the acquisition of wealth or status is a guarantee of being complex and interesting. The lower classes were not manipulated by music hall because they lacked sense or sophistication; but several factors worked in conjunction. The construction of reality offered by the halls was confirmed by most other available sources and thus became difficult to resist. It was being projected by masters like Formby, whose power to influence was indisputable. Furthermore, those relaxing away from the slog and tedium of the factory had limited energy for critical questioning. So the music hall beckoned: a palace of delight where the tyranny of foreman and machine could be forgotten. Not that the entertainment was undemanding: frequently, for instance, it was necessary to appreciate both an enactment of life's absurdities and the enacter's ironic commentary. Behind the performer's mask is ... a performer's mask: the intensely private Harry Relph would, as Little Tich, play a rôle and puncture illusion by standing outside it and commenting. His style, which perfectly fused spontaneity and artifice, made it hard to separate accident from contrivance. One critic was persuaded that, during his rendering of the Tax-collector Song, Tich fluffed his usual trick of flicking his hat on his head with his boot:

> First he kicked it into the orchestra by mistake. Then he kicked it into the back-cloth. Then he got it into the air all right, but muffed it with his head. So he had to get on with the last verse, and was so convulsed with amusement himself that he could scarcely get the words out.[192]

Walking off and having to be recalled was another way Tich had of destroying illusion – or creating different dimensions of it. R. G. Knowles, recognized as one of the great reshaping forces on the halls following the heyday of the *lions comique*, did the same thing. He was credited with having introduced the 'walk', and although that was not quite true, Knowles's example effectively disposed of stage immobility.[193] Also innovative were 'the quaint interruptions and "ad libs." with the orchestra which Knowles dropped into his performance as a kind of side-dish'.[194] Again this caught on, demanding more attention from audiences than the techniques of the red-nosed comics.

For all the pressure towards passivity, audiences were more versatile than those at the regular theatre. The collective mood was more potent and might colour or transform what was being purveyed out of all recognition. There might be collusion across the footlights, in those specially charged moments when more seemed to be offered than the censor might allow. But it was all part of the game, with no serious end in view; like the licence taken in carnival time. 'Extra Turn' points to some of the 'ways of getting *en rapport* with your audience. You may manage it by scolding them, like George Robey, by smiling on them like Florence Smithson, by walking up and down among them like Shirley Kellogg, by hiring a confederate in their midst like Wilkie Bard, or even by treating them as if they were dirt beneath your feet.'[195] These various means are not without hazard. The dangers attending the Kellogg technique are touched on by Mistinguett: 'Once over the footlights and you're on your own. The spectators see you at close quarters, without your kindly halo of stage lighting; you are made of flesh and blood now, just as they are ... so one false move and you're for it.'[196] But the chorus song might involve a different kind of danger, which is why managers in the late nineteenth-century halls sometimes banned appeals to the audience to join in, and other forms of direct address.[197] Belcham comments on the perennial popularity of 'the chorus song': 'Its strength lies in its direct demand for co-operation, and co-operation means sympathy.'[198] It became an act of special complicity when wartime audiences were called to join in a patriotic chorus. Here control neared completeness since, no matter how fractured the nation's sense of identity, the war came as a great binding force. From the stage, as from Westminster, the call was for unison, for a chiming of viewpoint. Even so, influence is not a one-way process: audiences do affect performance as well as being affected by it. They complete meaning, and it might vary from one night to the next even while the artist aimed at sameness. It will do no harm to cite as example of this instability of meaning one of the most popular of soldier songs, since Tommy's demeanour is regularly claimed to have been shaped by experience in the halls.[199] It is the alleged source of the smiling Tommy, a stereotype perpetuated in countless later films where he serves as comic relief, allowing no room for seriousness and sensitivity. Given this constant smile, the singing of 'I Want To Go Home' can never be an expression of *défaitisme* – or so John Brophy and Eric Partridge affirm.[200] However, the many references to the song in soldier memoirs show otherwise, indicating that interpretations went through the entire gamut from mockery to literalism. No doubt the same outfit could sing the song from one time to another with quite different intent and meaning. But it never got them one step nearer home; quite the reverse, as it helped them through another wearisome time. And to just that extent audiences in the music hall exerted control over what they made of the material presented there. Even so, Little Tich found this 'terribly trying to the artiste. One night they are all applause, and the next night, for no apparent reason you find them perfectly cold and sometimes spiteful.'[201] However studied the artistry, there was always that unknown quantity which had to be reckoned with night by night. Yet for all the occasional surprise, some poll-tax provocation of resistance, the balance of power rests with the capable performer.

The development of the halls increasingly confirmed this artist ascendancy. In early days, exchanges between performer and audience were common. Later, until the early 1890s when he disappeared under pressure from the LCC's new authority, the ritual was enacted between chairman and audience where, far from producing dislocations, it was more likely to supply cohesion and continuity. But by 1914 informal interventions from the audience had been so ruthlessly discouraged that when they did occur they received considerable press notice. The topical gags of a double act at the Wood Green Empire elicited groans from 'some convalescent American soldiers ... But later in the week the Doughboys gathered in force' driving the offenders off the stage with a bombardment of eggs and tomatoes. This affair was treated lightly because of the status of the interrupters. But a different tone was adopted in the same weekly[202] when Lady Forbes Robertson earned the displeasure of the Coliseum gods.[203] That allegedly objections came only from that part of the house prompted thoughts of repressive measures: 'One advantage of a high-priced gallery would be that the less intelligent would not be inclined to pay the price asked', so that a higher type of entertainment could be introduced successfully. It is unnecessary to probe the implications of 'the less intelligent'. More interesting is the attraction of imitating the West End theatres in shedding cheap gallery seats, since their original purpose of undercutting old-style halls had long been achieved.[204] This is reflected in Maidie Scott's response, when Gertie Gitana pointed out that her singing was growing ever quieter and those at the back of the hall might be unable to hear, that her work was 'for the stalls and the dress circle. To hell with the pit and the top shelf!' Harry Lauder was evidently of a like mind. Addressing the audience at the end of his turn he was indifferent to an appeal from the back of the pit to speak louder: 'Why don't you pay a wee bit more and get nearer?'[205]

Before considering single-turn responses to the war it may be worth examining the process of compromise and containment by way of two of the most discussed artists of the period. Fergusson calls Gus Elen 'a stark Cockney realist as compared with Albert Chevalier, who was a brilliant Cockney romanticist'.[206] The difference, then, lies in the convention adopted by each, the careful artifice of Elen's performances being evidenced by his professional notebook.[207] Film of him performing reveals crisp co-ordination between word and gesture; and his recordings show a sturdy response to life's rigours, although flecks of falsetto hint at unexpected vulnerability. The war drew him out of retirement in October 1916, as it had other old-timers. The process was partly exigent, but also a consequence of that nostalgia generated by the war. Elen's first real success had been with the song, 'Never Introduce Yer Donah To A Pal', but he was able to consolidate it with the still more popular ''E Dunno Where 'E Are'. Harry Wright's lyrics deal with knowing one's place. The person who forgets this virtue, unable to comport himself suitably in his new-found affluence, arouses disapproval and resentment. But the title-tag was appropriated for various uses besides that of affirming caste. One old man, in his anguished uncertainty, wrote a poem, 'Missing', about his soldier-grandson Jimmie: 'He's a "dunno where 'e are".' Here it connotes pain, perhaps idiosyncratic though it may be an experience which the song offered to others. Certainly Elen's coster-rival, Albert Chevalier, dealt in pain. If Elen exudes sturdy working-class independence, it is on sufferance. There is always the prospect of the economic garotte squeezing it out of existence, and this is the situation represented by 'My Old Dutch'. The song, portraying a love-match of forty years' standing, addresses not the inevitable separation of death but the ignominious sexual segregation imposed when the couple enters the workhouse. There is frustration as well as anguish at the way that lack of money renders the husband impotent to care for his wife and prevent this separation. Chevalier had been singing it for years, and it presumably moved audiences because he himself was moved: Finck heard him sing it 'twice in one day at Eastbourne and both times tears streamed down his cheeks as he sang'.[208] Eugene Stratton wept unashamedly at the 1916 play founded on the song.[209] Cyril Fletcher, in a 1977 broadcast, called the song 'a music hall classic', but then reconsidered: 'No, no, an art song of classical dimensions, worthy of performance on *any* music platform.' The present tendency to dismiss it as 'saccharine' is neither accurate nor helpful. At the Coliseum in early 1916 it was reported that the song 'again kept the house in a wondrous silence',[210] and Knowles observed that Chevalier's 'coster creations were accepted in the East as well as the West End'.[211] It worked somewhat in the mode of 'Gunga Din', with its awesome portrayal of a coloured man who belies the symbolism of his pigmentation. 'My Old Dutch' offers a similar revelation in a world where the haves and have-nots were so rigidly separated that it became a convenient fiction that the latter were calloused people, incapable of finer human feelings. The song quietly and poignantly asserts that this is untrue; and that, furthermore, a system designed to relieve the poor imposes additional barbarisms on people already at a low ebb. This accorded with official policy since it nudged towards improving the existing order rather than transforming it, thereby distracting attention from the need for a more comprehensive approach to social injustice. There was an Arnoldian message for middle-class audiences about comfortable reforms aimed at the betterment of the lower orders, which in turn would lock them closer to middle-class interests, helping to make them politically quiescent. The song was a sop, then, though not therefore without real feeling; but it was also concessionary. One irony was that the very demotic speech used helped to give credibility to a process which marginalized parallel cultures and dissent. Another showed in the illusion-breaking change of mood with the song that followed, reminding audiences that in front of them was not one of the destitute but a highly paid, and consequently powerful, variety artist.

The dislocation would be especially marked during the war, when the coster Chevalier was apt to scramble into French uniform to sing the 'Marseillaise'. Chevalier, half-French, would be more plausible than Coborn, who recalls, on the declaration of war, telegraphing from Kirkaldy 'for the uniform that I had of a French *sous-officier*, and the band music of "La Marseillaise"'.[212] The halls ('still cesspools of slushy sentimental patriotism and blatant cock-suredness', as one commentator sourly put it[213]) made their contribution to the hysteria which marked the war's opening phase, though Boardman, as a manager, had some anxiety: 'An outbreak, even on the score of patriotism, is something to be avoided in a crowded theatre, ... Programmes had to be revised; patter to be most carefully edited and ruthlessly censored. Patriotism was to be the order of the bill, and jingoism to be avoided.'[214] It was the jingoistic excesses of the Boer War which had borne in on people the need to attempt a distinction. While that war was still in progress, J. A. Hobson had written a devastating critique of the way in which the mind of the nation had been captured for base ends under the mask of patriotism, and made a chilling prophecy: 'It is of the gravest importance to understand the methods of this manipulation of the mind, for the combination of industrial and political forces which has operated in this instance will operate again, and will copy the methods which have been successful once.'[215] He saw the music hall as perhaps the most potent educator amongst 'large sections of the middle and labouring classes', and since the halls presented ideas of national or imperial destiny, coupled with distrust of non-Britishers, the shift into war mode required only an addition of particularity.[216]

So what Hobson described was being gruesomely re-enacted at this new conflagration, his warnings heeded only insofar as the more sensitive strove to evade the taint of jingoism. Hence the claim that variety audiences in the first months of war were 'out of patience with War sketches as a whole' since the country showed 'none of that spirit termed "Jingoism"'. Tommy was said to squirm when someone slipped in a jingo song, such things having 'died a natural death during the Boer war'.[217] In reality, the first month of war saw so much jingoism on the variety stage that 'managers of certain houses [were] already requesting their artistes to refrain from overdoing the patriotic business'.[218] Apologists for the excesses strove to displace them onto 'the uncultured', responsibility for whose conditioning was left carefully unprobed: 'A certain class of alleged comic cannot fail to be ready with doggerel rejoinders of the crudest kind to Lissauer's "Hymn of Hate." He blatantly tells his listeners what we'll do when we get to Berlin. Such lines invariably excite ignorant gallery hobbledehoys to exhibitions of vehement stupidity.'[219] But *Era* was not always so nice, its representative delighting in Whit Cunliffe's 'parody on the "Hymn of Hate"' (21 March 1917, p. 14), just as its closest rival consistently praised Tom Clare, who delighted the 'hobbledehoys' with 'My Cheery Little Hymn Of Hate' and 'Who Killed Bill Kaiser?'[220] In any case, unease seems not to have affected those eminent songsmiths Weston and Darewski, whose 'By Jingo! I'm A Jingo' (1916) boldly adopts the Decatur precept: 'If the lingo of a Jingo is "My country, right or wrong!"/By Jingo! I'm a Jingo!'

Even Coram (Tommy Whittaker), along with Arthur Prince the finest ventriloquist of the day, was not above jingoism. Along with gags like 'What did you do in the great war, daddy? – I minded you while your mother went out selling flags' were the other kind: 'Why is a German's funeral like the tail of a pig? – Because it is the end of the swine!'[221] Charles Austin's series of Parker sketches, which began in 1911 with *Parker PC*, includes *Parker Captures the Kaiser*, a comic fantasy which continued serviceable in Chaplin's 1918 *Shoulder Arms*.[222] Another topical subject, the tribunal, proved so popular in *Parker's Appeal* that it was lifted into the 1918 Liverpool *Cinderella*.[223] Still more popular was the medical board, which furnished 'the subject for songs and patter at pretty nearly every other hall'.[224] But the reality was no laughing matter, the methods of the Mill Hill Medical Board, described as 'one of the best' in the Army, being exposed at the Middlesex Appeal Tribunal by an applicant who complained that when he was passed for general service only one doctor was present instead of three. Asked why he did not protest against this, he replied that another man who did was told that if he did not keep quiet he would be put in the guardroom. In spite of this the Tribunal dismissed the appeal.[225]

For someone returning from a rough time in Salonika to hear a music-hall songster burble 'If you don't want to fight, go to Salonika'[226] must have prompted thoughts like those of Eighth Army personnel towards Lady Astor after her remarks about 'D-Day Dodgers': 'You're the nation's sweetheart, the nation's pride,/But your mouth's too bleeding wide.'[227] But this was not a regular topic. The favourites in later 1917 were air raids, the beer crisis and allotments.[228] London had recently suffered the notorious air-raid week, but as an earlier commentator put it, 'there is much to be said for the comic view, in spite of the welter of bloodshed in the background'.[229] Interest fluctuated according to circumstances. In spring 1918 'Extra Turn' noted 'that air-raid jokes, which have for some weeks been in abeyance, are now as numerous as they have ever been, whereas rationing is being given a well-earned rest – pro tem'.[230] But the beer situation had perennial appeal. Wilkie Bard, as a fireman, refused to turn out until hearing that a brewery was alight, the joke being made topical in *Hotch Potch*, where a squire tries to raise a company of volunteers from 'a most apathetic crowd' with talk of air-raid outrages. Indifference greets the threat of 'Westminster Abbey in ruins – Buckingham Palace in flames – the House of Commons blown up' ('By its own gas', suggests one). But each is ready to fight at the prospect of the German raiders reaching Burton, destroying 'all those lovely breweries'.[231] Comedians eagerly utilized the ban on treating and restricted bar-opening. However, it was the Lloyd George administration, prejudice joining hands with wartime exigence, which gave most scope. In 1917 the Prime Minister cut beer production from an annual 26 million barrels to ten; and he anticipated the danger 'of driving the population from beer to spirits' with 'a corresponding restriction' on them.[232] This combined with reduction in the quality of beer, hotly denied by the trade, and spirits 'of the vilest description [being] supplied in some of the working-class districts'.[233] Right on cue Ernie Mayne began singing 'Lloyd George's Beer', allegedly 'the worst thing that has happened in this war. "Feed your hens with it, Fill the pens with it," he wails – sweep the floors with it – squirt the Germans back with it – anything so long as you don't drink it', sentiments sung as if from the heart.[234]

Shortages prompted a whole clutch of songs from him: 'My Meatless Day', 'Have You Got Your Ticket For Coal?', 'Sugar', 'Eat Less Bread'. 'Eat Less Bread' was the slogan of Lord Devonport's campaign, as official food controller, urging people to limit their consumption to 4lbs a week.[235] *The Times* (9 April 1917, p. 3) reasonably noted: 'The appeal obviously cannot be addressed to the poor. Bread is their staple food.' It was vital that the well-to-do should eat expensive food and leave the basics to the less fortunate. It had been noted in the first days of war that 'cornering of the food supplies by the wealthy and the consequent advance of prices to the poor demand immediate and drastic action'.[236] Yet Devonport was still resisting 'compulsory rationing, with its cumbrous system of tickets', as *The Times* (21 April 1917, p. 3) disparagingly described it.[237] Although 19 June 1917 saw Devonport's replacement by Lord Rhondda, at that time not only a member of the government but Masonic senior grand warden, the old prejudices remained. But eventually Rhondda was forced to recognize that soaring food prices supplied too crude a solution since, although this catered for the leaders, the led were apt to be inadequately fuelled to undertake the long hours of heavy labour which war conditions demanded from many of them. Hardly a triumph for democracy, then: Lyn Macdonald[238] contrasts the 'mess-tin of what appeared to be warm water with raw mutton fat floating on top', which passed for a hot meal up the line, with the seven-course lunch provided for George V some 14 miles away during his visit to Fourth Army Headquarters.

Treatment of rationing followed depressingly familiar lines, with the poorer sections of the audience sucked into participating in a ritual mockery of the very restrictions which allowed them to eat. Typically, at the Kilburn Empire the Royal Bartles chorused: 'Monday is our jamless day,/Tuesday is our meatless,/Wednesday is our hamless day,/Thursday is our sweetless.' And so on until Sunday, with 'no grub at all'. Jack Lane made fun of his wife's big mouth: 'what a repository for three ounces of meat!'; then described an S. O. S. meal: 'Pudding S. O. S. – short of sugar; beer S. O. S. – short of strength; and diner himself S. O. S. when it came to the bill – short of splosh.' Finally the situation was 'summed up by Edie Veno, who, singing "Whatever Is The

World A-coming To", ... displayed a series of placards representative of her tickets – her Sugar Card, her Ration Card, her Insurance Card, and, last, her Right-to-Live Card!'[239] In this same period Malcom Scott was dealing briskly with 'Lord Rhondda, Sir Arthur Yapp, Marie Corelli, and other celebrities of the commisariat'.[240] Novelist Corelli, found guilty of large-scale food hoarding, made a court appearance more entertaining than many a variety sketch: 'I am a patriot, and would not think of hoarding. I think you police are ... upsetting the country altogether with your food orders and what not. Lloyd George will be resigning to-morrow, and there will be a revolution in England in less than a week.'[241] (In accordance with the prevailing bias, food hoarding only became an offence on 10 April 1917.)

Another topic for light satire was the renovation and lavish appointing of Donington Hall, a dilapidated Leicestershire mansion, to accommodate 320 German officer-prisoners. There would have been those who entertained suspicions about owner Frederick Gretton's good fortune; but the skit sung by Tom Woottwell, who rounded off a fine career as Bert in Bairnsfather's *The Better 'Ole*, confined itself to the pampering of prisoners (including provision of billiards rooms and 80 internees sent as unwilling officers' servants).[242] Surprisingly there was still mileage in the subject two years on, when Leslie Elliott introduced her new song, 'Dear Old Donington Hall'.[243]

Thus much criticism of official policy could be accommodated, as could a touch of irony in the unending torrent of music-hall patriotism. Newsome, Mills and Scott's '"Send a Photo of the King to me", which might be a patriotic ditty judged by the title, is really a very funny comedy chorus song.'[244] The joke, about wanting the portrait stamped on silver or gold, had done service in the armies of Charles I,[245] and Lily Morris's rendering at the Holborn Empire evidently awoke 'responses in the hearts of the many Tommies present.'[246] But there was an invisible line which the artist crossed at his peril. Will Evans, 'supreme in burlesquing domestic scenes', was told to stick to his safe topics instead of making 'fun of the over-age volunteers and the middle-aged soldiers at the time when the Government is calling them up'.[247] Clearly Evans's tilting ever so gently at current absurdities had evoked those clownish arts of insurrection which cause the conformist to quail.

To offer direct opposition to the war would have been legally impossible (DORA, section 27), not to say professional suicide. Often enough the stars, insulated from reality by vast salaries, would pretend to address the reality of war, their patriotic hobbies helping to furbish their star image. Harry Lauder was serious enough, but breathtakingly arrogant. Addressing front-line troops, he began: 'Boys, do you know what you are fighting and dying for? I'll tell you.' He described a lamplighter at work 'driving away the darkness of the winter evening. Boys, you are lamplighters. You are dying every day in order that your children and your children's children shall enjoy the light of civilisation and the comfort of freedom.'[248] Lamplighters, like war veterans, would soon become redundant. The only overlap between Lauder's homespun nonsense and Knowles's early 1916 reflections, also based on some extensive touring of the Front, is a recognition that the troops had no idea of why they were fighting. But Knowles would never have presumed to try telling them. For him, no one really knew 'what caused the war. It seems it was in the air, and Europe [went] mad over it.'[249] Having exchanged Canadian nationality for American, Knowles enjoyed a measure of detachment, seeing that the war would do no more than prove that courage 'is not the monopoly of any nation in particular'. Such sentiments could not be permitted on stage: like politicians, entertainers are in the business of persuasion. A *Musical News* columnist, regarding stage patriotism as 'either an impertinence or a failure', naïvely supposes that it is the entertainer's rôle merely 'to entertain' (16 January 1915, p. 41). But Alfred Barnard knew better, reflecting, after experiencing Julien Henry's war appeal at the Coliseum: 'Great artistes possess the power of impressing their audiences with anything according to their own individual desire.'[250] It was thus necessary to harness that power to the cause, and Captain Thomas Whiffen, recruiting staff officer at the War Office, provided a text in the shape of Harold Begbie's 'Fall In', set to music by Frederic Cowen. He also arranged for Lyell Johnston to sing at the halls, without fee, his own 'John Bull's Catechism', followed by 'a five minutes' address inviting young men to answer their country's call'. And once Johnston had 'roused the audience to a proper pitch of enthusiasm', a recruiting sergeant seized the moment. Commented Belcham: 'This power of the halls to sway feeling, though it has been recognised in an incidental way by Cabinet Ministers, has never been previously so clearly acknowledged by the Government.'[251] Here, then, was naked admission of what that long process of refinement of the halls had been designed to achieve.

The music-hall's pre-war deflections away from domestic hardship and injustice to global issues could now be openly practised in the name of patriotism. The Kaiser as ogre obliterated any sense of the manipulating ogres at home. Will Hay's stage schoolroom was now that of Dame Europa: 'The present-day schoolboy, as mischievous as ever, becomes a sergeant in the Volunteer Civil Force – Music Hall Platoon – and invites all his friends in the profession to join. Drill takes place every morning ... at Ruskin House, Rochester-row, Victoria, S. W.'[252] This sums up the disorientating techniques which caused fantasy and reality to blur. There was one manifestation at the Birmingham Empire, when a party of Kitchener recruits in the stalls took leave by singing 'Comrades In Arms' while the war films were being shown. Responding to this 'pretty incident', the manager called forth three hearty cheers from the audience.[253] During a patriotic *scena* with miniature naval battle at the Devonport Hippodrome news arrived of the sinking of the *Scharnhorst* and *Gneisenau* off the Falklands. A perfect coda to the stage enactment, this was 'immediately thrown on the screen' and the audience went wild.[254] At the other end of the war, announcement of land victories added similar spice to the patriotic turn. When, instead of Nellie Wallace, the Kilburn Empire's manager appeared before the tabs with the 'glorious news' that Haig had 'advanced five miles, capturing 7,000 prisoners and 100 guns', hysteria followed. Then Nellie capered on, 'bobbing her apology for an osprey, ... shrilling out, "That's the stuff to gi'e 'em,"[255] and so incarnating the prevailing spirit' that it seemed like Mafeking night over again.[256] It was noted, too, that sudden calls for troops to rejoin their units 'are more exciting when they take place in a music-hall, and occasion much enthusiasm among the audience' (presumably that part not required to abandon its recreation).[257]

Even ideas of the accredited stage performer became blurred, and Newton waives objections to unmediated politics 'seeing that topping the bill with Bottomley at the Empire last week proved such a financial success'. Besides, he introduced little politics: support of King and Empire are seen as beyond politics.[258] *The Times* reported him approvingly:

> A chronic attack of Anno Domini prevented him from being actively engaged in the war. At that moment the men who used to sit in the stalls of that theatre were shivering in the trenches in defence of this country. If any demagogue should sneer at the aristocratic young men of England, the battlefields of France and Belgium would be his answer.[259]

Mrs Pankhurst similarly appeared at the Pavilion, pleading for national unity and castigating 'the sentimental "internationalists" and peace-at-any-pricers in characteristic Pankhurst fashion'. Earnings were to go to war charities since she professed to be 'no variety artist'. But this was thought a trifle disingenuous considering her theatrical contrivance of two children in the wings, clad as Tommy and Red Cross nurse, who brought her flowers and were rewarded with a kiss.[260]

The personality cult, whether projected images of national celebrities or that of the Kaiser to the strains of 'Hold Your Hand Out, Naughty Boy',[261] featured prominently. The supreme icon was the king, as Edmund Goulding's topical sketch, *God Save the King*, demonstrated. The protagonist, a young man with a weak heart whose loyalties are assailed by a German spy, is recalled to a sense of duty by hearing 'the strains of the National Anthem' at the music hall and seeing 'a portrait of King George thrown on the screen'.[262] Hurrying home, he 'chokes the life out of the German spy, and falls dead himself as a result of the over-excitement'.[263] Emphasis on the elite is one more irony of a war said to be ushering in the age of the common man. Admiral Wemyss, applauded in Oswald Williams's magic act as a master magician, preferred dictatorship to that 'spurious democracy' which he associated with Lloyd George.[264] He need not have worried: the common man had scant post-war recognition apart from the burial of an unknown soldier in Westminster Abbey, it being vastly cheaper to make a symbolic fuss over one dead soldier than to create a land fit for the host of survivors.

But during the war it was politic to give prominence to the Tommy, especially through the contrivance of decorations. In an earlier conflict, Kipling's 'Absent-minded Beggar' (1899) had made its populist pitch: 'Cook's son, Duke's son ... it's all the same to-day!'; although this was rather undercut by the jocular expansion of DSO to Dukes' Sons Only. During the Great War, lesser decorations were often said to come up with the rations; and Ted Waite's 'First I Went And Won The D.C.M.' (1918)[265] humorously hints at the wealth of political calculation and cynicism behind these gongs. But for that very reason authority took them very seriously; hence, when one of the Ten Blighty Boys (music-hall performers who had all been wounded and discharged from the army) was found guilty of wearing on stage a DCM to which he was not entitled, he received six months' hard labour.[266] For all that, the VC retained its aura, serving to make the representative of the common man uncommon; though *John Bull* notes how members of the Bootle Board of Guardians, invited to join in honouring a VC, 'questioned the advisability of a gold watch for a farm servant' (13 October 1917, p. 11). The cult permeated stage performance as much as popular fiction: Cecil Gray, directing an act called Haig's Happy Heroes, was delighted to add Corporal Williamson, a fine baritone but also one of Australia's Gallipoli VCs, to the group. [267] Following Hugh McIntosh's example of providing free life-passes for VCs at Australian theatres, special facilities were often provided by British managers. Stoll made a box at the Leicester Palace available to Private William Buckingham, 'the Poor-Law V.C.', whenever required; and he managed to avail himself of this several times before taking up more permanent occupancy of a box on the Western Front.[268] Fêting recipients became part of the show, confusing war hero with his stage counterpart. Clara Beck (who had been the first to sing Finck's 'I'll Make A Man Of You' in *The Passing Show of 1914*) sang to Sgt Issy Smith, the first Jewish VC, at a Belfast pantomime; and at the Coliseum, Vesta Tilley bowed to Piper Laidlaw, VC, whose presence had been announced to the audience by way of a 'specially lowered screen'.[269] Bradford's first VC, Sgt Meekosha, did rather better at his local Empire, where a collection was held for him while some of the chorus girls kissed him; and Sgt-major Daniels, hero of Neuve Chapelle, was drawn into making a recruiting speech at the Wood Green Empire.[270]

Many performers made recruitment part of their acts, and the would-be hero could have his moment of glory by getting up on stage as volunteer. F. V. St Clair, whose 'Follow The Drum' was the first recruiting song of the war, performed in conjunction with recruiting authorities (*Era* 17 November 1915, p. 16), and Neil Kenyon combined his crisp brand of Scotch humour with 'a few apt words', which secured 100 recruits during his month at the Oxford (*Stage* 18 March 1915, p. 16). Bransby Williams, who succeeded him there, carried on the good work in a still more integrated way. As *The Lounger; or One of the Overworked*, he would start to exit when Sgt-major Linden detained him, trying to rouse his patriotism. But there was no response until he heard 'what the "German dogs" did to the women of France and Belgium and what they would do if they reached England. Smashing his clay pipe from his mouth to the stage, and shouting, "By God! I'm with you," Mr. Williams [set] off to enlist arm in arm with the recruiting officer.'[271] Lauder devoted much time to recruitment and fund-raising. He could well afford to: at a breach-of-contract case involving Vesta Victoria it was stated that Lauder 'gets £600 a week in this country, and £1,000 a week in America'.[272] At his most tactless, Lauder recruiting 'at Montreal remarked that if the French-Canadians were not willing to do their duty in this war they had not the pure blood of French ancestry in their veins. Prominent French-Canadians present strongly protested against the remark ... and the anti-conscriptionists were greatly advantaged.'[273] (Montreal's French-Canadians were apt to feel little enough in common with republican France.) Returning from America, Lauder was entertained by the London Burns Club. After trumpeting his exploits (travelling 36,000 miles to address two million people and collect £60,000 for the cause) he mentioned seeing in the morning paper how pacifists were to hold a demonstration in London. If the government refused to intervene 'then they should stop it. Run them into the Thames; ... Cutting the throat would be too quick for them.'[274] (Newspapers, in publicizing these events, were very effective in having them broken up.)

But outdoor meetings and demonstrations on the other side were regularly undertaken by variety artists. The magician Carlton was so energetic (he secured 57 recruits at the Grand, Henley) that the National War Aims Committee appointed him 'to run a patriotic propaganda in opposition to the pacifists'.[275] A stage erected at the base of Nelson's Column, in Trafalgar Square, accommodated, amongst others, Leo Dryden clad in the scout-style hat and spurs of the League of Frontiersmen, and Seymour Hicks by official request.[276] When Harry Tate spoke there he was said to consider it 'the most serious engagement he ha[d] ever undertaken'.[277] But the spillage from stage to street could be a good deal more ambitious than this. 'Military bands, soldiers, reservists, and scouts marched in procession from the residence of the Mayor of Wandsworth' one Friday night to the Grand, Clapham. A final 'military and naval tableau was presented on a flag-bedecked stage' while the mayor and local MP delivered exhortations.[278] Often the procedure was reversed: 'Thousands of people lined the streets at Tottenham, Stamford-hill, Harringay, Hornsey and Crouch-End ... to witness a recruiting pageant, a mile in length, which left Wood Green Empire at noon, ... headed by 1,400 men of the 19th Middlesex Regiment, under the command of Colonel Ward, M.P.' Glamorous Liane D'Eve, who represented France in one of the tableaux, doubtless aided recruitment, victims returning to the theatre to be entertained by Stoll.[279]

But the sexual ploy was already familiar at Wood Green. Nat Lewis and five of his revue ladies in the aptly titled *Ever Been Had?* secured 35 recruits there in a week.[280] It was there, too, that Lily Lena (Marie Lloyd's cousin and the first to sing 'The Moon Shines Bright On Charlie Chaplin' in the halls) spoke of engaging a young tenor to sing the chorus of one of her songs, 'but he joined the Army, and so his old father deputised for him, ... she thought every young man should be "in it"'. And she promised to appear at the recruiting office 'to enrol any local man who was ready to enlist'. Indeed, so successful were her efforts (she added the gift of a cigarette lighter to her persuasions and had drawn in over 500 recruits) that she was said to have 'converted the music hall into not the least productive sphere of enlistment operations'.[281] Artists were selling kisses in Cardiff;[282] and picking up strange men on the streets became approved behaviour. When Maie Ash and the Red Heads were appearing at the Stratford Empire, they formed themselves into a press gang; and while at the Royal Hippodrome, Dover, Queenie Leighton followed up her patriotic act with an expedition about the town, depositing 'half a dozen stalwart recruits ... at the Dover Town Hall'.[283] Ada Vivian and a sweet-voiced confederate (sharpshooter and siren) offered a different pattern of seduction at her native Manchester, recruiting 42 men by 'making each one a good shot ... She has to her credit the names of over 2,000 men she has taught to shoot since the outbreak of war.'[284] Most of the women stars were involved. Even Gertie Gitana who, according to a recent biographer, 'always refused to have anything whatsoever to do with recruitment', set aside conscience for the 23rd London Regiment's third recruiting meeting at the Grand, Clapham, 2 April 1915, when Mrs Pankhurst was principal speaker.[285]

Music hall, like pantomime, responded to the changing rôle of women under wartime pressure with a quickened interest in sexual ambiguity. A new example of a particularly convoluted kind was provided by Fennel and Tyson. Ostensibly 'a lady and gentleman in a rag-time medley', the lady astonished her partner by removing her wig and 'revealing herself as a "him"'. After a change into male attire, several rag-time numbers and dances are presented by the duo, and the act concludes by the pseudo "male" again removing his wig and disclosing himself as a lady after all.'[286] Freud had yet to invade the European consciousness; but a gossip columnist experienced some unease in noting the 'masculine airs' adopted by 'girl war-workers', addressing one another as 'old boy'.[287] Likewise, Hetty King recalls breaking the theatrical mood with 'a little smile, or a little wink' if things threatened to grow too intense,[288] which is not to suggest that male impersonation had the same effect on audiences a century ago that it would have today. Like the can-can, these masquerades entered the halls at a time when voluminous skirts encouraged forgetfulness that women moved on legs, much like their male counterparts. During the war King, cutting 'a picturesque figure in a Staff Officer's uniform', was admonished 'that such a uniform demands a certain dignity of stage action, and [she] should confine her amusing imitation of a Tommy's jaunty walk to occasions when her kit is more in keeping'.[289] But it was Vesta Tilley who most fully realized the patriotic potential of cross-dressing. She describes how her 'war songs' were always selected 'for their cheery nature',[290] even 'A Bit Of A Blighty One' sung in hospital blues. However, this only entered her repertoire in the last weeks of the war. Her favourite recruiting number was 'The Army Of To-day's All Right', sometimes staged with 'a squad of men wearing the khaki armlet'.[291] At a luncheon held to mark the contribution made by theatre people to the war effort, Horatio Bottomley described how recently, at South Hackney, Tilley's efforts brought 300 recruits, known locally as 'Vesta Tilley's Platoon'.[292] A 95 year-old veteran of the Royal North Lancs recalled her less favourably: 'She'd come on stage dressed as a soldier, singing patriotic songs, then she would invite men up onto the stage to join up ... Of course, there were a couple of recruiting sergeants standing ready in the wings ... Yet she had the nerve to refuse to go over and entertain the troops like many other artists did, saying she couldn't spare the time.'[293]

By the end of the war uniforms were out and jazz was in, courtesy of the American forces. Anthony Bennett[294] concludes that music hall now lost its hold because 'it could find no support in a musical language which was essentially Victorian'. But Leo Dryden, who took to street singing after the war, going 'direct to the public since he lacked the chance to have the public brought to him',[295] was surely right in believing that his style of singing had not become outmoded overnight. The principal factor in musical reorientation was less a shift of taste or sensibility than the overwhelming force of commercial interest. Indeed, the old style retained an informal hold for some years after World War II, when a billion-dollar popular music industry, ideologically opposed to co-existence, steamrollered it into oblivion. In commenting on the decline of the halls, Harry Randall points to the malign influence of a new kind of management. Even revue, he insists, 'pushed the individual artist from the boards not because the public tired of "Variety", but because it suited the managements better'.[296] He knows what he is talking about. Under the ever-increasing pressure of commercial logic, working-class patronage decreased in importance. Leonard Henry recalls how things were 'all right until about a year after the War when all the gratuities were spent'.[297] By that time wages had slumped, unemployment soared and there were no more khaki concessions. Gracie Fields was one who maintained the old rôle of cultural representative; but that style of close identification with the artist gave way to social blandness in the battle for audiences. Largely abandoning community allegiances, variety had to compete on level terms with an increasing number of leisure activities, never quite establishing new roots to match the old.

Notes

1. *Era* 29.11.16, 7.
2. The Marlborough in Holloway had this arrangement (*Era* 1.3.16, 16).
3. *Era* 30.6.15, 12.
4. G. H. Mair, 'The Music-Hall', *English Review* 9 (1911), 122–9.
5. This should not be taken to exclude stylistic variation in these circuits: 'Dump me down in the middle of a music hall, and, equally good as they both are, I could tell the difference between a Stoll and a Gulliver entertainment with my programme closed' (*Era* 21.11.17, 17).
6. Henry Chance Newton, *Idols of the 'Halls' Being My Music Hall Memories* (Heath Cranton, 1928), p. 98. Newton had his own axe to grind about blue songs; and a London performer of Marie's experience would hardly need instruction concerning the varying levels of tolerance in its different districts. Credibility finally vanishes when Newton adds that he just happened to be at hand to witness Marie's discomfiture.
7. *Era* 29.3.16, 18; *Era* 12.6.18, 14; *Era* 21.4.15, 12, mentions a baby in the Coliseum's gallery.
8. Dave Russell, *Popular Music in England, 1840–1914* (Manchester: Manchester University Press, 2nd edn 1997), p. 97.
9. *Encore* 22.4.15, 6.
10. *Era* 4.10.16, 16.
11. *Stage* 25.3.15, 15; *Era* 9.8.16, 12.
12. *Era* 8.9.15, 18.
13. 'Lancelot', *Referee* 5.11.16, 5; *Era* 17.7.18, Music Suppt 1.
14. *The Times* 23.6.17, 9; *Era* 23.6.17, 9.
15. *New Age* 13.5.15, 31.
16. Mair, 'Music-Hall', p. 127; *Era* 11.8.15, 13.
17. C. Jesson, *Era* 2.6.15, 21.

18. *Era* 29.12.15, 15.
19. *Stage* 14.1.15, 18.
20. A. T. Settle and F. H. Baber, *The Law of Public Entertainments* (Sweet & Maxwell, 1915), p. 47.
21. George Robey, *Looking Back on Life* (Constable, 1933), pp. 63–4.
22. George Bernard Shaw, *The Bodley Head Bernard Shaw: Shaw's Music*, ed. Dan H. Laurence (Bodley Head, 1981), vol. 2, p. 713.
23. *Era* 5.1.16, 9.
24. *Era* 22.11.16, 14.
25. *Era* 19.8.14, 10.
26. *Referee* 27.9.14, 3.
27. *Era* 9.9.14, 10. Lockhart's seven elephants were commandeered by the French government, though later they were back competing with Rossi's musical elephants. It was one of the latter which, at the Metropolitan, 'poked his trunk into the pocket of a chief stage hand', consuming its contents including 'the man's military discharge papers' (*Era* 2.9.14, 10; *Era* 28.2.17, 14).
28. *Era* 2.9.14, 10.
29. *Era* 17.3.15, 7.
30. *Era* 19.8.14, 10.
31. Cf. *Encore* 17.8.15, 6, on Board of Trade figures indicating record employment levels: 'Wages have risen, ... want has been banished.'
32. *Stage* 2.3.16, 14.
33. *Era* 27.12.16, 11.
34. *Era* 18.11.14, 17.
35. Marks, *Referee* 12.12.15, 4; *Era* 15.12.15, 15. Rivalry between the two showed itself in the poaching of artists; when Butt lost Ethel Levey to Stoll, he retaliated by reclaiming George Graves for his forthcoming Empire revue (*Sunday Chronicle* 11.6.16, 3).
36. *Referee* 9.8.14, 2.
37. W. H. Boardman, *Vaudeville Days*, ed. David Whitelaw (Jarrolds, 1935), p. 245.
38. *The Times* 10.8.14, 7.
39. *Ibid.*
40. *Era* 21.4.15, 12. The VAF's 'masterly handling of the present situation' even persuaded Vesta Tilley to join (*Performer* 17.9.14, 11). But George Formby, recognizing how performers earning £10 and under bore the brunt, suggested that those like himself at the top of the bill should stand any loss; after all, if they were worth their money, there would be none (*Era* 26.8.14, 10).

41. *Era* 19.8.14, 10. *Performer* 24.8.14, 11, noted that the Morecambe Tower manager continued to pay full salaries.
42. *Era* 9.9.14, 6.
43. *Era* 4.11.14, 9. Again, with the 50 per cent increase in rail fares and new baggage surcharges it was indicated that 'the Government has sounded the death-knell of innumerable poorly-paid variety acts' (*Performer* 11.1.17, 22).
44. *Era* 19.8.14, 10.
45. Newton, *Referee* 16.8.14, 3; *Era* 3.11.15, 15.
46. *Era* 9.9.14, 10.
47. *Era* 4.11.14, 9, records the agreement reached on 28 October, 'That all single turns in receipt of a salary of £5 or less shall be paid in full' as well as 'all turns consisting of more than one person in receipt of a salary of £10 or less'.
48. *Era* 20.1.15, 14.
49. *Star* 29.3.17, 2.
50. *Era* 30.9.14, 6.
51. F. V. St Clair, *Performer* 17.9.14, 19.
52. *Era* 2.6.15, 21.
53. *Era* 21.4.15, 12.
54. *Stage* 2.3.16, 14.
55. *Stage* 29.4.15, 15.
56. *Evening News* 12.6.16, 3.
57. Hitherto objection to women in music-hall orchestras had hinged on physique rather than morals: 'It is not like theatre music, for the musicians have to be at it all the time. Women are not physically capable of playing brass instruments throughout the evening' (*Evening News* 12.6.16, 3).
58. *Era* 8.11.16, 13. Cf. *Era's* characteristic attempt (2.8.16, 14) to undermine a pay dispute at Golder's Green Hippodrome by misrepresenting it as impotent, while the hazards of giving a performance 'without the assistance of stage hands' are downplayed: 'little of noticeable importance happened' (apart from the collapse of wings and scenery!). 'The directors, in refusing to accept the demands of the Trade Union concerned, are supported by other well-known places of amusement in London': evidently taken as proof of the rightness of their position. However, Askwith arbitrated an award, though this still meant many employees were earning between 32s. and 12s. (*Performer* 13.9.17, 21).
59. *The Times* 3.11.16, 6; *The Times* 29.11.16, 5.
60. *Era* 1.12.15, 15.
61. *Encore* 29.4.15, 6, warned that 'very low salaries are paid by the Picture

Theatre proprietors for their variety turns', regarding '£3 or £4 a week as quite substantial remuneration'.

62. *Stage* 20.7.16, 13.
63. Cf. Darewski's 'Coupons For Kisses' number in *Buzz-Buzz* (1918).
64. *Era* 10.4.18, 6; Marks, *Referee* 14.7.18, 5.
65. *Era* 2.10.18, 12.
66. Rose updated with *The New Bloomsbury Burglars* (*Love Letters*) in 1916. The sexual ambiguity of a scene 'in which the burglars get into the heroine's bed, vulgarly discuss her garments, and "cuddle" one another, after one of them has donned her night-dress', prompted censorship (LC 1916: 17/364).
67. *Era* 11.8.15, 13.
68. William Archer, 'The Music-Hall, Past and Future', *Fortnightly Review* 100 (July–December 1916), 259.
69. *Era* 2.8.16, 14; *Era* 17.1.17, 14; *Stage* 3.8.16, 14.
70. Boardman, *Vaudeville Days*, p. 276; *Referee* 25.7.15, 4.
71. The new scale of allowances for servicemen's wives and widows caused apprehension. Those who had been bringing up nine children on 21s. a week might find themselves with 37s. 6d., and 'not know what to do with it' apart from the public house: very few working-class women 'could stand such a change of circumstances' (*The Times* 10.11.14, 9).
72. *The Times* 2.12.15, 9.
73. *London Life* 8.1.16, 10. Only the skilled workers got a decent wage (*Era* 27.9.16, 12).
74. Pianos figured amongst the 'extravagancies' ascribed to Sheffield munition-workers (*The Times* 3.1.16, 17), the £20 paid by one family said to be considerably more than the 'value of the furniture in the house'. However, the *Manchester Guardian*'s investigation (6.12.15, 4) revealed that far more sewing machines were being bought than pianos, a sign not of extravagance but of prudence and industry. Subsequently the paper seems to have come under pressure, reporting (8.12.15, 3) that there were probably 'more pianos in working-class homes in Manchester than ever'. Whatever the truth of that, the claim that munition workers had 'kept the retail trade up to the average level or even beyond it' is refuted by Board of Trade figures, the pre-war average of 115,000 pianos sold plummeting to 38,000 in 1915 (*Era* 29.3.16, 13). A piano was 'a desirable investment' for those ignorant of 'stocks and shares' (*Guardian*), as well as a symbol of self-respect. Revenge came with the Means Test, which deprived many labourers' homes of their pianos.
75. LC 1916: 22/457.
76. LC 1916: 17/374; *Stage* 3.8.16, 14. *The Times* 5.12.16, 11, notes 'that the audience did not always applaud quite at the proper point'.

77. *Era* 6.12.16, 1.
78. *Stage* 13.1.16, 16. *The Times* 3.1.16, 17, grumbled that Sheffield munition workers 'who formerly drank beer have changed their refreshment to the more expensive whisky-and-soda'.
79. *Era* 12.1.16, 19.
80. *Era* 17.11.15, 24.
81. The propaganda was relentless: a *Times* report (23.4.17, 9) that survivors from the sunk hospital ship *Lanfranc* were abused 'by British dockers, ... who earned high wages in perfect security' gained wide currency from repetition in Wilson and Hammerton's weekly *The Great War* (Amalgamated Press, 1917), IX, p. 256. Robert Graves testifies to the effectiveness of this divide-and-rule ploy, telling Bertrand Russell that his men would open fire unhesitatingly on strikers if ordered to do so: 'they loathe munition makers and would be only too glad of a chance to shoot a few' (*Good-bye to All That* (Cape, 1929), p. 308).
82. *Era* 9.12.14, 15.
83. *Era* 23.8.16, 11; *Era* 20.3.18, 12.
84. *Era* 11.7.17, 5.
85. *Era* 1.11.16, 21.
86. Cf. Gordon Williams, 'Newsbooks and Popular Narrative during the Middle of the Seventeenth Century', in Jeremy Hawthorn (ed.), *Narrative from Malory to Motion Pictures,* (Arnold, 1985), pp. 56–69 (61).
87. LC 1914: 3/3023; *Era* 25.11.14, 16.
88. *Era* 13.10.15, 14; *Era* 17.11.15, 9.
89. Fred J. Morris's one-act *Deserter* also involves the honour of an old veteran and sentimental evasion of harsh realities (*Era* 6.9.16, 11).
90. *Era* 6.1.15, 6; *Era* 23.6.15, 14.
91. *Era* 4.10.16, 16; *Era* 8.5.18, 14; *Era* 4.12.18, 14; *Era* 16.8.16, 16. Boardman (*Vaudeville Days,* p. 249) mentions an instance at Brighton concerning a man robbed of his speech at Loos, in Easter 1916; and Seymour Hicks (*Me and My Missus* (Cassell, 1939), p. 227) another where a two-year silence was broken at a performance of Cohan's *Broadway Jones*. Robey (*Looking Back on Life,* p. 183) performed the 'miracle', as Lady Tree called it, at one of the hospital concerts which she organized; as did Nelson Keys at the Palace, on a victim of Hill 60 (*Performer* 15.7.15, 21).
92. *Era* 20.9.16, 18.
93. *Era* 29.9.15, 20; *Era* 6.10.15, 23. For the last scene, where women relaxed after a hard day's toil, Karno recruited a platoon of the Women's War Work Emergency Corps.
94. *Stage* 8.4.15, 16.
95. *Era* 29.6.16, 7; *Era* 12.6.18, 14; *Era* 7.8.18, 4.

96. *Era* 29.11.16, 14.
97. *Era* 19.12.17, 6. Cf. Frederick Lonsdale's *The Patriot*, where an upper-middle-class suburban family objects to having a Tommy billeted on them, until they learn that he is a baronet (*Era* 19.5.15, 20). With the use of accent, cf. Victor Grayson's *War, Wine, and a Woman*, where a British woman agent in enemy hands 'wheedles round the German officer' by adopting a cockney accent, conventionally associated with comic and 'inferior' characters (*Era* 3.3.15, 15), an attempted embrace drawing the response: ''Ere, ole cock – None o' yer Scarbro' tricks on me!' (LC 1915: 5/3228).
98. *Era* 1.9.15, 7. There is a hint of *Pygmalion* in Jack Williams's *Show Me the Way to Your Heart*, where a munitionette, 'beloved by the master's son', is allowed to marry him when she has been 'trained to take her place in Society' (*Era* 16.2.16, 11).
99. *Era* 4.9.18, 14.
100. *Era* 15.8.17, 1; *Era* 29.8.17, 14.
101. Alfred Sutro, *The Marriage ... Will Not Take Place* (French, 1917), p. 24.
102. Thus William J. Shiller's *A Daughter of Belgium* (premièred 29.3.15) and *My Friend Thomas Atkins* (*Era* 16.12.14, 14).
103. *Era* 10.5.16, 14.
104. *Era* 9.10.18, 5.
105. M. Van Wyk Smith, *Drummer Hodge* (Oxford: Clarendon Press, 1978), p. 78.
106. *Referee* 21.3.15, 10.
107. *Stage* 20.1.16, 16.
108. *Era* 5.8.14, 6; *Referee* 9.8.14, 2.
109. *Era* 20.9.16, 18; *Performer* 29.6.16, 18.
110. *Era* 16.12.14, 14.
111. *Era* 10.11.15, 23; *Era* 1.9.15, 14.
112. *Era* 23.12.14, 14; *Era* 4.10.16, 16.
113. *Era* 23.12.14, 14.
114. *Era* 9.6.15, 7; *Era* 17.10.17, 14.
115. Hicks, *Me and My Missus*, p. 213.
116. *Era* 19.12.17, 14.
117. *Era* 8.8.17, 7.
118. *Stage* 27.5.15, 14; *Era* 2.6.15, 7.
119. *Era* 30.12.14, 27.
120. *Era* 22.11.16, 14.
121. *Era* 22.9.15, 14.
122. F. Anstey [Thomas Anstey Guthrie], 'London Music Halls', *Harper's New Monthly Magazine* 82 (January 1891), 190–202 (192). This may have

been Annie, whom J. H. Littlejohn, *Scottish Music Halls 1880–1990* (Wigtown: G. C., 1990), p. 73, records appearing with her father Professor Beaton at Clark's Music Hall, Dunfermline, February 1888. But during the old Aquarium days Beckwith and his two daughters performed a similar act (Herman Finck, *My Melodious Memories* (Hutchinson, 1937), p. 27).

123. Pete Collins, *No People Like Show People* (Muller, 1957), p. 218.
124. *Performer* 22.4.15, 28. They were rivalled by Miss Olga and the Diving Norins, returned to Britain in 1915 after a successful American tour (*Performer* 25.3.15, 19).
125. *Performer* 19.8.15, 29.
126. *Performer* 22.4.15, 28; *Performer* 17.6.15, 22; *Encore* 4.3.15, 13.
127. *Era* 28.4.15, 16; *Era* 14.7.15, 18.
128. *Performer* 8.7.15, 26; *Era* 25.8.15, 7; *Era* 7.7.15, 14.
129. *Era* 16.8.16, 12.
130. *Era* 12.5.15, 13. Gerald Robinson's story, *The Voice of the Tempter*, in *Performer*'s 1915 Christmas issue (136), takes a similar sexploitation line: 'Do you think that every girl in your chorus parades in her flimsy attire simply because she likes to do it? ... It is only the fear of dismissal, ... of starvation, which' overcomes shame. But a woman in the same line of business took the view on television recently that exploitation lies in being underpaid rather than underclothed.
131. *Era* 11.10.16, 13; *Era* 29.12.15, 15.
132. *Era* 27.12.16, 11.
133. *Era* 11.10.16, 13. Smith-Dorrien chose to take the sarcasm as compliment (*The Times* 25.10.16, 5).
134. *Morning Post* 29.8.16, 6.
135. *Performer* 21.9.16, 24.
136. *Weekly Dispatch* 3.9.16, 5; *Performer* 5.10.16, 31.
137. *Star* 4.9.16, 2.
138. *The Times* 16.9.16, 5.
139. *The Times* 4.11.16, 3; *Era* 11.10.16, 13. Possibly 'Another Little Drink Wouldn't Do Us Any Harm' gave offence: 'I went to a Ball dressed as the map of France,/Said a girl "Show me how the French advance,"/When she reached the Firing Line I shouted in alarm' (*The Bing Boys Are Here* (Feldman, 1916), p. 28). The libel case reached a friendly settlement (*Evening News* 4.4.17, 3).
140. *The Times* 25.10.16, 5. There is little substance to this ritual blaming of the provinces: Wigan audiences refused 'the blue-nosed comedian with the signal red gags' and the Birmingham Empire's manager was fined £5 for permitting Harry Champion to sing songs which had been heard 'in

London and elsewhere without complaint' (*Era* 6.12.16, 16; *Era* 22.12.15, 22). Manchester's Watch Committee had disapproved of performances 'given without objection both in Liverpool and London', though Liverpool's Licensing Committee worked at purging music-hall indecency (*Era* 27.12.15, 11; *Era* 1.11.16, 14).

141. *Era* 16.6.15, 13.
142. *The Times* 21.9.16, 5.
143. *Referee* 3.12.16, 3.
144. *Era* 29.11.16, 8. Cf. VAF chairman Fred Russell's divisive line, defending music hall by denouncing *Hindle Wakes*, where dialogue left 'little or nothing to the imagination' (*Performer* 12.10.16, 25).
145. *The Times* 11.6.17, 11.
146. *The Times* 25.9.16, 5; *Era* 26.7.16, 13.
147. *The Times* 19.5.16, 5
148. According to John Cowen, 'Music Halls and Morals', *Contemporary Review* (November 1916), 611–20 (614), his source was a Canadian officer who supposedly traced responsibility for an infected soldiery 'directly to one or two London music halls'.
149. *Stage* 3.8.16, 14.
150. Philip Gibbs, *The Pageant of the Years* (Heinemann, 1946), p. 227.
151. *Era* 20.9.16, 12, ironically observes 'that the reporter whose work is thus challenged has in his possession his notes of the speech. In those notes the word "every" appears.' The disputed 'everys' also occurred in *The Times* 13.9.16, 5.
152. *Weekly Dispatch* 27.8.16, 2.
153. *Era* 15.5.18, 7.
154. Fred Kerr, *Recollections of a Defective Memory* (Thornton Butterworth, 1930), p. 265. Pope notes that the Australian troops were 'a real headache to all theatre managers, for they were quite unruly'; and when several created a disturbance at the Islington Empire, the manager was presented with the ear of one of them by a friend who took exception to their behaviour (W. J. Macqueen-Pope, *Ivor* (Allen, 1951), p. 141; W. J. Macqueen-Pope, *Ghosts and Greasepaint* (Hale, 1951), pp. 112–13).
155. St John Ervine, *The Theatre in My Time* (Rich & Cowan, 1933), p. 118.
156. Gilbert Frankau, *Gilbert Frankau's Self-Portrait: A Novel of His Own Life* (Hutchinson, 1940), p. 45.
157. Paul Fussell, *The Great War and Modern Memory* (Oxford University Press, 1975), p. 23.
158. Edward Knoblock, *Round the Room* (Chapman & Hall, 1939), p. 201.
159. *Era* 29.11.16, 13.
160. *The Times* 3.11.16, 6.

161. *Era* 3.5.16, 20.
162. *Era* 6.2.18, 12. However, the reverend headmaster was not the only one to be perturbed by Scott, Marks (*Referee* 9.12.17, 5) urging her to 'drop her "Youngest of the Family" ditty forthwith' (*Referee* 5.5.18, 5, brought another remonstrance).
163. Charles Cochran, *I Had Almost Forgotten* (Hutchinson, 1932), p. 79.
164. Louis Fergusson, *Old Time Musical Hall Comedians* (1949), p. 26.
165. T. Murray Ford, *Memoirs of a Poor Devil* (Philpot, 1926), p. 157.
166. *Referee* 10.9.16, 7.
167. She recalled: 'I used to be able to sing three new songs in one evening without a shiver. But now it takes me days and days to pluck up courage to sing one' (*Era* 27.9.16, 18).
168. Naomi Jacob, *'Our Marie': Marie Lloyd. A Biography* (Hutchinson, 1936), p. 197. Laurence Senelick, 'Politics as Entertainment: Victorian Music Hall Songs', *Victorian Studies* XIX (1975–6), 149–80 (176), assigns this to the Boer War period, presumably confusing it with Harrington and Le Brunn's 1900 'Girl In The Khaki Dress', in which she mocked 'the latest craze' of 'khaki this and khaki that', confiding that she even wore khaki bloomers (Richard Anthony Baker, *Marie Lloyd* (Robert Hale, 1990), pp. 80–2.
169. *Stage* 27.1.16, 14; *Era* 19.1.16, 20.
170. 'Extra Turn', *Era* 26.12.17, 12. It is worth emphasizing the date since both Baker, *Marie Lloyd*, p. 137, and Russell, *Popular Music*, p. 108, assign it to 1919.
171. Fergusson, *Old Time*, p. 28.
172. *Observer* 8.10.22, 15.
173. 'Extra Turn', *Era* 3.4.18, 12; *Era* 27.11.18, 14.
174. Letter to her POW boyfriend in Bavaria (5.9.18).
175. Colin MacInnes, *Sweet Saturday Night* (MacGibbon and Kee, 1967), p. 23.
176. Boardman, *Vaudeville Days*, p. 252.
177. *Era* 30.12.14, 22; *Era* 16.12.14, 14.
178. Harry Randall, *Harry Randall: Old Time Comedian* (Sampson Low, Marston, 1930), p. 217.
179. In a 1971 BBC interview Wee Georgie Wood claimed that Lloyd was indeed invited in 1912; but Graeme Cruickshank, *Call Boy* 37 (Spring 2000) 1, 8, dismisses this as one of his tall stories. Albert Chevalier was another strange omission, moving him to make a full-page protest in *Era* 6.7.12, 24. So there was evidently some score-settling by the organizers.
180. Daniel Farson, *Marie Lloyd and Music Hall* (Tom Stacey, 1972), p. 100.
181. *Era* 12.8.14, 11.
182. *Era* 21.4.15, 12.

183. J. B. Booth, *The Days We Knew* (Werner Laurie, 1943), pp. 59, 61.
184. *Dial* 72 (January 1922), 510–13 (513).
185. *Stage* 15.4.15, 15. Both were Robey's own compositions, which he recorded for the Gramophone Co. in 1915.
186. H. G. Hibbert recalls that when the Stoll group took over, the Middlesex gave 'a series of revues by one of the lower grade Parisian companies, ... scantily dressed French beauties marching a "joy plank" across its once sanded floor to its once impeccably virtuous stage' (*A Playgoer's Memories* (Richards, 1920), p. 243).
187. Newton, *Referee* 20.1.18, 2.
188. Richard Gruneau (ed.), *Popular Cultures and Political Practices* (Toronto: Garamond Press, 1988), p. 25.
189. Terence Prentis (ed.), *Music-Hall Memories* (Selwyn & Blount, 1927), p. 17.
190. *Era* 13.10.15, 9.
191. Robin Daniels, *Conversations with Cardus* (Gollancz, 1976), p. 29.
192. *Era* 28.11.17, 14.
193. Once the halls were equipped with proscenium stages these had to be filled, and the walk was a means by which the single artist might achieve that. Revue, with the singer supported by a bevy of chorus girls, helped to make it redundant.
194. *Era* 18.11.14, 20.
195. *Era* 2.10.18, 12.
196. Mistinguett, *Mistinguett: Queen of the Paris Night*, trans. Lucienne Hill (Elek, 1954), p. 226.
197. In 1877, Charles Coborn, calling upon the audience at a Leicester hall to join in the chorus, was told that it was not permitted; and his contract with Morton at the Palace expressly forbade any addressing of the audience (*'The Man Who Broke the Bank'* (Hutchinson, 1929), pp. 89, 234).
198. *Era* 11.8.15, 13.
199. Typical is this *Performer* report (25.1.17, 25): 'That he believed music halls had been an active cause of the patience and good humour of the soldiers at the Front under the most trying circumstances, was the statement made by Bishop Frodsham in an address at Cheltenham Town Hall.'
200. John Brophy and Eric Partridge (eds), *Songs and Slang of the British Soldier: 1914–1918* (Partridge, 1930), p. 8.
201. Mary Tich and Richard Findlater, *Little Tich* (Elm Tree, 1979), p. 35.
202. *Performer* 7.11.18, 17; *Performer* 23.11.16, 21.
203. Robertson, otherwise Gertrude Elliott, had made her variety debut at the Victoria Palace (*Era* 1.3.16, 16).
204. Newton, *Referee* 28.4.18, 3. That the process was already under way

shows in the remodelling of the Bradford Empire, which sacrificed the 'old balcony and gallery' to make 'one upper circle' (*Era* 2.8.16, 8).

205. Ann Oughton, *Thanks for the Memory* (Edinburgh/Cambridge/Durham: Pentland Press, 1995), p. 15; *London Opinion* 14.9.18, 170.
206. Fergusson, *Old Time*, p. 58.
207. Adrian New, 'Zola of the Halls', *The Times* 19.12.70, 13.
208. Herman Finck, *My Melodious Memories* (Hutchinson, 1937), p. 39.
209. *Era* 12.7.16, 14. A film version which Chevalier made in the same year must rank amongst the most popular British movies (*Era* 7.6.16, 8).
210. *Era* 26.1.16, 16.
211. R. G. Knowles, *A Modern Columbus* (Laurie, 1916), p. 152.
212. Coborn, '*The Man Who Broke the Bank*', p. 275.
213. *WAAC*, p. 41.
214. Boardman, *Vaudeville Days*, pp. 244–5.
215. J. A. Hobson, *The Psychology of Jingoism* (Richards, 1901), pp. 108, 3.
216. Robey, *Looking Back*, p. 44, emphasizes the point: 'There was as much patriotism at the Oxford in 1891 as there was at the Coliseum in 1914–18.' Indeed, in the *Manchester Guardian* 24.8.14, 4, it was wondered whether the music hall's efforts 'to reflect the national life' at that time were the less effective 'because its ordinary stock in trade is patriotic sentiments and martial choruses'.
217. E. M. Sansom, *SYB 1915*, p. 22; *Era* 22.3.16, 15.
218. *Performer* 10.9.14, 18.
219. *Era* 2.6.15, 13. *Era* 21.10.14, 10, is predictably scathing about Butt's *By Jingo* revue title; but even Bransby Williams received withering notice for grafting 'on to three of his Dickens characters the personalities of two English statesmen and the Kaiser': the appeal of '"Wilhelm-Fagin" relieving his tortured soul in Dickensian phrases' was strictly 'to the unthinking' (*Era* 4.10.16, 16).
220. *Stage* 22.6.16, 28.
221. 'Extra Turn', *Era* 25.12.18, 12. Marks (*Referee* 21.11.15, 4) raises no eyebrow over this, but complained earlier (*Referee* 28.2.15, 4) of Kaiser-baiting comedians, who must surely include Ernest Shand, a popular and distinctive humorist. *John Bull* 5.9.14, 3, and *Era* 16.9.14, 10, quote Shand's 'To Wilhelm' approvingly: 'He's a humbug, not a fair man/He's a rotter, he's a German/For he'll violate all treaties that are made;/He may win a smallish battle,/Shoot the citizens as cattle,/But he hasn't made a single soul afraid.'
222. LC 1915: 5/3217.
223. *Era* 25.12.18, 6.
224. *Era* 4.9.18, 14, deploring the plagiarism which resulted in two comedians

giving virtually 'the same "Medical Board" turn', and urging whoever 'was first in the field' to take action. Cf. *Era* 31.10.17, 6: 'An unscrupulous person was recently caught red-handed taking down all Fred [Duprez]'s patter in shorthand on a programme.' Sydney Blow, *The Ghost Walks on Fridays* (Heath Cranton, 1935), p. 157, indicates that entire plays were still filched in this way.

225. *Star* 25.8.16, 2.
226. Letter (25.3.17) reproduced in Peter Liddle (ed.), *World War One: Other Fronts* (Longmans, 1977), p. 22.
227. Roy Palmer, '*What a Lovely War!*' (Joseph, 1990), p. 178.
228. 'Extra Turn', *Era* 14.11.17, 17.
229. *Stage* 18.2.15, 17.
230. *Era* 22.5.18, 12.
231. *Era* 1.12.15, 16; LC 1918: 1/1337.
232. *The Times* 31.3.17, 3; *Times* 24.2.17, 10.
233. *The Times* 16.1.17, 5. A woman in Gertrude Jennings's *Allotments* (French, 1918), p. 14, who gets mustard in her brandy, immediately suspects 'the Government'. *Weekly Dispatch* 4.8.18, 2, noted that beer cost 300 per cent 'above pre-war prices', while being 100 per cent thinner than in 1915.
234. *Era* 4.9.18, 14.
235. Cf. Fred Curran's 'Bread, Bread, Bread' and Harry Barrett (of Barrett and Knowles) with *War Bread* (*Era* 20.2.18, 14; *Stage* 17.1.18, 20).
236. *New Age* 13.8.14, 338.
237. Much earlier Walter Runciman, President of the Board of Trade, told a gathering of organized labour at the Central Hall, Westminster, that 'He did not think the people of this country [politicians' code for the establishment] would like to be limited in their diet by ticket' as the Germans already were (*The Times* 2.12.15, 9).
238. Lyn Macdonald, *Somme* (Joseph, 1983), p. 108.
239. *Era* 10.4.18, 12; *Era* 27.2.18, 14.
240. 'Extra Turn', *Era* 27.3.18, 14. Yapp, the recently knighted national secretary of the YMCA, had been made director of food economy in co-operation with Rhondda (*Times* 20.9.17, 6).
241. *The Times* 3.1.18, 3. The same issue reported that Lady Mabel Gore Langton had been found guilty on a similar charge, having 'enough tea to last the household more than a year'.
242. *Era* 23.2.16, 16; *The Times* 25.2.15, 10; *The Times* 2.3.15, 9; *The Times* 6.3.15, 9.
243. *Era* 8.5.18, 14. One curious aspect of the affair was the scandal attaching to Margot Asquith, the Prime Minister's wife. Her daughter

noted in her diary on 1 June 1915: 'The *London Mail* has surpassed itself by saying Margot daily plays tennis with German officers at Donington Hall' (Cynthia Asquith, *Diaries 1915–18* (Century, 1968), p. 35). The libel was taken up in the *Globe,* which accused her of treachery. The affair, fully reported in the *Manchester Guardian* 22.12.15, 12, prompts the question of who stood to gain most from smearing the Prime Minister's family.

244. *Era* 19.7.16, 19, reprinted in the Star Music Company's *10th Planet Song Annual* (1916), pp. 42–3.
245. Cf. anonymous pamphlet *The Brothers of the Blade* (1641), p. 4.
246. *Era* 1.11.16, 18.
247. *Era* 24.7.18, 12.
248. *Era* 11.7.17, 12.
249. Knowles, *A Modern Columbus,* p. 297.
250. *Era* 5.1.16, 15.
251. *Era* 16.9.14, 9.
252. *Era* 14.4.15, 7. The following week it was carefully noted that Will himself was 'a sergeant in the Music Hall Platoon, and very keen on the responsibilities of drill'. Ray Seaton and Roy Martin, *Good Morning Boys* (Barrie and Jenkins, 1978), p. 36, wrongly assert that Hay's development of a schoolmaster sketch with a boy 'feed' occurred post-war, after his experience with Karno (*Era* 26.1.16, 7).
253. *Era* 7.10.14, 10.
254. *Era* 16.12.14, 14.
255. One of the most popular catchphrases of the day, though by this time it had reached the parody stage. 'Extra Turn', *Era* 31.7.18, 12, noted two variants at the Wood Green Empire: '"That's the guff to sti'e 'em," and "That is the stuff to give unto them." This latter was delivered in very precise and scholastic tones by Sam Hilton, the "Chippie Chappie in Chintz".' In his 'gaily flowered cretonne suit' (*Era* 19.5.15, 18), Hilton was clearly an inspiration to 'Cheeky Chappie' Max Miller (serving in Mesopotamia at this time).
256. *Era* 14.8.18, 12. Similar emotional scenes at the Palladium followed the announcement that Bulgaria had surrendered (Marks, *Referee* 6.10.18, 5).
257. *Performer* 11.2.15, 13.
258. *Referee* 31.1.15, 3.
259. *The Times* 26.1.15, 5. Bottomley's concentration on the sacrifice of the aristocracy was a regular theme in the pages of *John Bull,* hence the surprise expressed (*Era* 19.12.17, 4) at Whit Cunliffe's representing Bottomley 'as running "a penny paper of a Socialist trend"'. Patrick MacGill's response, which could be made only post-war, was that young

aristocrats had more reason to fight for their country than common folk, who possessed no more 'of England's earth [than] stood in the flowerpots on the window sills' (*Fear!* (Jenkins, 1920), p. 34).

260. *Stage* 11.3.15, 15. Pankhurst's deal with Lloyd George had alienated a significant part of her following; hence the appearance of two suffragists in the gallery of the Apollo at the first interval of *Hobson's Choice*, scattering handbills and hurriedly abusing the government before being hustled out (*Era* 1.11.16, 8).
261. *Performer* 20.8.14, 19.
262. This scene entails a 'sudden transference of the action from stage to auditorium', the hero 'sitting in a Palladium box watching the screening of patriotic features', which proved disconcerting for *The Stage*'s reviewer (20.8.14, 11).
263. Newton, *Referee* 23.8.14, 3; *Era* 19.8.14, 10.
264. *Era* 7.8.18, 4; R. E. W. Wester-Wemyss, *The Navy in the Dardanelles Campaign* (Hodder and Stoughton, 1924), pp. 195, 203. In the interest of discipline he coolly 'ignored both the law of the land and the King's regulations and Admiralty instructions'.
265. *Lawrence Wright's Song Annual* (1919), p. 20. At the war's end, the lack of discrimination with which campaign medals (Mutt and Jeff) were distributed aroused a contempt in combatants anticipating that of the WW2 song 'Africa Star'. Cf. G. S. Melvin's 'See that medal? Do you know what I got it for? For a penny' ('Extra Turn', *Era* 25.12.18, 12).
266. *Performer* 2.11.16, 23.
267. *Era* 24.10.17, 14.
268. Marks, *Referee* 1.9.18, 5; *Performer* 5.9.18, 17.
269. *Era* 19.1.16, 18; *Era* 1.3.16, 16.
270. *Stage* 3.2.16, 15; *Stage* 6.5.15, 17.
271. *Stage* 15.4.15, 15; *Stage* 22.4.15, 16. This account appears almost word for word in *Encore* 22.4.15, 12, and *Era* 21.4.15, 12.
272. *The Times* 15.12.14, 3. Terry, *Era* 12.1.16, 14, finding the clergy equally intemperate whether denigrating or praising the stage, mocked the Rev. G. H. Hazlehurst's comment on Lauder: '"God has given him the gift of humour, and he was using it for God"! M'yes, and a few hundreds a week!'
273. *Era* 5.12.17, 14.
274. *Era* 3.7.18, 14. There was little criticism of Lauder. J. D. B., *Saturday Westminster Gazette* 5.10.18, 16, guardedly wrote that he did 'not wholeheartedly endorse Mr. Lauder's views on the war'; while the comedian who gibed at 'Larry Hoarder' was not thought worthy to be named in *Era* 6.12.16, 15.

275. *Performer* 4.11.15, 19; *Performer* 7.3.15, 19.
276. Hicks, *Me and My Missus*, p. 224.
277. *Era* 1.9.15, 14.
278. *Stage* 18.3.15, 16.
279. *Era* 11.8.15, 14.
280. *Era* 21.4.15, 6. Lewis had been found 'medically unfit owing to a broken ankle'.
281. *Era* 3.11.15, 16; *Era* 17.11.15, 16.
282. *Era* 28.10.14, 10.
283. *Era* 9.9.14, 13; *Era* 9.5.14, 10.
284. *Era* 10.11.15, 25. Vivian played 'Tipperary' by firing at musical bells (*Era* 3.11.15, 16).
285. Oughton, *Thanks for the Memory* p. 23, her source presumably being Gertie's husband in the BBC's tribute, *The Idol of the People*; *Encore* 8.4.15, 10.
286. *Performer* 15.10.15, 20.
287. *Sunday Pictorial* 4.6.16, 7.
288. *Guardian* 14.4.72, 9.
289. Marks, *Referee* 16.4.16, 7.
290. Vesta Tilley, *Recollections* (Hutchinson, 1934), p. 141.
291. *Stage* 6.1.16, 15.
292. *Era* 1.3.16, 11; *Era* 9.2.16, 15.
293. Terry Cunningham (ed.), *14–18: The Final Word* (B. C. M. Stagedoor Publishing, 1993), p. 15. Tilley attempts to explain away her non-appearance in France through the impossibility of taking 'over with me all my stage suits and props' (*Recollections*, p. 142).
294. Anthony Bennett, 'Music in the Halls', in J. S. Bratton (ed.), *Music Hall: Performance and Style* (Milton Keynes: Open University Press, 1986), 2–22 (22).
295. M. Willson Disher, *Winkles and Champagne* (Constable, 1938), p. 88.
296. Randall, *Harry Randall*, p. 234.
297. Leonard Henry, *My Laugh Story* (Stanley Paul, 1937), p. 104.

5

War and the legitimate theatre

On the whole, the first half of 1914 had been a poor time for the legitimate theatre, and hopes were set on the autumn season to rescue the year. Then war intervened: Ruby Miller mentions 'very bad business' done during those 'first few weeks of the war, before the readjustment to a new way of life became habit'.[1] Attempts to evade the blackout included earlier starting times and matinées;[2] and there was also a brief favouring of revivals. The latter were encouraged as much by managerial uncertainty as by a desire for economy.[3]

Another easily achieved economy was to dispense with the orchestra, relic of those still recent days when practically every theatrical performance had a musical element. In Annie Horniman's experience, this would save about £1000 a year.[4] But the clearest sign of West End anxiety was when a number of managers reduced seat prices, a tariff ranging from 1s. to 10s. 6d. becoming 1s. to 7s. There had been agitation for this before the war, since West End theatres were, 'with some in Paris, the dearest in the world'.[5] But as soon as things settled down, there was a return to the old prices, managers having discovered that, despite changes in audience composition, people were ready to pay top prices.

However, a corollary of price reductions was cuts in salaries, and managements were much slower to restore these to the old level. The stars, of course, were in demand and therefore exempt from (or even party to) the exploitation. In mid-1915 Grein considered 'six shillings for a stall' ample, provided that landlords and stars were not pandered to. But managers believed in stars rather than plays, often paying out £80 and more a week for aura rather than talent, at the expense of the rank and file.[6] Bernard Weller deplored the way that 'the long-delayed revision of West End prices' was abandoned while many actors were still receiving only half or even a third of their normal salaries.[7] He pointed out that managers were blaming the war for salary reductions resulting from their own cut-throat policies.[8] It suited them to play up the mood of uncertainty when it induced a man who had been 'earning £50 a week as a tango dancer in the principal Continental capitals' to grab the part of a German soldier in *England Expects*, though he had only to appear for a few seconds and be shot. The reality was that by Christmas things had largely righted themselves: 26 of the 29 West End theatres which had been open at Christmas 1913 were operative,[9] the number increasing to 28 'out of a possible 31' by the start of 1915, usually 'playing to full houses'. But by now it was clear that the war, far from bringing disaster had brought a boom: 'unprecedented runs ... unprecedented fortunes', with more theatres open in London and the provinces 'than in the average peace year'.[10]

Initially the provinces were harder hit than London, where rich syndicates could stand a temporary loss and transport difficulties had minimal effect. During that first autumn, some itinerant groups disbanded and the number on tour was 'about a quarter below the average'.[11] But recovery was rapid, and Christmas saw as many provincial theatres open as ever. Alfred Harding, who spent much of the war on the road, found business 'very good indeed' and couldn't 'remember playing to a bad house since war was declared'.[12] But good business was no guarantee of a living wage for those on tour. Seduced into accepting war contracts (euphemism for cut rates) as a means of spreading the supposed losses sustained by theatres, touring players frequently worked for half-salaries (starvation level for the small-part majority).[13] At the end of 1915, with business booming, Weller reported an overall salary decrease of 25 per cent in the provinces;[14] and this despite the way that the twice-nightly system was finding favour, calling for double work at those half-salaries. Twice nightly naturally affected theatrical employees generally, though one issue of *The Stage* (18 March 1915, p. 19) juxtaposed stories of the theatrical boom and of the short shrift given to stagehands striking for more money at Kelly's Liverpool theatres. The leader in a subsequent issue (6 January 1916, p. 18) criticized the normalizing of war contracts, insisting that even a return to 'former salaries' would be inadequate given 'the prevalence of twice-nightly performances in the provinces'.

It was widely recognized that performers on the legitimate stage suffered more acutely in salary terms than did their music-hall counterparts, for which two reasons were offered: public preference for bright and informal entertainment, and the existence of the VAF to look after some of the interests of music-hall performers.[15] Reason one fails to acknowledge differences in seat prices: if the theatre public could 'get a considerable dramatic element in the music halls at half the price, and [often] with double the comfort in the cheap parts', some shift of allegiance might be expected. After all, the West End theatres were 'shut off by a high ... tariff from the bulk of the London public'; in 1918 Henry Irving's important *Hamlet* 'came to an abrupt conclusion after a run of only three weeks', whereas the Old Vic's 'Shakespeare at cinema-prices ... held the boards more or less throughout the whole year'.[16] Until the provincial theatres extensively adopted the twice-nightly system, the price differential could be explained through the halls' 'double earning capacity of seats per night'. Thereafter it showed as rank profiteering.[17] Reason two is entirely pertinent: one important achievement of the VAF was to bring the reduced-salary phase to a definite conclusion.[18] It is indicative of the level of wartime exploitation that the deeply conservative acting profession became unionized by the end of 1918.[19]

There was never a shortage of actors, though the Derby scheme had its effect in the provinces. One touring manager complained to *The Stage* about the difficulty of finding men for his productions, 'The few men who are vacant ask[ing] exorbitant salaries.' But his grumbles were quashed by an editorial response: 'many managers, while they could afford to do so, failed to re-establish actors in the salary-rates paid before the War.' Having exploited 'supply and demand', they could hardly complain if actors now applied 'the same principle'.[20] But the pressures felt elsewhere were never experienced in the West End, cushioned by big budgets and prestige. Whereas conscription found the Old Vic employing women in men's rôles, this possibility never went beyond discussion amongst the leading managers, only George Alexander showing enthusiasm.[21] It would have been healthier had the West End been under greater constraint, one well-known dramatist deploring the way that 'syndicates and combines' operated exclusively for profit.[22] Those being exploited were impatient of managerial moans 'when everyone knows that the theatrical business has seldom enjoyed greater prosperity'.[23] Spero Mehora, a theatre musician, complained that, whereas during the initial phase of poor business he had 'submitted to a reduction to his hand-to-mouth salary', the 1915–16 boom was benefiting only the shareholders.[24] (One columnist contrasts the way that reduced salaries still prevailed at some houses while an officer on leave seeking a seat at a West End theatre tried eleven without success before paying a guinea for two returns at the twelfth.[25]) London saw still greater profits in 1916–17. 'There aren't enough theatres even for all the people who want to go to them or all the plays that are waiting to be born; and manager-people *roll* in Treasury Notes.'[26] Only twice was theatrical business hit by the war: several weeks of heavy raids in 1917 kept London audiences at home; and the period following the 1918 Spring Offensive saw all available troops despatched to the Western Front. Even so, 1918 was a remarkably good year: 'in every big centre, business has been sustained above normal, in proof of which the excess profit tax is an unimpeachable witness.'[27]

It might be expected that the spate of revivals caused by the onset of war would have drawn comment about artistic decline. Instead, in *Sphere* (19 December 1914, p. 298) it was claimed that London had never enjoyed 'a better collection of dramas on the stage at one time'. As for the revivals, most of them were 'of the lightest description', fairly indicating that choice of such material was not so much demanded by as imposed upon audiences.[28] This makes nonsense of those leading articles in *Era* (28 July 1915, p. 13; 9 August 1916, p. 11) claiming: 'After many plucky and energetic attempts to gauge the inclination of wartime audiences, managers have discovered precisely the kind of fare that suits the taste of the present day, and have provided plays light, bright, entertaining, and of sufficient interest to distract attention temporarily from the war.' Cochran, writing on behalf of the commercial manager just a week before the Armistice, adopts a similarly flawed stance. The theatre's wartime 'condition of extraordinary prosperity', he claims, was due to managers finding 'plays that have appealed to the taste of an exceptional public'; exceptional since, unlike the pre-war habitué, the new breed 'is unsophisticated, eager for entertainment, and, thanks to the incessant mutation of the London visitor from the war front, from the provinces, from abroad, he is innumerable'.[29] Carter is more blunt about the process in which Cochran was participating. He alludes to 'changes of mood corresponding to the fluctuations of the War', and the way that people turned to the theatre 'for an insight into the meaning of their moods'. What they received was a packaged 'meaning which sold the best seats', theatrical controllers adroitly exploiting 'the public moods as these appeared in turn'.[30]

Yet even normally perceptive commentators often overlooked the way that suppliers were creating rather than responding to a demand. Asking 'Is Our Drama Declining?',[31] Grein could exonerate the provinces, especially with the Birmingham Rep under the daring management of Barry Jackson. Yet he still uses '*la guerre*' to account for a trivialized London theatre: 'for when one great problem hovers over life the thoughts of the average man are not disposed to burrow into smaller problems.' Unfortunately, this implies that Birmingham had not its share of average men, and that the 'one great problem' hovered over London and not the Midlands. As for London's rejection of the 'serious play' in favour of 'the merry and the bright', generally descending to 'the silly and the frivolous', he is quick to blame audiences, supposedly impoverished by the absence of a society element far too busy with war work to have much leisure for theatre attendance. This is one of Grein's dafter comments: the increased proportion of women in wartime audiences included a fair number of the fashionable set, there 'merely to see the dresses and sit patiently through the Russian Ballet in the hope of picking up new ideas for colour schemes'.[32]

He slips into a commonplace that the stage has been 'handed over to the business of entertaining subalterns on leave' and their womenfolk. This is too glib for another critic, who points out that the war has merely 'emphasized an already established tradition'.[33] Pre-war 'the jaded worker' turned to the theatre to forget 'his daily routine'[34] just as now he came to forget wartime anxiety. Even so, there had been sufficient response to continental developments to allow Belcham's claim that 'Before the war we were welcoming new thought in the theatre, and looking for a new vision in everything.'[35] This dimension of theatrical activity is a casualty of war chiefly because it had seen the domination of a new style of management which favoured standardizing. And whereas Grein might deplore the disappearance of a progressive strain, for Hope it meant a 'new lease of life' for a theatre 'no longer intimidated by the "intellectuals"'. He was pleased to reflect that audiences need no longer mark the play but only relish the stars, indulging their 'preference for comedy and "happy endings"'.[36] What these critics share is a professed belief that 'the public wants plays which can make it laugh, or cry, or feel excited, and not plays that make it think'.[37] But in reality the demand was made *of* them, a demand for unthinking acceptance. There had been those pre-war for whom thought and theatre were incompatible; now it became a patriotic necessity to insist on the disjunction since thought-provoking theatre might well unsettle convictions about Britain's war-rôle. Fortunately, even restricted by emergency powers, the theatre showed enough resilience to defy Hope's philistine optimism. As the opera amply proved, the vices of the star system were not an inevitable price to be paid in order to enjoy that accomplished playing which inspires audience confidence.

The Old Vic was also conspicuous, appealing to Tommies, many of whom liked some substance to their theatrical entertainment. It was recorded how, when an inane conjugal infidelity farce was performed for the troops at Colchester Barracks, two-thirds of them quietly left after five minutes.[38] According to Ervine, 'it was commonly said in the trenches that the War Office was subsidising the performance of appalling twaddle in order to make the soldiers glad to go back to the Front'.[39] H. M. Wallbrook regrets wasted opportunities, with so many people looking for a theatre that would 'lift us, not merely out of ourselves, but up from ourselves'. Looking back over 1915, he and Weller wonder that so few managers grasped the fact, which they believe to account both for West End failures and for the eagerness, in the absence of first-rate plays, with which audiences sought out solid second-raters like *Quinneys* and *The Man Who Stayed at Home*.[40]

However, it should be noted that some good plays, for differing reasons, failed to hold their place, notable amongst them being Knoblauch's *Marie-Odile* and Basil Macdonald Hastings's *Advertisement*. The latter, after just 20 performances was packed off to the Liverpool Rep while the Liverpool company took its place at the Kingsway. *Advertisement* pillories some of the same follies and vices as Pinero's *Big Drum*; but whereas Pinero views them through a smoked glass of formality, Hastings's treatment is raw and immediate. One critic found the play possessed of 'so much that is interesting and unusual that it is a thousand pities that it is not more coherent'.[41] But it is hardly incoherent, despite hitting at a range of targets, some of them sensitive enough to earn the play some damaging notices. Critics disliked being shocked. When reporters arrive, looking for a story following news that Sufan's son has been killed in action, Sufan first shows numbed indifference; but then his interest quickens as he sees the chance to introduce a 'puff ad.' for his new product into the story. 'This unedifying scene is handled ... with great power',[42] the more so as Sufan has experienced real anguish. And there is rending pathos, even while it testifies to Sufan's warped values, when he woefully misinterprets a last letter from the dead boy declining to accept any more money from his despised parent: 'Oh, my dear, my dear, he must have liked me after all. He didn't want my money'.[43] But then comes doubt: to refuse money shows 'He wasn't the son of his father' (p. 64); and there is poignant irony because this is the literal truth. By the war's end, Sufan has acquired a fortune and social position; but his wife, distressed at the way in which his useless products have 'been forced on the public by clever advertising' (p. 87), can take no more. Faced with having to choose between her and a lucrative tobacco deal, he is struck by the poisonous nature of the cigarette industry: 'Ten for twopence or threepence. Smoke 'em and let your kids smoke 'em. Kill yourself and kill your kids. Ye gods, is there anything in the world so unscrupulous as the commercial side of a newspaper!' (p. 107). And he denounces a press which, for all the moral posturing over 'the little quacks that can't spend much', is complicitous in large-scale rackets. The play was assailed for its treatment of the Jew.[44] In fact, it hits at racial prejudice. Despite his Christian upbringing, the son is a 'Yid' to his Cambridge associates, though his double blue prevents him from being 'avoided' or 'snubbed' (p. 31). Nor is the father's 'greed for money' inherent. In his young days, 'keen on business as he was, he had a soul for other things – beautiful things – and especially for music. He played the violin like an angel.' And he finally returns to his violin, to his faith and to his wife.

Although it was his picture of the grieving Jewish father which attracted most condemnation, Hastings was consciously treading on corns with that anti-smoking diatribe. The war gave a huge boost to the tobacco habit, and soldiers' letters (Hastings was himself a ranker) show how many of them had become dependent on cigarettes. The Smokes for Soldiers and Sailors Fund had huge momentum, entire profits from theatre matinées being devoted to it.[45]

The tobacco industry, with government connivance, used the same ruthless saturation methods to sell its product as the government did to sell the war. Pressure was unremitting: George Wills, chairman of the Imperial Tobacco Company, not satisfied with the huge increases in profit brought by nearly four years of war, urged the government to remove import restrictions on tobacco, claiming that shortages would be 'bad for the temper of the nation' and cause people to eat more at a time of food shortage.[46]

Official encouragement of the drug is nicely symbolized in royal gifts. Victoria had chocolate dispatched to front-line soldiers in South Africa at the end of 1899, the 'coffin nails' nickname for cigarettes being already well established. Yet it was cigarettes and tobacco which were sent to soldiers on active service at Christmas 1914 under the patronage of Princess Mary. The situation with hard drugs was more confused. The late nineteenth-century practice of selling heroin as relief from coughs and influenza persisted, and it was not until the summer of 1916, with recognition that they could damage the efficiency of servicemen and war workers, that DORA, section 40B was modified to make unauthorized distribution of hard drugs a criminal offence.[47] Meanwhile, Hartley Manners, author of the hugely successful *Peg o' My Heart*, had written his drug play *Wreckage*, designed to encourage 'legislation for exterminating the evil'. Since the problem was far graver in America, he doubted if it would be acceptable on the London stage; but Bourchier was keen to play the protagonist, who almost dies through drug abuse. However, it never reached production over here,[48] though Ardeen Foster's *A 'Woman's Soul* was given at a Kingsway charity matinée (28 July 1916). Here a New Yorker addicted to the 'Devil's needle' emerges from one of his 'frightful dope-dreams' raving for morphine and ransacking his room until he finds half a tablet. The scene is remarkable for its detailed portrayal of preparation and injection.[49] Often, however, gritty realism yielded to exotic romance, John Brandon's crook play, *The Yellow Fang*, being set in a Frisco opium den[50] (scene for a song on 'the attraction of the drug' in *Pell Mell*).[51] Traffickers dislodged from the Continent by war and anti-drug laws encouraged cocaine-sniffing amongst 'girls in revues and musical comedies'.[52] But it took the sensational death of revue artist Billie Carleton, following the Victory Ball at the Albert Hall at the end of 1918, to bring general awareness of the growing drug scene.[53]

On the whole, dramatists were more interested in sex than drug abuse, though the wide gap between early and late twentieth-century morality is underscored by responses to the Canadian J. G. Cambridge's *The Love Thief*. This had 30 performances at the Queen's, its sordid subject made 'almost entertaining' by maladroit handling. But it is less the disapproval aroused by its 'skirt-chasing' which points the difference than the attitude to children born out of wedlock contained in one reviewer's final, depressing phrase: 'Almost every character in a piece presumably meant to be taken seriously ... may be said either to be an illegitimate child, to have had an illegitimate child, or to be the possible parent of such unwanted offspring.'[54] The specific issue of the war baby will be touched on later, but it was not only illegitimacy which raised problems. In Walter Ellis's *A Little Bit of Fluff* (p. 29), it is deemed necessary for one man to whisper to another that a doctor has been out delivering a child, only the tip-off phrase 'both doing well' being audible. This absurdity is addressed by Violet Pearn in *Hush!*, where a young wife is 'so badgered into reticence about her baby before it is born that she cannot get out of being ashamed of it after it is born'.[55]

H. V. Esmond's *The Law Divine* is more effective in its approach to marital difficulties, but, while dealing with the 'new woman' beloved of problem playwrights, it promotes love and marriage as no self-respecting problem play is supposed to do. It reverses the familiar situation of emotional deprivation resulting from a spouse's total absorption in business, since here it is the wife, altogether wrapped up in her war committees, who is in danger of losing her husband. He ruefully assures a girl that 'it's damned difficult to keep on loving a woman who thinks the most important thing in her bedroom is the telephone' (p. 29). Like Mrs Pankhurst, the preoccupied heroine even postpones suffragism until after the war. But it is the war, or at least an air raid, which finally brings her to her senses. The idea that everyone should seek shelter is upset first comically: 'There's blackbeetles in the cellar, so cook's gone back to bed'; then romantically, as the husband suggests that he and his wife repair upstairs. As he holds out his arms she comes to him shyly as a bride, pretending that her anxiety is due to the guns which have temporarily ceased their clamour. He murmurs reassuringly: 'If they come again – we'll hide our heads under the blanket – and let the blighters bomb.' The curtain descends as they kiss, then rises on an empty stage, while distant bugles sound a symbolic 'all clear' (pp. 71–2). According to Esmond, 'special permission had to be obtained from the authorities' for this air raid scene, 'not because of any matter of the "blue-pencil" needing kind', but to conform with DORA. Even so, it was described as 'daring in the extreme'.[56]

Although the stress of war was revitalizing some of the older values, this alone would not account for the play's 368 performances at Wyndham's. It offers an agreeable contrast to the turgid emptiness of sexual emancipation plays like Sutro's *Freedom*.[57] Yet while the latter reminds that not all opposition was grounded in the anti-Ibsenite view that problems 'have nothing to do with art',[58] there was a too-convenient identification of problems with tedium. Walter Saltoun's *The Girl Who Wouldn't Marry*, when it reached the Elephant and Castle, prompted the instructive comment: 'Were it in more pretentious surroundings it might easily be classed as a play with a purpose.' Whereas the plebs was supposedly oblivious to problems, critics reacted badly when, instead of having the values of their world reaffirmed, they were 'invited to listen to four acts on main drainage and the housing question or the relationship of sweated industries to prostitution'.[59] The Lodge Percys' *The Heart of a Shop-Girl* seems to have pleased Brixton audiences more than some of the critics. Sexual harassment today has become so all-inclusive as to lose meaning. But this play represents an extreme form, and evidently irritated because of its refusal to defer to any hierarchical principle: 'Even the worst of employers could not devote the whole of his time to making improper overtures to the ladies behind his counter nor tolerate the presence of promiscuous old colonels [with] a facetious interest in underwear.'[60] But sexual harassment (even when, as here, its victim is manoeuvred into prison for clinging too tenaciously to her virtue) attracted little attention, whereas the government had given sexual disease high priority. As a result, Ibsen's *Ghosts* and (especially) Brieux's *Damaged Goods* became theatrical moneyspinners. The latter might 'not be a "play" in the technical sense, but it most certainly grips you, and thereby answers the whole purpose of the theatre, which is to divert you – whether it does so by appealing to your laughter or your tears, or any of your social interests'.[61] Confronted with this phenomenon, A. Campbell, who thought the war not wholly bad if it had brought about the 'Death of the Problem Play', has to remove them from that category: 'They are thesis plays – pathological ... rather than amorist.'[62]

Far from seeing, in Campbell's words, the end of 'the Drama of Gloom', the theatres were enjoying what another columnist dubbed a 'Gloom boom'.[63] In the wartime career of the problem play *Damaged Goods* is pivotal. It answered both of the necessary criteria, making a lot of money and posing problems and offering solutions in accordance with current orthodoxies. Such matter remained only a relatively small part of wartime theatre production, yet the huge success of *Damaged Goods* brought a spate of what were now called propaganda plays: 'there seems a probability that almost every evil under the sun will ere long be shown up by means of a stage production written for that express purpose ... Whether the theatre is the proper medium for the exposure of social evils or doubtful practices is an open question; but such plays as "Tainted Goods" may be cited as offering the most striking contrast possible to the frivolous type of contemporary stage productions.'[64] The latter play, by Clifford Rean, blatantly designed to cash in on the success of *Damaged Goods*, similarly stresses how ignorance of the world is a prime cause of trouble: 'There is plenty of time for girls to learn the realities of life after they are married.'[65] A brilliant woman doctor of the new stamp warns how 'Thousands of babies' are consigned annually to blindness caused by congenital gonorrhoea, because neither the law nor society will 'strip the question of sex of its vile secrecy' (p.102).

That play was at the Dalston almost simultaneously with the same author's *Ignorance* at Stratford's Theatre Royal. *Ignorance* goes far to confirm that Rean was less interested in social enlightenment than in riding a bandwagon. The man of the family is at the Front, and those left at home exhibit all the clichéd problems: 'the mother with a craving for drink',[66] a son whose large earnings 'on munitions' turn him to betting and crime, 'the youngest girl, whose one desire is to "go to the pictures" ', and her sister seduced by the slum landlord. Only one child has struggled free of ignorance to become a schoolteacher, joining with those other authority figures, doctor and vicar, in an attempt to bring light to her benighted family.[67] Patronizing triteness rules.

Although a welcome relief from overworked sexual themes, *Retribution*, an anti-vivisection play, seems curiously ill-timed during a horrific war when experimental surgery had an endless supply of human subjects. Besides, whatever gross exploitation of animals was taking place in the laboratory hardly matches the terror and suffering to which unwitting horses were exposed on the battlefield. These war horses, too, were being used to bolster huge commercial interests, the most compelling argument against vivisection. However, argument weighs no more here than it does in similarly contrived recruiting plays, the doctor's conversion from vivisection resulting from the death of his daughter, after accidentally cutting herself with the knife he has used on a cat.[68] Even more remarkable in the 1914–18 context is Eugene Walter's *The Knife*, which raises the question: 'Should the bodies of criminals be used in place of those of heroic volunteers for medical experiment?' This is considered well worth raising 'when comrades and nurses are risking their lives daily in the transference of blood and so on'. It is an American play, in American hybrid style: part problem play, part crook melodrama; so the ethical question is snarled up with a revenge plot. A doctor's sweetheart is abducted and raped and the doctor (Aubrey Smith) proposes to use the perpetrators in his research instead of handing them over to the police. Once again the drug issue comes into play, one of the criminals being a 'dope fiend'.[69] He is also credited with second sight; so the heroine, a Virginia girl who has absorbed black superstition from her mammy, falls an easy victim.[70]

Hence the play caters for yet another current preoccupation, that fascination with spiritualism which, stimulated by Darwin, greatly intensified during the war. An entire page of the *Weekly Dispatch* (27 August 1916, p. 5) was shared by those ardent spiritualists Sir Oliver Lodge and actress Estelle Stead in providing hope for the bereaved. These at least were genuine in their desire to help people; but there were hordes of 'harpies, posing as clairvoyants, spirit-controlled mediums, crystal-gazers, and fortune-tellers' fastening on to anxious or grieving relatives of soldiers at the Front, many of the victims paying money they could ill afford to have 'protective thoughts' sent out there or to receive messages from the dead. Apart from being fleeced, warned 'Olivia' (*Sphere* 24 February 1917, p. ii), people risked mental, moral and physical damage from dabbling in the occult. It was in part to frustrate this knavery that 'The Golden Gipsy' made a timely appearance on the stage. Upon a glass platform, fully lit, she reproduced 'all the most convincing tests of the mediums', emphasizing that there was nothing supernatural about her act (describing unknown objects 'dropped by spectators into a box suspended above her head [being] merely an odd sense that anyone can acquire').[71]

There is no need to trace interest in the subject on the legitimate stage beyond a few instances. It would certainly have been a large part of the appeal of *Peter Ibbetson*, adapted by John Raphael from George du Maurier's novel, and given at His Majesty's in aid of the Allied Forces' Base Hospital at Étaples. Constance Collier, who was deeply involved in the production, and S. R. Littlewood found the final scene of reunion in the Other World while earthbound characters weep over a deathbed both finely realized and a 'very spiritual and uplifting approach to death'.[72] In quite different vein is Bayard Veiller's *The Thirteenth Chair*. De Courville, who brought it from America, describes how 'the thrills come from spiritualistic seances in which the audience will, as it were, take part ... Speaking for myself, I have never seen a play which held me so spellbound throughout. It ran a year in New York, and there are six companies on the road out there.'[73] The medium (Mrs Patrick Campbell 'admirable ... as the instinctive, quick-witted woman on the defence') has been hired not to contact the dead but to assist in the trapping of a murderer. She is pretty honest about her profession: 'most of the time it is tricks with even the best of us', though she had experienced inexplicable things, 'messages from them that 'ave passed on'. But this happens seldom and unpredictably: 'if you waited for it you would starve to death.'[74] Walter Hackett's *The Barton Mystery* utilizes clairvoyancy, by way of a more dubious medium, to solve a murder. The charlatan rôle gave H. B. Irving's 'fantastic humour a splendid opportunity'; he revelled in cunning opportunism, while the re-enactment of the murder, where psychic powers unexpectedly come into play, was 'breathlessly exciting'.[75]

These latter plays belong in the crime category, to be considered later. First, the major contribution of comedy needs to be examined. In the early phase Louis Parker's adaptation of *David Copperfield* was outstanding. Tree triumphed in the parts of Micawber and Dan'l Peggotty: 'our greatest living character-actor ... has never for sheer rich, broad humour beaten his Micawber. And assuredly never for gentle, homely fun and intense pathos has he ever excelled his Dan'l Peggotty.'[76] Nares, who had the title part, describes how Tree managed both rôles by means of a lift concealed in an enormous mast fixed centre stage, a double emerging from behind the mast to saunter slowly off as

Peggotty. As he disappeared, Tree, 'as Micawber, thrust his head through a ... hatch in another part of the deck'.[77]

Haddon Chambers's *The Saving Grace*[78] has at its centre a Micawberish retired colonel managing to break down the opposition of a titled matriarch to her son's union with his niece. The same concern with yoking ill-matched fortunes governs Douglas Murray's *The Man from Toronto,* though there is also some toying with class issues. The heroine disguises herself as her own servant, the fad for mistaken identity plots at this time doubtless having sombre roots in war experience. She tells her Canadian admirer: 'I needn't be a servant if I don't want to be, but I think it's ripping. Before I started I never thought domestic life could be so jolly!'; but the real servant, who has been kissed by a house guest, makes the difference fairly clear: 'When a gentleman kisses a girl like me, we know what 'e's up to and we like it because it makes us feel that our flesh ain't dirt any more than 'is is.'[79] But it is more effectively handled in Jerome K. Jerome's *Cook,* when a gentleman unknowingly spends an evening with his cook: 'I'm sorry, sir. Of course, if you had been an ordinary gentleman, I should have guessed what had happened and have put you right. But – well, you being a Socialist, sir, and remembering all you've said and written about the absurdity of class distinctions, it did just occur to me that perhaps you did know who I was, and that it made no difference to you.' And she is tart when he foolishly asks if she has 'always been a cook': 'I wasn't born one.'[80] Indeed, the only thing wrong with this cook is that she is 'Just the sort of young woman that makes you fancy things ain't so bad as they are' (p. 76).

During the Depression, Hollywood peddled the idea that rich people are just poor people with money. But the war was a period when Britain's manipulators found it expedient at once to emphasize and minimize class difference. A nice stage example of having it both ways is provided by Besier's *Kings and Queens.* It is not much of a play, but critical responses are interesting. Clearly 'the author, by inserting on the programme the quotation "My dears, they have five fingers on each hand, And take their meals regularly" wishes to instruct us that kings and queens are very much like other people'.[81] But it is objected: 'If you show your personages ... in the aspect wherein they are just like anybody else, why trouble to give them Royal labels? The answer is that Kings and Queens are not, and cannot be, *exactly* like other people even in their private lives.' What this *Times* reviewer (18 January 1915, p. 5), too refined to notice anything as disagreeable as money, fails to mention is that the difference lies in wealth, which means power and prestige. His *Athenæum* colleague (23 January 1915, p. 78) is similarly restive at royals being shown as far below average 'in intelligence and behaviour' when they are 'rightly expected to be well above it'. When the Queen Mother 'bullies her daughter-in-law, just as though the pair were Mrs. Brown and Mrs. Brown, jnr., of

Brixton, we begin to wonder whether Mr. Besier is not confusing likeness to the common people with identity'. Even if 'Marie Löhr's Queen is nearer the average girl we know than the dignified goddess we expect anyone of royal rank to be,' writes another, 'the average middle-class theatre-goer is flattered at being shown royalty thus humanized, and at finding he has so much in common with the "highly born" '. Yet another critic, noting that the play appealed to those 'who dearly love a lord and who read "society" papers', adds optimistically: 'This terrible War is creating an entirely new aristocracy, an aristocracy of worth and deeds, and one of its finest results will be a total disregard for the label on the box, be the label never so attractive.'[82]

The changes wrought by war apparently impeded the success of Maugham's wartime productions. Revival of his 1913 play, *The Land of Promise,* was considered 'risky', it being 'as primitive as "The Taming of the Shrew" '.[83] Indeed it ended after 60 performances, barely a third of the pre-war number. It was his 'cynicism' which was thought to have limited his 'brilliant, witty society comedy' *Caroline* to 142 performances.[84] Newton had expected 'the wisdom of the worldly and the gospel of the bored' which it projects to make an appealing contrast with 'this genuine, industrious, anxious War life of ours'.[85] And real success eluded him again when *Love in a Cottage* ended after 127 performances at the Globe. This play promoted 'the old lesson that money is a delusion and a snare'. But *The Times* reviewer (28 January 1918, p. 9), commenting on the way that the heroine's suitors largely disappear on learning that she will lose her money on marrying, considers Maugham 'rather harsh ... to hold them up to contempt. It is certain that if matrimony always beggared both parties, the marriage-rate would appreciably decline.'

Without Maugham's reputation, Henry Maltby had great difficulty in arousing interest in *The Rotters.* In his introduction to the text he describes how he wrote it in 1915, though it was not until July of the next year that he persuaded the manager of a repertory company in New Brighton, Cheshire to play it for a week. It was a hit, and there followed a production at the Garrick (86 performances) and provincial tours continuing for a decade. Maltby gives two reasons for the initial lack of interest. It was a 'pioneer' in dealing with a family of 'nasty' people, and readers mistook his 'broad comedy ... for a problem play'.[86] In reality, only Clugston senior, head of what the sub-title ironically terms 'a respectable family', is nasty. His youngest child, thought 'to have learnt a lot' at the school from which she has just been expelled, explains that her contrivances and duplicities were acquired at home: 'When you've got a father who thinks it is a sin to breathe, you've got to learn how to live by artificial respiration' (p. 40). Mrs Clugston's shortcomings seem limited to having a vague fancy for the chauffeur and failing to disclose that she has had a previous husband, both faults a direct consequence of Clugston's obsessive respectability. The play was regarded in *The Times* (31 July 1916, p. 9) as neither particularly interesting nor pioneering; rather, it seemed a familiar type 'in which Town Councillors do furiously rage, and impossibly stern parents have incredibly naughty children and the Lancashire accent can be cut with a knife. It is a formula [threatening] to become as conventional as the formula of Mayfair manners and epigrammatic dukes which it superseded.' This is no more perceptive than taking its burden to be 'that parents who worship respectability are cursed with peculiarly disreputable children'. Although these uses of the plural seem to inculpate Mrs Clugston, she is neither severe nor a worshipper of respectability. Clugston is a hypocrite, a dishonest lout who operates with some success in a world as morally bankrupt as himself. In a race for mayoral office he has discredited one opponent (described as 'very nice' by Mrs Clugston, though caught in the wrong bed), and is now defending himself against similar attempts by another rival. Scandal threatens because his son has been caught at illicit gambling. A police inspector arrives to explain that the arresting constable 'didn't know who he was, or that his father was on the Bench'. But when his identity became known, a second charge of resisting arrest (necessitated because he was in slightly battered condition) was dropped. The inspector is well disposed towards Clugston, who has 'always convicted every case' brought before him, 'without sifting the evidence – as some does', so advises him on suborning the press. A few shafts of this kind add piquancy to the fun.[87]

There was also good fun to be had from Maltby's all-woman farce, *Petticoats*, with 'women taking possession of the State in the absence of the men, yet secretly longing for the men to come back'. But reviewers' unease over its 'light-hearted jokes about the war', only partly mollified by the fact that Maltby had been a bombardier in France, may have communicated itself to the public.[88] All the humour about a woman-dominated society (lady lawyers, doctors, even parsons) is present by implication in Zangwill's *Too Much Money*, another farce which met with undeserved failure. All reference to the war is excluded, yet it takes its inspiration from current circumstances: 'Man being so thoughtless as to make war, has left his place open to woman, and she has occupied it.' Massingham, in his searching review, traces the graph of the play where Mrs Broadley exhibits all

> the caprice of despotism. Given money for the adornment of her person and the satisfaction of her whims, and having nothing to do with the making of it, she can become a monster of affectation and extravagance, ... Evicted from her pleasure-house, and presented with the choice of work or starvation, she will hoard pence like a miser, and when she has learned what money can do, become drunk with the power of it, and still use man as her footstool.

The same tendency shows in the other women: one controls her artist-husband, keeping 'his honesty down and his prices up', and another loses 'patience with her man as soon as his plays begin to succeed'.[89] For Massingham, the play's one real deficiency is a lack of tenderness 'both to the general absurdities of life, and to the rascals who feed upon them'. But Shakespeare's Falstaff, the example chosen for elaboration, is only one possible model. Zangwill moves in a quite different direction opting, like Maltby, for alienation,[90] and has no qualms about giving his farce a satirical edge.

But a spice of satire, like Maugham's mildly cynical outlook, was something which 'Our English entrepreneurs' put little faith in. Anxious to 'run as little risk as possible', they looked to the lightweight star vehicle for the coveted long run.[91] *The Stage* (27 July 1916, p. 16) noted that the average run of pieces in the West End during 1915–16 had been longer than the previous year, more theatres had been open and there had been 47 pieces produced by British (excluding colonial) authors as against 28 the previous year. But one favoured (profitable) line was American sentimental comedy, things like *Romance, Peg o' My Heart*[92] and *Daddy Long-Legs*. Although they will hardly stand close analysis, 'in each there is a freshness of observation and characterisation. Moreover each play enables the principal actress to make a distinct success'. Although no more than 'the average number of American plays was produced', their success rate might suggest an 'American invasion'.[93] That was certainly Farjeon's impression: 'London is being deluged with American farces, and the British Drama is in a state of siege. We should have thought that there was enough trouble in Europe already [and] that this bombardment even constituted a breach of neutrality.'[94] Although the acting in Zellah Covington and Jules Simonson's *Three Spoonfuls* was 'full of push and go', he found 'the types portrayed ... so American as to be completely unfamiliar to us'. But these were early days of colonization; later on such things would become as familiar as stage representations of the British scene.

Although an analysis of runs for 1917 suggested that comedies and farces could be 'rather hazardous speculations',[95] with a good deal of 'stronger fare' on view as the taste for 'war melodramas' increased,[96] in general light comedy and farce were amongst the war's most successful forms. The popularity of light comedy is largely owed to market strategies, but that of farce is more complex. The 1915 Chaplin craze came about not simply because Chaplin had found a perfect vehicle in that little tramp figure, or even because the war was allowing Hollywood to gain world dominance in the film industry. But war *is* a major factor in provoking a special need to escape from moral responsibility. This is why the war years found farce so congenial on stage and screen, why the zany humour of the halls moves so smoothly into mainstream theatre through the medium of revue. Not the least source of strain during the war, for those whose sense of moral dislocation went deeper than a prurient concern with what munition-girls got up to on a Saturday night, was the way in which it was sanctioning every kind of dirty trick. Generations of public schoolboys had been educated in the fair-play ethic, only to be told that its operation must be suspended during hostilities. The way that the abandonment of values so carefully instilled produced disorientation is indicated by a letter from a Q-ship commander to his superior, Captain Herbert Richmond of the Admiralty Special Service Branch, asserting that the order to take no prisoners was 'damnable'.[97] Those theatrical offerings which traded on suspension of moral responsibility were escapist in a very special way. Ellis's *A Little Bit of Fluff*, the most successful farce of the war years, undoubtedly took leave of such responsibility. That it largely took leave of ingenuity in its complications and wit in its dialogue seems not to have mattered since the opening night audience, and evidently many more, roared at its nonsense loud enough to drown 'a Zeppelin raid'.[98] One reviewer noted, apropos of Avery Hopwood's successful *Fair and Warmer*: 'The farce-writer has his privileges, and among them is the immunity with which he can present situations which would shock in actual life.'[99]

However, such immunity was circumscribed by the censor. He rejected the title of the American farce, *Twin Beds*, by Field and Mayo; so it appeared at the Apollo as *Be Careful, Baby*. The play is quite innocuous, but Farjeon's description of the 'heart-fluttering' set makes it clear why the title was changed: 'are not those twin beds an earnest of all those farcical complications which any confirmed farce-goer has a right to expect?'[100] A line about twin beds ('so noticeably alongside each other. Looks too suspicious') was amongst those censored in Lawrence Cowen's *Double Dutch*. Several about growing sexually overheated ('You had better go and sit on the refrigerator') were blue-pencilled, along with definition of a wife as 'a sort of connection' and superficial acquaintance with a woman as 'all on the outside'. Exception was taken to dialogue about God having denied a couple children: 'You leave an important matter like that to a third party! Haven't you read ... Smiles on "Self-Help"?' But with deletions of this kind the play was passed in 1916; and at the Apollo the next year audiences found it very amusing, though *The Stage's* critic (12 April 1917, p. 14) wanted lines about busts and figures 'toned down'. Interestingly, the censor's reader Street claimed that 1917 had seen public opinion swing against suggestiveness and the play should now be banned as 'extremely repugnant to the taste of the time'; but a visit to the Apollo caused a further *volte face* due to 'the real funniness of the chief comedian, Mr. Bentley, and the fresh and graceful playing of Miss Dorothy Minto'.[101] Reassuringly, the humour of *Double Dutch* was not 'of that saucy Frenchy kind we have had foisted upon us in some plays'.[102] Seemingly, only the French had the 'gift of being improper without being improper';[103] so

Arnold Bennett and his wife, 'a Parisian to her finger-tips', could enjoy 'the fun' of Pierre Wolff's *Dieu! Que les hommes sont bêtes*, which 'the censor wouldn't pass' in English.[104]

Sight gags involving dress and undress ran into intricate taboos. A neat example is supplied by a Pavilion sketch, *Temptation*, with Harry Pilcer as the gambler and Teddie Gerard as the Spirit of Gaming: 'There is a good deal of bodily contortion and some squirming about Pilcer's realisation of amorous infatuation, but the thrill of the sketch is reached when the satyr-like victim of play chases the tempter round the stalls. As she gets back to the footlights he clutches her dress, but she escapes him, leaving a portion of the diaphanous robe in his hands.' Terry (*Era* 10 March 1915, p. 12) adds that decency was not offended, though Mrs Grundy 'must have had some anxious moments during the progress of this "high art" production'. This suggests how anxiety rather than titillation is to the fore; indeed, the act was somewhat modified in later performances, having caused some people *too much* anxiety. Both responses are implicit in a comment on Morton and Niccodemi's *Remnant*, to the effect that Hilda Moore's *peignoir* requires 'such frequent adjustment that we gather that she would be bitterly disappointed if we went away with the idea that she had anything on underneath it but her decorative "nightie" '. The same critic considers the start of Gallon and Lion's *Felix Gets a Month*, with Felix 'stretching his arm through the window and helping himself to a sofa-cover' to hide his nakedness, not very happy: 'The suggestion of partial or total nudity on the stage is an exclusively feminine privilege not to be rashly usurped by the mere male.'[105] Where both sexes are involved, even though only in the imagination, the censor, an especially sensitized embodiment of audience anxiety, is particularly heavy-handed. The climax of Fred Rome's one-act farce, *What a Change*, comes with a curate and his wife and Jim the bookie having to exchange clothes following a sartorial mix-up. They do so in a darkened room at a police station, and 'the remarks heard from the bookmaker and the curate's wife suggest all sorts of nastiness' to the censor.[106] Had it been left in its original form the result on stage would have been amusing enough. Clearly 'Steady on, Missis, yer tickling my beauty spot' and 'Oh lor! I've shoved my finger in the ink pot' were inadmissible; but it was over-fastidious to remove 'Horace, my love, how do these – er – garments – unbutton?' Out, too, went the wife's 'Oh – who is that tickling my legs? *Curate*: It is only me, I am looking for my stud. *Jim (Tearing sound heard)*: Lummee, I've torn all the lace off one leg. *Curate*: Dear me, whatever's that? *Jim*: That's my funny bone, Guv'nor.' Even the denouement is marked in blue. However, this episode, where Jim has dressed and left the room with the clothes of the other two, raising the blind to reveal them 'dressed only in bathing costumes', survived when Joe Elvin appeared as Jim at the Camberwell Palace.[107]

But, as already intimated, the official censor was not the only force of conservatism in the theatre, or even the most troublesome. Managers and critics could be still more damaging; indeed it was the former who, when the Lord Chamberlain was hard beset in 1909, petitioned in his support ensuring that Britain would not follow the French example of dispensing with an official censor. Managers clearly feared that abolition of a government censorship would only add to the uncertainties of their professional activity. For the same reason they frequently deferred to the staider critics in the national press, as if those critics were mouthpieces of public opinion. Although his own weekly was only too happy to participate, trial by the press is something Belcham deplores when writing of 'Mrs. Grundy in America', [108] where she is assumed to have journeyed but recently, braving U-boats. It perhaps suits him to ignore the fact that she was amongst the matrons accompanying the Pilgrim Fathers so that he may set a fresh aberration beside that of America's failing to join us in the war to end war. The lady's latest folly concerned the Ballets Russes at New York's Century Theatre. That city's *Tribune* critic found *Schéhérazade* demoralizing; even to those north of the Mason–Dixon line: 'the remarkable impersonation of the negro favourite of Zobeida by M. Bolm was repulsive. Yet it is a scene whose Oriental splendour, colour, animality, and lust will long remain with all who saw it.' Of *L'Après-midi d'un faune* it was recalled that at its Paris première 'Nijinsky was hissed off the stage', and now Bolm's impersonation was hardly less disturbing: 'humorous, natural, and – well, Greek.' Such reviews brought a strong reaction from the Catholic Theatre Movement and intervention from the magistracy, the latter forcing modification of the orgy scene in *Schéhérazade* and requiring Bolm's faun to restrict himself to kissing the nymph's scarf instead of falling upon it. These scenes, insists Belcham, caused no qualms at Covent Garden just before the war, and left audiences enraptured. However, Beaumont remembers *L'Après-Midi* creating a sensation not only 'for its novelty of presentation' but for Nijinsky's final audacity: the audience gasped when he 'proceeded slowly to recline, face downwards, on the scarf'.[109] But there was no call for changes, so thus far Belcham is justified in pointing a contrast with events in America. His main thrust is against local and 'spasmodic bowdlerising'. But his rebuke of America's Catholic organization might have been addressed more profitably to Britain's equivalent when it forced the premature withdrawal of Knoblauch's *Marie-Odile* the previous year, though he kept his head down during that sorry affair.

Events in New York prove that, in the midst of all that Bakstian colour-in-motion, the old folk-tales had not lost their bite. It might even be cause for satisfaction that the Ballets Russes aroused controversy instead of being received with the awe due to 'great art'. Presumably it was some such awe which allowed the sensuality to pass in London, like Victorian acceptance of the classical nude. Indeed, like that classicism, the Ballets Russes were conveniently distanced from British standards of respectability, for this was 'a company whose inherent savagery had not yet been dulled by prolonged absence from Russia'.[110] At any rate, there is no question about the company's popularity over here. When Stoll brought it across war-torn Europe, the proposed six-week season at the Coliseum extended to over six months. Although Bolm and Karsavina had left the company, in *Schéhérazade* ('undoubtedly the most popular item in their extensive repertoire'),[111] there was Massine who, avoiding Nijinsky's explosive animalism, 'hovered about Zobeida with quick nervous steps and caressing gestures in the manner of the true voluptuary'. Then there was Lopokova, supreme comedienne of the dance. She excelled as an airy Columbine in *Carnaval*, a 'mischievous variation on the theme of the *commedia dell'arte*'.[112] The latter form made a strong appeal outside the ballet, silent cinema ensuring that the conventions of mime were well appreciated. The success of the wartime revival of *L'Enfant prodigue* resulted in a flurry of such pieces in both the regular theatre and the music hall. A puff pastry of humour and pathos drew audiences to the spectacle of Pierrot's thwarted love in Ferdinand Belasier's *A Pierrot's Christmas* and Sybille Ginner's *Et Paris bon-soir*, in which Ginner herself played the ill-fated Pierrot.[113]

The belief, widespread in more advanced theatrical circles, in physical expression over the verbal was probably assisted by the latter's having become contaminated through new excesses of official lying. Body movement, an equally effective conveyor of messages, was not necessarily more immediate and spontaneous, but had not thus far been subject to the same debasement. Whether or not this encouraged Pierrot plays, that they were a step away from the tyranny of the text is undeniable. Along with Victorian rhetoric had gone a whole rich vocabulary of gesture, replaced by an understatement which is hamstrung without speech. The theatre's imprisonment in text was in large measure due to the critics and theorists achieving an unholy alliance between Shakespeare and Victorian naturalism. This naturalism was designed for 'the class of playgoer who would be as uncomfortable in a morality that was not ready-made as he would be in a suit of clothes that was'. It was theatrical form as well as moral content which had to be ready-made to fit him.[114] Fortunately, he had a more redoubtable opponent than Pierrot in Bernard Shaw. Shaw's campaign for something of the recognition in this country which he had already won in Germany and the USA was one of the most notable features of the London theatre in the first decade of the century. By 1914 his position was assured.

But if Shaw, like 'most of our important dramatists', went into 'hibernation' during the war, this was not as Grein alleged, 'because art needs clear vision, and for the time all is cloudy and obscure'.[115] Authority would allow him scope for only the occasional gnat-bite, though he must have been working on his finest and most Chekhovian play, *Heartbreak House,* which London saw in 1921. Chekhov himself was largely invisible except for his slighter pieces. The one-act *Proposal* had its British première at the Birmingham Rep in 1916;[116] and *The Bear,* updated version of the Widow of Ephesus and somewhat off-key, where grieving widows had become an awful commonplace, accompanied a film programme at the Scala in 1914.[117] But Chekhov, as supreme poet of inertia, was represented only by a Dublin production of *Uncle Vanya* in February 1917. Inertia was too much at odds with the vitalist flavour of the war period. Yet *Vanya's* mood of degradation, beyond the saving reach of grief or horror, is dangerously expressive of that deadening futility which lay behind the febrile energies and excitements.

Other Russians received brief airings, though their works were so much at odds with the safe offerings of the commercial theatre that one was scandalously deleted from a Russia's Day matinée at the Alhambra. This was Evreinov's *The Theatre of the Soul* (1912), due to be given by Edith Craig's Pioneer Players but summarily banned by manager Charlot on the morning of the matinée. In the introduction to her (and Marie Potapenko's) translation of the play, Christopher St John[118] mentions how Charlot's business manager advised against submitting the play to the censor: it would not be passed, and was in any case unfit 'for the Alhambra audience'. She chose to interpret this as meaning that it contained 'neither inanity nor nudity', pointing out that it was not intended for an Alhambra audience, but for distinguished supporters of Russia's Day. So it was left to Charlot, after watching the final dress rehearsal, to issue what even *Era* (24 November 1915, p. 15) saw as a 'calculated slight' to artists of the calibre of Ethel Levey and Lillian Braithwaite who had been rehearsing for three weeks. However, their efforts were not wasted; Churchill's mother availed herself of the production at a Shaftesbury matinée in aid of the servicemen's buffet at London Bridge station soon afterwards. Craig's production was striking: the three entities of the soul were reduced to 'faces appearing at different levels out of intense darkness. The heart was represented by a glowing red space which appeared to pulsate owing to an effect of light. The concepts of the women were seen in the foreground and were brilliantly lighted.' They are products of the protagonist's subjectivity, the conflict occurring between his rational and emotional perceptions while the subliminal dozes. 'The idea was ingenious, and well supported by the double presentation of the man's wife as in one guise a shrew and in the other a noble sufferer; and of the dancer as in one guise lovely and witty, in the other a horrible hag.'[119] The 'horrible hag' is exposed by the old device of stripping off beauty's trappings, in this version stopping short at teeth and wig. One rumour had it 'that it was the repulsive incident of a woman's wig being taken off', displaying her bald head, which provoked Charlot's intervention;[120] but it was in reality a clash of ideologies, the dominant ideology, commercial theatre, refusing hospitality to an alternative even in the name of wartime charity. Staider critics were resistant both to Evreinov's form and to his Freudian exposure of murky impulses. One complains that the conflict is of so 'sordid a nature as to be unworthy of treatment, although the unreflecting majority might be cajoled by the supreme cleverness of staging and presentation'; and another splutters about 'schoolboy rubbish with a strong dash of bad taste'.[121] There is seldom any sense that 'bad taste' on stage can sometimes prove illuminating; much less that no stage event could be so murkily impelled or so monumentally tasteless as the European conflict. Not that the idea of man destroyed by the irreconcilable elements of his own nature is the play's prime motive; though even for *The Times* reviewer (9 March 1915), who finds it 'original and interesting', it is 'ruined by the postulate that the emotional side of a man craves nothing but low vice'. He is much nearer the mark when, on renewed acquaintance (4 December 1915, p. 11), he discovers the leg-pulling element which coexists with the cynicism, something most of these critics miss. The introductory section is not primarily a way in to the play but a parody of academic discourse. Yet *The Stage's* reviewer (11 March 1915, p. 21) declares the professor's lecture 'far too abstruse for the ordinary audience', though such an audience might have related that basic image of the train journey and communication between emotions and brain by telephone to the zany Futurism of Harry Tate's 'Motoring' sketch. Absurdity triumphs over bourgeois realism as the subliminal unconcernedly leaves the train at the end of the journey either indifferent or not noticing that this is no scheduled stop but a comi-tragic derailment. When the emotional entity strangles the rational and uses the telephone to persuade the self to suicide, Evreinof both takes advantage of the high drama of the well-made play and parodies it relentlessly.

Although groups like the Pioneer Players gave too few performances ever to aspire to being a people's theatre, they managed to keep in view an alternative to the commercial mainstream. The Pioneers introduced another of Evreinov's plays, *The Merry Death*, where Harlequin derides bourgeois anxiety over death.[122] For him it is a consummation devoutly to be wished now that he has sung all his songs, laughed all his laughter and revelled away all his merriment. Pierrot's direct address explodes social along with theatrical convention: 'I'm a betrayed husband, and ought to revenge myself, because all nice people do.' Then, shaking his fist at the audience: 'Bad, wicked people, it's you thought out such silly rules! It's because of you I've got to take the life of my best friend!' This would have had sombre point in 1916, as he literally turns his back on the audience. At the end he drifts out of his rôle as Pierrot, speaking confidentially and apologetically. If the author preaches that nothing in life is to be taken seriously, then neither his play nor audience response to it is of consequence. Even now 'Harlequin has probably risen from his deathbed, ... tidying himself in anticipation of a call'. One perceptive critic found it 'an engaging mixture of the grotesque and macabre', perhaps a shade 'pretentious, but ... rare and exciting'. With unconscious irony Newton pronounced it 'typically Russian in its complete lack of a sense of humour'.[123] Another agreeable little satire put on by these Players was Andreyev's *Dear Departing*.[124] It is slight enough and fails to manage a satisfactory resolution. But again it is pretty clear why they thought it worth presenting in those khaki days since it hits at the way people derive a theatrical frisson from the spectacle of apparently real tragedy.

They also gave Krasinski's *The Undivine Comedy* (c. 1832),[125] its grim pessimism spanning the gothic world of Bürger and the Expressionist nightmares of the early twentieth century. Krasinski's Shelleyan split-mindedness makes the bloodthirst of the new paganism only a re-enactment of that of the old Christian aristocracy, whose last bastion, fortress of the Holy Trinity, also hides its torture chambers. It would not have been difficult to see in the war between an old, decayed elite and a young, virile, yet equally compromised proletariat, not only an applicability to contemporary events in Russia but to the larger conflict between British conservative interests and PanGermanism.

Social realism, too, showed best in this society theatre. Before the war the Pioneers turned to Herman Heijermans, a Dutch Jew, for his best-known play, *The Good Hope*. The war saw them follow up that success with *The Hired Girl*, where again Heijermans shows his preoccupation with the effects of poverty. *The Hired Girl* personifies and personalizes the class war, the servant Marie being not only born into an inferior position but without any evident means for rising above it. Ugly and unloved, cunning rather than intelligent, she can only simmer with resentment at her mistress who, of like age, enjoys all the advantages of money, education and general admiration. Even love, wrote Hope, comes to the mistress 'as though by natural right';[126] and Marie, materially and emotionally starved, seizes a chance opportunity to bring her mistress to an equality of degradation. But Marie's experience, limited to the humiliations attending a life of drudgery, finds her unequipped to take real advantage of the situation. Hers is 'a sorry triumph, made more horrible by the relentless malignity with which she inflict[s] her petty persecutions upon her mistress'. The critics ignored the lessons of this, though Hope had never experienced a more revolting portrayal of the sex war than that on the husband's return, when the wife seeks to extract from him a confession of infidelity and so 'establish a precedent of forgiveness'.

There was also interest in what was regarded as continental decadence. Birkett Winning's adaptation of Daudet's novel, *Sapho,* was in the repertoire of more than one touring company, a girl in Hertfordshire writing to her POW boyfriend that she'd seen it: 'no wonder you didn't want me to read that book. I guess I read it now.'[127] In February 1918 the Pioneers moved in a similar direction with Pierre Louys's *Girl and the Puppet,* Edith Craig's 'colour schemes [being] beautiful and original'; though neither they nor the good acting could appease Newton, who denounced it as 'a dirty play', designed 'to tickle the palates of a (of course) crowded audience with suggestiveness'.[128] The Stage Society turned to D'Annunzio's *Dead City*. That he had been instrumental in bringing Italy into the war would have done nothing to damage the Society's success with his ingenious and florid first play, where the house of Atreus seems to cast its spell in an atmosphere heavy with pending adultery and incest, averted only by an impulsive act of sororicide. The parched Greek landscape was a contrast to the altogether harsher one, visited earlier by the Society when the Icelandic playwright Jóhann Sigurjónsson's *Eyvind of the Mountains* was put on. This climaxes with the protagonists going mad with starvation before recovering their wits and their old love as they die in the snow. One reviewer noted that 'the spectators were appalled by the horror of the scene', concluding that 'it is not the business of art to appal'.[129] He and most of his fellows were more comfortable within the limits imposed by commercial theatre; with a theatre of reassurance that people have control over their experience. It may be that, had there been more to appal on the London stage, there would have been a diminution of those appalling events being enacted just 200 kilometres from the Queen's Theatre.

Yet the capacity to break out was there if required: the always-popular Barrie could vie with the Russians (or revue) in theatrical self-consciousness. His occasional piece *A Strange Play*[130] opens in a law court, with the several cases being presented as separate episodes. Then there is a return to the court for sentencing, with a final confusion of fiction and reality as fines are exacted from the audience in the shape of war charity donations. This is amply prepared for as several of the episodes play around with conventional ideas of reality. In the first, Nelson Keys falls for a woman known to him only on film: 'She holds out her arms [but] can't break through the screen.' In some sense he will abandon the stage for the screen, the only way to reach her, appearing to enter a window through which she is visible: 'The picture changes to the interior of the room and we see Keys now as a genuine film figure.' In another episode the wife 'innocently speaks her stage directions except when they are within brackets'. 'I will burn it', she says of the letter in which Charles Hawtrey has announced his intention to murder husband Dion Boucicault; then continues: '*She finds there is no fireplace.* I don't think I'll burn it. I'll throw it out of the window. *She finds there is no window.*' Eventually she thinks of a way of foiling the plot: 'Dear, if I don't give him his cue, he won't be able to come on!' In the last episode of this matinée piece Barrie mocks society involvement in matinées, the curtain rising on an empty stage. The orchestra plays a few preliminary bars, but tails off; and the audience is left staring at the empty stage for long enough to realize that something is amiss. The prompter peeps out, agitated by the titled performers' disregard for time. The orchestra tries again, but there is another awkward pause before an 'extremely classy' lady flounces on in outdoor dress. The prompter, scandalized, tries to get her to withdraw; but, 'imperturbably good-natured', she reassures him: 'I'm not one of the actors, but I'm a friend of theirs.' She is delighted to hear that the audience can see her: 'How jolly for them!'; and, peering through her lorgnette, she spots a familiar face: 'Bobby, isn't it splendid of our *people* to come and play?' And he shouts back: 'Rippin'! Of course, they're the attraction.' When the titled players eventually appear, this lady seats herself at the side of the stage and comments on the action. Beaumont had adopted the same technique in his *c.* 1607 *Knight of the Burning Pestle*, and it was surely a revived taste for such things which caused the old play to be given as the 1919 Christmas production of the British Rhine Army Dramatic Company, despite the heavy censoring which must have been required.[131] Even so, Barrie was probably addressing a rather rearguard audience, one wedded to its illusions both within and without the theatre. No other British dramatist would have had the status, nerve or adroitness to mock society's stage pretensions while he was in the process of opening its collective purse.

The self-reflexive style had been adopted in Wilfred Blair's *Whimsies*, given by Horniman at Manchester's Gaiety, but not brought to the West End. A dramatist approaches the public to see what kinds of characters might find favour in his next production. An 'upper-class girl would like to see the kind of middle-class woman who is generally seen with parcels;[132] the middle-class woman fancies a butler, because she can't afford one; and the middle-class girl frankly announces that she does not approve of [the author's] plays at all, but might do so if he would renounce the usual set of impossible stage types' in favour of some who behave naturally. After the induction these characters transpose to 'the desired characters in the play', with ironic discordances and a riot of comic invention.[133] But Horniman's valuable work lost out to commercialism, her company's demise drawing mordant comment: 'As an illuminating sidelight on public taste it has to be recorded that the provincial company of "Romance" recently played at the Gaiety for eight weeks to an average of £1,000 per week, and returns next year for an unlimited season.'[134] Sheldon's *Romance* had been extremely successful in America before running for over 1000 performances at the Duke of York's, a record for an allegedly serious play. It is full of mawkish morality, its climactic third act (subject of 'an uproarious skit' in *Shell Out*)[135] requiring belief that a night of passion with an Italian diva will place the immortal soul in jeopardy. The protagonist, a bishop in the making, is brought to his senses and his future career preserved by the sound of a street choir improbably chanting 'Ein Feste Burg'. Although the play's cautionary tale of abnegation backfires (it is told by the old bishop to his grandson, who promptly rushes off to marry his actress-sweetheart), it warrants condemnation on grounds other than those of chapel morality. However, a certain Adelaide Farren, writing to *Referee* (8 September 1918, p. 3), evidently has this play in mind[136] along with Esmond's *The Law Divine*: 'Is it pleasant to be asked to give the name of "a clean play – something I can go with my son to see," or to sit through the exceedingly suggestive last act of a piece, played in semi-darkness, with a boy-officer by one's side, or to hear, on coming out, a wounded youngster ask, "Mother, who was Cora Pearl?"' (Surely it would not have strained the mother's moral sensibility unduly to answer that Pearl was a woman of unsavoury reputation whose father had written 'Kathleen Mavourneen'.)

Promotion is what gives *Romance* the edge over the altogether worthier productions of Horniman. Two with oblique relevance to wartime circumstances will suggest something of her activity in this final stage. The Glamorgan schoolmaster D. T. Davies's *Where Is He?*, which had its Welsh-language première at the Cripplegate on 5 February 1913, received its first production in English dress at the Gaiety on 4 September 1916, and Horniman brought it to the Court early the next year. The play turns 'upon the mental anguish of an orthodox chapel-going wife who has lost, in an accident, her heterodox husband, and cannot reconcile her sense of his human worth with the apprehensions as to his destiny conjured up by her gloomy creed'.[137] The reviewer might have noted that the husband has been turned off chapel by the trite words of consolation offered by the minister following his daughter's death;[138] what *is* noted is that the kind of heart-searching represented in the play had become all too common in the dark days of war. Horniman also premièred *'The Joan Danvers'*, by Frank Stayton, a lesser figure of the Manchester School. The title alludes to a ship owned by a wealthy Bristol merchant who, having insured her heavily, has no qualms about sending her company to its death since both ship and lifeboats are rotten, though given a lick of paint to deceive the inspector. He squares his conscience by attending church at least three times on Sunday and bullying his family into doing likewise. There are prospects of a seat in Parliament and a baronetcy: he is altogether a pillar of society, and the resemblance to Ibsen's play is hardly fortuitous. But the terse economy is not Ibsen's. There is crisp dialogue, fresh characterization, and even the patriarch can rise to a grim wit: told that his son has borrowed a sovereign from his daughter ostensibly to buy her a present, he remarks: 'James has the makings of a great financier.' James has been 'cooped up, stifled, caged' like his sisters in a household resembling a prison and a country 'so damned respectable it makes you sick'.[139] In running away on the *Joan Danvers* he serves as paradigm of those countless volunteers in 1914–15 who sought to escape the petty tyrannies of home and office and find adventure by donning khaki. Like them he jumps out of the frying-pan into the fire; and although there is no insistence on the *Joan Danvers* as ship of state, it may be that an author who had been 'wounded at the Dardanelles'[140] hesitated about showing that ship to founder. Even so, it is a pity that he followed Ibsen in ending on a note of reconciliation.

After its disappearance from Manchester, it was the Jackson–Drinkwater regime at Birmingham which did most (on the mainland at least) to keep the repertory flag flying.[141] In a Prefatory Note to Rupert Brooke's *Lithuania*, Drinkwater mentions the attention given to poetic drama at the Birmingham Rep, but points out that Brooke's playlet is in prose, aligning him 'with some of his fellow poets in believing that if poetic life was to be brought back into the modern theatre it would be in prose and not in verse form'.[142] Drinkwater did use blank verse for *X=0*, a Trojan War anecdote but reflecting 1917 war-weariness as soldiers kill out of duty when the cause is forgotten. But he adopted prose for *Abraham Lincoln*, a play acknowledging America's recent entry into the war while using her civil war as distancing device. Lincoln serves to show how total commitment to the war may coexist with compassion. He deals magisterially with the question of reprisals, and effectively rebukes the warmonger: 'I accepted this war with a sick heart, and I've a heart that's near to breaking every day. I accepted it in the name of humanity, ... And you come to me, talking of revenge and destruction, and malice, and enduring hate.' As he continues, the doubling of Germany with the South is particularly telling: 'These gentle people are mistaken, but they are mistaken cleanly, and in a great name. It is you that dishonour the cause for which we stand – it is you who would make it a mean and little thing.'[143] It is strange that Eden Phillpotts's *The Farmer's Wife*, given at Birmingham in 1916, had to wait until 1924 for a London production. It plays with the clichés of unsophisticated courtship ritual, but there is a solidity of observation and moments of low-key wit which make it the perfect complement of bright and elegant comedies like A. A. Milne's *Belinda*.[144] The Birmingham Rep also premièred on 14 April 1917 Gilbert Cannan's one-act *Everybody's Husband*, which cleverly contrasts 'the romantic ideals of marriage and the sardonic facts that lie in wait', the scene ironically laid in a young woman's bedroom on the eve of her marriage. There is a lovely dispute with the bride-to-be's grandmother, who still wears the crinolines of her girlhood: 'I don't wonder you have forgotten that you have legs, with a 5-barred fence all round you.' Pondering whether her granddaughter's outburst is 'the effect of bi-cycles', the old woman is told: 'And motor-cycles, and cars, and aeroplanes – Certainly I have legs. Look at them!'; and the ample display as she bounds on to her bed prompted the censor to call for 'discretion'.[145]

Of the commercial theatre, there remains to be considered melodrama and the war play. The former, combining the discords of hearty, even callous, humour and blood and thunder thrills, was enjoying a revival.[146] It had its clichés of language as well as action, the vehement 'No, a thousand times no' achieving popular semi-comic currency. Such lines needed a style of acting which was rapidly on the wane; but then, so did Shakespeare. Genevieve Ward's playing of Margaret in 'Shakespeare's Melodrama' *Richard III* represented 'a survival of the high days of Shakespearean acting'.[147] A clash of styles was noted at a celebrity matinée of *Henry VIII* when Owen Nares 'played Cromwell with great sincerity, but with the curiously ultra-modern note in his voice that unfits him for Shakespearean plays'.[148] Ward could 'dominate the stage without rant and ... be distinctly heard without noise';[149] and there is no reason why naturalism's pursuit of intimacy should be at the expense of projection. But the trap quickly claimed those following Gerald du Maurier's style of reserved acting. A 'Galleryite' wrote complainingly of a visit to Sheldon's *Romance* at the Lyric, which only held 1200, that the players' 'conversational tone and dropping the voice in order to be impressive' made them largely inaudible to a crowded gallery, one patron of which vainly exhorted, 'speak up, please'.[150]

Melodrama fell victim to this process, its old-fashioned style inviting parody; but in its heyday it demanded a complexity of response. Shakespeare's Othello has been subject to urgings away from murder by 'unsophisticated' audiences, just as the general in Melville's *Female Hun* was warned by a voice from the Lyceum's pit not to mention war-plans since his spy-wife lurked 'behind the curtain'.[151] Involved here is an imaginative suppleness beyond the fashionable houses, enabling audiences to switch easily from immersion in terror and excitement to the amused detachment with which one helpful voice from the gods answered a heroine's 'What shall I do?' when faced by a hulking gorilla: 'Chuck him a nut, Miss!'[152] Terror is present, but also a means of controlling terror, even of enjoying or mocking it. This double perspective effectively challenged the prevailing naturalism. Furthermore, while in an irrational world which guarantees neither success to the virtuous nor protection for the weak, melodrama's settlements necessarily seemed arbitrary, its falsifications were more innocent than those of naturalism. Melodrama reflected a world of foreman-villains and rent-collector-villains, of hardship and ever-threatening disaster. It was a world which the new theatre-going public had chosen to ignore in favour of staider and stabler aspirations. But the values of sobriety and discipline covertly fostered their opposite, resulting in the vitalist explosion of war. Now everyone's life was touched with the melodramatic, and theatres saw new possibilities in what had become a despised form. As will be seen, numerous war plays followed this pattern.

The change in attitude was signalled by no less a person than George Alexander of the St James's, who expressed concern that 'this cry against melodrama has caused some of our dramatists to be led into losing what I might call "grip" in play work'.[153] Accordingly he revived James Fagan's 'drawing-room melodrama', *Bella Donna* (1911), with Mrs Patrick Campbell in her old husband-murdering part,[154] and played in Louis Parker's *Aristocrat*, 'a typical piece of stage carpentry dealing with the French Revolution according to the traditional view of our drama'.[155] Meanwhile manager C. P. Crawford was looking to American-style punch and thrill, obtaining British rights to 17 sensational pieces which A. H. Woods was touring on the popular-priced Stair and Havlin circuit in America. These included Theo Kromer's *Bertha the Sewing-Machine Girl*, all horses, automobiles, fire-engines and 'a river of real water', the latter used when Brooklyn Bridge was blown up and a car in which Nellie was riding ended in the water. Earlier she had been subjected to the hazards of the movie-serial queens, lashed to a railway line and almost crushed by a lift, finally triumphing in a knife-fight with the villainess.[156]

Drury Lane, with its spacious stage and a tradition shaped by Augustus Harris, had long been associated with spectacular melodrama. A return to this old tradition was made in 1916 with Ernest Bendall's *Best of Luck*, which opened splendidly on the deck of a Spanish galleon in 1588 (thus catching the mood of thwarted invasion). It had hatchways that disgorged hordes of Spanish seamen, while overhead the great mainsail was worked by ropes. The ship lay off the west coast of Scotland, bathed in a warm, golden light rendered hazy by the summer's heat; the water reflecting 'the gold and purple of the hills and the deep blue of the sky'. But this was mere prologue to a modern-day treasure hunt and a heroine of the times. Accused of sharing 'the British prejudice against what you call foreigners' (naturally by an exotic villain), she answers proudly: 'If it *be* a prejudice to prefer my own countrymen.' Villain and hero do battle in diving suits in an extraordinary scene where past and present converge. A submarine slowly sinks to a seabed created by lighting, 'waving seaweed and ... slimy rocks',[157] resting beside the wreckage of that ancient galleon. Indeed, the villain is a descendant of that galleon's captain, and he finally succumbs on its planking, his sliced air tube 'emitting real bubbles'. However, a match for this is the scene where the heroine crouches low on a motor cycle, 'hair flying in the wind', as she tears across a bridge which is under repair. She is pursued by the occupants of a powerful car, and a workman who hears its approach rushes forward waving a red warning lamp. One of the car's occupants throws 'himself towards the plank crossing', screaming as he misses, and the vehicle 'plunges ... into the darkness below'. Just how this was staged cannot be gleaned from the script; but *Era*'s reviewer (4 October 1916, p. 1) could 'recall nothing more thrilling'.[158] It clearly had its hazards: in a court case, stunt-man Fred Zarinella (William Baylish) described how the manager required him to leap 'six feet sideways ... from a travelling motor-car', firing 'a revolver at a young lady' in the process. The stage manager conceded that wrecks were frequent, the management having 'to keep cars in reserve'.[159] But in Rudolf Besier's *A Run for His Money*, produced by Matheson Lang, effective results were achieved by modern lighting techniques: 'The audience sees two pin-points of light winding down the steep decline from the chateau. Then shots ring out as the car flashes through the town.' After a curtain, 'stage and the auditorium are in pitchy blackness. Then the headlights appear in the gloom of the stage, ... looming larger every second. Suddenly there is a crashing of timber, a girl's cry of terror, and the stage springs into light, revealing the damaged car standing derelict across a railway, [heroine] prostrate on the ground, and [hero] leaning, dazed, over the side of the car.'[160]

The cinema could achieve these effects more readily, but the ingenuities contrived in the live theatre exercised their own appeal. In any case, there was continual interaction between the two theatrical modes. Elmer Reizenstein's *On Trial* 'opens in a court-house, where the murdered man's wife is giving evidence. A dark curtain falls, the stage is turned, and we see the actual murder committed; the dark curtain falls again, and we are back in court hearing the witness finish her evidence. And so on through the three acts.'[161] This was recognized as 'a cinematograph principle' (flashback), achieved 'In the absence of a revolving stage, ... by means of rollers ... the changes [being] accomplished with incredible smoothness and swiftness'.[162] But when it was imitated in Hackett and Vachell's *Mr. Jubilee Drax*, despite the advantage of the Haymarket's revolving stage, the result was disappointing.[163]

It was because of the prevalence of the crook genre in the cinema that the stage censor felt impotent to resist representations of 'clever and resourceful criminals escaping from the police', despite unease about their effect on the young.[164] Crime in a Parisian setting had a certain stage vogue, Charles Darrell's 1913 melodrama, *When Paris Sleeps*, being revived at the Lyric, Hammersmith.[165] This followed the Raffles pattern with a society cracksman, but more often the apache underworld was evoked as in *Women of Paris*.[166] This was by Landeck and Bellamy, its white slavery plot taking place in Algiers. Landeck had collaborated with Arthur Shirley on *Kit Carson, the Blind Detective* (1911).[167] This may have been the first appearance on stage of a blind detective, but it was superseded by Bramah and Heron's *In the Dark*, dealing with 'a gang of international crooks (who are incidentally in the pay of Germany)'.[168] This featured Bramah's 1914 fictional creation, Max Carrados, most famous of blind detectives.

But overwhelmingly the crook play, like the crook film, was American. Popular melodrama, it was claimed, had been 'largely ousted by the American crook-play', or 'the American "surprise" melodrama'.[169] Typical of the latter is *Inside the Lines* by Earl Biggers (creator of Charlie Chan) who happily flouted the old precept 'Never keep your audience in the dark.'[170] Those who resented this habit 'of spoofing the audience instead of letting it into the secret' were swimming against the tide; as a reviewer of Hackett's *The Barton Mystery* points out: 'We demand from a good detective story to be persistently baffled until the end.'[171] That such things, with their emphasis on ambiguities and problems of identity, should come into their own in the age of Kafka and Freud (as well as Ludendorff and Haig) is scarcely surprising. In the autumn of 1915, when Charles Eddy's tabloid thriller, *The Dandy*, opened at the Oxford, 'the public taste for "crook" plays' was so far from being 'satiated or the source of production exhausted' that they were vying in popularity with revues.[172] By 1918, American star Shirley Kellogg had migrated from revue to play the female gang-boss in Max Marcin's *Cheating Cheaters* at the Strand. Reviewing it, Koopman describes the recent evolution of the crime thriller:

> The police lost their cunning and our interest with the advent of the sympathetic criminal of the Raffles and Leah Kleschna type, ultimately redeemed by love from their evil courses, meritoriously self-sacrificing throughout. They were superseded in their turn by the "crook," the cute, self-confident, friendly American crook, on excellent terms with the police and the audience, alert and cheerful to his unrepentant end. Now the game is to mix up the characters and make it impossible to tell which is the hunted and which the hunter until five minutes before the fall of the final curtain.[173]

A key year, however, was 1915. It not only saw a revival at Brixton of Paul Armstrong's *Alias Jimmy Valentine* (a 1910 trend-setter based on O. Henry) but the arrival of Willard Mack's New York sensation *Kick-In*, the latter more geared to American popular taste with its 'vivid exposition of the fears and frenzy of the young morpho-maniac'.[174] It was commended by popular American comedian Augustus Yorke, at the Playgoers' Club, as 'a faithfully drawn picture of the New York underworld, [though], too, the sentimental side of the American character was brought out in Chuck's tender-hearted landlady'.[175] It was one of the many melodramas which prompted 'sympathy with the "crook," and indignation with the police' ('if we are to judge the police of America by imported American dramas, what a terrible lot of bullies and traitors and low-down ruffians they must be!').[176] But a different kind of opposition was explored in Broadhurst and Hackett's *He Didn't Want to Do It* at the Prince of Wales's: 'Unlike the majority of "crook" plays, sympathy is not with the criminals, but with the simple, guileless youth who gets mixed up with their schemes.'[177] This was followed at the same theatre by another variant, O'Higgins and Ford's *The Dummy*, concerning a boy who develops 'the "sleuth-hound" fever badly' from reading too many penny dreadfuls; he is full of 'Bowery slang and mannerisms',[178] which *Kick-In* had shown to have piquant appeal for British audiences.[179]

'Time was when the New York police – as shown us by the New York stage – seemed the greatest villains in the world, next to the Russian police – as shown us by the English stage. To-day we know of worse villainies than anything ever dreamed by the most bloodthirsty of dramatists.' Here a *Times* reviewer (30 August 1915, p. 9) intimates that the war has become the natural subject for melodrama; and throughout the war writers for the theatre showed themselves fully alive to the fact. Late on, Cyri Gilbert's *Jack on Leave* (Grand, Croydon) was using all the 'old melodramatic tricks as marked cards, poisoned wire, a plot to ruin Jack's wife, Mary saved from the villain's clutches by Jack, dire poverty, and happiness at last'.[180] It was in this fourth year of hostilities that comedian R. G. Knowles concluded that the war was 'too vast for condensation at present. Beyond a few melodramas, it has hardly been touched. And these melodramas positively reek with improbabilities, without the art that makes improbabilities seem probable.'[181] At the outset there was obvious confusion about what to prescribe: 'There used to be a good deal of sentiment and romance about war, and these are the essence of drama. The Germans have shown us only its seamy side' and have thus '"knocked the stuffing" out of war for amusement purposes.' Thus *Era*'s leader-writer (26 August 1914, p. 9), who adds: 'The public will resent flippancy or *chauvinism*' in war plays, their writers needing 'to avoid boastfulness and brag' while yet preserving 'a tone of quiet confidence'. On the whole he thinks a more successful and satisfactory alternative might lie with the theatre of fun or sensation. A subsequent leader (8 March 1916, p. 15) addressed the problem of bringing the real tragedy of war to the stage, especially when the actor was resistant 'to appearing on the stage to spout cheap patriotism as a khaki hero'. It escapes notice that spouting 'cheap patriotism' would have little to do with representing the grimness of war, except as searing irony. There was a multitude of reasons why the stage could not be used to bring home something of war's realities, despite a glut of those willing 'to spout cheap patriotism'. Any wariness about donning khaki for the purpose came about through growing audience hostility to such masquerades. But there were no such inhibitions in the early days, which saw a wild scamper after topicality, and sometimes a lack of scruple about how it was achieved. Rollo Balmain's *A British Soldier*, given at Walsall as a piece treating recent events on the Western Front, was virtually Hal Collier's play of the same title written during the Boer War which Balmain had 'produced and toured' at that time.[182] One manager recalled how a similar rush for war plays at the start of the Boer War bred a surfeit: 'This has happened again. War drama is taboo.' This was early in 1916; but by the end of 1917 an *Era* leader recorded a shift. The war play had been taboo only 'for a time'. The writer was undecided whether the disfavour into which it had fallen by the end of 1914 was due to a shortage of 'good work' or to a growing sensitivity about treating the war as amusement. At the same time, it was noted that sustained feasting on patriotic fare in the halls had not diminished people's appetite for it.[183] A more likely explanation is that, once again, this was managerial prescription. John Raphael complains that London managers fight shy of the war, 'and in particular, its dramatic side', though 'if you ask any member of the London public whether the mere fact that a play touches on the war is sufficient to keep him out of the theatre he will laugh at you'.[184] It was its dramatic side that Bourchier thought inappropriate: early on it was recognized (by whom?) as 'almost indecent to present plays showing actual fighting' when so many of the audience had a 'personal interest' in the war.[185]

But if declarations about civilian taste seem haphazardly provenanced, a scattering of anecdotal evidence was sufficient for the pundits to pronounce on that of the Tommy. Whereas Tommy with his experience of the real thing will have no desire to see 'mimic encounters arranged by a hack dramatist', such things undoubtedly 'appeal to the unlettered masses, who swallow with a simplicity that is astounding the impossible happenings, the unconvincing characterisation, and the crude absurdities of the war play'.[186] But this patronizing makes no allowance for the likelihood that many amongst the unlettered masses were relishing what they well understood to be theatrical exaggerations and fantasies, something which Tommy, only temporarily distinguished from them, may also have enjoyed. Their response could be hardly more naïve than that of the reviewer of Eva Elwes's *Joy, Sister of Mercy* who, when the heroine loses her sight, regrets that she 'does not recover from this blindness'. That was when it was playing at Manchester's Metropole; by the time that it reached the Theatre Royal, Stratford, the blinding had become temporary.[187] The pattern was thus set for plays like Hughes and Howard's *The Silver Crucifix*, Dorothy Mullord's *Married on Leave* and Clifford Rean's *On Leave for His Wedding* where the soldier-hero has his sight 'miraculously' restored.[188]

It is that so-called 'taboo' phase at the start of 1915 which is hardest to pin down. Its contradictions are addressed by a *Times* columnist (5 February 1915,

p. 11), who discerns a shift from pre-war taste for 'smart and vacant cleverness' to a theatre 'either of thrilling incident or of hearty humour'. 'Patriotic plays, from Shakespeare to George R. Sims, do well', whereas 'Stage pictures of atrocities and "frightfulness" meet with no welcome.' But qualifications have to be made constantly: 'that engrossing mixture of laughter and tears', Fonson's *La Kommandatur*, upsets the belief that 'Serious plays about the war are not wanted ... It would probably be found that those who read their newspapers most and with the most lively imagination want no war in the theatre, while to the rest the theatre is the force which crystallizes the ambient rumour. And thus, between the desire to learn about the war and the desire to forget about the war' the theatres are crowded. F. P. , writing just a month earlier about the West End, also recognizes different constituencies: 'If you exclude the music halls, where the tradition of full-blooded Aristophanic topicality is maintained by beating the patriotic drum till it cracks, the theatres are ... silent about war – with three exceptions.'[189] There is Hardy's *The Dynasts*, which confronts 'the horrors of war, but it is all transfigured into a kind of wistful distance', intellect softening the blow as sentiment does in the bourgeois theatre. This latter is represented by *The Flag Lieutenant* at the Haymarket, a revival of a 1908 play by active majors W. P. Drury and Leo Trevor: 'Honour is the key note – a queer, exalted conception of honour which lingers on in the well-made military play from the days of chivalry.' During the war, with Shakespeare's acid view on chivalry's relation to *realpolitik* dissembled, things were refashioned into a mythic 'contrast between Teutonic "Kultur" and the British love of fair play'.[190] And if the honour code of *The Flag Lieutenant* seemed a trifle dated for a war of the present kind, the *Times* reviewer (30 November, 1914, p. 11) found a contemporary ring in 'the indomitable cheerfulness of the rank and file. Listen to Sloggett, A. B., and Private Borlaise of the Marines cracking jokes over their rations, "grousing" over some tedious bit of routine, or making linguistic experiments on a captured enemy, and you might be reading extracts from those jolly, schoolboy letters from our men in the trenches.' For F. P. this is to gaze 'happily through a rosy mist of sentiment in which the dirt and squalor that goes with real heroism is softened away. There is a wounded soldier sitting next to me. He, if he liked, could bring the thing to the touchstone of reality, but clearly it never occurs to him to do anything so extraordinary.' This well-dressed audience seasons its theatrical emotion with chocolates, while in the gods at the Lyceum bottles of beer circulate, produced surreptitiously from beneath shawls. Here F. P.'s third exception is another revival, *The Soldier's Wedding* (1906), by Walter Melville who, with his brother, managed the theatre from 1909. Jack Brown, the soldier hero, 'is a symbol of human nature as it lives in the vision of poor streets and hard lives'. His very unreality 'is there to give a glimpse of life as it might be if all the sorrows of the street were purged away and simplified by emotion. His red coat is a ticket of admission to the love of the gallery.' He is a folk hero, who might as easily right wrongs in Flanders as in the galleryites' own environment, thereby supplying justification for the war: oppression (which they all know about) actually challenged and defeated.

F. P. mentions another war play, Temple Thurston's *The Cost* (Vaudeville), which had been hastily withdrawn: 'There are many who do not relish seeing the delicate processes of conscience butchered to make an evening holiday.' He supposes that audiences want to be spared the serious as they do the real: 'If they put ten minutes of this real war on the stage we might bolt for the doors.' Elsewhere, exception is taken to 'some rather purple passages about the appalling horrors of work in the trenches and about John's white face and almost convulsive gestures on his entering into his first engagement. This latter speech might be excised, as it seems cruel to ascribe to John any suggestion of physical cowardice.'[191] If abject terror is a common battlefield experience, it is presumably confined to those whose cause is not just! For Baughan, the play's chief impropriety lies in the way that John eventually joins the colours not in the alleged spirit of those who are naturally averse from war, recognizing it as 'a fight for freedom', but simply 'because the war spirit has entered his veins'.[192] There must be no exposure of irrationalism; and another critic manages a more sympathetic view by ignoring this offence, concentrating on John as unfitted for war intellectually and emotionally, yet reluctant to 'urge others to fight for England till he has joined himself'.[193] Most reviewers found the play inopportune. Everyone understands that 'in times like these one's whole nature changes', as brutishness is encouraged over higher feelings. But such things are felt 'too acutely' to be welcome on stage. Hence the stabbing irony that these comments adjoin a favourable review of a Jekyll and Hyde play, *The Double Mystery*, adapted by José Levy from Louis Forest and Henry de Gosse's *Le Procureur Hallers*.[194]

However, a few plays were regarded, in some quarters at least, to combine truth with sensitivity so as to achieve lasting importance. Of these, Fonson's *Kommandatur* survives best. The English version (by Celia Storm and Ina Cameron) was premièred at Liverpool. Although with British actors melodrama overtook genre study, Imeson's Siegfried offered a gain in subtlety, being less of a 'Uriah Heep from the first entrance' than in the Belgian production. And Belgium under the jackboot was literally realized in the view of the invaders' 'great clumsy boots through the windows' of the Brussels basement-home.[195] *Armageddon*, held over for the next chapter, couples the moral coarseness of the more lurid melodramas with a blank-verse pretension which makes it intolerable. Much better, since it gets dramatic purchase on a serious moral dilemma, is Maeterlinck's *Burgomaster of Stilemonde*. Here the burgomaster must decide whether to sacrifice his own life or that of a worthy old gardener to what the Germans have decreed to be military necessity. The burgomaster, with much to live for in his children and his botanic garden, is exposed to temptation by the old man's readiness to end a life which has lost its savour, and by his German son-in-law's setting his importance to the local community against the gardener's insignificance. But there is no wavering; he behaves as any decent Belgian must, a patriotic note which somewhat deflates dramatic tension. Complications follow as the son-in-law too faces a dilemma. Having been ordered to command the firing party, he is persuaded by his wife to disobey and join her against the firing wall with her father. The burgomaster will not allow this additional sacrifice; but after his death his daughter renounces her bewildered German husband. This final rift would give no trouble if it could be accepted as the result of shocked horror. But earlier moments (a 63-year-old having to await the coming of the Germans to discover that life is not always just, or a young wife, raised in the cockpit of Europe, asserting that 'There has been nothing like this in any war in history') argue propagandist contrivance.[196] If the burgomaster, as his creator Martin Harvey avers, exhibits a philosophy of forgiveness, this (understandably) is not Maeterlinck's.[197] Zangwill is right to see in this ending a symbolic estrangement from the German people.

To an extent Maeterlinck exhibits the limitation posited, after a year of war, by Littlewood when he decided that no great war plays or novels were emerging because there was no room for debate, no scope for fresh perspectives: 'Everybody knows that the Allies are right.'[198] Littlewood could not countenance the likes of Stephen Moor, who in Galsworthy's *The Mob* makes the mistake of weighing the rights and wrongs of his country's cause when Britishers are fighting and dying. Thurston was no Moor: one reviewer suspects that in *The Cost* he 'stopped halfway' from fear of alienating his audience;[199] but at least he had clouded the water slightly. However, by 1918 he was as platitudinous as the rest: 'I do not think I could sit for five minutes now and listen to a real play, expressing real and genuine emotions. I want the injection of the anaesthetic as much as everyone else. But when the war is over' (that is always the plea), then writers 'must and will say what is in their minds'. When it is too late, all those things will be said 'which, for reasons of patriotism and the will to victory, [people] neither have dared nor have they wished to say'; and (how bold he makes this sound) no one 'in the world will stop their being said. This is what the playgoer after the war will demand, the thoughts he has cherished in silence for the last four years and a half – and, directly peace is declared, we shall find the whole tone of the theatre changing to reality.'[200]

Some of these thoughts are adumbrated in society productions. The Pioneers introduced Gwen John's *Luck of War* (Kingsway, 13 May 1917), where having a husband among the first volunteers is seen as no cause for pride: 'I never thought 'e showed much consideration, leaving me with the childer an' all ... I do blame a man does that when 'e 'as a good 'ome ... All t'neighbours said it semt as if I'd not done right by 'im.'[201] The commercial theatre, whose commitment to the cause ruled out Kate Searle's wish for an end to 'the recruiting sketch',[202] floated such thoughts only for them to be shot down. Thus *The Recruit* offers some semblance of debate, *one* young woman flaring up on hearing that her boyfriend is volunteering. The newspapers have misled him: 'Pretty picture you've made of yourself smothered with medals an' gold lace and French women throwing daisies in your face', while the reality is either getting 'blown in bits' or 'coming 'ome half of you here an' half left there and never see who you've been fighting'.[203] But the prevailing view is that exemplified in Myers and Murray's *Kitty's Catch*, where Kitty tells her beau that his love is only self-love in the face of that love of country for which 'men are dying in thousands'. She is a mouthpiece for the current cant: 'I cannot wholly love you until you prove yourself the man I want you to be. The price of a woman's devotion to-day is in the sacrifice to her country of the man she loves.'[204]

J. E. Macmanus's *The Man Who Wouldn't* opens up a different perspective when the title character suggests 'There are plenty of men who haven't much to give up ... let them go and fight.' This makes his daughter wonder why such people *should* fight for a country that has given them 'Very little wages for very hard work – and often they can't even get work. The less a man has, the less he has to fight for.'[205] But again the point is settled, just as Matthew Boulton's *Sword and Surplice* disposes of the clergyman's troubled conscience. The latter is converted from sermonizer on the text of 'Thou shalt not kill' to fire-eating recruit through the clumsy expedient of losing his little boy in an air raid. He ends up declaring himself still 'a man of peace! It is for peace that I am going to fight',[206] a fallacy trenchantly nailed during the Gulf War when someone scrawled on a wall in Swansea: 'Fighting for peace is like fucking for virginity.' But the vicar's wife is allowed to mouth a yet more pernicious cliché on the subject: 'it cannot be yet – the Allies have suffered too much to think of peace yet' (p. 9). Sometimes recruitment was built into the action, a pattern set by Hicks and Knoblauch's *England Expects*. Newton saw Bertrand Davis's *A Call to Arms* first in the suburbs and then, a few weeks later, at the Palladium, by which time it had shaped into a 'neat and terse' recruiting vehicle. It 'received official testimony' for 'its recruit-drawing powers', with Bertram Wallis cutting 'a splendid figure as the merry and bright and very musical ... Recruiting Sergeant' who in his final speech hands over to the genuine article 'in the vestibule'.[207] This also included 'Dorothy Rundell, as the now ubiquitous Girl who causes the slacker to unslacken', dodging the column being equated in the Lodge Percys' *The Slacker* with shaming virgins and seducing soldiers' wives.[208] In Charles S. Kitts's sketch of the same title, the slacker considers it 'pretty cool' that he has Tommies billeted on him rather than officers.[209] The Tommies are such as think 'conveyances' are 'public 'ouses' (not lavatories: coyness mixes with condescension) and that a serviette is used 'To wipe your nose.' They fail to persuade him to join up, but a vivid dream of invasion, in which his wife is blinded by an enemy shot, does the trick.[210]

There were many comical asides on the war. Captain E. C. Baker's *A Cushy Job* was written out of his own experience in a recruiting office. Spelling the name of Jewish recruit Yitychrock Goldsilverstein gives trouble: 'You don't spell it, you play it on the trombone'; and a mother asks that her 14-year-old son be accepted: he is deaf and dumb so 'won't hear the shells bursting'. By this time the officer is ready to return 'to the trenches for a little peace and rest'.[211] *Rights and Wrongs* depicts the interview by an official of the Military and Naval Aid Association of a soldier's cockney wife applying for rent money. She receives it despite being unable to substantiate her claim, or even to name her husband's regiment. However, although she and her children face eviction, she deposits the money in the Belgian relief box while 'Your King And Country Need You' is 'played very softly as the curtain comes down, swelling out *forte* afterwards'.[212] Such complacency about the resilient poor at once reassures about provision for destitute soldiers' wives and calls for the indigent to help foot the war bill, so that their betters may not have to cut back on their Coronas. Knoblauch's *War Committee* is slight enough on paper but obviously acquired flesh on stage. It depicts the committee mania which affected society women of the time, and Maud Tree as the titled lady raising the committee was a brilliant 'embodiment of soulful silliness'. A small committee acquired its own dynamic for growth, even co-opting an 'oh, so racy' cockney charwoman as the voice of the people: 'Every dropping of an "h" opens new vistas of smoking chimney pots and squealing children',[213] until 'finally the whole meeting broke up in an uproar upon Miss Ethel Levey singing a ragtime song'. This was too much for Newton: 'What we want from the stage just now is patriotism, not neutral ridicule' (Knoblauch at this time was still American).[214] And in the same column Newton worries about Ada Abbott's *The Love-Child*, set in 1924, where, 'owing to the shortage of men *after* the war, all sorts of posts have to be filled by women'. It would be much better set in the present, thus avoiding the idea 'that nearly all our men will have been killed in the war'. His attitude to Gertrude Jennings's *Poached Eggs and Pearls*, set in a servicemen's restaurant staffed by the aristocracy, is unrecorded. This might have been inspired by an anecdote retailed at the opening of a YMCA recreation hut about 'An Aspiring Soldier' who sought a date with a young society lady behind the counter of such a hut. The tone of the anecdote, which is not Jennings's, drew sharp comment from a YMCA woman in France who had received marriage proposals from 'two gallant soldiers (without asking my pedigree)'. This only made her proud: 'To make a joke of it as Mrs. Stuart-Wortley has done is in the worst taste.'[215]

In 1917 a determined theatrical assault was launched on the pacifist, headed by Henry Arthur Jones's *The Pacifists* and Harold Owen's *Loyalty*. One critic dubbed the latter a 'war problem play', though its hero belabours 'problemmy' theatre for urging expenditure on needless social reforms rather than armaments.[216] This authorial mouthpiece presented difficulties even for contemporary reviewers. In July 1914, he shows 'such amazingly bad manners as to mimic a German's accent to his face, ... launches into a tirade against democratic government in a speech which, borrowed closely from Pericles, would make President Wilson blink his eyes, ... declares passionately that what he wants is Home Rule for England, which is not the sort of remark you make to people whose intelligence you respect, [and crassly] suggests that pacifism is due to purely "party" motives.'[217] Farjeon found the play 'too puerile a piece of Jingoism to do any good to either its political or its commercial backers'.[218] It lasted at the St James's for only 21 performances, though aided by a superior cast (Fisher White, Aubrey Smith, Viola Tree). It had been presented anonymously, and it was not until it had been running for a week that Owen acknowledged responsibility.[219] His one aim, he declared, has been 'to smash Pacifism', a necessary step towards smashing a hated Germany.

As noted earlier, 1917 provided a good deal more than these anti-pacifist statements. Farjeon, contrasting the start of the war, when 'we flattered ourselves we took war far too seriously to import it into our playhouses', remarks 'the steadily increasing popularity of war plays' during the year.[220] Particular favourites were spy plays like *Inside the Lines*, which 'made a fortune at the Apollo', or *Seven Days' Leave*, 'going so strong' at the Lyceum 'that the customary pantomime was for once abandoned'. The latter was written, according to its author Walter Howard, 'to please his brave young soldier son';[221] and the enthusiasm which it aroused in an audience of wounded showed that they harboured 'no "stop-the-war" heresy'.[222] Why this proved the most durable type of war play[223] is explained by 'Candida', who found the London theatre at the start of 1916 offering 'scarcely a war problem'. Indeed, the only one pretending to address 'ruthless realities' was a spy drama, 'romance and adventure masquerading under the name of realism'.[224] Always realism had to be avoided. Thus C. B. Fernald's *The Day Before the Day* was reckoned a good play, but 'war is too near us to be staged in [this] way'. It presents the crisis 'on lines that are not helpful. It is a story of a German spy conspiracy carried on on the East Coast with such an air of verisimilitude that it becomes more than ever unreal – if you understand the paradox ... The whole affair is – chilling.'[225] The alternative might be thought still less helpful since, as some critics pointed out, no one was going to worry about the kinds of simpleton-spy characteristically represented on stage. But this approach contented many critics: 'The spy is the only article made in Germany now tolerated by the British public, and then solely that he may be held up to ridicule.'[226] This is implicitly endorsed by Baughan, who resents the way that 1918 has seen too many German spies, with their loyalty and courage, given the dramatic advantage over the 'profound inefficiency' of slang-spouting British officers. Yet he has not been duped into taking Lawrence Cowen's piece of crude 'dramatic journalism', *The Hidden Hand*, seriously;[227] though Horatio Bottomley, present at the first performance at Liverpool's Royal Court, with customary patronizing flatulence urged the value of 'such educational plays' in awakening 'people to the hidden danger in our midst'. (*Pick-a-dilly* satirized Bottomley as 'The man who clutched the Unseen Hand'.[228]) The play was credited with bringing 'home the established fact that among England's most dangerous enemies are those who, occupying prominent social positions, are least suspected'. In reality it aimed at nothing so subversive, confining itself to those of British nationality and German origin – always a safe xenophobic target which contrived to leave the delicate position of the royal family untouched. Here a German born baronet, hiding behind a Scottish name, attempts 'to bring about strikes among his own shipbuilding firm' (industrial disputes were regularly ascribed to enemy agency).[229] He is foiled by a patriotic clergyman-soldier, clumsily named St George and played in an absurd aureole of limelight by William Stack, whose 'appeal to the workers not to strike carried his audience with him'.[230] (Stack deserves, says Carroll, 'a better fate than to be drafted into such work, notwithstanding the distinction and vitality he is able to impart to it'.[231])

It became almost axiomatic that naturalized Germans would favour the fatherland, so it is refreshing to find H. A. Vachell introducing one into *Searchlights* who, although cutting a somewhat ludicrous figure in his kilt, is amiable and genuinely committed to the interests of his adopted country. 'He drinks English lager, and has bought a Gillette safety razor, because his razors were made in Germany.'[232] The commercial implications of this had already been spelt out in a version of 'Belgium Put The Kibosh On The Kaiser', recorded 6 October 1914 by Mark Sheridan: 'We won't buy his German goods,/and we'll never taste his lager any more.'[233]

But Hall Caine was content to slip into the well-greased 'enemy within' track for *The Prime Minister*, a more ambitious play than Cowen's, but hardly worth more than its 67 performances at the Royalty. The Prologue demonstrates the prime minister's humanity by having him interrupt a vital cabinet meeting to attend to the needs of his motherless daughter (and incidentally to allow for some soggy exposition). Hope derides the playwright for making his cabinet ministers 'drivelling idiots, who do not know that mid-European time is one hour fast on Greenwich';[234] alas for the reputation of cabinet ministers, Caine in a prefatory note to the play (p. x) emphasizes that Asquith and his cabinet, waiting for Berlin's ultimatum in August 1914, made exactly this blunder, 'so that Great Britain was an hour at war before the country was aware of it'. The prime minister hires a Swiss governess to tend his child, but Margaret Schiller takes her place. This young woman has sought to replace loyalty to the land of her fathers by loyalty to that of her birth: 'But they wouldn't let me' (p. 35). As a result she heeds her cousin: 'If the Government of this accursed country have determined to treat us as conspirators, why shouldn't we be conspirators?' (p. 41). But he dupes her with rationalization since his Goethe Club already fronts a spy ring. The play is set in the future, with 'the war to end war' over and another beginning and the authorities determined not to repeat old mistakes regarding enemy aliens. Attention is directed towards 'the professional classes, who in the previous war so often evaded observation', and there will be no more 'interning the men and leaving the more dangerous sex at liberty' (pp. 57, 61). Unbelievably, power has neither corrupted nor compromised Caine's prime minister, though this, as one reviewer puts it, makes him 'an unmitigated bore'.[235] Recognizing his virtue, Margaret determines to save him from assassination at the expense of her own life, just when he has yielded to Vansittartism: 'You are all alike. It is the mad, bad blood in such as you that is deluging the world in crime' (p. 154).

During the course of the London run Caine tried to energize it with a more dramatic conclusion to the third act, in which Margaret curses the Kaiser and hurls an ink-pot at his portrait (p. 129). This would have been impermissible on the British stage at the time when the play was written, just as reference to Britain's all too effective naval blockade would have become unwelcome by 1918: 'Think of it! Seventy millions in the Fatherland to be starved to death – men, women and little children!' This policy made abuse of the Zeppelin raiders as babykillers the veriest hypocrisy.[236] However, there were more central concerns which caused licensing to be recommended 'very dubiously': 'the audience would almost certainly think of the present war, and therefore of the present Prime Minister.' The factual aspect of the time difference was embarrassing, and the basic situation 'would revive in people's minds the story about a German governess in the Asquiths' house'.[237] By the time that it appeared in London, it would have been more likely to prompt thoughts of the

Wheeldon case, a fantasy plot to poison Lloyd George which the authorities used to discredit suffragettes, conscientious objectors and even the Industrial Workers of the World.[238]

That earlier phase of restiveness about war plays found critics both complaining about unrealism and insisting that war's reality was unwelcome.[239] One way around the problem was to write domestic drama which used the war incidentally. Women were particularly adept in this field, Jessie Porter's *Betty at Bay* being full of 'old-fashioned sentiment, illegitimate appeals to tears and laughter alike, and such conventionalities of plot and situation as we had thought discarded for good'.[240] Gladys Walton's *If Love Were All* makes daring use of such familiar wartime features as memory loss 'and the restoration of speech by shock',[241] while Dorothy Mullord's *The Story of the Angelus* is positively spectacular, including a German's escape, after signalling from a church tower, by means of 'a rope dropped from a passing Zeppelin'.[242] The Lodge Percys' *Mary From Tipperary* is one of a number of plays reflecting anxiety over the U-boat menace, the threat to 'a liner conveying a portion of the Canadian contingent' obviously recalling the *Lusitania*.[243] Sexual circumstances resulting from a soldier's absence at the Front have the changes rung on them constantly. The prolific Eva Elwes's *John Raymond's Daughter* engineers reunion with a soldier-lover after the wicked squire 'is killed in a motor smash'[244] (apt as well as convenient since this was the rich man's toy until the Ford era of mass-produced vehicles, destined to cause more destruction of town and country than all the bombardments of both world wars). Vernon Proctor's *The Wife with Two Husbands* renders the Enoch Arden situation which had become all too topical with so many false death reports emerging from the confusions of the battlefront.[245] Proctor's *The Unmarried Mother* functioned as a recruiting aid, but interestingly portrayed a parent's murderous response to unceremonious pregnancy.[246] Street regretted 'the frequency of the "unmarried mother" in contemporary melodramas'.[247] But there was extensive anxiety over war babies, as munition girls moved away from home for the first time and army camps sprang up everywhere. Although the Committee on Illegitimate Births, chaired by the Archbishop of York, concluded that 'the rumours which have been circulated have been proved beyond doubt to have no foundation in fact',[248] this by no means dissipated anxieties. In Millane and Carleton's *Somewhere a Voice is Calling*, the heroine has been deserted and wishes to terminate an undesired pregnancy, but the doctor chides her: 'There are women deeper wronged than you in Belgium – who are victims of a cruel victor's lust; even they have not the right to slay the life the Lord has allowed to spring from them.'[249]

If factors within the theatre helped to give impetus to these domestic dramas, there was also an important external factor. This was the Lord

Chamberlain's office, which imposed various restrictions on playwrights dealing with war topics: there should be no opposition to government policy; no serious attempt to convey war's reality (though representations of the frightfulness practised by the enemy were broadly acceptable); and respect should be maintained for authority and for the king's uniform. Bendall, as censor's reader, approved of Dreda Boyd's *John Feeney, Socialist* for 'showing how the Socialist theories which prevent a sturdy North Country miner from enlisting for what he calls a Capitalist war, are knocked on the head by the *argumentum ad hominem* of an unhappy Belgian refugee, who describes some of the Hun horrors which, together with the policy inspiring them, provide the worthy motive for our war with Germany'. Claims that the coal master is propelled by 'gross greed' are countered by the fantasy that the miner is cossetted to a degree (his children 'fed, clothed, educated by the State') which has pauperized his 'spirit of independence'.[250] Were Feeney half the radical he is supposed to be, he would demolish this in a couple of sentences, pointing out that where state provision has any substance (in education) it has been enforced out of entirely interested motives. But this would be no more allowable than the satire in Myddleton Myles's *War, Red War*. Bendall censors the contention that 'bastard' is 'an ugly word when mentioned in connection with poor or common people, and becomes quite romantic when associated with a royal or noble indiscretion'. A later speech, emphatically blue-pencilled, denounces those in the war 'who consider they have done their share by taking up some of the Government Loan and helping their country at 4 per cent interest', traders who have raised food prices to a starvation level for the poor, civil servants who have allowed middlemen to make huge profits out of government contracts and 'the ruthless tax on the commodities of the poor, whilst the rich have been, comparatively, allowed to go free'. Finally, it is urged that those 'risking and giving their lives for their Country' and their families should not be dependent on charity, but should be properly provided for by the state.[251]

As for the more fundamentally 'critical and even insurgent' drama, that must wait until after the war. Why the state should have been 'frightened of it' even then, as Massingham alleges, is hard to understand, 'first attempts to construct the "morality plays" of the war-period' having been effortlessly suppressed.[252] Amongst these were Miles Malleson's *'D' Company* and *Black 'Ell*, published together in 1916 in an edition which, according to Nicoll, was 'destroyed' by government order. But surviving copies seem to have emerged in 1925 and *Black 'Ell* was produced the next year. *'D' Company* had a matinée performance at the New Theatre, Oxford, by officer trainees: 'The little play, full of touching pathos in places, had a very cordial reception' (*Era* 14 February 1917, p. 21). The author's preface describes how he wrote it in Malta while serving briefly as a private in a territorial battalion. The two most striking bits occur in letters read out, the first from a mother who has just lost her youngest boy Tom: 'They says in the papers here mothers ought to be proud to give their sons, but them what writes that ain't mothers with sons to give ... Alf, don't go if yer can help it. I must close now. I can only think of my Tom and you all the time sitting here' (pp. 23–4). The other letter has been written by a gentleman-ranker: 'I think if I aimed at a German officer, the obvious symbol of Prussian Militarism, I should be sure to miss him, and hit a private who would probably be a Social Democrat with many an idea in common with me, or a musician who has felt as I have over the passion of Wagner, or a man who simply loathes fighting as much as I do.' He adds, of his lieutenant: 'He is as fresh from Cambridge as I am – except that he comes from Oxford! But, oh, the great gulf that our uniforms make between us. You should hear my deferential "Sir" and his haughty look – which is food for thought' (pp. 27–8). The playlet ends with the men *'drinking in their letters like a thirsty soldier at a pot of beer. Of a sudden all the lights go out. From the blackness comes a howl of execration. Howl after howl – and on this the Curtain slides down'* (p. 31). The title *Black 'Ell* alludes to the place where a parlour maid would consign those who have killed her sweetheart; though her mistress and friends are off to 'the Royal Opera House to hear St. John Bullock on "War – the new Religion" ' (i.e. Bottomley, whom the family patriarch 'used to call ... the biggest scoundrel unhung before the war', p. 45). The central event is the homecoming of an officer-hero, who has despatched six Germans and been awarded the DSO. But he is horrified at being feted and decorated for an act of butchery, and calls for an end to the madness. He describes how he has overheard a German in a trench 'talking against the war', but his comrades 'got furious with him' and replied with atrocity stories that 'were just the same as we say about them'. He glimpses how the mind-benders make 'everybody believe it's somebody else's fault', using war as an evasion, a distraction (p. 61). He has come to know Tommies from the nearby slums, which he and his family studiously ignored pre-war. These men should 'join together and get a more decent share of life' instead of being seduced into fighting their own kind. And the horrible part is that they fall for it: 'We put 'em in uniforms, and yell "Form fours! as you were!" at 'em till they'll do *anything*.' But in frustration at finding no practical solution he can only fantasize about letting all the statesmen, newspapermen and parsons go at it with knives and bombs until they are ready to 'start negotiations' (pp. 61–2).

The need to deal with this same group of warmongers is confronted in R. C. Trevelyan's *The Pterodamozels: An Operatic Fable*. This was obscurely published by the author, who could have had no thought of production.[253] The play is a fantasy, though its targets are sharply enough defined: 'Tribunals, churches, trenches, patriotism, Daily-Mail government' (p. 2). With those 'bellevolent big-wigs', exploiters of 'frontiers, rent and monopoly', removed from their thrones of power, the war stops forthwith (pp. 27, 63). The central characters are 'three conscientious objectors To compulsory race-suicide', seeking 'a trenchless and Timesless land, where speech is free and the soul unattested' and 'the average man as reasonable And sane as Socrates or Shaw, or – well As a woman' (pp. 22–3).

Later twentieth-century history has killed the belief that women would lead in a more pacific direction than men, but it is one of the less satisfactory propositions offered in Marion Wentworth's anti-war play, *War Brides*, popular enough in America for it to be translated to the screen in 1916 as a vehicle for Alla Nazimova. Early that year Nazimova, married to British actor Charles Bryant, was hoping to play it on the London stage, but its theme rendered that impossible.[254] It is a little like *Riders to the Sea*, except that it is not a cruel nature but a heartless government which destroys all the young men. And there is also a dash of Aristophanic revolt against becoming a 'breeding-machine' to restock the country 'for the next generation's cannon'.[255] Another American war-play which failed to cross the Atlantic was Davis and Sheehan's *Efficiency*. On the face of it this one is unexceptionable in sentiment, though stylistically more Greenwich Village than West End. The central character is No. 241, a kind of bionic man who has been reassembled after being blown up, along with a million more, to create an unstoppable army. But he is disenchanted at the prospect of being brought 'twice-to-slaughter', and demonstrates 'Ef-fi-cien-cy' (he talks in stilted Dalek accents) by strangling the Kaiser.[256] This, for all the play's assault on the Kaiser, might have revealed a double edge, aligning it with Gertler's 1916 canvas 'Merry-Go-Round' (in the Tate Modern), which explains the war as man gruesomely trapped in the workings of his own technology.

War's horrors could not be staged in pacifist terms, but they could be ascribed to an unscrupulous enemy. This provoked protest in the *Deutsche Tageszeitung* against nightly representations of 'German "barbarity" and "cunning" '.[257] Deliberate efforts were made to stamp out any idea of the good German. A recitation about a German boy-soldier's remorse delivered to Canadian troops was instantly answered by their chaplain, who denied the existence of such remorse and pronounced: 'There is only one good German and that's a dead one.'[258] Indeed, one reviewer suggested that 'no living dramatist could at this moment put a real live German on the stage', and another thought Barrie's *Barbara's Wedding* remarkable for 'the rare admission that German subalterns may sometimes have been decent young men – at least before the War'.[259] Even so, signs of German humanity made a fitful stage appearance. *It's a Long Way to Tipperary* introduces a kindly German professor who helps a British soldier; and in R. W. Mockridge's *Remember Louvain* a young German soldier 'denounces the war upon women and children', disobeys an order, and 'is at once shot dead' by his officer.[260] There are compensations for the ugliness in Chris Davis's dramatic sketch, *The Enemy*. A German officer surprised in sleep by a small child instinctively shoots her. Mortally wounded, he repents, but the child is discovered to be only stunned by a bullet graze 'and the curtain falls on a scene of forgiveness and happiness'.[261] The Uhlan in Louise Heilgers's *The Bridge* does no more than echo Newton's 'soldiering is at best a brutal business' when he responds to an accuser: 'Of course we're brutes. You don't win battles by wearing kid gloves.'[262] But the ideas immediately evoked are 'burning of a convent, shooting of nuns', all those unspeakable things which accompanied the invasion of Belgium according to Dorothy Mullord's *The Princess and the Soldier* and innumerable other dramatizings.[263] Standards of acceptability were uncertain. The safe route was to provide thrills without being 'distressingly "lifelike" '.[264] On the other hand, even the St James's audiences had 'the colours laid on thick' in the American Chester Fernald's *The Day Before the Day*. Here a German secret agent thinks 'it will be a good joke for his friend the Führman to outrage an English girl while her chained lover looks on'.[265] Alfred Noyes's *Rada* is a less useful example since it was never produced; but, published in elegant form, it clearly aimed at the discerning. One reviewer asks: 'What is the use of the gratuitous harrowing of our feelings with blood and "belly wounds", and drunken Germans threatening with outrage a girl of twelve, ultimately shot by her mother, ... gramophone sounding "Adeste Fideles," while blood trickles under the door and cannon sound without?'[266] But more striking than this are some of the lines allotted to an old, half-witted schoolmaster as he ponders the war dead: 'perhaps if Goya were living to-day he would prefer to pack them into Chicago meat factories, with the intellectuals dancing outside like marionettes, and the unconscious Hand of God pulling the strings.'[267] This wedding of Goya and the Chicago canneries works devastatingly. The latter had been in use as a symbol of ruthless capitalism since the publication of Upton Sinclair's *The Jungle*, recently filmed with 'revolting' images of the canning process.[268] The image of the war in mass-production terms, with the soldier as its raw material, was altogether too pertinent to be allowed wide circulation.

Noyes's play and Fernald's at the St James's serve to undermine the facile convenience of viewing response to atrocity portrayals in purely class terms: 'However we may question the wisdom of the attempts to portray the horrors of war and the loathsomeness of German Kultur on the stage, there can be no denying the fact that such incidents appeal to popular audiences.' The play prompting this remark is Myles's *War, Red War*, first seen at the Brixton (31 May 1915). Here one woman in a torn chemise is told that to be raped by

German soldiers is an honour; another, musically inclined, is tied to a tree and told to listen for the music (shots announcing the despatch of her husband); a third is scarred saving a war baby from a burning house, only for an attempt to be made to knock out its brains on a door-post (an attempt thwarted by a snarling bulldog). A little British boy raising a toy gun is shot as a *franc-tireur*, a widespread motif also found in R. W. Mockridge's *Remember Louvain*.[269] Armies are jealous of their killing privileges and view harshly any civilians bearing arms against them. Hence the *franc-tireur* issue was a sensitive one. It came to the fore during the Franco-Prussian War, and the British were faced with its complexities when fighting the Boers. The censor objected to a scene in Andrew Emm's *For England, Home and Beauty* where nurses remove their insignia preparatory to doing battle. Indeed there is objection within the script, to which the heroine retorts: 'There is no power on earth that can prevent a woman defending her honour; come Betty hand round the rifles and the ammunition; give your commands Captain Leyton we are ready.'[270] This play also includes a scene where a German general throws water in the face of a wounded British prisoner. This is of a piece with the ill-treatment of wounded prisoners from Mons described in Owen's *Loyalty* (p. 165): 'soup held to their lips and then snatched away' or drink either spat in by nurses or poured over them. On the first night, when Fisher White recounted 'the appalling tale we have all read of the treatment of British prisoners in German camps the house was hushed with a deep and you might almost say, a tragic silence'.[271] Watson Mill goes one better in *In Time of War*, 'a play for the unsophisticated' which was not to be taken seriously despite 'scenes that are particularly painful at the present time'.[272] Here a nurse, actually a German spy, poisons the drinking water of the patients (though the real poison is the hatred which such representations generate). This occurs in what is perhaps the first of those tasteless comic hospital episodes, rendered the more indecent by being mixed up with 'scenes of horror, ... of women mad from insult and grief, of men delirious with agony, of wounded and sick and dying'.

Another noteworthy scene shows German spy Baron Guggenheim taunting a wounded British officer and being bayoneted in the back by the officer's estranged wife, who has somehow managed to follow him to the Front as a Red Cross nurse. (The saturation point which this cliché had reached is acknowledged when Sheila Walsh's *Up Boys, and at 'Em* is approved because its author avoids the temptation to make her heroine a nurse.)[273] What is interesting about Mill's heroine is that she kills an enemy without alarming the critics, thus anticipating the action of Lillian Gish in Griffith's 1918 film, *Hearts of the World*. A comparable episode in J. G. Brandon's *The Pacifist* misfired for several reasons. Although the pacifist, who appears in British naval uniform, has guided air raiders 'in a poor neighbourhood the night before', it is claimed that the doctor-heroine is unnecessarily robbed of sympathy when she poisons him, since he could 'so easily poison himself by mistake'. The fault is compounded by allowing 'this patriotic heroine ... a sentimental love outburst over his body'. At the performance under review this speech was 'resented and derided by the audience', spoiling 'the intense enthusiasm' which the play had aroused thus far.[274] Yet in Melville's *Female Hun* the general's shooting of his wife, the female Hun, achieves a gain in emotional intensity from the fact that he still loves her. Nor is the difference merely that it is in order for a general to kill, his very uniform entitling him to do so.

In *The Toast* the Germans are declared 'Shocking outsiders' for respecting 'the White Flag as little as they do the Red Cross on the Ambulance Waggons'. But the censor draws the line at a Prussian officer telling a young woman: 'I'll whip you first and dishonour you afterwards', and commanding her to take off 'every stitch' of her clothes. More interesting as regards censorship is G. Henderson's *Beast of Berlin* (John Lawson was evidently part-author too). The censor comments that it was refused a licence as *The Bloody Beast of Berlin*, but had now jettisoned passages calculated 'to inflame the passions of an audience against alien-enemies, as bread-poisoners and so forth. In their place we have attacks upon "the Crown Prince" as looter and instigator of the bad treatment of "poor Belgiums".'[275] However, Newton saw it under the latter title, and the technique adopted, altering 'the piece night by night in order to drop in all the latest war episodes', would have been wholly unworkable without evading the Lord Chamberlain. Newton went expecting to see a 'Zeppelin descent episode', but it was replaced by a more topical and 'most realistic scene representing the anti-alien Deptford riots and the smashing of certain German shops. This wild and whirling patriotic pasticcio teems with rousing recruiting appeals and denunciations of our treacherous enemy.'[276] The Deptford riot had all the signs of being carefully orchestrated, especially as similar, though smaller, outbreaks occurred simultaneously in Camberwell and Southwark. A force of 200 police was unable to cope and 350 soldiers were called in.[277] Belcham virtuously reflects that 'the self-control and sobriety of the middle-classes prevent them from ebullitions like the recent riots in the East End'.[278] He might have considered, firstly, that German pork-butchers were not a common feature of refined suburbia; and, secondly, that people of refinement had worked hard to inflame those considered less refined with a barrage of hate propaganda. In some ways these riots become a paradigm of the war itself: the working class manipulated into doing the dirty work of a socially superior class. But in this case the latter kept aloof from the violence and was thus able to repudiate it after the event. Pieces like Henderson's not only recorded but incited such incidents. That this one was allowed to run for a while unlicensed suggests that its inflammatory rôle was not unwelcome.

In Henderson's resubmitted text Belgian girls coming to Britain as refugees are met at the station in eighteenth-century fashion by bawds who whisk them off to prostitution. Amongst the crowd are representatives of 'The Peace Loving Party' who, appealing to the tax-payer, are told: 'The tax payer of this country knows exactly what he is doing', and, for the sake of his children, is determined 'to see it through'. As far as the censor was concerned it was open season on notable members of that 'peace loving party': as seen earlier, the most vicious insults could be directed at Keir Hardie and Ramsay Macdonald without reproach. But otherwise there was careful policing where well-known figures or the socially elevated were concerned. The ordinary citizen had no protection if his name was used for the darkest of stage villains; but a chorus lady in Barrie's *Rosy Rapture* could not be labelled 'The Hon. Lady Lascelles' because that was 'an actual aristocratic name'; and Allsopp (family name of Lord Hindlip) was deleted from Willie Benn's *Pass On Please*.[279] The censor found the name Sir Carl Spielmeyer, given to the enemy agent in Harris and Valentine's *The Lads of the Village*, too 'near Sir Carl Meyer'; and it was changed to Sir Karl Swinestein.[280] Of a similar figure in Lawrence Cowen's *The Hidden Hand*, the censor decided that making him a privy councillor owning a portrait of the King presented 'by his Gracious Majesty himself' was going too far (especially as it concealed a 'wireless installation').[281] Royalty came in for the most rigorous protection. In Neil Lyons's *A Bit of a Lad*, an agreeable conversation in a Paddington shop between a shy soldier and 'a high-spirited cockney girl' behind the counter, the latter was found a touch too high-spirited for the censor, who disliked her response on hearing that the soldier's name is George: 'The same as Mr. Robey and our King.'[282]

The instinct to maintain the dignity of the Kaiser was sound but hardly feasible. Faced with an unmistakable Kaiser-figure in Barrie's *Der Tag*, critics asked why he was not made up accordingly, Newton pointing out that the rules forbade it.[283] The same applied to Eustace Ponsonby's curiosity, *To-day and To-morrow*, where Britannia croons 'Oh, Willie, I have missed you', and the Kaiser (who, says the censor, 'must not be made up as such') tows in 'a profile property Little Willie after the celebrated Haselden cartoons'.[284] Mill's *In Time of War* was considered 'probably the first melodrama to put the German Emperor on the stage', although transparently disguised as 'Prince Siegfried, the War Lord'. He 'marches around in his great helmet with the eagle on top, and boasts of ruling the earth for all the world like Herod the king in the old miracle plays'.[285] But the pass was already sold with Austin and Ridgwell's *Parker Captures the Kaiser*. *The Stage*'s reviewer (18 February 1915, p. 17), acknowledging that there are 'those who object to such things, notwithstanding the drastic treatment' accorded the Kaiser in newspaper caricature, considers the sketch saved by its sheer comicality.[286] But there was still concern not to allow satire on the private life of the Turkish commander Enver, or of Field Marshal von der Goltz, commander of the Turkish 6th army, desiring Enver's wife.[287] And even in 1917 it was deemed 'unfair', though allowed to stand, that a spy in Howard's *Seven Days' Leave* should be described as 'the Crown Prince's mistress'.[288]

There was concern about any kind of authority figure. Street was given pause by Charles Longden's *Doing His Bit*, where a medical examiner passes men who are too old for active service: 'A real doctor would hardly do such things.'[289] And he regrets that British policemen are not 'protected from ridicule, as soldiers are now'.[290] Critic and censor were equally zealous about the latter. Even in a light comedy like Jesse and Harwood's *Billeted*, Newton found portrayal of sexual stirrings in a colonel inappropriate: 'Most of the current colonels that I happen to have met have been keen, able men', too committed to make 'fools of themselves over chits of girls'. Since the play is set in 1915 and Harwood is a serving captain, Newton allows that there may have been some such colonels around at that time ('No wonder we made a mess of things'); but they 'have been cleared out now'.[291] *The Little Soldier*, a comic-strip spy play, made Street uneasy because an English captain throws in his lot with a female German spy, as did *In the Secret Service* where a naval captain tells his wife official secrets; but the pieces were thought too trivial to worry about.[292] It is pointless to deride the censor for inconsistency. Insistence that a naval officer's garb in Martin Byam's *That's Enough* should be non-regulation, though the character was 'not meant to be ridiculous and service uniforms are so common on the stage', was due partly to the revue context and more especially to the Admiralty's having 'become very particular about Navy uniforms'.[293] The censor was concerned about the dignity of the uniform and its accessories in Sewell Collins's *The Quitter*, where an American has had a rough time serving with the RAMC and decides to seize the opportunity of a short leave to take ship back home. His gesture of throwing his 'water-logged uniform into a corner' was disallowed; it had to be returned to the wardrobe. Likewise, 'To Hell with the medals, they can take the medals and hang them on Christmas trees' was softened to read 'reputation' in place of 'the medals'.[294]

While ensuring 'that any barbarity exhibited should not be too horrible or disgusting' was reasonably straightforward, the censor experienced more trouble in guarding 'the King's uniform' from ridicule since 'the comic relief man generally enlists and continues to be comic relief: I take that to be unobjectionable provided he is made a decent fellow and does nothing derogatory to the character of a soldier.'[295] But performers were warned to enact Tommy with respect,[296] and Cris Hamilton had to eliminate a soldier-rogue from *What Happened to Jane?*[297] Preston's *Constantinople 1915* opens in the slave market of the Turkish capital, and the delightful stage direction 'some

Harem women scream ... pursued by British sailors laughing' is marked 'undesirable'.[298] Even Ruritanian armies had to be spared burlesque, so the 'skit on army drills' in John Tiller's *Monte Carlo to Tokio* was blue-pencilled; and so was a comic inspection of Indian soldiers in Norman Lee's *The Dream Girl*.[299] An acceptable solution for the presentation of the private soldier was found once focus shifted somewhat from the officer-hero. The innovator here was Bruce Bairnsfather, a captain in the Warwickshire Regiment, who brought the flavour of his immensely successful Old Bill cartoons to the stage. There were depths to his humour. As he said of his 'Better 'Ole' cartoon: 'It is, I hope, not only humorous chaff of Mr. Atkins about a shell-hole he has known, but a human cry from the bedrock of war-life, "Oh, Lord, deliver us," an appeal against man's inhumanity to man, which makes countless thousands mourn, a cry to the heights for a "Better 'Ole".'[300] His most important stage work is *The Better 'Ole*, a visit to which at the Oxford Brigadier L. H. Harris recalls as the highlight of his leave in August 1918.[301] But there were a couple of exploratory ventures before that. In conjunction with fellow soldier Macdonald Hastings, a lance-corporal at this time, he provided a scene for the revue *Flying Colours*, entitled 'Bairnsfatherland, or The Johnson 'Ole'.[302] At the censor's office it was thought that 'The authorship is a guarantee of lifelikeness and ... takes away any possible offence there could be in treating trench life lightly.'[303] A running joke is the supposed general who has fallen into a Johnson hole, and Bert's anxiety about whether he should 'let him drift or fish 'im out'. A follow-up, 'Where Did That One Go?', was introduced into *See-Saw*, with the landlord of a ruined estaminet in which Bairnsfather's Tommies have been sheltering, recovering his savings from beneath the staircase. Bendall insists that 'there is no suggestion that, even if the Tommies had found the money, they would have done anything with it but the right thing'.[304] Golsworthy (*Bystander* 21 March 1917, p. 568) took a more realistic view, stressing the Tommies' excitement over discovering a few francs in the ruins when they had 'missed the real prize, ... the proprietor's strong-box'.

Bairnsfather's initiative spawned numerous imitations. But Unger and Lyons's *London Pride* achieved freshness by an ingenious splicing of the Bairnsfather element with a picture of coster recruiting, complete with ' "moke" and barrow', which had already done service in Delome and Foley's *Get over There*.[305] *London Pride* follows the career of Tunks, 'a cheery young costermonger', who enlists, leaving his donkey and barrow to his sweetheart Cherry.[306] Worried about Cherry, and having his leave stopped, he first performs a deed of gallantry and then deserts by exchanging identities with a dead comrade. The play acknowledges that desertion was a capital offence when a pal warns that for his seven days he will get seven years if he's lucky, 'And a seven foot hole' if he's not. However, as Daphne du Maurier puts it, his 'discreditable performance was glossed over' by his heroism, fitting the needs of 1917. Seventeen years on (sobering comment on our hectic civilization), she found the play 'as antiquated and as buried as the words "Blighty," "Hun," and "Tommy" that lie stored away in the dusty places of men's minds', though at the time 'it helped in a not inglorious fashion to foster some measure of hope and belief in the hearts of those who saw it'.[307] Although episodic, moving from dugout to 'café behind the line where a body on a stretcher was borne past the open door, and thence to the hospital haunted by an impossible lady visitor', finally returning to the world of pearlie king and queen, *London Pride* scored rather through atmosphere than construction. Gerald du Maurier caught 'the lightheartedness, the unfailing humour and sensitiveness of the Cockney most admirably'. But just occasionally 'his voice betrays the cultured intonation of the well-bred man'; so Tunks, splendid symbol of London pride and war hero, is for all that uncultured and ill bred.[308] The great social divide shows all too clearly in these reviews, though *Athenæum*'s man (December 1916, p. 616) took a fairly impressive shot at wartime readjustment. He was enchanted by the second scene with its 'barrow and real "moke" ', and admired the resolve of those left behind to 'carry on' after the two coster comrades had enlisted: 'Any one who sees them smother their grief and drive off on their first round without realizing it as a glimpse into the intrinsic worth of the "lower" orders must either be very callous or must just have returned from trying to retain some "indispensable" relative in a position of more authority than utility.' In such scenes, 'real humanity made players and audience one'.

The Lads of the Village (Valentine's book with music and lyrics by Tate and Clifford Harris) was told in flash-back, and included a recruiting bioscope, sinking of a U-boat and Mesopotamian trench scenes embellished with 'a number of discharged wounded soldiers'.[309] It anticipated the mode of Bairnsfather and Eliot's *The Better 'Ole*, which it preceded at the Oxford, so Newton's claim that the latter pioneered 'the singing melodrama, which is so essentially a War-time revival', is inaccurate.[310] But *The Better 'Ole* established the genre; for Cochran it was 'The only product of the stage that can be directly traced to the influence of the war, and will probably become a classic', breathing 'the very essence of the humanity of the war'.[311] When he took on the play it had already been turned down by Butt, de Courville and Charlot. He was fortunate in being able to mount it at the Oxford, 'a theatre with an atmosphere of "Old Bill" and beer'.[312] The crudity in plotting and construction hardly weighed against simplicity, unflagging humour and 'the Bairnsfather types, [standing] for the optimistic philosophy of "Tommy" in the tremendous conflict ... It was the exact psychological moment for a war play without false heroics.' Energetically, Cochran turned the Oxford's box office into a dugout and hid the lobby under sandbags,[313] his one concern being Bourchier's Old

Bill, a character the actor never fully grasped. When John Humphries, who had 'given a masterly performance of Old Bill' in *Any Old Thing* (Pavilion, 1917), took over from Bourchier, he proved the best Bill in Cochran's experience, though not quite equalling Tom Woottwell's Bert. [314]

Findon waxed lyrical: 'Through Flemish clay and Leeds khaki cloth, shines forth the unsophisticated humour and the sturdy commonsense of a man of the people ... In the depths of his nature Old Bill stands equally for peer and peasant.' He and his comrades, who to the ordinary eye might seem 'rough, uncultured', show, through Bairnsfather's 'instinctive grasp of character, ... as unconscious heroes, as the salt of Empire'.[315] Having something of revue's flexibility, the play could comfortably accommodate additions. French cartoonist Poulbot's *Les Gosses dans les ruines*, adapted by Brigadier-General Cannot as *Kiddies in the Ruins*, was 'neatly introduced into the second act ... by Old Bill starting to tell the story thereof to Alf and Bert'. The scene fades and blackened ruins are disclosed. 'While his children in their Somme village play amid the relics of Hun savagery, prancing like their enemy or making believe to be the Kaiser, a tragedy is all prepared and waiting for their father on the march with his comrades. But though the discovery he makes of their mother's fate makes him see red' – Sybil Thorndike, in only her second West End rôle, played the distracted woman – 'they go on with their play. Truth here supplies its own moral.'[316] Poulbot's piece was deleted at the Armistice, but Armistice night saw its own interpolations. Seated outside a café the pals discussed the mysterious paper which Bill first obtained from the spy, and then sold him for £80. Alf thought it might have been the peace terms, but 'Bill replied with a snort' that they'd 'want more than eighty quid for them'. Eventually Bill received a letter: ' "Best wishes to you all and to the audience. A far, far better 'ole has been found at last. – Bruce Bairnsfather." The audience yelled itself hoarse.'[317]

That was the end; but well before the end people like Thurston had pondered which way theatre might go after the Armistice. Grein imagined the pioneer societies preparing managerial opinion for a completely new type of problem play. He was not only over-optimistic about the receptivity of commercial managements, but curiously adrift in supposing that aspects of the women's war would continue to hold interest after the event.[318] More percipiently, Farjeon saw an immediate reaction against the war; then, a few decades on, war would be approached and appraised in terms quite different from those currently obtaining: 'no great ado about spies', nor about pacifists or women workers, who by that time would have become commonplace; and 'no realistic representations of submarines, as in "Seven Days' Leave" ', since such scientific marvels would appear too shabbily obsolete to thrill. The Russian Revolution would be popular, though less so than the French had been;[319] but the Kaiser would vie with Napoleon as a popular stage figure. Indeed, Farjeon saw the war celebrity theme as dominating, with plays on Lloyd George rivalling those on Disraeli, while Haig, Kitchener, Northcliffe and Gaby Deslys would also serve as protagonists.[320] There was no suspicion that the very events of the war, along with some politic manipulation, would help to shift dramatic focus from leader to led.

Notes

1. Ruby Miller, *Champagne from My Slipper* (Jenkins, 1962), p. 61.
2. It was the Shops Act of 1912 which originally popularized the matinée, and it was new social factors in 1916 which made them a practical means of evading air-raids in the West End.
3. The war months of 1914 saw in the West End 'some 16 new plays' compared with '21 revivals (not counting Shakespeare)', the earlier part of the year having produced only six revivals (Baughan, *SYB 1915*, p. 1).
4. *Stage* 12.3.14, 34. *Daily Sketch* 14.9.14, 5, noted that already the Apollo, a theatre associated with musical plays, had dispensed with its orchestra, though the surplus of musicians made it an easy matter to reconstitute one when necessary.
5. Grein, *Sunday Times* 27.6.15, 4.
6. *Sunday Times* 27.6.15, 4.
7. *SYB 1916*, pp. 10, 12.
8. *Stage* 13.8.14, 18.
9. Baughan, *SYB 1915*, p. 12.
10. Grein, *Era* 29.11.16, 13; Weller, *SYB 1917*, p. 15.
11. Baughan, *SYB 1915*, p. 12.
12. *Era* 12.6.18, 6. Ernest Irving, *Cue for Music* (Dobson, 1959), p. 63, touring *The Count of Luxembourg* in the early weeks of war, found it lucrative to fill in for disbanded companies. Weller, *SYB 1916*, p. 11, discounts *Era*'s worry (4.8.15, 13) about the precarious state of the provincial theatre: if some 'business is not good, ... it was not good before the war'.
13. *Graphic* 14.11.14, 692 ('by a well-known actress'). *Daily Sketch* 21.9.14, 5, printed an appeal for distressed small-part players.
14. *SYB 1916*, p. 13.
15. *Performer* 19.11.14, 12.
16. Baughan, *SYB 1915*, p. 13; Farjeon, *'Era' Annual 1918*, p. 36. Before the introduction of entertainment tax, seating at the cheaper suburban halls ranged 'from a shilling in the stalls to threepence in the gallery' (*Era* 22.9.15, 13).

17. Baughan, *SYB 1915*, pp. 11, 13. In some regions twice-nightly did entail some reduction in seat prices, especially when dark nights discouraged attendance at second houses (*Era* 22.12.15, 20).
18. *Era* 20.1.15, 14.
19. After intensive campaigning the Actors' Association voted overwhelmingly on 1 November 1918 to reconstitute itself, ratifying on 22 November 1918. As an avowed believer in the survival of the fittest, Kerr deplored this 'socialistic' move, as well as Sydney Valentine's heroic work in securing a standard contract, which ensured that 'all artists engaged at a salary of ten pounds a week and under were to be paid a certain amount for rehearsing'. He quotes Irving approvingly that, far from being paid, 'a great many actors ought to pay very highly for what they learn at rehearsals' (Fred Kerr, *Recollections of a Defective Memory* (Thornton Butterworth, 1930), p. 215). Tree, just before the war, had 'initiated the principle of payment for rehearsals, and it was predicted that his example would be generally followed' (*Era* 6.9.15, 11). But it took more than goodwill to change a practice which usually meant six weeks' saved salaries (Maisie Gay, *Laughing through Life* (Hurst & Blackett, 1931), pp. 251–2).
20. *Stage* 24.2.16, 19; *Stage* 2.3.16, 16.
21. *Daily News* 13.9.16, 3, reported that the Academy of Dramatic Art had just 'two male students as against 40 before the war'.
22. Frank Stayton, *Weekly Dispatch* 8.9.18, 5.
23. *Era* 11.9.18, 9.
24. *Era* 22.3.16, 19.
25. *Pall Mall Gazette* 15.3.15, 4.
26. *Bystander* 7.2.17, 228.
27. *Era* 16.10.18, 11.
28. Baughan, *SYB 1915*, p. 1.
29. *Sunday Times* 3.11.18, 4.
30. Huntly Carter, *The New Spirit in the European Theatre 1914–1924* (Benn, 1925), p. 25.
31. *Era* 28.2.17, 13.
32. 'Candida', *Graphic* 19.10.18, 444.
33. *Athenæum* 8.17, 395.
34. *Era* 4.3.14, 19.
35. *Era* 10.11.15, 15.
36. *New Age* 20.4.16, 588.
37. *Graphic* 5.2.16, 208.
38. *The Times* 1.1.15, 3. Lena Ashwell, *Era* 27.12.16, 5, reinforces the point. She rebuts the idea 'of the superior person ... that an expensively

cultivated mind [is] necessary for real appreciation' with her experience of soldier audiences, who offer 'a quicker response to the real thing when they meet it' than any high-toned audience. Cf. Jesse and Harwood, when a woman is asked where she takes soldiers on leave in London: 'Musical comedies if they're officers and Shakespeare or Westminster Abbey or something of that sort if they're men' (*Billeted* (French, 1920), pp. 11–12).

39. St John Ervine, *The Theatre in My Time* (Rich & Cowan, 1933), p. 117.
40. *SYB 1916*, pp. 1, 9.
41. Fenton, *World* 20.4.15, 630.
42. *Era* 21.4.15, 11.
43. Basil Macdonald Hastings, *Advertisement* (French, 1915), p. 62.
44. Grein (*Sunday Times* 18.4.15, 6) found it offensive to Jews and insensitive to present conditions, so that 'in any other capital involved in war, it would have aroused a scene of indignation'. *Athenæum*'s notice, on the other hand, takes in its stride 'racial attributes, such as acquisitiveness and love of display' before veering off into naïve fantasy of a post-war world when the 'blatant advertisement of a worthless article' will no longer yield success, and the 'nation will have to concentrate on satisfying needs instead of ephemeral wants' (24.4.15, 389).
45. *Era* 20.11.18, 12, quotes Charles Gulliver on the Palladium Cigarettes and Comforts Fund, which 'had enabled him to send 23,000,000 cigarettes to the troops' as well as more for canteens. F. V. St. Clair, patriotic songwriter, devoted all the profits from the sale of his songs to war charities including 'over £1,500 worth of tobacco and cigarettes' for soldiers on active service (*Era* 18.9.18, 20).
46. *Graphic* 9.3.18, 320.
47. *London Gazette Supplement* 5.12.16, 11915. When Harrods ran foul of this, *The Times* (5.2.16, 3) emphasized how 'exceedingly dangerous' morphine was for men on active service.
48. *Era* 27.10.15, 10; *Referee* 25.7.15, 2.
49. LC 1916: 17/367. According to one reviewer, the play's only merit was that it was earning money for the Blue Cross Fund (*Era* 2.8.16, 10). Earlier, Charles Hannan's *The Opium Eater*, first produced in New York, was shown at Richmond (*Era* 27.10.15, 11).
50. *Era* 1.5.18, 13.
51. *Era* 7.6.16, 13. This 'weirdly-lighted' scene 'with smokers dimly discerned reclining on their bunks' echoed one in *Everything New – Not Likely!* (*Stage* 8.6.16, 18; *Graphic* 26.12.14, 892). *Beauty Spot* had its *Hashish Dream*, Régine Flory being flung about with reckless abandon by Jan Oyra, a Russian who had been badly wounded in the war with Japan

(*Referee* 23.12.17, 3; W. J. Macqueen-Pope, *Gaiety: Theatre of Enchantment* (Allen, 1949), p. 449).

52. *Evening News* 13.6.15, 3; *Evening News* 14.6.16, 3.
53. *Daily Sketch* 10.12.18, 5. In typically self-reflexive style the revue *Summer Boarders* features a revue star deserted by her lover because 'she is addicted to the opium habit' (*Era* 20.12.16, 6).
54. *Stage* 9.3.16, 18.
55. *The Times* 8.5.17, 3.
56. *Era* 21.8.18, 8.
57. Due to be produced by Harley Granville Barker, it fell under Tree's prediction at the outbreak of war 'that sex problem plays will not be popular for the moment' (*Referee* 23.8.14, 3).
58. Desmond MacCarthy, *Drama* (Putnam, 1940), p. 208.
59. Ervine, *Theatre in My Time*, p. 102.
60. *Era* 6.12.16, 11.
61. *Graphic* 24.3.17, 358.
62. *Era* 15.8.17, 11.
63. Farjeon, *'Era' Annual 1918*, p. 37.
64. *Era* 30.10.18, 11.
65. Clifford Rean, *Tainted Goods* (Birmingham: Moody, 1918), p. 11.
66. This was a common aspersion directed at soldiers' wives from working-class districts; cf. *Times* 20.1.15, 10, for a rebuttal. But Lloyd George's temperance concerns found rather less support on stage than might have been expected; a scene in Wylie and Parker's *Kisses* where a drunk journeys to Manchester 'to act as a horrible example at a temperance meeting' was the kind of send-up which William Poel found depressingly widespread (*Stage* 3.2.16, 14; *Era* 20.9.16, 13). When a version of Zola's *L'Assommoir* was played at the Battersea Palace there was reference to drink as 'one of the most popular – or unpopular questions of the hour' (*Era* 5.5.15, 12). Temperance themes occur in Leonard Mortimer's *The Lane Without a Turning* and *Damaged Lives*, a playlet given at Burslem incorporating film of Burslem street scenes (*Era* 8.8.17, 8; *Era* 12.9.17, 14).
67. *Era* 20.11.18, 5.
68. *Era* 9.10.18, 5.
69. *Referee* 14.4.18, 3.
70. *Era* 17.4.18, 1. Barbara Gott, who 'gave a vivid and menacing little sketch of the prophetic old Negress', relates how a chance encounter with a 'coloured gentleman' from Virginia enabled her to translate her 'part – for it was mostly in ordinary English – into proper coloured Virginian English' (*Stage* 18.4.18, 14; *Era* 21.5.18, 4).

71. *Era* 31.1.17, 16; *Era* 7.2.17, 14.
72. *Referee* 20.6.15, 4; *Referee* 25.7.15, 3.
73. *Referee* 30.9.17, 5. This is impresario's puff: it only had its première (in Schenectady) on 16 October 1916. But it ran for 251 performances at the Duke of York's.
74. *French,* 1922, p. 14; MacCarthy, *Drama,* p. 296.
75. *Era* 29.3.16, 13. Hackett followed up with another play hinging on the influence of the spirit world, *The Invisible Foe,* again played at the Savoy by Irving.
76. Newton, *Referee* 27.12.14, 2.
77. Nares, *Myself and Some Others* (Duckworth, 1925), pp. 160–2, thought his Micawber 'magnificent', but Fenton, *World* 29.12.14, 248, mightily impressed by his Peggotty, considered Micawber 'very amusing but rather over-burlesqued'. One perceptive critic (*Times* 26.12.14, 9) spotted affinities between the latter and Richard II, Tree's finest Shakespearean assumption.
78. Heinemann, 1918.
79. Douglas Murray, *The Man from Toronto* (French, 1919), pp. 73, 75.
80. Published as *The Celebrity* (Hodder and Stoughton, 1926), pp. 27, 29.
81. *Sphere* 30.1.15, vi.
82. *Stage* 21.1.15, 22.
83. *Graphic* 17.2.17, 206.
84. Koopman, *'Era' Annual 1917,* p. 30.
85. *Referee* 13.2.16, 3.
86. Henry Maltby, *Rotters* (French, 1925), pp. 7–9.
87. *Stage's* reviewer (3.8.16, 18), enjoying the 'caustic and pungently diverting dialogue', was gratified that, since the play's première, the chauffeur was no longer an incognito KC, but merely the son of a KC.
88. *The Times* 12.3.17, 11; *Graphic* 17.3.17, 332.
89. *Nation* 1.6.18, 224; Israel Zangwill, *The Works of Israel Zangwill* (Globe, 1925), p. xiii. Notably, Zangwill was a women's rights activist (*The Times* 26.2.15, 5).
90. Allardyce Nicoll credits Maltby (*Rotters*) with originating the alienation principle (*English Drama 1900–1930* (Cambridge: Cambridge University Press, 1973) p. 365).
91. *Era* 10.11.15, 15.
92. *Peg* was aptly named; the point is made in *Illustrated London News* (17.10.14, 556) that Manners had done no more than provide a peg for exploiting the personality of the star, his vivacious American wife Laurette Taylor.
93. Baughan, *SYB 1917,* p. 4.
94. *Cartoon* 29.4.15, 362.

95. *Era* 2.1.18, 21.
96. Baughan, *SYB 1918*, p. 5; *SYB 1919*, p. 4.
97. Letter from Lt C. A. P. Gardiner (20.4.15) in Richmond MSS (National Maritime Museum RIC/7/4).
98. *Era* 3.11.15, 15, where it is described as 'real, old-fashioned, wildly extravagant, knockabout farce'. In Redvers Dent's war novel, *Show Me Death!* (Toronto: Macmillan, 1930), p. 320, an officer mentions *The Bing Boys* and *A Little Bit of Fluff* as 'the best shows I have seen for a long time'.
99. *Illustrated London News* 25.5.18, 624.
100. *Era* 24.4.18, 1.
101. LC 1917: 7/871, reports dated 18.3.16, 13.3.17 and 26.4.17.
102. White, *Era* 4.4.17, 8.
103. *Era* 27.6.17, 1.
104. *Passing Show* 29.5.15, 19.
105. Golsworthy, *Bystander* 21.3.17, 566; *Bystander* 21.2.17, 349.
106. LC 1916: 17/372.
107. *Era* 9.8.16, 7.
108. *Era* 15.3.16, 15.
109. Cyril W. Beaumont, *The Diaghilev Ballet in London* (1940, rept. Putman, 1945), pp. 51, 54.
110. Beaumont, *Diaghilev Ballet*, p. 13. Asche complains of the controversy aroused over the orgy scene in his *Cairo*: 'It was daring, but not more so than the Russian Ballet' (*Oscar Asche: His Life* (Hurst and Blackett, 1929), p.173).
111. Marks, *Referee* 13.10.18, 5. *The Times*'s reviewer (11.10.18, 6) found it 'a strange contrast to pass from the surroundings of the glorified fair ground of Trafalgar-square to those of the Persian harem as imagined by M. Bakst'; though presumably Bakst's 1910 Paris designs, with bare-breasted odalisques and the Red Sultana in transparent trousers which enhanced rather than concealed her bare bottom, had been toned down. But one amazing Bakstian effect is recalled by Carter, 'obtained by a wide range of colours brought in by the slaves and eunuchs and set vibrating against a great mass of emerald green, and by the swaying lines caught up and repeated by every object and agent in the scene' (*New Spirit*, p. 108).
112. Beaumont, *Diaghilev Ballet*, p. 119; *Era* 18.9.18, 19.
113. *Era* 23.11.16, 21; *Era* 29.12.15, 24. Ginner's piece was played throughout the war. The wartime appeal of Pierrot is glanced at in a review of Eric Lyall's *Two Pierrot Plays* (*Bookman*, 9.18, 194), which describes him as the elusive 'spirit of Romance' carrying 'us far enough away from the racket of battle into the world of dreams'. Lt Lyall had written one of the plays while hospitalized after his return from Gallipoli.

114. *Era* 18.11.14, 6.
115. *Era* 7.2.17, 13.
116. Its first London performance was at a St James's matinée, 3.12.18.
117. *Era* 25.11.14, 6. This had been done at the Kingsway in 1911, and the Birmingham Rep gave it in September 1918. Another of Chekhov's shorts, *The Wedding*, was performed by the Pioneer Players at the Grafton Galleries, 14.5.17.
118. Nikolai N. Evreinov, *The Theatre of the Soul, a Monodrama*, trans. M. Potapenko and C. St John (Hendersons, 1915), p. 9. St John had already detailed Charlot's antics in *New Age* 25.11.15, 95.
119. *The Times* 9.3.15, 11.
120. St John, Introduction to *The Theatre of the Soul*, p. 11.
121. *Era* 10.3.15, 8; Newton, *Referee* 14.3.15, 2.
122. It was also done by the Birmingham Rep, 26.10.16.
123. *Daily Telegraph* 3.4.16, 5; *Referee* 9.4.16, 3. *Era* 12.4.16, 9, approved it as 'a beautiful, weird little fantasy'. A full translation appeared in *New Age*, 25.11.15, 86–9.
124. Trans. Julius West (Hendersons, 1916). A vicar's shouted absolution to a man thought to be in imminent danger of falling to his death was considered 'very bad taste' by Newton, *Referee* 6.2.16, 3. Andreyev's *The Life of Man*, given at Edinburgh's Lyceum in 1915, had its mordant pessimism overtaken by events, whereupon he produced *The Sorrows of Belgium* (Macmillan, 1915).
125. *Referee*, 25.11.17, 3.
126. *New Age* 12.4.17, 565. Marie has known love only from a sickly mongrel, and it is notable that she can respond with genuine grief at the creature's death.
127. Letter dated 23.5.18.
128. *Referee* 24.2.18, 2.
129. *The Times* 15.6.15, 9.
130. LC 1917: 4/792.
131. Links between this Cologne company and the peripheral excitements of the London stage are clear from the presence of Inez Bensusan, starring in her own comedy, *The Singer of the Veld*, immediately before the Beaumont production. Bensusan, who appeared frequently with various theatre societies, was also in the 1914 West End productions of Zangwill's *Melting Pot* and *Plaster Saints*.
132. Cf. the girl in *Flying Colours* (LC 1916: 22/457): 'I loathe carrying parcels. It makes one feel so middle class.'
133. *Era* 10.3.15, 15.
134. *Weekly Dispatch* 5.8.17, 6.

135. *Stage* 10.2.16, 22.
136. Edward Sheldon, *Romance* (Macmillan, 1918), p. 86.
137. *Star* 11.1.17, 2. *Star* 18.1.17, 2, notes only one Welshman in the cast, Wordley Hulse as Simon Morris the deacon; *The Times* 9.1.17, 9, comments that he 'was the only member of the company who came near to the right Glamorgan accent'.
138. Stratford-upon-Avon: Shakespeare Head, 1917, p. 21. An incidental interest is the play's attention to South Welsh working-class enthusiasm for education (pp.11, 21).
139. Frank Stayton, '*The Joan Danvers*' (French, 1926), pp. 19, 36.
140. Newton, *Referee* 13.2.16, 3.
141. *Era* 8.12.15, 15, notes that the early uncertainties of war had not seriously affected receipts at Birmingham. However, Liverpool's repertory theatre had become commercialized before the end of the war.
142. Rupert Brooke, *Lithuania* (Sidgwick & Jackson, 1935), p. vi.
143. *Plays of To-day*, vol. I, (Sidgwick & Jackson, 1925), p. 122.
144. Milne had no trouble establishing himself on the West End stage. For Newton (*Referee* 14.4.18, 2) his work sparkled with 'clean-bred wit'; and his first offering, *Wurzel-Flummery*, 'was the most delightful and cultured comedy of the year' (Farjeon, *'Era' Annual 1918*, p. 36). Irene Vanbrugh defines his characters as 'real flesh and blood seen behind a gauze of true fantasy, without being whimsical' (*To Tell My Story* (Hutchinson, 1948), p. 118).
145. LC 1917: 9/899; Robb Lawson, *Bookman* 3.18, 194.
146. *Era* 19.7.16, 15.
147. *Manchester Guardian* 24.5.16, 4.
148. *Era* 7.7.15, 13.
149. *The Times* 7.1.16, 11.
150. *Era* 27.9.16, 12. Cf. Newton at the Court, *Referee* 2.4.16, 3: 'the amount of needless talk in a play is not lessened by speaking it so that only half the audience can hear.'
151. Newton, *Referee* 6.10.18, 2. At another point, 'when one of the characters speaks of Germany conquering the world, a woman, on the first night, shouted out with passionate conviction, "Never!" ' (*Graphic* 12.10.18, 410).
152. *Performer* 31.10.18, 15.
153. *Era* 7.4.15, 8.
154. *Era* 7.6.16, 13. It was noted that the new war-woman had put 'insolently wicked women [temporarily] out of fashion' (*The Times* 1.6.16, 11).
155. Farjeon, *'Era' Annual 1918*, p. 40.
156. *Era* 13.9.16, 9.

157. Stanley Lupino, *From the Stocks to the Stars* (Hutchinson, 1934), pp. 194–5.
158. LC 1916: 22/452. Interest in spectacle translated easily to the war play. The battle of Jutland and the assault on Zeebrugge were re-enacted respectively in Frank Price's *Mother's Sailor Boy* and Hicks and Shirley's *Jolly Jack Tar*, the latter 'so realistically that there were quite a number of casualties' according to Charles Graves (*The Cochran Story* (Allen, 1951), p. 68). Characteristic exploitation of the air war occurs in Wallace's *The Enemy in Our Midst*, with 'a most effectively worked Zeppelin raid', where the airship is eventually sent down in flames by a British aircraft (*Era* 20.9.16, 18; *Era* 4.12.18, 13; *Era* 15.9.15, 8).
159. *The Times* 10.3.17, 4.
160. *Era* 4.10.16. 8. Besier took the idea from a play produced in Berlin about a year before the war, when the author and company, all natives of Alsace-Lorraine, were imprisoned for *lèse majesté* (*Era* 20.9.16, 8).
161. J. M. Bulloch, *Graphic* 8.5.15, 606. Resemblance was detected to 'the famous Stanford White and Thaw murder case', in which the celebrated architect was shot dead by Harry Thaw in full view of the Madison Square Garden first-night audience on 25.6.06.
162. *World* 4.5.15, 709; *Era* 5.5.15, 13.
163. *Era* 4.10.16, 15; *The Times* 2.10.16, 11.
164. *Get-Away* (LC 1916: 22/461).
165. *Era* 18.11.14, 12.
166. *Era* 16.12.14, 9. Leon Pollock's brutal play *The Rat* (LC 1916: 3/69) exemplifies how the apache play tended to overlap with grand guignol.
167. *Era* 21.2.17, 22.
168. *Era* 14.2.17, 14.
169. Newton, *Referee* 20.1.18, 2; Baughan, *SYB 1918*, p. 2.
170. Grein, *Era* 30.5.17, 1.
171. *Graphic* 27.10.17, 526; *Era* 29.3.16, 13.
172. *Era* 15.9.15, 20; *Era* 29.9.15, 13.
173. *Era* 6.2.18, 1. Raffles and C. M. S. McLellan's Kleschna were memorably played by du Maurier and Ashwell respectively.
174. *Stage* 2.9.15, 20.
175. *Era* 22.12.15, 18.
176. *Era* 1.9.15, 13.
177. *Era* 10.3.15, 11.
178. *Graphic* 2.10.15, 442. Under the title of *Some Detective, The Dummy* was adapted for the variety stage, with Wee Georgie Wood as the office-boy detective, and the action was eked out with 'film pictures' (*Era* 21.3.17, 14). O'Higgins and Ford's *The Argyle Case* (1912), concerned with graft amongst members of the New York police, reached this country during

the war, Julia Neilson and Fred Terry starring at the Strand (*Stage* 29.4.15, 19).

179. Fenton, *World* 31.8.15, 212, says of *Kick-In*: 'Five years ago an English audience would have needed a glossary ... but we are being swiftly educated up to American idioms, and their apt expressiveness causes them to take root in our effete vocabulary.' A song in *My Lady Frayle* (1916), p. 15, refers to 'Yankee slang, Now ... so much in vogue'.
180. *Era* 29.5.18, 5.
181. *Era* 20.3.18, 12.
182. *Era* 7.10.14, 12; *Era* 14.10.14, 9.
183. *Era* 2.2.16, 24; *Era* 19.12.17, 13.
184. *Era* 15.11.16, 15. De Courville came back from America with an option on *Under Fire*, but shelved it since there was no immediate 'call for War plays ... especially those with trenches, fights, and other battle horrors' (*Referee* 14.11.15, 3).
185. *Era* 14.2.17, 13.
186. *Era* 2.6.15, 13.
187. *Era* 6.1.15, 8; *Era* 11.8.15, 8.
188. *Era* 1.9.15, 8; *Era* 24.4.18, 5; *Era* 21.8.18, 8. Blindness received on active service also figures in Waldron's *Should They Marry?* (*Era* 8.9.15, 21), the Whitlocks' *The War Baby* (*Era* 28.7.15, 9) and Whitbread's *The Soldier Priest*. In the first two a soldier is afflicted and in the third a Red Cross nurse (*Stage* 3.2.16, 16).
189. *Manchester Guardian* 7.1.15, 10.
190. *Era* 14.8.18, 8.
191. *Stage* 15.10.14, 18. John's pregnant wife hopes for a boy 'to carry a knapsack', a fate destined for most British males born during this war.
192. *SYB 1917*, p. 2.
193. *Illustrated London News* 17.10.14, 556.
194. *Era* 21.10.14, 8.
195. Littlewood, *Referee* 31.1.15, 2; *Referee* 21.3.15, 2.
196. Maurice Maeterlinck, *The Burgomaster of Stilemonde*, trans. Alexander Teixeira de Mattos (Methuen, 1918), pp. 58, 88.
197. John Martin Harvey, *The Autobiography* (Sampson Low, Marston, 1933), p. 490.
198. *Referee* 22.8.15, 5.
199. Fenton, *World* 20.10.14, 42.
200. *Era* 9.10.18, 15.
201. *Plays of Innocence* (Benn, 1925), p. 56.
202. *Era* 30.6.15, 12.
203. *The Recruit* (French, 1914), pp. 13-14.

204. LC 1916: 3/65.
205. LC 1915: 9/3317.
206. Stockwell, 1916, p. 28. Cf. Louis Parker's *The Masque of War and Peace* (Bickers, 1915), p. 20, where Frightfulness, claiming to be War, is repudiated by War: 'Thou art not War! . . . I am the Spirit of War! Behold I fight To shield the weak, and to uphold the right.'
207. *Referee* 6.12.14, 3; LC 1914: 28/2926.
208. *Era* 29.3.16, 19.
209. Contrast Desmond Flower, *Fellows in Foolscap* (Hale, 1991), p. 18, on how the billeting officer gave his parents the choice of 'two officers or ten other ranks'. His father opted for the other ranks to save himself 'dressing for dinner every night'.
210. LC 1914: 33/3016. The dream device had considerable currency. It occurs twice in *The Call of Conscience* by 'Ruth Melvill' (Mortlock-Brown), a curiosity which players from the Cotswold village of Birdlip brought to the Margaret Morris Theatre, Chelsea. Both a hear-all-sides publican and a striking munition worker are converted by dreams to a sense of war's realities (*Era* 26.7.16, 9).
211. LC 1918: 1/1333.
212. LC 1915: 5/3236.
213. Edward Knoblauch, *War Committee* (French, 1915), p. 11.
214. *Referee* 4.7.15, 3; *Referee* 18.7.15, 3, found him still grumbling at this slur on women's war activity; though Cynthia Asquith, the Prime Minister's daughter (p. 54), considered it 'excellent farce', with 'Tree perfect in it'.
215. *John Bull* 20.11.15, 4.
216. Harold Owen, *Loyalty* (Hodder & Stoughton, 1918), pp. 170, 47, 19.
217. *Era* 28.11.17, 1. One line, 'The common people never have ruled . . . and never can' (p. 83), drew cries of protest from the gallery (Newton, *Referee* 25.11.17, 2), but Owen defends this '"anti-democratic" sentiment', written 'months before the course of the Russian Revolution showed its essential truth'. Similarly, Golsworthy (*Bystander* 26.1.16, 164) likes the observation in Layton's *Parish Pump* that 'working men will elect anybody to represent them except one of their own class, . . . since leaders of men are born and not made'.
218. *'Era' Annual 1918*, p. 37.
219. *Evening News* 28.11.17, 2. That very day, *Era*'s leader pointed out that it infringed the new regulation against anonymity, which strictly should apply not only to pacifist authors.
220. *'Era' Annual 1918*, p. 37.
221. *Era* 8.8.17, 8. The play had triumphed in the provinces, and overseas rights were eagerly bought up.

222. *Graphic* 26.5.17, 627.
223. *Weekly Dispatch* 1.9.18, 2, reports 'five spy plays running in London'.
224. *Graphic* 8.1.16, 68.
225. *Sphere* 26.6.15, 322; *Graphic* 29.5.15, 704.
226. *Era* 11.9.18, 13, reviewing Stevens's *In the Light of Day*.
227. *SYB 1919*, pp. 2–3.
228. *Era* 29.5.18, 5; LC 1916: 9/192.
229. Tonally unusual is Leonard Mortimer's *When Love Creeps in Your Heart*, where a strike at an ironworks, caused by German chicanery, strands a revue company in Monmouthshire, allowing for the introduction of sundry musical items (*Stage* 20.1.16, 22). His *Deliver the Goods* more plausibly focuses on the unscrupulous profiteer, making a powerful plea for harmonious relations between capital and labour after the war by bringing 'the brave boys who have done their "bit"' back into employment (*Era* 12.12.17, 22).
230. LC 1918: 10/1588; *Stage* 11.7.18, 12. Cowen, deciding that bad reviews resulted from 'interpolations and alterations' made by presenter Ernest Rolls, applied for an injunction to prevent the play from receiving further performances at the Strand in that form (*Era* 4.9.18, 11).
231. *Sunday Times* 7.7.18, 4.
232. H. A. Vachell, *Searchlights* (Murray, 1915), p. 103.
233. Cf. the father in Thurston's *The Cost*, peeling the German label off his lager bottle (Newton, *Referee* 18.10.14, 3).
234. *New Age* 11.4.18, 468.
235. *The Times* 1.4.18, 7.
236. LC 1918: 2/66. Cf. *Her Mother's Crucifix* (LC 1915: 34/3927): 'The Huns think that they can murder helpless women and children from the safety of their airships and then slink home unscathed – but there is not one man in the RFC who would not give his life to bring one of their cowardly murdering gas bags to the ground.'
237. Popular anxiety over German governesses was thought to have its origin in Worrall and Terry's *The Man Who Stayed at Home*, which certainly spawned the idea of illicit wireless aerials in chimneys (Basil Thomson, *Queer People* (Hodder and Stoughton, 1922), p. 39).
238. *The Times* 5.2.17, 4.
239. *Stage* 24.2.16, 14; *Stage* 3.8.16, 16.
240. *Illustrated London News* 20.4.18, 474.
241. *Stage* 6.7.16, 19.
242. *Stage* 10.2.16, 14. He is only sheltered in the church because the priest would marry him to the heroine, so avoiding the disgrace of unmarried motherhood.

243. *Era* 18.8.15, 8. The sinking of a U-boat was staged in Eva Elwes's *Heaven at the Helm* (*Era* 22.11.16, 8).
244. *Stage* 27.1.16, 22.
245. *Stage* 27.7.16, 18.
246. *Era* 28.7.15, 9.
247. *Heaven at the Helm* (LC 1916: 17/361).
248. *The Times* 18.6.15, 11.
249. LC 1915: 14/3466.
250. LC 1915: 14/3474.
251. LC 1915: 14/3464.
252. *Nation* 12.1.18, 487.
253. R. C. Trevelyan, *The Pterodamozels* (Pelican Press, November 1916). Srgjan Tucic's *The Liberators,* dealing with the second Balkan war, was banned in Croatia, and R. W. Seton-Watson, in his Preface to Fannie Copeland's translation (Stratford-upon-Avon: Shakespeare Head, 1918), p. x, contends that it is no 'pacifist tract'. But it proved too near the mark for performance in Britain until 1920. Even Marie Stopes's *Conquest* (French, 1915), hardly pacifist although it proposes meeting the problem of war by way of a league of nations, could only manage a reading at the Lyceum Club (*Era* 30.5.17, 8).
254. *Era* 2.2.16, 10; *Performer* 30.3.16, 29.
255. Marion Wentworth, *War Brides* (New York: Century, 1915), pp. 31, 33.
256. *Era* 29.5.18, 7.
257. *Era* 12.5.15, 20.
258. *Weekly Dispatch* 22.9.18, 4.
259. *Times Literary Supplement* 3.6.15, 185; *Punch* 23.12.18, 424.
260. *Referee* 6.6.15, 3; *Era* 14.7.15, 21.
261. *Era* 2.12.14, 19.
262. LC 1914: 31/2993; *Referee* 18.10.14, 3.
263. *Era* 10.11.15, 10. Her play was originally given as *In the Hands of the Hun,* a modification of *The Hun and the Nun* censored along with the stripping and whipping of the mother superior (*Stage* 15.4.15, 15; LC 1915: 10/3342).
264. *The Times* 26.12.14, 3.
265. *Era* 26.5.15, 11; Littlewood, *Referee* 23.5.15, 2.
266. *Referee* 21.3.15, 2.
267. Alfred Noyes, *Rada* (Methuen, 1915), pp. 14–15.
268. By New York's All-Star Feature Corporation, its first London showing mentioned in *Referee* 29.11.14, 8.
269. LC 1915: 14/3464; *Era* 9.6.15, 10; *Era* 14.7.15, 21.
270. LC 1915: 12/3392.

271. *The Times* 22.11.17, 9. Cf. David Wilson's notorious 'Red Cross or Iron Cross' poster depicting a nurse pouring water on the ground to torment one of the thirsty wounded: 'There is no woman in Britain who would do it. There is no woman in Britain who will forget it.'
272. *Era* 26.5.15, 11.
273. *Era* 14.4.15, 16.
274. *Referee* 3.11.18, 5.
275. LC 1914: 33/3028.
276. *Referee* 25.10.14, 3.
277. *The Times* 19.10.14, 8.
278. *Era* 23.6.15, 13.
279. LC 1915: 5/3226; LC 1917: 4/813.
280. LC 1917: 11/975.
281. LC 1918: 10/1588; *Stage* 11.7.18, 12.
282. LC 1917: 4/798. Further modification was required when, hearing that several of her soldier-acquaintances had saved George's life, she asked: 'Pardon me, Sport, but are you a bloody cat?'
283. *Referee* 27.12.14, 2. When Tree was planning to put on *The Ultimatum* at His Majesty's, which avoids overt allusion to Germany, Street expressed confidence that Tree would 'not have the bad taste to spoil the play by indicating the Kaiser in make-up' (LC 1915: 3/3174).
284. LC 1915: 9/3323; cf. W. K. Haselden, *The Sad Experiences of Big and Little Willie* (Fine Art Society, 1915).
285. *The Times* 24.5.15, 9; *Referee* 23.5.15, 3. The subliminal link with Herod is spelt out in a cartoon by Jan Sluyter (*Die Nieuwe Amsterdammer* 23.6.17, 1) dealing with the baby-victims of air raids, where Wilhelm and Herod shake hands.
286. LC 1915: 5/3217. When the pre-war revue *A Year in an Hour* arrived at the Middlesex, its Political School scene had been updated by making the naughty boy 'Kaiser Bill' (*Era* 24.2.15, 10). The same paper (p. 9) comments on Leonard Mortimer's 'impressive portrayal' of the War Lord in his patriotic musical comedy, *The Glorious Day*.
287. John Preston's *Constantinople 1915* (LC 1915: 9/3341).
288. LC 1917: 2/753; Newton, *Referee* 18.2.17, 3.
289. LC 1915: 14/3459. Bendall intervened over a vicar in Turner's revue, *Bubbly*, to prevent him from becoming the butt of jokes (LC 1917: 9/923).
290. LC 1914: 33/3015. The comment is prompted by the 'tipsy manner' of a policeman in Tom Nelson's *On Night Duty*; but elsewhere (*The Cockney Sport*, LC 1916: 3/68) he notes grudgingly: 'Policemen in undignified attitudes are sanctioned by custom.'

291. *Referee* 26.8.17, 2.
292. LC 1916: 17/366; LC 1916: 22/454.
293. LC 1917: 2/751. On the other hand, for *The Fringes of the Fleet* 'The Admiralty kindly helped to get the exact kit copied for Mr. Chas. Mott and his three companions' (*Era* 27.6.17, 12), the combination of Elgar and Kipling evidently a sufficient mollifier.
294. LC 1917: 11/960. Quaintly, Newton (*Referee* 20.5.17, 3) protests that the Americans who persuade their friend not to desert should likewise 'do their bit' and enlist.
295. Andrew Emm, *For England, Home and Beauty* (LC 1915: 12/3392).
296. *Encore* 20.5.15, 6.
297. LC 1915: 9/3331.
298. LC 1915: 9/3341.
299. LC 1915: 5/3235; LC 1915: 28/3795.
300. *Graphic* 1.12.17, 691.
301. L. H. Harris, *Signal Venture* (Aldershot: Gale & Polden, 1951), p. 37.
302. *Era* 20.9.16, 13. Bairnsfather designed scenes and costumes, and took advantage of sick leave to superintend rehearsals (*Era* 9.8.16, 12).
303. LC 1916: 22/457.
304. LC 1917: 4/809.
305. *Era* 23.6.15, 14.
306. LC 1916: 27/571
307. Daphne du Maurier, *Gerald: A Portrait* (Gollancz, 1934), pp. 175–6.
308. *Era* 13.12.16, 1.
309. LC 1917: 11/975. Cf. the 40 dischargees who populated the Western Front scenes in M. P.'s *For the Flag*, presented by Carter Slaughter for the Federation of Discharged and Demobilised Sailors and Soldiers (*Era* 18.9.18, 19).
310. *Referee* 30.6.18, 2. He thought *Soldier Boy* 'the finest example we have yet had, ... less broad in its humour [and] more delicate and artistically elaborate' than *The Better 'Ole*, while the dialogue sparkles with clean English and American wit'. Findon (*Play Pictorial* 33.197, 17) sought to dampen his enthusiasm by pointing out that the book was adapted from the German and the composer, 'S. Rombeau', was in fact the Austro-Hungarian Sigmund Romberg (based in New York since before the war). The London version was adapted by Edgar Wallace, who interpolated a 'spy scene ... which was one of the funniest moments in any play' (Albert de Courville, *I Tell You* (Chapman & Hall, 1928), p. 162).
311. *Daily Express* 28.11.17, 2.
312. Charles Cochran, *The Secrets of a Showman* (1925, rept. Heinemann, 1929), pp. 234–5.

313. The example was followed on tour. At Nottingham's Empire, 'the whole of the main vestibule and stairway' was disguised as a slice of the Western Front (*Era* 22.5.18, 7). 'Five companies went into the provinces, and five companies played it in the U.S.A.' (Cochran, *Secrets*, p. 241).
314. Cochran, *Secrets*, pp. 237–8, 242.
315. *Play Pictorial* 32 (191), 18.
316. *Illustrated London News* 6.7.18, 24.
317. *Performer* 7.11.18, 21; *Era* 13.11.18, 8.
318. *Era* 7.2.17, 13.
319. It received some theatrical attention during the war. In Perceval Sykes's *The Cry of the Children* (LC 1918: 1/1325) a Russian soldier asks for British rates of pay: 'Give us officers like yours – who love their men and treat them well, not with blows and curses, fill our stomachs, then we will fight.'
320. *Era* 24.10.17, 13.

6

A classic theatre?

The war had been in progress for just five weeks when a *Manchester Guardian* critic (8 September 1914, p. 7) wrote that trivial plays had been exposed by the glare of conflict 'as sunlight finds out rouge'. There would be a hunger for great art (the specific production under review was Annie Horniman's *Twelfth Night*) 'though the nations fight for a generation'. At first sight this writer seems to have been sadly mistaken. By 1918 controversy over the state of the theatre was widespread. Lawson imagined

> the dramatic historian of posterity ... pondering over the ironic fact that an epoch, which might have wrung out of the souls of its dramatists a series of plays vibrant with those basic truths which strike at the roots of humanity, should have had as its main product a series of feather-brained revues.[1]

During the skirmishing which took place in the *Sunday Times*, S. W. Carroll (18 August 1918, p. 4) continued optimistic despite few 'revivals of the Classics'. Conceding that little of consequence had emerged from the established dramatists, he considered *General Post* 'one of the finest comedies written for years', while du Maurier's 'study of the murderer' in *The Ware Case* was an outstanding example of tragic acting. More important were Hardy's *The Dynasts*, 'several delightful stage fancies' from Barrie, and proof 'that the British public can appreciate the work of Brieux'.

R. W. King replied (*Sunday Times* 25 August 1918, p. 2) by reasonably claiming that some of 'the wretched stuff named by S. W. C. will [not] be worth reviving even twenty years hence'. He blamed the managers for supplying 'nothing but war soporifics', as if 'Beecham left Mozart and Wagner alone and took to musical comedy'. Beecham's experience bore out the prediction of that *Guardian* critic in finding a wartime 'mood of simplicity and gravity [leading] many to the solace of great art'.[2] And as soon as opera is put into the equation, especially with that cultural appropriation of continental works through the success of the 'opera in English' mission, things look tolerably healthy. But King is right about the West End's shortcomings, which actor-manager Dennis Eadie located in the virtual monopoly achieved by business syndicates and speculators, making art wholly subordinate to profit. He is one amongst many blaming these for seducing people 'into swallowing little else but *risqué* farce, ragtime, and *spectacle*, so that now our audiences find it difficult to digest any other form of diet' (*Sunday Times* 27 October 1918, p. 4). As part of a circular process, Shakespeare and the old comedies 'are shelved entirely, because the powers that be tell us there is no money in them'. This supplies a troubling paradigm of the myth and reality of war aims: Shakespeare's works, the grand expression of values for which the war is ostensibly fought, lose out to the profit motive.

If Eadie overstates his case somewhat, the demise in quick succession of Tree and Alexander certainly made for despondency. That the latter's St James's Theatre was likely to fall to Alfred Butt brought a strong reaction from the editor of *Play Pictorial*: 'Managerial men of his type are not concerned with original manuscripts or any patriotic desire to foster native art. Their desire is to buy the goods ready-made, with some sort of a hall-mark of success on them.'[3] But if there was a 'Syndicate of Soullessness [holding] the London theatres in fee',[4] the *Weekly Dispatch*'s gloomy financial picture (5 August 1917, p. 6) of handsome box-office takings 'eaten up by excessive salaries to actors and the enormously increased cost of all materials of production' helps to conceal it. Hibbert notes how widespread was such press misrepresentation, printing 'without question the figures of managers, who had been prodigally extravagant to avoid the tax on "excess profits" '.[5] The *Dispatch*, like Lawson, blames low artistic standards on audiences 'Composed for the most part of soldiers on leave and munition workers', *Era*'s leader-writer answering by reference to the success of Ibsen and Brieux. That this involved more than a *succès de scandale* is solidly testified: 'In the midst of the eruption of revue, ... it is extremely gratifying to see such strenuous plays as "Ghosts," "Damaged Goods," and "The Three Daughters of Monsieur Dupont" conquering the average young playgoer.'[6] Cochran, during the successful run of *Damaged Goods*, was persuaded as much by the nature of the heavy post he received as by box-office takings that audiences had 'a genuine love of serious drama', while Farjeon recognized that the excitement it aroused 'was due less to the audacity of the subject than to the unhappily topical flavour which it had acquired during the war'.[7]

Until just a few weeks before the war, Britain was said to be the only country where *Ghosts* was not licensed for public performance. But when that sorry situation ended, the immediate result was just one celebratory matinée at the Haymarket (14 July 1914), organized by Grein whose championing of the play since 1891 had made him *persona non grata* in certain circles.[8] Brieux's *Damaged Goods*, also confronting the subject of venereal disease, had similar difficulties. But by 1917 both plays were enjoying a healthy run in London, and their popularity swept over into the provinces.[9] They had been banned 'through mere stupidity', alleged *Era*'s leader-writer (27 June 1917, p. 11), blaming the Lord Chamberlain for the theatre's reputation in some quarters as a 'Sink of Iniquity' by censoring 'plays of serious moral purpose, while allowing Palais Royal frivolities free passage'. But if now 'under the lash of war we are facing facts frankly and gladly, as a people who would learn',[10] the facts to be faced were carefully selected. That the one play was licensed as Britain was poised on the brink of war, and the other when she was in the midst of it, shows that this was no disinterested relaxation. The huge expansion of the military provided a rich breeding ground for the syphilis spirochæte. And there was much anxiety over the moral health of young women, sometimes leaving home for the first time, who had taken war work. As Ervine noted, there was a physical threat: 'in terror lest the troops should become physically incapable of waiting in a hole in the ground to be bayoneted or blown to pieces because they were syphilitic, the Government annulled the ban.'[11] But there was a psychological threat too, with the cheery, singing Tommy as liable to succumb to a venereal disease as to a combat wound. Marie Stopes's recognition of this had caused uproar. But the relentless process of war brought the need for a new perspective, and the government saw the theatre as the neatest way of achieving this. Hence a full-scale production of *Ghosts* ran for 96 performances at the Kingsway. As Walkley noted, the part of Oswald was no less horrifying than in the brave old censorious days, yet 'we have all seen many worse horrors since then, on and off the stage'.[12]

Damaged Goods had run for two years in America before it was 'licensed for public performance and approved by the War Office authorities etc., for propaganda purposes'.[13] It was staged by a specially formed company at Cochran's new luxury theatre, the St Martin's, all profits destined for institutions specializing in treatment of venereal diseases. It ran for 282 performances, raising £14,000; but when £6,000 had been disbursed as intended, the government stepped in claiming £11,800, though eventually settling for the remaining £8,000.[14] That some of its most notable tour successes were achieved in variety rather than regular theatres[15] drew protest from *Performer* (22 March 1917, p. 17; 26 April 1917, p. 18) that audiences would suffer 'incalculable harm' just when the music hall had been rendered fit for Sunday-school classes. There were seven tours of *Ghosts* in progress by 23 September 1917 (*Referee*), and still more of *Damaged Goods*. In the latter, Ronald Colman, discharged from the army after the retreat from Mons, played the diseased husband, holding Liverpool audiences 'spellbound'.[16] Response to the play's arrival at Hitchin, Hertfordshire is glimpsed in a letter (dated 28 June 1918) written by a young woman to her POW boyfriend. She toys with it as something scandalous: 'for Adults only (I wonder why). Eva said she's not going so I shall (not).' Her hero is safely shut away from such perils at Ingolstadt, so she need make no imaginative leaps to preserve him unsullied though syphilitic.

Although, unlike *Ghosts, Damaged Goods* is rather a tract than a play, the brittle happiness with which the second act opens is still very painful, several ladies on the opening night at the St Martin's being 'overcome with emotion'.[17] And Brieux's *Three Daughters of M. Dupont*, another exploration of sexual problems, is much better. It ran for 161 performances at the Ambassadors', with Ethel Irving scaling 'heights of nervous passion that electrified the house' and earned her the lead in Caine's *The Prime Minister* (Introduction, p. xi). Earlier scenes, which gave her scope for delicate comedy, would only have underscored the tragic futility of that final reconciliation: 'everything comes right when once you make up your mind to be like the rest of the world.'[18] Besides French-language productions of Brieux, his *La Robe Rouge* was adapted at His Majesty's as *The Arm of the Law*, with Bourchier as the unscrupulous magistrate. Bourchier employed a sourer ending than that in Miall's translation, the magistrate being promoted instead of murdered. He explained that Brieux 'originally intended Yanetta to be thrown on the streets, and that the stab was brought in for Réjane's benefit'.[19]

Ibsen fared less well in the West End. *Rosmersholm*, 'gloomy enough in itself' according to *The Times* (6 June 1917, p. 9), was turned 'into a burial service' at the St Martin's; but *The Master Builder*, running for a couple of weeks at the Court, was admired for its treatment 'of the eternal paradox, the failure of success and true success which is conventionally called failure'.[20] Also at the Court for eight performances was *Realities*, which Ibsen never took beyond the preliminary stages, but which Austin Fryers (William Edward Clery) now fleshed out as a sequel to his version of *Ghosts*.[21] Unfortunately, only the key figure of Mrs Alving, played by Madge McIntosh, was thought up to Ibsen's standard.[22]

Of our own modern 'classics', a conceptual anomaly more or less authorized by Ben Jonson, George Sampson lists several. Contending at the end of the war that the contemporary theatre was far superior to that of twenty years earlier, he cited Galsworthy, Masefield, Barker, Shaw, Hankin, Houghton, Murray, Bennett and Barrie.[23] Wilde was ineligible; and in any case he was meagrely produced in wartime London, though popular in the provinces. *A Woman of No Importance* was brought to the Kingsway by the Liverpool Rep (*Stage* 20 May 1915, p. 20) and *The Importance of Being Earnest* was given at the

Little Theatre, used for much of the war as a retreat for Canadian soldiers but which in August 1918 reopened as a theatre with this play, given by the Canadian YMCA Company.[24] *An Ideal Husband* had closed at the St James's some ten days before war was declared, and the West End's only wartime production was the privately performed *Salomé* at the Court, given by Grein's Independent Theatre Company, with music for Salomé's dance composed and conducted by Granville Bantock. It was made notorious by the libel action of its star Maud Allan, who had produced shock-waves long before with her unrelated dance, *The Vision of Salome*. *The Stage* considered Wilde's dialogue, 'rouged and painted like a courtesan's face, ... very repellant to a healthy taste' (18 April 1918, p. 14), whereas *Era* found much of it 'wonderfully written' and impressively delivered (17 April 1918, p. 8). Dunton Green wrote of 'a large and enthusiastic audience', with Allan emphasizing the child in Salomé, a 'child full of vague aspirations, full of wild visions'; while George Relph's neurotic Herod was 'instinct with a sombre and tragic grandeur'. [25]

Otherwise the Irish theatre was represented by Shaw and the Abbey Players, responsible for bringing Synge to the London stage. The way in which *The Playboy of the Western World* projected and punctured myths of Irish sex and Irish nationalism had led to riots at the Dublin première in 1907 and again when the Abbey Company visited New York in 1911–12. But London audiences had grown accustomed to the play, if not to its special wartime nuances. Synge's Western Irish villagers, like most Britishers before August 1914, were too shut off from the world of heroism to see through its sham. However, a play where killing acquires a kind of ritual acceptability, not to say sexual appeal, took on new meaning as tales of the 'hardened slayer' became mediated through every newspaper's war news. So too, the drear topicality of *Riders to the Sea* was growing insistent as parents outliving their sons became a terrible commonplace; doubtless mindful of this, *Athenæum*'s critic (27 May 1915, p. 474) was affected by 'the relief (automatic and unconscious, but inevitable) of the old woman who knows, with the death of her last man-child, that the sea can take nothing more from her'.

During the war, Shaw was gaining more publicity (not to say notoriety) outside the theatre than in it. That he trod on some influential corns with his views on the war may be why he had little share in the revival boom. He thought *Pygmalion*, given its English-language première in early 1914 when Tree considered it 'the pinnacle of the twentieth-century drama', ripe for revival, since it 'came off at His Majesty's at the end of the season to big business'.[26] But the West End was not to see it during the war, though Charles Macdona's company made it the Dalston Theatre's 1918 Whitsuntide attraction. Indeed *Fanny's First Play* was his solitary West End revival, achieving 49 performances at the Kingsway.[27] Its revival was hailed in the

Illustrated London News (20 February 1915, p. 226) both for the 'surprising good-nature' of its satire and for Lena Ashwell's performance, all 'nervous intensity', as the modern 'woman-rebel'. But V. V. V. in the *Sphere* (27 February 1915, p. 234), deeply hostile to Shaw, gloated that *The Times*'s critic found its humour 'very jarring in war time'. *Mrs Warren's Profession* was denied a showing, thanks to a censor determined to 'protect the public from being made to feel uneasy in its habits and its conscience', though objections from Dublin Castle failed to stop an intensely played production at Dublin's Little Theatre.[28] The Abbey Theatre's abrupt abandonment of plans to put on his new play, *O'Flaherty, V.C.*, was unofficially ascribed to the mutilations of the censor.[29] It had a few throwaway lines calculated to raise hackles: 'You'll never have a quiet world til you knock the patriotism out of the human race'; 'Don't talk to me or to any soldier of the war being right. No war is right; and all the holy water that Father Quinlan ever blessed couldn't make one right'; or, on the war's supposedly uplifting effects: 'It's like the vermin: it'll wash off after a while.' The play, which had to wait until 1966 (Mermaid) for its first commercial production in London,[30] was premièred at the 40 Squadron base in Trezennes, Belgium (17 February 1917), Shaw having sent a script of this and *The Inca of Perusalem* to the actor Robert Loraine, then serving in the Flying Corps. Shaw, touring the Western Front at that time, actually caught a rehearsal which he found unintentionally uproarious.[31] It was performed by the officers, while the rankers were assigned *The Inca* (notable for endowing the Kaiser with a touch of Shavian irony). *Era*'s reviewer (11 October 1916, p. 8) missed the irony when it was premièred at the Birmingham Rep, either because a Prussian dress uniform proved an insurmountable barrier or because the production chose to underscore William's 'bombastic megalomania'. But following its single London performance, as part of a triple bill given at the Criterion by the Pioneer Players, Walkley commented on Shaw's Kaiser: 'He talked a good deal of sound sense; he talked a good deal of shrewd wit; he talked a good deal of mere nonsense; ... But he talked well.'[32] For Newton, however, Shaw was sneering 'at the very blood our boys are shedding'; making 'out that the Kaiser has done good by taking them from "the horror of their homes" ' blends 'pretentious ignorance with execrable lack of taste'. There is no horror about British homes, insisted Newton, smugly thinking of his own suburb which accommodated 'a duke, two earls, a princess of Royal blood, and a member of the War Cabinet'.[33] But this is wilful misunderstanding since Shaw, writing as a member of a sanitary authority concerned with slum clearance, had already provided a gloss: 'comparison of what the Germans have done to Albert with what I should like to do to London or Manchester would make the Kaiser seem a veritable Angel of the Passover beside me.'[34]

Annajanska, the Bolshevik Empress, written for the Coliseum, fared better. It was thought an amusing spoof on the Revolution, except that 'it is scarcely Shavian, and certainly not British, to raise laughs at the expense of anything unfortunately Russian, even though Russia has raised loans at our expense to carry on a war which she has abandoned'.[35] But the real irritant is that, like Wesker's *Chips with Everything*, it endorses the view that even revolution must be led by one of the élite. The only other new Shaw item was *Augustus Does His Bit*, given by the Stage Society at the Court in January 1917. Here a pseudo-spy plot is a peg for jocularity directed at the old boy network. The wartime commonplace that military discipline will dispose of dangerous radicalism is neatly sent up: 'There's no more law for you, you scoundrel. You're a soldier now. Thank heaven, the war has given us the upper hand of these fellows at last.' And the playlet ends on an amusingly self-reflexive note when a ritual reference to 'our gallant fellows ... perishing in the trenches' prompts the thought that some of them have come on 'a few days hard-earned leave; and I am sure you won't grudge them a little fun at your expense'.

Shaw never went beyond 'a little fun' on the wartime stage. Although his essay 'Common Sense about the War' (*New Statesman*, 14 November 1914) caused some to scream 'traitor', the government knew better; this was fortunate, he wrote in 1924, 'or I should have been shot'. Like many another, he set aside his principles until the war was over, since 'The danger of discouraging enlistment during the voluntary period and of weakening the national *morale* was too serious.' Frank Harris quotes this disapprovingly, adding: 'I lacked Shaw's talent of choosing and championing the "right" side in a quarrel of two scoundrels whose aims are identical.'[36] Shaw's split-mindedness shows in the preface to *Heartbreak House*: 'When men are heroically dying for their country, it is not the time to shew their lovers and wives and fathers and mothers how they are being sacrificed to the blunders of boobies, the cupidity of capitalists.' Had they died for their country or been criminally sacrificed on the altars of cupidity and stupidity? As for timing, Harris is unanswerable: wartime is the only time when saying these things can make a difference.[37] But Shaw was loth to risk *Heartbreak House*, which he showed to Lillah McCarthy in the summer of 1918, on the wartime stage.[38] He harboured uncharacteristic doubts about what proved to be his finest work. If it was begun pre-war, as he claims, it had been drastically reshaped by events. It is Zeppelin raids which he uses to show the impossibility of reclaiming Mrs Hushabye from her moral torpor. In crassness she outstrips Eliot's women who 'come and go/Talking of Michelangelo', by hearing aerial bombardment as a Beethoven symphony. No thought of casualties is allowed to intrude: 'what a glorious experience! I hope they'll come again tomorrow night.'

The play ends with the diplomat Randall, who had been too dry-mouthed during the raid to sound a note, rendering 'Keep The Home Fires Burning' on his flute. In Galsworthy's *A Bit o' Love*, the central character, a new Orpheus, uses a flute to commune with the birds and beasts. Although he has none of Shaw's sinewy ebullience, Galsworthy shows boldness for these times in confronting the need to love one's enemy. The play was introduced at the Kingsway (May 1915) by the Liverpool Commonwealth Company. It clearly relates to Galsworthy's *The Mob*, first performed just over a year before, which deals with the destruction of a young member of the government who cannot accept his party's bellicose policy towards the Boers. In *A Bit o' Love*, circumstances require more oblique treatment. Definition of a Christian at confirmation class, 'He don't drink, an' he don't beat his horses, an' he don't hit back', provokes objection: 'father says if yü hit a man and he don't hit yü back, he's no güde at all.' This is the rule: 'When Tommy Morse wouldn't fight, us pinched him – he did squeal!'[39] And the curate's ideal of St Francis as one 'full of love and joy' draws the unconsciously ironic comment: 'I expect he's dead.' Cuckoo emblems signal the curate's cuckolding; and his understanding attitude attracts the disapproval of the rector's wife: 'It's a priest's business to guide the people's lives ... There are times when forgiveness is a sin.' But he resists her, having been moved not by forgiveness, but by an all-encompassing love which not she, the villagers, nor *The Times* reviewer can comprehend. She has warned the innkeeper against allowing scandal in his bar, but he acutely identifies her responsibility: 'If there weren't no Rector's lady there widden' be no notice taken o' scandal; an' if there weren't no notice taken, twidden be scandal.' Her rejoinder that 'This is a Christian village' becomes a condemnation of the country at large through his ironic repetitions at every moment of crisis. It is of a piece with the footman's left-handed praise of his master in Galsworthy's other wartime play, *The Foundations*:[40] 'I've had experience with him, in the war ... Why! he didn't even hate the Huns, not as he ought. I tell you he's no Christian.' The curate of *A Bit o' Love* has his moments of doubt, though those who take the lead against him are far from pure of motive. When one of them drunkenly pushes his fist into the curate's face, his own aggression is used to propel him through a window. Later the curate will apologize, but for the moment his other principal enemy marvels: 'Whü wid a' thought it?' As so often with those swimming against the tide of public opinion, the curate's strength has been mistaken for weakness. His suicidal impulse results not from inability to live with the consequences of his action but a feeling that he cannot live without his wife. However, the unorthodox court public shaming. In *The Mob*, the minister is subjected to jubilant horseplay by a mafficking crowd and finally killed. What the curate suffers is less drastic: an attenuated form of that 'rough music' which people in former times inflicted on neighbours who failed to control their wives, as the villagers gather to hiss him after evensong.

That Galsworthy had no wish to incur what was also a recognized sign of disapprobation in the theatre meant that he wrapped up his message pretty carefully, probably too carefully for it to have real impact, hence the play's quick disappearance after seven performances. *The Foundations*, whose message could be rendered more distinctly, at least lasted for 23 performances. But that it was no comfortable message for 1917 is recognized by Grein: 'In these times, it is a courageous thing to picture London in revolution after the war, with a mob massed in Mayfair, and aristocrats speechifying from palatial windows.' Further, it is as witty as it is bold: 'its very wittiness is bold, for such a subject can only be treated lightly by a master-hand.'[41] The play opens in the cellars of one of those Mayfair palazzi, and amongst the choice vintages is discovered what appears to be a bomb aimed at the visible foundations of the establishment.[42] But the real 'foundations' are that mass of sweated labour, like Mrs Lemmy who stitches and sews trousers at 'tuppence three farthin's a pair', which is being discussed and exhibited upstairs. As Grein concludes: 'Old Mrs. Lemmy may become a by-word, terrible and inspiring, if we do not look to the "foundations".' But he fails to note that Galsworthy's innate conservatism has prevented him from offering any workable solution. In proposing loving kindness Galsworthy ironically indicates that this 'strikes rather a new note'. The benign aristocrat, asked by a press representative how far he would apply it 'in practice', counters: '*Can* you apply it in theory?' But parading the amiable and concerned Lord Dromondy lends no credence to Galsworthy's idea that loving kindness will work the trick; as he concedes at one point, the country is amply stocked with the other sort. A call for loving kindness has no more chance of healing a painfully divided society than it had of diverting the countries of Europe from war. It is so much piety unless there is legislation to compel the rich and profiteering to share some of their surplus with the poor and the exploited. Yet although Galsworthy only toys with the deeper issues, as when the butler tells Miss Stokes that she wants it both ways in thinking that she can raise the lower classes without the necessity of herself coming down a notch or two, the play is not to be despised. There is a delicious moment when Dromondy asks, of the lower orders, 'Why do we always call them *they*?' His wife is simply puzzled by the question, but Miss Munday, a kind of Joyce Grenfell parody of a do-gooder, is suddenly struck by its aptness: 'Quite right, Lord William! *Quite* right! Another species. They! I must remember that.' Again, the chatter of a child of the slums about what she is taught in school is strangely discordant. She has learned to play the piano a little, but not any of the skills which might help her to acquire one. She can recite poetry which has as little bearing on the life she leads as the values that are inculcated: respect for fast cars and the need for a revolver to 'shoot the people that steals my jools'. But when Mrs Lemmy asks, 'Du they tache yu to love yure neighbours?', the answer is in the negative. There is wry comment on war aims from the younger Lemmy, obtusely (or defensively) described as 'addle-pated' in *The Times* (27 June 1917, p. 9): 'they said, ... ye're fightin' for yer children's 'eritage. Well, wot's the 'eritage like, now we've got it? Empty as a shell before yer put the 'igh explosive in.' And there is more than a touch of authorial disquiet behind another of his speeches: 'Yer thought the Englishman could be taught to shed blood wiv syfety. Not 'im! Once yer git 'im into an 'abit, yer cawn't git 'im out of it agyne. 'E'll go on sheddin' blood mechanical – Conservative by nyture.' Fortunately, that same conservatism would also produce a counterbalance; but Lemmy later touches on a more interesting aspect of trench experience. Deriding the empty talk about unity and a new spirit in the country, he addresses Dromondy as representative of the governing classes: 'Noo spirit! Why, soon as ever there was no dynger from outside, yer stawted to myke it inside, wiv an iron 'and. Naow, *you've* been in the war an' it's given yer a feelin' 'eart; but most of the nobs wiv kepitel was too old or too important to fight. *They* weren't born agyne.' Dromondy has already acknowledged how standing side by side in the trenches with working men has allowed him to recognize the present insurgents as 'thorough good chaps at bottom'. This anticipates Harold Macmillan's maiden speech in the House of Lords, delivered (shortly before he died) at a period as divided socially as that imagined in the play: 'A terrible strike is being carried on by the best men in the world. They beat the Kaiser's army and they beat Hitler's army.'[43] It was when the likes of Dromondy, junior officers in World War I, achieved senior positions in government after World War II, that some sort of social reformation was undertaken. But the basis of this reform, an understanding won in the mud of Flanders, finally disappeared with Macmillan.

'That Sir Arthur Pinero is an author whose work will rank as classic I take to be undeniable.' Thus C. K. S. on the appearance of his new play, *The Big Drum*, at the St James's.[44] *Athenæum*'s critic (11 September 1915, p. 182) touches most of the bases: 'Sir Arthur seizes upon the foibles of an age when (as one of his characters declares) bishops and politicians play to the gallery, and duchesses vie with the cheap draper in energetic advertising – when blessed Charity herself is clothed in the garments of the cheapjack, mourning is made a parade, and those who cannot beat the drum strain every nerve to reach the stick just beyond their reach.' It is the hero, Mackworth (George Alexander), who attacks these things in a new novel which shares the play title. But he, too, in his own more honourable way, fancies seeing himself in print, 'and strikes a preposterous bargain with the Comtesse which makes their marriage dependent on the desired notoriety'. She adopts the simple expedient of 'buying up several editions of her lover's book "for export" ', an act prompted partly by love but also by an inherent strain of vulgarity in her nature which she eventually owns would prevent her making him a suitable wife. By the third performance critical pressure forced Pinero to improvise a marital conclusion, and *Era*'s leader-writer (15 September 1915, p. 13), while claiming for it no 'added grace', saluted Pinero's wisdom in yielding to people's 'very natural desire' in these depressed times (the people referred to being a pretty unrepresentative but highly influential group). On the same page, Newton called for Pinero to return to 'his earlier kindlier dramatic outlook', though later acknowledging the falseness of this happy ending.[45] Facetious old *Punch* (13 October 1915, p. 315), taking the new ending to be an experiment in fluidity promising 'great changes in the drama of the near future', gives a post modern air to the play. But Fenton sees the change as a failure of nerve which still leaves Pinero trapped in 'Victorian artificiality', taking 'five minutes to say something which an American dramatist would compress into three racy words … The world is in the melting-pot, and we are in no mood for minor philosophy and unimportant ethics.'[46] However, as Koopman summed up at the end of the year, the play 'had a fair measure of success', one medically unfit theatre-goer writing that he enjoyed it 'despite the fact that a whole row of stalls had been presented to wounded Tommies, who somehow brought the flavour of war into the theatre and made me feel as if I ought to have been elsewhere doing my bit'.[47]

So much, then, for *The Times* reviewer's delight that the play 'is dead-silent about the war' (2 September 1915, p. 9). And Pinero's other full-length play of this period, *Freaks: An Idyll of Suburbia*, although ostensibly having no war reference, may well glance at the need to come to terms with those freaks which the past three and a half years had created in quantity; a complement to that German Expressionist film, *The Hands of Orlac* (1924, after Renard's novel), with its dark comment on the traumas experienced by the war-mutilated. Pinero was said to have 'done a very daring thing' in transporting 'a number of human monstrosities from the atmosphere of the circus booth, where their physical differences are exhibited to the public at a penny a peep [to] the atmosphere of a West End theatre, where the innermost workings of their souls may be observed at half a guinea a stall'. It was at the New that the play for six weeks demonstrated the proposition 'that ordinary mortals may be more freakish than freaks'. But reviewers found less merit in the central theme than in incidental details such as Pinero's gift for 'depicting the mean side of relatives' in all its comic ugliness. This is personified in Sir Norton and Lady Ball-Jennings, the former played by Fred Kerr, who thought the play had been 'worried into a rather early grave by incessant air-raids'.[48] When the titled couple, somewhat thawed towards the freaks, give photographs of themselves in fancy dress as parting keepsakes, the recipients amusedly recognize superior material for a freak show. But the effect is spoilt because finally the line drawn is as rigid as that of class or colour: when two suburban siblings (one of them

Leslie Howard, adumbrating that amiable urbanity which he brought so often to the cinema screen) and two of the freaks fall in love, the latter realize they must depart for ever in order not to cause upsets in polite society.

This time there was no critical clamour about violating 'the tradition of concluding a comedy with a marriage',[49] any more than there was over the refusal of the governess to wed with her 'betters' in *The Hillarys.* This play, begun by Houghton, whose *Hindle Wakes* (1912) was revived at the Duke of York's, was completed after his death by Brighouse. Brighouse's *Northerners,* premièred at the Gaiety, Manchester, in August 1914, was overtaken by events. The London theatre could do without anything but the most loaded representation of industrial strife, albeit set in the 1820s. Although his *Road to Raebury* made the trip from Manchester to the West End, its stay was brief. Like *The Hillarys,* it was an attempt 'to evolve a new sort of "country-house comedy" in place of the provincial-suburb genre' with which the Manchester school had been concerned hitherto. But Littlewood found nothing fresh: 'The time has long gone by now for a penniless baronet's widow to be in any way shocked at her house being let to a commercial magnate or to raise any objections to her son marrying his daughter.'[50] But the next year Brighouse's *Hobson's Choice* arrived to general acclaim, though London managers had refused to touch it prior to its American success. This meant that now the US owners of the rights claimed nearly 50 per cent of the London profits.[51]

By late 1917 Brighouse had evidently written 'a kind of "Conscientious objector" play, with a strong war-incentive undercurrent', called *The Golden Ray*; though it was not licensed.[52] But Barrie's contribution to war topics was significant. *A Well-Remembered Voice* is a gentle counselling piece for the war-bereaved. The mother holds a séance, but it is to his quietly grieving father that the dead boy appears, their talk of simple domestic things bringing them closer than ever before. The father thinks first of his wife's grief: 'You should have gone to her, Dick';[53] but the boy explains that he has appeared to the parent who needs him most. Dick's girlfriend confides guiltily that she sometimes feels 'quite light-hearted'; but Dick has anticipated this: 'If you are sad, I have to be sad. That's how we have got to work it off. You can't think how we want to be bright.' So his father can reassure her that she is not being heartless: 'Perhaps, nowadays, the fruit trees have that sort of shame when they blossom, Laura; but they can't help doing it. I hope you are yet to be a happy woman, a happy wife.' Veteran Johnston Forbes Robertson played the father 'with exquisite tenderness and a fine dignity', his task the more difficult because most of the time he was playing to the disembodied voice of Gerald du Maurier. Walkley concluded: 'wonderfully simple; but wonderfully beautiful.'[54]

This is not the only play to remind us that Barrie had adopted informally five orphaned brothers, one of whom, Lt G. L. Davies, was killed in action on

13 March, 1915. The father–son relationship is again at the centre of *The New Word*: really two words, '2nd Lieutenant', according to the script. But one reviewer proposes 'that the new war-engendered word is "dear" ', the exit line being 'Good-night, dear father.' This 'truthful study of the commonplace' introduces the son in subaltern's gear causing mother to sentimentalize and sister to gush. But the interest lies in father and son's efforts 'to admit their mutual affection without expressing it. If the sentimentality of the play is sometimes glutinous, what matter, for the characters are always decently inarticulate.'[55] But the play has its moments, quite apart from the delicate charting of the central relationship. When the boy chides his mother for having 'knitted enough things already to fit up my whole platoon', his sister is enchanted: 'Have you noticed how fine all the words in -oon are? Platoon! Dragoon!', and father adds drily, 'Spittoon'. Nor does the doting mother's patriotic fervour have quite the irresistible recruiting appeal detected in *The Illustrated London News* (27 March 1915, p. 386). Her declaration that she wouldn't have had one of her sons stay at home, though she had had a dozen, acquires unexpected spin when she adds: 'That is, if it is the noble war they all say it is. I'm not clever, Rogie, I have to take it on trust. Surely they wouldn't deceive mothers.'

This was a curtain-raiser to *Rosy Rapture*, Barrie's own revue at the Duke of York's, which grew out of the contribution he had made to *Hullo, Ragtime!* over two years earlier. Unfortunately it never quite took off despite the high-octane presence of Gaby Deslys 'as a chorus girl who married a lord and hankered after her former triumphs to the neglect of her baby and her home'. Indeed the domestic hearth provides a link between this and *The New Word*, in which the first object revealed to the audience was the back of a metal fender placed before the footlights, so that the characters enjoyed their intimacy before the fire set in that missing fourth wall. In the revue 'we see the footlight *milieu* from the standpoint of the hearth, and in consequence note all the ridiculousness of its conventions – the sillinesses of "musical comedy" with its "incompetent chorus," the grotesqueness of melodrama, the more irritating side of the cinematograph, and so on'.[56] But this 'attempt at a comic thesis – the disappearance of the *tertium quid*, the "lover," from the "eternal triangle" ', despite the comic efforts of Leon Quartermaine, in that rôle, to reinstate himself – was thought perhaps 'too intellectual, too "high-browed," to get a fair chance in competition with bare backs' (notably Gaby's).[57] A good third of the revue was devoted to a cartoon film, drawn by Lancelot Speed. Speed's *Bully Boy* series of patriotic sketches for the cinema, begun within two months of the outbreak of war, was still being issued by the Neptune Company,[58] which owned the screen rights for Barrie's works. The subject of the present film was Rosy's baby, who, pursuing various adventures in his automobile perambulator, discovered for his restless mother 'how to be happy though at home'. This worked well, while Deslys as French peasant girl and Norworth as Tommy making 'love with the help of a phrase-book and with Lord Kitchener's homily to soldiers in mind',[59] was good enough to have a separate life in the music hall.

Barrie was probably the most popular British dramatist at this time, his earlier work frequently revived and new items continually in demand for war matinées. But his customary deftness was absent from *Der Tag*. Squire considered it 'the worst thing on the war that has yet emanated from a distinguished writer', shaking his head sadly over posters which boomed it as 'the burning words of a great mind on a great subject'.[60] It makes 'a crude and specious appeal to the minds of the unwary and the ill-informed by an assault upon their emotions'. The Kaiser and his aides 'discuss diplomacy in alluringly simple terms', and even the former's recantation at sight of all the havoc he has wrought is only a dream. The patriotic Newton would still disallow it, and is only appeased by the concluding scene when the 'murdering maniac' is handed a revolver by the Spirit of Culture, 'to blow out his brains withal'.[61] But the play was promoted energetically, the text being printed in full in both *Daily Chronicle* and *Telegraph*. C. K. S., who found it tasteless and regrettable, conceded that it was drawing 'crowds to the Coliseum'.[62] And *Era*'s reviewer (23 December 1914, p. 14) was confident that it would 'be talked of in every neutral country, and probably Berlin. It was not only 'an impeachment of Germany's lust for world conquest [but reflected] the workings of the Kaiser's soul'. His determination to take it seriously faltered only at its best moment – where Kaiser and Epicure Mammon become kin: 'I could eat all the elephants of Hindustan and pick my teeth with the spire of Strasburg cathedral.'[63]

In quite different vein, and balancing those depictions of father-son relationships with another of soldier and surrogate mother, *The Old Lady Shows Her Medals* was part of a triple bill at the New; along with *Seven Women*, adapted from the first act of his *Adored Ones* with Leonora no longer a suffragette but organizing a government department, and Captain Rattray as submarine-chaser. Barrie's old lady is a Scotch charwoman who, unlike her neighbours, has no man at the Front. Reading of a brave deed done by a Black Watch soldier with the same name as herself she 'adopts' him, sending him food parcels under an aristocratic name and showing her neighbours packets of his supposed letters. By chance soldier and charwoman meet, he, without kin, being as lonely as she. But he will not accept her as a 'mother' until she proves herself worthy:

> we watch him thawing to her, spoiling her, rejoicing in her, until at the end of his leave comes the parting. And that we could hardly watch.

> Odd, comical Scots though they were, their parting summed up all the partings. It was far easier to watch, in the last scene, the old lady, alone now for ever, "showing her medals," her dead "son's" little belongings.[64]

Critical reception was generally favourable. Sentimentality yields to 'the finer note of sentiment and pathos, not least as the curtain falls, when we hear the ghostly piper of the Black Watch wailing the "Flowers of the Forest," to tell the old lady, as she puts away the lad's bonnet, that he has paid the great price somewhere in France.'[65] But a lieutenant who saw it while on leave took a sourer view. A third or more of the audience were soldiers due to return to France who had gone to the Coliseum looking for a cheery 'send-off', not 'Pawky sentiment'. This, he suggests, would 'help premature peace', a loading characteristic of those indoctrinated with the idea that only a victorious peace was tolerable.[66]

It is doubtful if Barrie would have been perturbed by this officer's response to the play, since it had established itself with the troops in France.[67] On the whole, his sentimental streak is absorbed by his grasp of theatre's power to weave magic spells. 'Compare him with others who attempt the light fantastic', wrote MacCarthy at the appearance of *Dear Brutus*. 'How stodgy and how over-solemn they appear when they introduce the playful supernatural!'[68] But that was not the only, or even the best, example of Barrie's whimsy to be found on London's wartime stage. His knack of 'carrying on into mature years the wonderments of childhood' enables him, like Dickens, to enter into the child's imagination. This shows extremely in *Peter Pan,* which had become a Christmas annual and was relished at its first wartime showing for the absence of those 'topical allusions or the strident patriotic songs which the purveyor of pantomime considers that his customers demand'.[69] But the war is pervasively present in another of Barrie's childhood fantasies, *A Kiss for Cinderella,* which also visited the West End for Christmas 1916 and 1917 as a climax to successful provincial tours. Before that it had run for 156 performances at Wyndham's. At the start it toys with spy mania, since the little drudge at the centre of the play has a few scraps of German, indulges in incessant questioning and is secretive about her private life. But the mystery is resolved by the discovery that, impoverished as she is, she adopts waifs: 'One is English, another French, another Belgian, and another – alien! ... In this terrible war we had been getting used to the rather un-British way of thinking that the best kind of alien, is a dead – alien; and here we have the gentle reminder that to us a helpless child has no nationality.'[70] The children are accommodated in rough boxes fixed high on the wall of Cinderella's room; and in the later ball-scene they are similarly elevated above the throne, nesting atop a baldachin in a kind of theatre box, since that is '*the grandest thing Cinderella has ever seen*'. From this vantage point they offer usefully sticky-fingered comments on the high-flown events. The ball takes place somewhere between the Never Land and Buckingham Palace, a hunger-and-cold-inspired dream out of which Cinderella awakens with a near-fatal dose of pneumonia. Cinderella has never attended a ball, but she has seen a horse show, and borrows copiously from that. In the arbitrary way of love and dreams, her Prince Charming resembles the policeman who has been investigating her secret life. The efforts of the several media to disseminate images of royalty have been lost on her since she can evidently afford neither newspapers nor cinema visits. Instead she draws upon playing card representations for her king and queen, who look '*as if they thought the whole public was dirt, but not so much despised dirt as dirt with good points*'. But one part of the propaganda has filtered through: when the prince arrives home from France for the occasion, the guests are bidden to 'make way'. At some point in the infant mind has been lodged this reflex response to the vague concept of Majesty. It is a matter of the awe it inspires rather than the power it wields, though power is decidedly present in Cinderella's vision. The wartime censor's rôle had its terrors, and here Cinderella sees it as the punitive arm of Majesty. In a reversal of Turandot's situation, those unsuccessful in their bid for the hand of the prince have a meeting with the censor-headsman. Naturally Cinderella not only solves the riddle but passes the goodness test, measured with a thermometer, though when she insists that the prince be similarly tested, he conveniently drops the thermometer after claiming a reading identical with hers. But their joining together in a ragtime dance means that two of her wishes have been satisfied by her fairy godmother who is also a Red Cross nurse. The third, that she be allowed to tend the wounded, is in a measure realized when she is admitted to a convalescent home where she makes friends with the soldiers as well as 'the Lady Charlotte something' who is skivvying as a lowly VAD. One of the wounded, formerly a plumber, flirts with Charlotte, who jokingly hopes that she will graduate from washing floors to washing him. Instantly he is parodying Kern's 'They Didn't Believe Me': 'And when I tell them that some day washed by her I'll be – they'll never believe me', Charlotte joining in with abandon, 'But when I tell them 'twas a jolly good thing for me – they'll all believe me!' Abruptly, as they link arms, she wonders 'what are we doing?', and Cinderella ascribes it to the war mixing 'things up till we forget how different we are'. But Charlotte has a sudden insight: 'Or it has straightened things out so that we know how like we are.' When he arrives after the war with his toolbag will she be a beast, or will there 'be at least a smile of friendship ... in memory of the old days'. 'That's up to you, my lady', responds the soldier, though Barrie thinks '*he will be wiser if he arranges that it is to be up to himself*'. And finally Cinderella is visited by her policeman-prince, who brings her glass slippers in place of the conventional engagement ring. As with Pinero, critics require a softer centre than the dramatist provides, one claiming that 'the curtain falls on a scene of universal happiness'.[71] But the final direction promises no living happily ever after: '*He presses her face to him for a moment so that he may not see its transparency. Dr. Bodie has told him something.*'

During those first uncertain days when revivals had seemed the safest option, Alexander, at the St James's, was able to bring all the old 'dash and intensity' to a part he had created in Pinero's *His House in Order*. A number of the original cast was available, including Irene Vanbrugh: 'She is never so good as when she has to be semi-hysterical and to abandon herself to a nerve-storm. Every quiver, every sob, every outburst of passion, seems not so much acted as wrung out of her.'[72] A year on, Pinero's *Trelawny of the 'Wells'* was brought to the Kingsway from Liverpool, and in 1917 the New saw a star-studded matinée performance including not only Gerald du Maurier, Genevieve Ward, Gladys Cooper and Gertie Millar, but Irene Vanbrugh and Dion Boucicault in their original rôles. Still more notable, perhaps, was Horniman's 'capital revival' of *The Amazons* during her last London visit, though Newton, deeming her unwise to compete with the West End in portraying high society, confounds theorics of theatrical representation and social hierarchy: 'Though West-End players have their faults, they can at least play the aristocracy, for the obvious reason that they meet the aristocracy.'[73] Horniman took it as a farce which reaches to 'the hidden tragedies of men's and women's lives' (never mind their class), producing 'an undercurrent of tenderness and sympathy beneath the light tone'.[74]

Henry Arthur Jones made his best wartime showing in revivals. *The Silver King*, a collaborative work from 1882, was welcomed as 'the finest melodrama ever written'. A more cautious estimate noted it as 'more long-winded and discursive than the present-day model ... When the play-goer of to-day is out for incident, he is in no mood for rhetoric.' But with H. B. Irving in the hero-part, 'who takes as much pains to interpret Wifred Denver as though he were interpreting Hamlet', there was scant cause to complain.[75] The play had been immensely influential on melodrama generally, and specifically for its presentation of the gentleman-cracksman, who had considerable vogue on the wartime stage. The most famous example, Hornung's Raffles, had not appeared until 1899, though a dramatized *Raffles* (1906) was another of these late 1914 revivals, with du Maurier so effective in the title rôle that it ran at Wyndham's for 180 performances. Jones's play, with 48 performances, hardly approached that, and his *Liars* (1897), an entertaining comedy, managed only 34 when it was given at the St James's in 1917, though the cast was impressively led by Aubrey Smith and Mrs Patrick Campbell. It seemed a little dated when Edward Falkner allowed love for Lady Jessica to stand in the way of service to his country: since the barrel organ outside the inn at Shepperton played 'Tipperary', Jessica might have been expected to sing 'I Don't Want To Lose You, But I Think You Ought To Go.'[76] *The Liars*, however, was hastily put on to fill the gap left by the spectacular failure of Jones's new play, *The Pacifists*. *Era*'s end-of-year summing up (2 January 1918, p.21) declares the latter 'bad', though when it was tried out at the end of August in Southport, the paper reviewed it very favourably (29 August 1917, p. 9). It was said to deal with the failure of a peace-at-any-price policy in the face of unjust force: 'It is necessary to call up a superior force, which, using the same methods as the unjust force, but acting in the common interest, eventually subdues the unjust force.' But presumably this is not quite Jones's point, since 'common interest' hardly operates at the end, when 'superior force' hustles the pacifist's wife to the seaside for a romantic week just as the opposition had planned to do. Or is this regarded as fitting retribution for the pacifist? Certainly Jones is not at his most lucid in dedicating his play to those who, having 'rabidly pursued an ignoble peace' in 1914, continue to pursue 'the tragedy of a delusive and abortive peace'. Since they were not be regarded as 'pitiable figments of farce', it was unwise for Jones to adopt the farcical mode for his parable, one reviewer pointing to a resultant falling between stools.[77] There follows a complaint that everything takes place off-stage: 'People came rushing in like the messengers in a Greek tragedy, to say it had happened outside', the dialogue being nowhere near good enough to sustain this procedure. Jones had achieved more of his old form in *We Can't Be as Bad as All That* which, after some measure of success in America, received its British première at the Croydon Hippodrome. Violet Vanbrugh was splendid as the heroine who finally escapes with her lover to the Argentine, leaving behind the 'veneered heartlessness' of Lady Camforth and the witty scandal-mongering of Lady Greenop.[78]

Arnold Bennett, who must count as a minor classic, wrote just two plays during the war, one of which was shelved until 1919. The other, *The Title*, amused audiences for 285 performances at the Royalty. It is an amiable satire on 'the political custom of bartering honours' (those 'artificial State-made distinction[s] between one man and another') along with the idea 'that it is the women rather than the men who keep the honours list going'. But the light approach was not universally appreciated: 'You would never guess as you listened to the pleasantries ... that the class at which they were aimed had drenched the world in blood.'[79]

Bennett's *Milestones* had been the great hit of 1912, but when it was revived at the Royalty, one reviewer put his finger on the problem: the play's several milestones are completely overshadowed by the *annus mirabilis* of 1914.[80] Even so, it did marginally better than the 30 performances Bennett's co-author, Edward Knoblauch, achieved with the first British production of his 1913 play,

Marie-Odile. Before 'this really beautiful play' opened, its producer Beerbohm Tree told a *Referee* representative: 'Delicacy combined with simplicity will be the dominant note' of this 'idyll within convent walls'. And at the end of its brief run he expressed the 'greatest pain and surprise' that it had 'apparently given offence in certain quarters'. It was Littlewood in the same weekly who identified Knoblauch's 'offence': 'there is no excusing his gross caricature of the Mother Superior, who is represented as a narrow-minded shrew.'[81] He insists that such people do not exist behind convent walls, though *The Times* represents a different view: she is one 'who in a convent might be called austere and outside it "catty" ' (9 June 1915, p. 11). Indeed the conventual picture is well-balanced: Sister Louise preserves it from a too easy contrast between love and sterility, reputation and innocence.[82] But the influential Catholic lobby (Tree had fallen foul of it once before in 1890)[83] forced the play to close. At the annual meeting of the Catholic Stage Guild (formed 1912), the chairman, incensed by a play which he claimed held nuns 'up to ridicule', outrageously considered it 'one of the mistakes of the war!'[84]

The plot, with the original Franco-Prussian War setting rendered tactically indeterminate (though Marie-Odile is significantly named after Alsace's patron saint), deals with the arrival of invading troops at a convent from which all the nuns have fled. By accident the little novice Marie, raised at the convent in ignorance of man–woman relations, remains, and a corporal amongst the invaders, another innocent, finds opportunity to initiate them both. A year on, the nuns return to find Marie with her baby, the mother superior's attitude towards this 'miracle' leaving Marie bemused. Littlewood objects to the ensuing banishment of mother and child. He wants, if not a 'happy ending',

> at least some hint of the probable future of her and her offspring. Does the Corporal survive? If so, does he find her again? Does she return to the convent? ... Personally, I should be all for bringing the Corporal back and letting the high-brows go hang!

Curiously, Grein takes a similar line, mouthing a Thomas Rymer platitude: 'The soldier should have come back, for soldiers are mostly honourable men.'[85] But he does appreciate the relevance of the war baby issue: often enough 'the young generation has gone to fight, and the burden of love has been left behind'. For Fenton, topicality is wrecked by the 'milk-and-watery soldiers' who do not 'suggest the ruthless invaders of the present'.[86] But this is viewed positively in *Athenæum* (12 June 1915, p. 535): the 'gentle-mannered' corporal had revived 'waning hopes that the stage may be of some use in helping us to a more considered view of the times through which we are passing'. But if Knoblauch deserves thanks 'for allowing some humanity to appear among rough soldiery not specifically allied to us', this 'should strengthen determination to crush a Power which has made of many such men tools for accomplishing devilry'. Such was the mood in 1915 that others dubbed Knoblauch 'an enemy propagandist' for mounting a play written before the war.[87]

Lurking here are notions of drama's function which cut across that problematic idea of the classic. Similarly, there are plays which, although without staying power, without that density of writing which makes them adaptable to any number of needs, are able briefly to touch depths which only a Shakespeare is supposed to reach. This is especially the case when a whole society is in a state of emotional turmoil, producing a kind of corporate response. Although Knoblauch's play was prevented from serving a much-needed purpose through irresponsible protest, others like Herbert Thomas's *Out of Hell* clearly hit the right nerve.[88] This play, in contrast to the quiet tones of *Marie-Odile*, allowed actors to let rip, venting grief perhaps on their own behalf and certainly on that of audiences. *Out of Hell* uses only two players, assuming double rôles as mother and son. It opens with the British mother saying goodbye to her son, Arthur, who is bound for France; 18 months later she welcomes him home on leave, only to discover that this is an impostor bearing a close resemblance to Arthur. He is a German spy, an unknown nephew, and her dilemma is whether to let him go or hand him over to the authorities, which will sentence Arthur, held hostage, to death. Meanwhile, her sister, who has been estranged since marrying a German years before, is faced with a similar conflict when Arthur turns up at her flat, a fugitive needing aid. Blood ties win and she helps him at the cost of her own life. When Arthur reaches home, his demented mother attempts to stab him, thinking he is the spy escaped from Donington Hall. Frances Ivor, who was on stage for almost the entire two hours, reached new heights in this scene before all was brought to a happy resolution. Koopman had 'found less enjoyment in many a better play', savouring the humanity and its 'setting forth of the finer instincts'.[89] Although blasé West End audiences only sustained it for 31 performances, the play was a great success in the provinces, Edith Blande (whose only West End appearance during the war had been in Ellis's hugely popular farce, *A Little Bit of Fluff*) scoring the triumph of her career. Her emotional reach was such, passing through scorn, anger, the resignation of the martyr, as well as tenderness, that one reviewer feared she would become 'a nervous wreck'.[90] Stage convention prevented the acknowledgment found in Private Wilfrid Halliday's poem, 'The Grave', that German women grieve for those taken by the war just as much as their British counterparts. Yet, despite the evasion in the play of making the two women sisters, one reviewer grasped the point in his reference to the playing of 'English mother' and 'German wife'. For all the play's crudities, its breadth of sympathy was evidently welcome to provincial audiences.

It is just this chiming of text and context which prompts Carroll to cite the production of George Pleydell's *Ware Case* for its great tragic acting, and another contemporary play, *General Post,* for its high achievement in a lighter vein.[91] Du Maurier's performance as Ware evidently transcended the play's limitations. If the piece was taken for more than a briskly paced and cleverly constructed crime drama, the cause must have been ephemeral. Perhaps witnessing a member of the upper class on trial for murder at a time when so many of his kind were being encouraged to murder introduced an ironic piquancy. Perhaps, too, there was further resonance from a war, somehow held to betoken the age of the common man, which was decimating the youth of Debrett. It is more than likely that the latter circumstance gave to another 1915 play, Phillpotts and Hastings's *Angel in the House,* an unconsidered twist with the replacement of ancestral portraits by Norman Morrow's strange Futurist canvases.

There is no indirection about confronting the effects of war on the class structure in Harold Terry's *General Post,* which even at the time struck some as trite. The author, in conjunction with Lechmere Worrall, had written a comedy spy thriller, *The Man Who Stayed at Home* (1914), popular enough to spawn a sequel.[92] Even there he showed a knack for picking the soft target for satire: white feathers were already drawing adverse press comment when Terry's hero coolly used one to clean his pipe.[93] With *General Post, Bystander*'s Arnold Golsworthy (28 March 1917, p. 618) adopts the right tone: 'The man who was hardly the sort you could meet socially a year or two ago becomes, under the reign of Mars, your superior officer. It is to the credit of most of such men in the Army to-day that they have had the tact to resist the temptation to emphasise their temporary advantage'; 'temporary' shows Golsworthy's flair for *le mot juste.* Indeed the one jarring note he detects is in the portrayal of the 'shuffling, illiterate' brother of one whom the army has lifted far above his station, though it was 'no doubt necessary to accentuate and justify caste prejudice'. What Golsworthy registers as illiteracy (for which there is not a glimmering of textual evidence) is the way that, according to a stage direction, the brother's '*speech is marred by a distinct burr*'.[94] The crudity of presentation of this new class structure – those contributing to the national cause and those not – is emphasized in *The Times* (15 March 1917, p. 5). Terry

> never swerves for one weak moment from the obvious. The war has turned this or that country gentleman into a Volunteer private and this or that tailor into a brigadier-general, V.C. So why not bring the two types into juxtaposition and (happy thought!) have a love-affair between the country gentleman's daughter and the ex-tailor V.C.?

The latter, it is pointed out, is not, even 'before the war, an ordinary tailor, but a philosophical tailor who can talk of Nietzsche and Sudermann'. Moreover, he is a tailor who knows his place: though if the war gives him a lift, well and good. For the moment he must refuse the girl of county family: 'You belong to one class, I to another – and the gulf between us couldn't be much greater if I were a Chinee' (p. 48). They only meet because she becomes, in Golsworthy's words, eccentrically 'engaged in the great work of what I believe is known as uplifting the masses'. 'What's going to happen when the war's over?' is the anxious question, and the old Tory knight answers confidently: 'they'll shake down all right. It's a way things have' (p. 57). Meanwhile, according to the jumped-up tailor, 'The new army's conducted on strictly democratic principles. Why, any day of the week, you may see Tommies dining at the Carlton whilst their officers feed at – er – .' But this is because 'the God of War's ... a most shocking old Socialist! Blue blood doesn't impress him one bit. It's red blood, new blood, the blood of healthy men that he demands' (pp. 71, 79). This has its reflex in the Bishop of Lincoln's comment on wartime organization: 'We have had a taste of Socialism, and we like it.'[95] But this resembled Roosevelt's adoption of socialistic methods to rescue a tottering capitalism; in late 1918, with the war effectively won though still awaiting its symbolic conclusion since a too abrupt cessation would have upset the market, a parliamentary committee, under Balfour's chairmanship, concluded that government policy

> should be directed towards the restoration of normal industrial conditions within the shortest possible time. We are strongly of opinion that State control of, and restrictions upon, industry arising out of war conditions will be found to be detrimental under normal conditions.[96]

Meanwhile, the play concludes with a nice double-take: society is allowed to feel complacent about making room for real merit, but it is also reassured that there can't be too many underlings who will achieve the rank of brigadier-general, win the VC and be in line for a title. No wonder West End audiences filled the Haymarket for 535 performances, one first-night field officer enthusing: 'It's all so true – hits the nail on the head.'[97]

Caste was conspicuous amongst Tom Robertson's concerns, the 1860s being as far back as the London theatre cared to venture except when consciously following the heritage trail. Robertson's *David Garrick* was in Martin Harvey's wartime repertoire, and *Caste* was revived in contemporary dress by Alfred Wareing's Brighton company, with Albert Chevalier. The original plot device of the soldier-husband posted to India, where he is reported missing, believed killed, was readily adapted to 1916 circumstances; and the discovery of unexpected virtues in each other by representatives of the upper and lower orders had its reflex in trench life, where the classes were thrown into alarming proximity. Although D. W. Marriott was slightly embarrassed at including it in his anthology of *Great Modern British Plays* (1929), the 1916 fuss over some very minor textual liberties indicates that the play had already entered the rarefied zone of 'classic'.[98]

The very idea of the classic, as far as British drama is concerned, is defined by Shakespeare. But before considering the wartime Shakespeare it is worth pausing over a few other early dramatists staged during the war, including Sheridan, the centenary of whose death in 1916 coincided with the tercentenary of Shakespeare's death. *The School for Scandal*, given as a royal matinée at Covent Garden, was largely an excuse for parading a galaxy of stars, though the Teazles were brilliantly played by Irene Vanbrugh and Tree. The latter's interpretation had mellowed, 'kindlier in the passages concerning the irresponsible young wife; more genial, more joyous in the humorous passages'.[99] A less glittering but highly successful matinée was given at Richmond Hippodrome in aid of the local Red Cross hospital, Bandmann Palmer emerging from retirement to direct and play Lady Teazle.[100] But in London it was the Old Vic which gave most attention to Sheridan (four plays), as well as Goldsmith's *She Stoops to Conquer*.

At intervals the Stage Society put on several of Congreve's plays, beginning with *The Double Dealer*. One reviewer at least decided that such plays were of more historic than dramatic interest, avoiding 'the normal and the natural' in their efforts to divert.[101] There was no beating about the bush over the next offering, *Love for Love*, which the *Weekly Dispatch* declared 'Disgusting'.[102] Farjeon scorns humbug, elevating Congreve and his fellows, who 'ridiculed the world of vice', over 'the modern farce-writers who turn it into a kind of fairyland of silk stockings and lace petticoats'. Shakespeare or Wordsworth may be bowdlerized, but not 'the Restoration dramatists or the official reports on atrocities in Belgium'.[103] *The Times* (17 April 1917, p. 9) recognized *Love for Love* as 'an organic whole brimming over with life', its characters 'all witty, even the serving men, and why not?' The reviewer, having cast his vote for democracy, also found the play astonishingly 'modern' – except that modern playwrights could never match its style. However, the same newspaper (15 May 1918, p. 8) found *The Way of the World too* modern, or at least the actresses' style of playing. But at least, unlike several over-solemn actors, they were effective, especially Edyth Goodall's '"chaffing" minx of a Millamant'. Earlier, the Society's revival of Farquhar's *The Recruiting Officer* had seemed ill-advised, with its uncomfortably familiar situations: 'The yokels of the time were coaxed, or bullied or driven senseless by drink, to accept the Queen's shilling'; and lower-class girls 'were mere cannon-food for the officers, who shifted them and possible consequences on to their subalterns'. For Newton, this was 'more pornographic than patriotic', and another critic puzzled over the motives for putting the play on 'at this particular moment. Is it intended as a hit at the "moral suasion" school of recruiters?' But it was splendidly played, Nigel Playfair giving 'a joyful performance' as Sergeant Kite.[104] Otherwise, early dramatists were unrepresented apart from Jonson revivals in connection with the Shakespeare tercentenary. Poel produced *Poetaster* at the Apothecaries' Hall, and the Birmingham Rep staged *The Alchemist.*[105]

The Shakespearean reputation had inspired a modern poetic drama, the outstanding production during the war being Granville Barker's adaptation of Hardy's *The Dynasts.* In its 19-act entirety it might have been done like Wagner's *Ring,* mused an *Era* critic, while Hardy visualized a stage arrangement of gauzes and veils, and 'monotonic delivery of speeches, with dreamy conventional gestures, something in the manner traditionally maintained by the old Christmas mummers'.[106] Although Hardy's folk-play conception hardly squared with Barker's epic approach, they co-operated sympathetically. Henry Ainley supplied cohesion by sonorously intoning from a lectern placed in the prompt position. The technique was much the same as he used for the *mélodrame* in *Carillon* (recorded with Elgar the following January); but for Hope, whose prejudices are transparent, he had been almost destroyed by Barker, 'drilled and directed and stage-managed until he seemed to have become a mere marionette . . . , and all the followers of Gordon Craig shouted for joy'.[107] Hope derides other staging arrangements: 'On each side of the proscenium arch, in high-backed chairs of grey and silver', were Esmé Beringer and Carrie Haase as cloaked and hooded Fates, commenting in strophe and antistrophe on a quick succession of events relating to Trafalgar, the Peninsula and Waterloo. Action took place before 'a white wall with three panels cut in it'. Thus a

> backcloth with the 'N' monogram, a settee placed against it, and a table to the left of the settee, seen through the centre panel, serves as the room at Fontainebleau wherein Napoleon signed his abdication; remove the backcloth, settee, and table, and the same scene serves for the hill at Waterloo wherefrom Napoleon witnessed his defeat; remove Napoleon, put a rail across the centre panel, and you have a street scene outside the Guildhall.[108]

For the most part, however, this simplicity and economy was admired. The audience was 'bewitched into seeing a whole battlefield in a perfectly blank grey curtain, from which came voices; one felt the cold night air, and the sound of the distant sea came faintly to one's ears when they laid Sir John Moore's body in his lonely grave, although there was no scenery but a little heap of earth and a dark backcloth'.[109] Moore's burial was one of two scenes cut in later performances 'because of the distress [caused] among the spectators who had just lost relatives in the war'.[110] Men in the audience were reduced to tears by the death of Nelson, observed *The Times* critic (26 November 1914, p. 5). Spliced into such grander scenes is the unwritten history of the underclass, drunken deserters at Corunna, stage-coachmen and camp-followers, or rustic customers in a Wessex inn, gossiping 'queerly ... about Boney and Pitt and their own everyday affairs ... Such a quasi-Shakespearean mingling as the whole thing is of high emprise and lowly humours, heroic deaths and the ignorant chatter of the common workaday world!' (Shakespeare endorsing what the reviewer takes to be the proper shape of things).

Stephen Phillips described his *Armageddon* as 'a modern epic drama', abandoning Hardy's and his own previous historical settings to demonstrate that blank verse could work in modern guise.[111] The London critics were unimpressed, though for differing reasons. Grein aptly wonders 'that such "rant" is allowed in a British theatre in 1915, after all the object lessons we have been given by Ibsenites and Barkers'. He does not care to see the stage misused 'for the purpose of denigration of one's adversaries and incitement of the crowd'.[112] *Era*'s critic (9 June 1915, p. 11) considers it 'exceedingly bad taste to put before the public ... the hideous happenings of the present world war ... There is one scene in particular that is inexpressibly lacerating [where] two women hear of the death in action of the son of the one and the betrothed of the other.' For women in the audience this could only intensify 'the ever-present fear of the telegram from the War Office'. Had the lacerations of 'this short but poignant scene' (the best in the play according to Walkley)[113] been calculated to shorten the war, they would have been justified. But the mood of the time was to accept the phoney consolation 'that he has met with a splendid death; that he is to be envied by all of us who are compelled to stay behind.'[114] The latter point is absurd, even leaving aside the likelihood that the soldier's death would have been squalid rather than splendid.

There is little common ground between the reviews in *The Times* and *Referee*, yet they do concur on one point. Walkley regards the play as 'a serious variety entertainment or revue ... with ratiocination in lieu of songs'; while Newton is reminded of the 'music hall war sketch', the episode of the German Press Bureau 'being useful only for some Graves-like gag scene in a revue – if it were allowable (which it ought not to be) to make comic capital out of such a subject'.[115] Newton raises no objection to the representation and rehearsal of most of the current themes of atrocity propaganda, but he dislikes intensely the final episode. Here, as the allies move victoriously on Cologne, the mood resembles that of Thomas More's *Dialogue of Comfort* where the Christians apprehensively await a Turkish invasion, steeling themselves for the inevitable atrocities. The German civilians are represented by Elsa, the burgomaster's daughter, who has befriended a young Belgian refugee: the only sign of German humanity in the play. Actresses 'Margaret Omar and Maud Rivers brought home to us the bonds of vulnerability which unite the womanhood of all nations', Elsa (Rivers) greeting the British general with rape very much on her mind, having learned what the Belgian girl has endured.[116] Hence she offers herself to him if he will persuade his French and Belgian colleagues to spare her city. He, 'spick and span' as generals are wont to be as they arrive behind their conquering armies, is tempted only momentarily before arguing disinterestedly against avenging Louvain and Rheims by destroying Cologne Cathedral. Yet even he wavers on hearing that his son has been killed and the body mutilated. Eventually Joan of Arc pops up to strengthen his resolve, causing Newton to bridle: 'Is there any British officer who need wait for Joan's ghost to appear in order to tell him his duty?' Newton's real trouble with this 'weak-kneed, weaker-willed' officer is spelt out by his colleague, George Sims: 'the Cologne scene belongs to a school of thought that may seriously delay our ultimate success and rob us of the fruits of victory when we have won. So long as we reply to Frightfulness and barbarity with sentimental humanity we shall be at a grave disadvantage.' Underlying this is acknowledgment that while the Germans have theorized about the rôle of Frightfulness in war, its practice is common to all armies. What is less honest is to relish the violability of Cologne's cathedral while keeping quiet about that of her womanhood. Phillips himself echoed the play's epigraph from the poet laureate ('This war is a war of Christ against the Devil') in hoping that the play stood 'for the teaching of the New Testament rather than that of the Old'. But *Referee*'s editor Richard Butler undercut by reference to the one scene of 'cheap melodrama': 'when every German on the stage had been killed by the explosion of a turpinite shell, the "savagery" was received with frantic applause in all parts of the house.'[117] *Era*'s critic, presumably unmoved by the commonplace horrors of lyddite, reacts with disbelief to the claims for turpinite: 'If this were true, and not merely a theatrical absurdity, we could hardly object to the subsequent use of asphyxiating gases by the Germans.' He could have read in the newspapers, as doubtless Phillips did, how a turpinite shell left a trenchful of dead Germans 'standing bolt upright, and still holding their rifles in the firing attitude'.[118] Walkley, knowing the representation to be 'true enough to fact', thought it none 'the more acceptable to the aesthetic sense for being true'.

Harvey's loyalty survived the 'savagery or ignorance' of press responses.[119] He played several rôles, most notably that of Satan to whose 'rich-voiced intonations' he imparted a certain dignity. Thomas Derrick's designs helped, setting the gothic upsoaring of Satan's wings against a clean-lined modernism.[120] The 'weirdly impressive' scene, with a mass of disembodied arms in the foreground waving enthusiastically as war was hatched, had Attila 'richly touched in colour', contrasting with the grey monotones of eternity. And at the final return to hell, a beam of light fell on Satan, making him cower 'stricken, to the ground under wings now limp and ragged'.[121] But Derrick's powerful austerity proved too subtle, and when the play went on tour all the chief denizens of hell were made colourful. Even so, it was on tour that the play proved outstandingly successful,[122] having been taken off in London after just 14 performances.

Masefield's wartime verse plays made no commercial impact, though the topical import of *Philip the King* was recognized, as Ainley prayed for his Armada's victory, buoyed by false news yet haunted by the spirits of those sacrificed to imperial ambition.[123] A similar 'war allegory' was detected in *The Faithful*, part Nõ play, part Jacobean revenge tragedy, which shifts between verse and prose. Although the lord Kira is described as a 'beast' who has burnt homes and scattered their occupants,[124] it is the wanton sacrifice of the best in this society which provides the most searing wartime parallel. Its mood was too bleak for the commercial theatre, though it proved 'a triumph' at the Birmingham Rep,[125] and the Stage Society gave it a London airing in 1919.

Something of the sombre power, the terseness and rhythmic impulsion found in Masefield at his best is also present in Bottomley's *Lear's Wife*. Here Maud Tree 'was intensely tragic as the unhappy, unwanted Queen', and there is grim Elizabethan humour when her corpse is laid out at the end. Viola Tree perfectly caught 'the spirit of the cold, chaste, unsullied' Goneril, 'unsullied', that is to say, if murder is considered unsullying, and her presentation constituted an interesting critique of a play avoided for most of the war.[126] The Old Vic company, in its mammoth undertaking to mount every one of Shakespeare's plays, produced it in 1918, but otherwise London had to make do with a dramatic reading at His Majesty's in 1916, by Bourchier and the British Empire Shakespeare Society. This reminds that the whole concept of the classic is politically loaded. Awkward art, like awkward morality, tends to be shelved by what is made to seem general consent for the duration. Newton thought *Richard II*, given at the Vic, unsuitable for wartime, since it 'makes you think'.[127] Likewise, if *Lear* would set people thinking, turn them away from fighting the good fight, then *Lear* should be set aside temporarily, to be taken up afresh when the need for it had abated, like Michael Morton's *The Yellow Ticket*.[128] But facile points could be made even with *Lear*. Sybil Thorndike recalls one night when an air raid coincided with Lear's storm and her brother Russell ventured a slight mispronunciation of 'all germens spill at once', yelling above the din of the bombardment, and causing the audience to shriek in response.[129] This might have reminded her that theatre, for all the pervasive doctrines of Romanticism, is not something autonomous and removed from day-to-day affairs, but is as functional as architecture. Responding to the claim that 'Soldiers home from the front want amusing', she decided that 'there are various sorts of amusement', and hoped that a visit to the Old Vic might 'have sent them back to their horrors with a vision and a faith, instead of a lulling drug which is all that a great many ask of the Theatre'.[130] The problem is to see that vision and that faith as something other than 'a lulling drug' to anaesthetize them against the horrors.

And there was always the danger that the anaesthetic would wear off. Eliot feared that war had destroyed the unity of traditional culture, despite Ypres and Louvain's providing ample fragments to shore up the rickety structure. But Shaw, in his buoyantly cynical way, pointed to a fraudulence at the heart of Eliot's tradition, denying consolation to

> those mourners for the Louvain library who have always voted against a penny rate for a library in their own parish ... What right had we to sponge on the middle ages for the beauty we would not produce ourselves? ... As soon as we really want an Ypres of mediæval charm we can have it. If we do not want it, nobody but a handful of members of the Art Workers' Guild will suffer the smallest privation by the smashing of the Cloth Hall and the cathedral.[131]

Shaw was articulating what many junior officers would learn in the confined world of the trenches: that their culture's underpinning of shared, stable values was an illusion. In the course of what one observer saw as inprecedented 'mental slumming', coming 'into actual contact with vulgar intelligence and popular feeling',[132] came the discovery that the lower orders were thinking, sentient beings, not necessarily content with a popular art that reassures, confirming known experience and values. Robert Graves was just one of many exposed to this culture shock, though he had the resilience to handle the discovery that the cultural interests of the working class could be just as intellectually solid and enriching as those of his own. For others it brought recognition that the real danger lay less in a debased version of high culture designed for mass consumption than in the possibility that working-class intellectualism would take an aggressively subversive turn.

Both problems were addressed by Lena Ashwell, in the concerts which she organized for troops on active service. Here was that prospect of a land fit for victorious heroes as she sought to persuade them that they had a stake in elite culture. That the Old Vic's missionary work with Shakespeare had similar motivation aroused enthusiasm amongst people of power and influence. H. B. Irving, speaking at a 'Fight for Right' meeting at the Æolian Hall in 1917, praised the Vic for undertaking the 'good work' neglected elsewhere, of making Shakespeare a morale-booster.[133] Although the Vic had 'not discovered how to make Shakespeare pay – pay, that is to say, as West End revues and musical comedies pay', it had demonstrated that there was 'an enormous Shakespeare public among the poorer classes' when reverence was kept at bay.[134] But there was some split-mindedness about a paying Shakespeare: *Era*'s leader-writer (16 February 1916, p. 15) had advocated making a Shakespeare tercentenary collection to set 'the Old Vic firmly on its feet, so that instead of being obliged to charge entrance prices of from two shillings downwards, it could open its doors to patrons at a uniform charge of 3d. per head'. The higher prices, by bringing in the 'well-dressed', kept some of the locals out: 'The coster has his class prejudices.' But Greet already felt constrained by a charter which required that Old Vic seat-prices be kept within reach of those simple folk who 'loved pictures and thought beautiful the poor scenery which ... serves to-day for Messina and to-morrow for Eastcheap'.[135] The patronizing note was there, too, when Mary Anderson came out of retirement to give a sample of some of her old successes in aid of war charities. At the Coliseum, where Beecham lent the balcony set used for Gounod's opera, she told Stoll that 'The soldiers in the gallery liked [her Juliet] quite as much as the people in the stalls.'[136] Newton, on the basis of a single night, tells a somewhat different story, noting with displeasure that Juliet's ecstasies caused fidgeting amongst the younger element (not necessarily galleryites, but undoubtedly including the soldiery) who seemed impatient 'for action – or knockabout'.[137] State education had helped to remove Shakespeare from the popular domain:[138] in mid-nineteenth-century Birmingham 'Shakespearean productions drew consistently good popular audiences';[139] and later, at Hoxton's Britannia Theatre, Sara Lane found a Shakespeare birthday festival week so far short of the demand that it was extended for some months. But in recalling this, *Era*'s columnist (10 April 1918, p. 8) cites the famed dictum of the old Drury Lane manager, F. B. Chatterton, 'Shakespeare spells ruin and Byron, bankruptcy', and the fact that a recent Shakespeare revival had brought a return of just £5.

Shakespeare's place in official integration propaganda was underscored by the war. In 1916 Israel Gollancz insisted: 'Shakespeare's boundless love of country is no mere poetic fervour; it is solidly based upon his belief that English ideals make for righteousness, for freedom, for the recognition of human rights and liberties.'[140] Hence the local vicar 'always urged his [working-class] congregation to go regularly to the Vic and learn their Shakespeare'.[141] Part of Ben Greet's strategy was to bring in the LCC schoolchildren on a curricular basis, which proved ideologically as well as financially rewarding.[142] According to *Era* (30 October 1918, p. 8), about 500 schools in the Greater London area participated, one of the chief features of the matinées being 'the mass singing of the National Anthem'. In an article written for that paper, Greet insists on the resurgent popularity of Shakespeare with the 'man in the street, the artisan, the mechanic, the twenty-two-bob-a-weeker', who 'prefers 'Hamlet' and 'As You Like It' to the lighter and more frivolous farce which he is generally offered'.[143]

Greet himself had the kind of credentials (son of a naval captain and brother of an admiral) to lift him out of that street of which he liked to talk. But there is no need to suspect cynicism in his missionary efforts, though advocates of a workers' theatre were pretty open about placing seduction above enlightenment. Rosina Filippi, who had been responsible for a season of plays at the Old Vic just before the war, began an article on 'A People's Playhouse': 'The art of the theatre is the most democratic of arts. From the stage the multitude can be influenced to a far greater degree than through the medium of any other art.'[144] She throws in the word 'democratic' with all the aplomb of a present-day cabinet minister, but, like Greet, who resorted to Shakespeare as a way of doing his patriotic bit, she gives primacy to mind-bending. Herbert Grover, in a letter to *Era* (24 April 1918, p. 8), expressed dismay that the anniversaries of Shakespeare's birth and death were passing unnoticed save at the Vic: 'And yet Shakespeare is being played now all over Germany' (and a Berlin publisher had just brought out Gerhart Hauptmann's new edition of the works).[145] He urged Shakespeare's propagandist value on those running a government department which had just allocated £30,000 for the making of a single film, but they 'calmly declared that they were not sufficiently acquainted with Shakespeare to express an opinion worth having whether his plays would have the desired effect'. In reality the government had been too wily to intervene on any scale when the theatre was doing voluntarily and inconspicuously far more than any direct government promotions were likely to achieve, and without any public money being spent. But now mounting pressure forced the appointment of Ben Tillett as official director of theatrical propaganda, though without producing the results looked for by *Era*'s leader-writer. He noted impatiently that, with the Actors' Association represented on the War Aims Committee, 'the machinery is there, waiting only to be put in motion'. And what better material could be found than

> the Chronicle Plays of our own national dramatist, for, taken singly, or better far as a cycle, they enforce invaluable political lessons, and one and all breathe the true spirit of sane and vigorous patriotism. Shakespeare's contribution to a scheme of war propaganda need not stop at the English historical plays, for the Roman plays as well offer great possibilities, ... especially 'Troilus and Cressida' with the great speech of Ulysses in I.3.[146]

Probably *Troilus* is the worst example that could have been furnished. Any tolerably impartial reading shows the moral absolutes in this speech already being undercut before the end of the scene, as Ulysses plans stratagems where honour is reduced to terms which Pinero found fit subject for satire in *The Big Drum*. Clearly more than one blind eye must be turned to a play which specifically confounds the 'fair play' ethic with *realpolitik*, so that amongst pre-war critics it was only the Germans who addressed it directly. A German version was given in 1916 at Zurich, a city crowded with German exiles from the war, concluding with Achilles in his chariot crowned with lasting fame as ironic glorification of murder.[147] The play was ignored in this country during the war, the Old Vic, in its heroic progress through the canon, leaving it until 1923, the very last of the series. But the company had a way of erasing the problems presented by Shakespeare. George Foss, who produced *Measure for Measure,* was persuaded that no 'mere *man* could play the part of "Lucio" as Florence Saunders did in November, 1918. The most unpleasant part in an unpleasant play was purged of its unpleasantness and became a joy to dream of forever.'[148] That she was relieved 'of most of the Hogarthian humours with Elbow, Froth, and Pompey' largely invalidated her performance and the entire production.[149]

Foss directed the 1918–19 winter season, after Lilian Baylis had got rid of Greet who in four years at the Vic had produced 24 of Shakespeare's plays. However, the first wartime initiative had come from Estelle Stead, actress and daughter of the famous journalist who died on the *Titanic*. She 'had the ear of the theatrical establishment', and interested Matheson Lang, and his wife Hutin Britten, as well as Andrew Leigh, in the Old Vic project.[150] The latter became a stalwart until his call-up in 1916. Meanwhile, Lang himself directed the first three productions, *The Merchant of Venice*, *The Taming of the Shrew* and *Hamlet*, his wife playing leads in two. (She supplied a fine display of 'rebellious anger' in *The Shrew*, though the audience was 'delighted at the punishment meted out to [this] Elizabethan suffragette'.[151]) For the remainder of the seven-month season, production was in the hands of Stead, Leigh and Greet, and by the end Greet seems to have conceived his grand patriotic design of working through the entire canon. It was surely this imaginative conception, rather than a convenient tendency towards stripped-down production or wartime uncertainties pushing actors to accept small salaries in return for guaranteed employment,[152] which supplied momentum for Old Vic Shakespeare. At the same time, the conception arose out of war, which also helped to foster team loyalty, making wages of '30 bob' acceptable.[153]

Greet had assisted Poel with the celebrated *Everyman* recovery, mounting his own production at the Vic. Although Greet tempered Poel's purism with practicality, his ideal was giving the 'complete' text on a plain Elizabethan-style stage. It is not clear whether he had absorbed Poel's contrapuntal technique, but he was certainly committed to quick flow: 'We on the stage race to get our scenery set to make the plays act as closely and rapidly as possible.' This derives from a much-quoted programme note written in November 1917, which makes unnecessary apologies for 'Acting versions' as opposed to scholarly texts: 'The intellectual ones and the youngsters who study the plays can supply with their knowledge the omitted scenes'.[154] *Era*'s leader-writer (25 April 1917, p. 13), relishing the way that Shakespeare was disempedestalled at the Vic, would have endorsed Greet's desire to make the plays 'entertaining and interesting'; and rejected special consideration for students and intellectuals.

Greet's scenic habits were necessarily more consistent than his textual. For a 1915 *Tempest* he craved 'indulgence for the paucity of scenery in a play in which it should play so important a part', but suggested that the interludes, with dainty sprites impersonated by Margaret Morris's Dancing Children, would compensate. This was an important element in Vic staging. The witches in *Macbeth* were 'weird, ghostly creatures', effectively lit and supported by 'fantastic dances', this time from 'the pupils of Mrs. Henry Wordsworth'.[155] Lighting created mood and atmosphere,[156] though Isaac notes the use of 'Trees' and 'Banks', and 'A kind of porch with double doors, and a balcony above, ... used for formal entrances and exits'. Juliet soliloquized from the balcony, and Russell Thorndike's Macbeth scaled it to murder Duncan 'while the audience held their breath'.[157] *Athenæum*'s critic (27 November 1915, p. 394) testifies to Greet's nimble approach in his first independent season: 'The management are to be congratulated on the speed and efficiency of the scene-shifting in this very long play' (*Richard III*). Apparently not much cutting had taken place here, nor with *Othello* which, as a result, seemed 'too long to be given in its entirety unless it begins at an earlier hour'. However, in the following season, the same reviewer attended an extensively cut *Hamlet* (March 1916, p. 152), though there were matinées when the play was given in its entirety: 4½ hours with 'Twenty minutes in the middle for eating and leg-stretching.'[158] 1916 also saw the Induction 'wisely omitted' from *The Taming of the Shrew*, with Sybil Thorndike playing up well to the 'excellent fooling' of William Stack's Petruchio.[159] A tiresome factor in the curtailing of performances was the LCC's squeamishness over indelicacies 'in "Cymbeline" and other Shakespearean pieces'.[160] However, that fairly full texts were being used early on is especially interesting, since at this period there was still an attempt to represent Shakespeare as part of a variety bill in order to circumvent the 'No smoking' regulation operating in the legitimate theatre until 23 November 1915. The 1915 *The Comedy of Errors* was item five on a mixed bill including 'some animated pictures of the warships of all nations'.[161]

That first season had produced a deliciously patronizing view of the Old Vic audience, 'as earnest as it was unsophisticated'.[162] The 'strained attention' of a well-filled house

> spoke very eloquently of the fact that Shakespeare, even in his serenest and most fanciful mood, is taken very seriously by a public which is not

> commonly credited by superior but mistaken people with a genuine interest in his works; and the hearty laughter produced by the antics of Stephano, Trinculo, and Caliban was no less indicative of an attitude of simple but genuine enjoyment.

Reasonably enough, Greet was concerned to get words and plot-lines across to an audience which on the whole was likely to be unfamiliar with the plays. He took pride in the company's ability to project to all parts of the deep house, for, as Grein put it, 'Not all are great actors, but nearly every one of them is an unimpeachable diseur.'[163] Stack played Hamlet 'as a gentle, sensitive youth, suddenly shaken from his dreams and distraught by a terrible shock. He appeared to best advantage in his scenes with his mother and with Ophelia, and Beatrice Wilson's clever impersonation of the Queen would have been still better if she had been word-perfect.'[164] (Under-rehearsal was a besetting problem for Greet's shoestring operation.) The treatment of *Julius Caesar* seems typical: no 'fining down of the rough edges' or lavish effects, but vigorously realized characterizations. Norman Norman, guesting as Antony, made him 'the hearty, robust soldier of fortune, something of a reveller', but quick of wit; 'That day he overcame the Nervi' becoming 'one of the spontaneous, uncalculated strokes with which he worked upon the passions of the mob'. The fickle mob, 'considering their few numbers, ... were remarkably effective' (sometimes numbers were augmented by members of the audience, bribed with 'lemonade and a sausage roll').[165] Greet's programme note for *The Tempest* describes it as 'too problematic ... for commercial purposes', and he certainly seems to have worked at ironing out the problems. He 'emphasised the benevolent aspect of the exiled Duke' and invested the love-scenes with 'idyllic charm'. Russell Thorndike's Caliban was 'raucous voiced and hideous', his ferocity 'not even softened in his cups'.[166] In *Othello*, 'Robert Atkins's unctuous villainy as Iago was a good foil' for Stack's Moor, deteriorating 'under the lash of jealousy'. But performance options were limited, as Stack affirmed, in bringing 'out the childlike moods of the primitive man that Shakespeare wanted his impulsive Moor to be'.[167] Newton, drawing on a long memory, compared him to Phelps and Charles Dillon for his 'agonising outburst' in Act III.[168] However, Fisher White managed some freshness. As Leontes, he exposed 'without exaggerating the psychopathic features',[169] and his Macbeth was 'a visionary [with] little outward show of the stalwart warrior'. Russell Thorndike supplied a more romantic Macbeth, mighty even in his fall, with the 'rugged features and gaunt frame' of some old-time Viking. Sybil's Lady Macbeth,

> Cold-blooded and ferocious, ... yet remains womanly throughout ... And so pity and sympathy are her due in the sleep-walking scene, rather

> than the awe at the contemplation of ruined grandeur awakened by Mary Anderson in her performances last year.[170]

Greet wanted Lady Macbeth played as 'truly wicked', but Thorndike resisted: 'I can't play her that way – she's not wicked – she's very like all women who are quiet and violent and want the best for the one they love, and despise anyone who gets in the way.'[171]

Although Greet took rather a black-and-white view of character, he evidently brought a comic richness to parts like Dogberry and, especially, Malvolio, which he developed over the years.[172] His programme note describes Shylock as 'an old rascal without a redeeming feature', yet he had long managed to project the character's 'bad side' whilst allowing him 'a remnant of dignity and pathos'.[173] When *The Merchant* was revived following Greet's departure, the Thorndikes guested, Sybil's Portia being less the great lady than a 'young, high-spirited girl, eager to love and be loved, shy and advancing by turns', and 'far too clever to make a show of her cleverness'.[174] One reviewer praised the Vic both for providing 'much more of the text' than was usual, and (aided by minimal scenery) for putting it across.[175] But Carroll plainly found Foss's direction no substitute for that of Greet: 'It was like listening to Beethoven on a barrel-organ.'[176]

Greet had shown his mettle at the Stratford Tercentenary Festival. In the summer of 1915, Benson had been in no doubt about the propriety of celebrating the Shakespeare season as usual, believing many people to be 'more in sympathy with a festival of culture than with a racket of revue'.[177] But in July of the following year he left for France on war work, and, with barely two months' notice, Greet repaired the breach with a dozen plays, ten of them by Shakespeare. His *Hamlet* revived some old traditions: Ophelia, in her madness, entered playing on a lute, and Stack, following Charles Kean, dropped a rose into her grave. Ophelia (Thorndike) 'gave away her flowers only in her distraught fancy. Throughout her eyes conveyed a kind of dazed expression as though she were moving in a circle of events beyond her understanding.' The idea, borrowed from Bernhardt, 'of sending the whole company with the King first and all the Court after him at full tilt across the front of the stage after the Play Scene, with Hamlet bringing up the rear, [was] singularly effective'.[178] *Henry VIII*, with which the season ended, was a new production, Lilian Braithwaite guesting as Katharine of Aragon and Norman Norman as the King. When he repeated the rôle at the Vic, Norman 'was much as we imagine unfriendly aliens' conception of Mr. John Bull to be'; overbearing, obstinate, relishing the way he achieved his ends 'under a cloak of open-hearted simplicity'.[179]

But it was *King John*, opening the 1917 autumn season with Philip Barry splendid as 'the impetuous and patriotic Falconbridge', which most surely hit the contemporary note. Some of the audience thought the line about 'Austria's head' to be a topical interpolation, and the fact that the first performance coincided with an air raid gave piquancy to the preceding phrases: 'Some airy devil hovers in the sky/And pours down mischief.' Falconbridge's final speech ('This England never did, nor never shall,/Lie at the proud foot of a conqueror') 'brought the house down', and the lines were inscribed over the proscenium arch for the remainder of the war.[180] As Constance, 'Sybil Thorndike's intense acting was something of a tour de force, especially under the circumstances': she had recently lost both her brother Frank (killed in action) and her father. Indeed the part provided a release, as Baylis observed: 'That mad tearing-of-your-hair scene is just right for you – you can't cry and go on like that in real life.' [181]

Greet persuaded Baylis that *Henry V* 'was just the play to draw all the soldiers in London'.[182] Its staging was spare: a 'curtained alcove between pillars at middle back of stage ... Some of the scenes are enacted within the recess, the curtains being raised or lowered when necessary by one of the two black-gowned boys who remain on the stage with the rest of the "props".' Otherwise, there was a section of 'breached Harfleur wall' which had already served for Pyramus and Thisbe. Only some 150 lines were omitted, but, barring 'one short pause', the play proceeded at a cracking pace. The chorus (armour-clad Estelle Stead) arrived on the run and used 'a breathless stop-press' delivery. Stack played the king, 'The mellow, modulating quality of his voice' fitting him best for the less stentorian moments.[183]

Sidney Lee had lectured that 'Henry's patriotism was of the spirited, wholesome type, and though he was a born soldier, he discouraged insolent aggression'. Frank Desprez, *Era*'s editor, disagreed, reminding how Shakespeare had made it plain that Henry's battles were fought, on his father's politic advice, 'to busy giddy minds with foreign quarrels'.[184] That internal problems in 1914, not least the Irish question, might have prompted a similar distraction ploy would have been apparent to anyone still working by intellect rather than emotion. However, Desprez implies that both Britain's people and their rulers have grown in moral stature:

> Shakespeare was writing for a public which was very different from that of our own day. It was cynically indifferent to international honesty, and adored strength and success. So that he risked little in demonstrating the mercenary policy of the Church, and its motives in finding Henry an excuse for the war he wanted.

Yet, although supplying the comfortable parallel of Bismarck in 1870, he nevertheless rejects the propagandist usefulness of a play in which the dramatist glosses 'over a crime by enlarging on the vigorous way in which it was committed'. When Shaw suggested that it was indiscreet to parade the hero Nelson during the visit of Joffre and Briand, he was told that this was tantamount to saying that *Henry V*, 'so much performed of late, ought to be withdrawn'.[185] But Desprez had already said it.

However, attempts to subvert the status of *Henry V* as a vehicle for wartime patriotism were easily contained. Wartime Shakespeare was non-problematic: as the great national poet he self-evidently respresented the nation's views. He served to justify the worth and rightmindedness of Britain's theatre as well as her foreign policy. Naturally no one was unwise enough to enter into debate with Desprez. The neatest way of disposing of his argument was to ignore it, to pretend that it had never been presented. When Benson brought *Henry V* to the Shaftesbury, Walkley made glancing reference:

> It would have been lamentable if so splendid an expression of the English spirit ... had been withheld from us at the present hour by blockhead misgivings about French susceptibilities. It celebrates French chivalry no less than our own, and might be as cherished a *livre de poche* for any French soldier in the Argonne woods to-day as for his British comrade-in-arms defending Ypres.[186]

He protests too much; later, reviewing Harvey's production, he discovers as saving features 'the difference between the France of Agincourt and the France of Verdun, and the alliance with which the piece concludes' (*The Times*, 30 May 1916, p. 9). But of the Benson production, he, along with most reviewers, alludes to Harcourt Williams's 'crazy French King', a nice justification for Henry's take-over. It is always hard to establish traditions in the playing of lesser parts, but Olive Jetley, in a matinée performance by Marie Slade's all-woman company, 'gave a clever study of foolish senility as Charles VI'.[187]

Benson's Henry was a total 'contrast in its kingly dignity to the impetuous virility of Mr. Lewis Waller's well-known impersonation'.[188] Walkley notes how Benson's 'voice trembled' over 'We few, we happy few, we band of brothers', and 'his performance throughout was marked by an unwonted fervour'. He was 'not merely playing the stage-part, but delivering a solemn message'. For J. S., the King's speeches reminded 'how England has always played the game – and always will'; and there was a clear indictment of the Kaiser in Williams's 'if the cause be not good the king himself hath a heavy reckoning to make: when all those legs and arms and heads, chopped off in a battle, shall join together at the Latter Day'.[189] Desprez had not reckoned on a conditioned audience's capacity for adjustment and displacement.

Reginald Denham recalls the startling 'thunder of applause' that greeted his feed line to Henry, wishing for 'But one ten thousand of those men in England/

That do no work today.'[190] It exposed the cannily opportunistic note in Henry's 'we happy few' speech that follows. And Benson, in an impassioned appeal which he delivered 'from behind the curtain of the past merely as an actor on the crisis of the present', emphasized that while Henry had 'fondled the idea of the honour and glory of the few', Britain's present need was for men and more men. He turned the Shaftesbury into a recruiting centre, his spirited call to arms bringing in 'some three hundred' recruits.[191] The most notable occasion was a performance dedicated to the 3rd London Regiment, when, during the first interval, the Lord Mayor spoke of 'the tremendous stakes at issue'.[192] Benson, who throughout the war enmeshed patriotism and a species of Shakespearean mysticism, insisted to the British Empire Shakespeare Society:

> If Europe had properly understood Shakespeare and all he has to say about the brotherhood of man – the one touch of nature making the whole world kin – there never would have been this War. If, on the other hand, our British Empire had fully understood the prudence, generosity, and high courage of Shakespeare's political philosophy, we should have been wise enough and strong enough to have ended the War in six months.[193]

The reporter adds drily: 'Precisely how this sort of miracle could have been accomplished the lecturer did not attempt to explain.' But that the Bard was *for all time* seemed, for the enthusiasts, to entail such possibilities.

John Martin Harvey, another Shakespearean intoxicated with wartime patriotism, included both *Hamlet* and *Henry V* in the five-week tercentenary season at His Majesty's, the latter a new production while the resources of Tree's theatre allowed his *Hamlet* to be staged adequately for the first time.[194] Inspiration had come from a conversation with Reinhardt, whose methods created momentum and a feeling of space in *Hamlet*'s outdoor scenes. A wide sky was achieved with a large concave semi-circle of white plaster, upon which coloured lights, 'high above the centre of the stage', could shift through 'mauve and grey and gold with an ease that [began] to flout the scene painter's brush'.[195] The cemetery scene was the most striking, adopting Reinhardt's solution of having the opening of Ophelia's grave set four feet above stage level. Disher vividly recalled Hamlet 'in a dip of the ground looking upwards to the skyline where Ophelia's coffin was borne towards the slanting tombstones around a gnarled, wind-swept tree in the fading light'.[196]

Walkley had been resistant to the romanticism of 'a Hamlet who immensely enjoys his own death-scene, turning up his eyes ecstatically while the organ swells louder and louder as in the last act of *Faust*'. But he was more approving of Harvey's work in *Henry V*: 'His is not a robust Henry, nor is it a Henry, heavy-burdened with the weight of kingship'; but the 'charming, boyish, frank' approach kept faith with the text. Also appreciated was the Elizabethan style of continuous production which lent pace.[197] To create an apron effect a false proscenium was built, with decorative and neutral curtains to suggest various kinds of interior on the fore-stage. The curtains might part to reveal the fall of Harfleur 'to the sound of booming cannon and trumpet peals',[198] or to simulate 'the great gate of embarkation', swinging apart to disclose 'on a blazing backcloth the English Fleet', surprising the audience into patriotic applause. As Disher added, this was the transformation scene of Christmas pantomime 'put to legitimate dramatic effect'.[199]

Between *Hamlet* and *Henry V* Harvey revived his *Taming of the Shrew* and *Richard III*. *Taming*'s 'swift, continuous action [was] achieved by the manipulation of curtains and three light screens in front of a single background'. Harvey's debonair Petruchio, acting responsibly as well as cheerfully, evaded the 'difficulties which the play is apt to present to a modern audience' (*Manchester Guardian* 17 May 1916, p. 10). Walkley approved the insight that 'Katherine is in love with Petruchio from the first; ... her wit, not her fear, mak[ing] her humour his caprice'. He was also pleased that the Induction was retained, with Rutland Barrington's Sly and wife enjoying the play from the jut of an apron: 'He applauded, he interjected "Tush!" he pantomimed to the players on the stage; and at the end of an act offered Petruchio a stoup of liquor', which was drunk 'with gusto'.[200] But, like the *Guardian* critic, Walkley 'feared that Shakespeare's Richard III has seen his best days'. Murder one or two near relations 'and you will be terrible; murder half a dozen and we only 'smile .... For one thing, we hardly know the victims; they only appear to be slaughtered.'[201] It is chilling that, in the light of Verdun and with the Somme offensive in active preparation, Walkley should write thus of escalating murder. But to the dramatic problem, Harvey's solution (following Irving) was to make Richard 'a kind of ghastly Punchinello', though with 'a certain elegance of style, as of a virtuoso in villainy who enjoys every *fioritura* and grace-note of his art'. *Graphic*'s reviewer (27 May 1916, p. 710) admired Harvey's neat bit of business 'when the lights go up in the Princes' room in the Tower, and he drops two white roses behind his back and then limps off in the darkness'. Genevieve Ward, at 79, was repeating her incomparable interpretation of the half-mad Margaret, and that 'blood-curdling laugh on her final exit' which had chilled audiences during Benson's season at the Kennington in October 1914.[202] Denham, who appeared with her at the Kennington, describes her as 'frighteningly elemental', and would 'never forget her crooked accusing finger and the little jets of flame in her eyes'.[203] She made Margaret 'a vital and genuinely tragic figure', wrote Newton. 'The rhetoric seemed like her natural language.'[204]

Harvey had undertaken this tercentenary season at His Majesty's because its manager, Tree, was busy in America throughout the year. After playing *Macbeth* before the Hollywood cameras, Tree went on to win acclaim for his own 12-week tercentenary season at New York's New Amsterdam Theatre. He then toured his production of *Henry VIII* which he had given as a royal matinée at His Majesty's, playing Wolsey to Bourchier's king. That matinée turned out to be the last time the West End would see either Tree or Lewis Waller in Shakespeare, the latter dying of pneumonia barely four months later on 1 November 1915. But both had played memorably. Tree managed to combine with 'the arrogant Prince of the Church and the broken figure of the final scene, ... the butcher's son from Ipswich'.[205] Waller's Buckingham avoided the cliché 'contrast between the virility of the hot-headed noble before his trial and the detachment of the man condemned to die in his final scene at the River Gate'. Instead, he gave a character who 'to the last was a man unjustly condemned, one who found death bitter, although his noble soul could face it with fortitude'.[206]

Tree's first wartime move had been to revive Louis Parker's 1912 pageant play, *Drake*, which had acquired new resonance. Belcham suggested he take up *Henry V*, 'with its magnificent appeal to the patriotism of the nation'.[207] But, as he told an interviewer, his Shakespearean choice would be nothing so obvious – not even *King John*.[208] He was evidently anticipating what Shaw was to say at the end of the war: 'People are sick of jingoism and fed-up with Agincourt speeches.'[209] Opting for *Henry IV, Part 1* allowed him to reprise his old success as Falstaff besides catching the wartime mood, but it also lost him money.[210] Owen Seaman's grumble about present interest not being in civil war found effective answer: Shakespeare wrote in the heat of Britain's 'desperate struggle against the Welt-politik and the world-grasping ambition of Spain', which so precisely anticipated present circumstances. He spoke across the centuries, adding powerfully to current clamour as 'the youth of England [was] reproached with idleness and pleasure-seeking, with indifference to their country's needs'.[211] But there were those who considered that 'Falstaff belongs to an England that has ceased to be'; his 'cowardice' caused discomfort, while 'His mutilation of Hotspur's dead body might surely have been omitted'.[212] For Seaman, 'the picture of that fat impostor lying supine in a simulation of death within a few feet of the fallen body of the heroic *Hotspur* was repellent to one's sense of proprieties'. But such proprieties would have meant little in Flanders. Later, the critic Sir Walter Raleigh was able to imagine Falstaff quite 'at home' in the trenches, recognizing 'a brother in Old Bill'.[213] Meanwhile, some enjoyed Tree's 'fruity, bibulous voice, the comic assumption of mock-courage, the ludicrous mixture of the grand manner and tap-room manners',[214] though the low-key modernism of Owen Nares's Hal disappointed those wedded to Waller-style pyrotechnics. But they had Matheson Lang's Hotspur, who, even as he expires, 'choked with blood, gasping out his last defiance, ... makes us realise very forcibly the undaunted spirit and the innate nobility of Henry Percy'. Lang's controversial stutter, suggested by Tree on the basis of textual evidence and a recent Berlin production, fairly expressed the 'impulsive and unbridled temper in the man'.[215]

London's tercentenary celebrations had been more handsome than was generally allowed. Horniman brought her production of *The Comedy of Errors* to the Duke of York's, playing without an interval to allow 'no opportunities for reflection on its incongruities'. Also helping was the 'finished acting' and effective painted scenery, including 'an exceedingly beautiful view of Ephesus' against which 'the street brawl was wonderfully well done'.[216] And three other productions ran successfully, including *The Taming of the Shrew* (Apollo). This provided 'splendid opportunities' for Lily Brayton, while 'Oscar Asche never had a better part than Petruchio. He plays it with riotous energy, and not in the mealy-mouthed way which a generation of feminism might suggest.'[217] Retention of the Induction assisted the breadth and pace of his performance, his 'lurking jovial relish'. Brayton, on the other hand, was 'termagant of termagants – a fearsome fury, until, famished and worn out, she [fell] tearfully into Petruchio's arms, ... greedily lapping up the soup'.[218]

Benson's *A Midsummer Night's Dream* (Court) opened during Christmas 1915, retaining the old Mendelssohnian musical comedy aspects whilst showing indebtedness to the Coronet production which had seized the pantomime possibilities of the play the previous year (Dorothy Green was a superb Hermia in both).[219] Celebrated scene-painter Joseph Harker had seldom excelled his contribution to this production.[220] The 'birch trees and bluebells' recalled Otho Stuart's 1905 landmark *Dream* at the Adelphi, 'the blue and silver note' being maintained throughout. 'The final picture of white arms waving in the moonlight and little flower-like figures flitting hither and thither on tiptoe to one of the sweetest melodies ever written' registered as a welcome return to Victorianism after Barker's modernist approach at the Savoy in the spring of 1914.[221] Florence Glossop-Harris, whose Portia had been pitted against Frank Cellier's powerful Shylock at the Prince's the year before,[222] was thought 'not quite self-sacrificing enough to forfeit her serious grace and dignity' as Helena, who appeared too 'deep and intelligent' for a mere country hoyden. A. E. George's Bottom posed another class crux, being not only too dignified for a rustic but returning from Titania's bower suggestively plucking 'wisps of hay from a wallet'.[223] Yet, noted the *Times* man (21 December 1915, p. 13), his business made 'the audience laugh; and after all that is the test. It is funny "business", and it nowhere violates the spirit of the scene.'

For his *Merchant* Lang sought authenticity through the help of 'Israel Zangwill and Mr. Dashman of the Yiddish Theatre',[224] contrasting the life led by the great Venetian merchant-princes and that of the ghetto where rich and poor 'were compelled to herd together'. In his own words, it was this ghetto life which made Jews 'often cunning, pitiless, and vindictive to those outside their race because they lived as outcasts and aliens, with every man's hand against them'. This formed the basis of Lang's impersonation, Newton describing how Shylock's murderous propensities developed out of the discovery of 'his daughter's elopement with a hated Christian and her reckless spending and feasting. Then, and only then, does this Shylock' determine on the 'merry bond' to get a little of his own back. Accordingly, the production underscored Jessica's vanity. After serving her father's customers with wine, she sat 'quietly in the background, admiring herself in a little handglass, arranging her becoming veil, etc.'. This was the scene in which Shylock was first discovered: not making his way 'over the bridge to the usual open place', but at home, 'seated cross-legged, ... bargaining with Bassanio'. His humanity showed even through his inhumanities, or 'his modernised affectations, the crossed-legs; the movement of hands with palms inward to denote contempt, doubt, indifference; the smacking of tongue; the spitting behind the Christian's back; the animal grunt after the gross act of injustice by mediæval law'. At the end he remained 'unbroken in spirit' even indicating 'by a playful handling of the knife that lay on the floor, that far from being submissive, he went hence longing for "the day" of reckoning'. Here is a man sustained by hate, who, as 'he leaves the Doge's Court, hisses at the Gentile crowd'.[225] Earlier, 'Miss Britten dashes into the Court in doublet and riding boots – quite a fine young fellow – and just throws her cloak around her when delivering her famous "judgment". This certainly looks more natural than stalking in in legal gown point-device – as all previous Portias have done.'[226] When Britten was indisposed she was replaced by an equally innovative Lilian Braithwaite. Now, 'instead of remaining standing in advocate fashion until the dismissal of the Jew', Braithwaite approaches the duke, 'painfully baffled' at the inefficacy of her mercy speech. Her back towards her husband and Antonio, she is moved to tears by the latter's poignant farewell. 'Suddenly you note that an idea has struck her. Getting back to the advocate's desk, she swiftly turns over a volume of the Law and then pours forth the solemn warning against any alien conspiring against the life of a Venetian citizen', heaving a sigh of relief when she finds that Shylock is utterly crushed.[227]

After the tercentenary year Shakespearean production tailed off. But a few post–1916 events are worthy of record. A new co-operative company, the Players of the Gate, began a season at the Kennington with *Romeo and Juliet*, the opening night being rather a comedy of errors. There was some good acting, despite the last-act scramble to meet the new 10.30 p.m. curfew. But the production was a compelling argument for Elizabethan simplicity, the delays having been caused by a plodding commitment to old-fashioned scene-changes and some attendant mishaps: the Capulets at home against a back-cloth representing the Mansion House, and a startling 'air-raid effect, the side wall suddenly falling over the orchestra'.[228]

This was in 1918, by which time 'Criticus' noted that managers were promoting the view 'that Shakespeare is out of touch with modern times', hence financially 'a back-number'.[229] But 1917–18 did see two important productions, H. B. Irving's *Hamlet* and James Fagan's *Twelfth Night*, given at the Court in the last days of the war. *Hamlet*, which ran for a mere 23 performances at the Savoy, was a carefully thought-out production emphasizing 'the dramatic, as apart from the literary, interest of the play'. Osric went, and so did Hamlet's advice to the players and that of Polonius to his son. On the other hand, intent on clarifying what happens to Hamlet between the murder of Polonius and his reappearance in the graveyard, Irving retained

> the talk about going to England at the close of the scene in the Queen's closet, ... the scene in which Horatio receives Hamlet's letter about his adventure, and ... brought in from the First Quarto a little scene in which Horatio tells the Queen of Hamlet's escape [showing] the Queen's unfailing sympathy with her son.

He also followed the First Quarto's arrangement of scenes in Act II, 'To be or not to be' and the Nunnery scene coming before the Fishmonger scene and the entrance of the players. Walkley challenged Irving's distinction between dramatic and literary, and reversed his criticism of Harvey's altogether different conception by complaining that Irving provided too little of the '*sweet* prince' as opposed to the 'sardonic, ironic, hortatory, contemptuous Hamlet'.[230]

Fagan's *Twelfth Night* fared better with both critics and public, winning approval because it was neither a 'starring' production nor 'rag-time Shakespeare'. Only a few details, such as 'Antonio's crossing himself before the image of the Virgin' and 'the girls dressed up as male attendants' which undercut Viola's adoption of the breeches, drew censure. If it was not 'the best all-round rendering ... within most folks' recollection', that was because Fagan chose to obscure 'the cynicism of the original story'. In this he was aided by Arthur Whitby as Sir Toby, a part he had played in Barker's long-running production at the Savoy in 1912, and which he had mellowed into 'one of the most richly comic conceptions of our stage .... The cruelty and coarseness of the man, his sottishness and knavery are skilfully softened, whilst his courage and adroitness, his family pride, his boyish love of practical jokes, his joviality' are emphasized.[231] This approach to Sir Toby evidently enjoyed current favour. It had been adopted in Andrew Leigh's 1914 production at the Vic, Basil Dyne's Toby being 'no mere conventional low comedian, but high-toned, of agreeable military mien, yet jovial withal, a true knight of the kitchen, a toper of fantasy!'[232]

In between his Stratford activities and succouring troops in France, Benson made a number of London appearances. He was honoured there in the tercentenary year, while playing Julius Caesar in Drury Lane's Shakespeare Day matinée. It was a comment on the theatricality of such events that he had been 'knighted in a theatre, in theatrical costume and with a theatrical sword'.[233] Benson was one of a number of celebrated Shakespeareans, including Lang and Ellen Terry, to bring Shakespeare to the wartime halls. Terry's Portia at the Coliseum was important since she ventured an interpretation which had been impossible when Irving's saintly Shylock needed a lively foil. Now 'the dignity and restraint with which her rendering is imbued point the path to all the Portias of the future'.[234] Benson was less successful at the Palladium with his patriotic anthology, which Newton ascribes to the monotony of his 'preachy' method.[235] Constance Benson recalls a ventriloquist complaining how Benson 'drops it all, and I've got to pick it up again, and all in ten minutes'.[236] What was needed was the explosive style and blazing passion of a Lewis Waller which were on display at the Empire in the first month of war.[237] His 'rushes downstage' in *Henry V*[238] would have recalled to music-hall habitués the irruptions of George Robey. An obituary notice for Waller mentions his way with the Agincourt speech: 'he showed no great modulation of voice, but carried his public with a rush of declamation and emotion.'[239] For Grein, 'His art was rhetorical in the finest sense of the word, ... In his delivery glowed such fervour that the harangue of Henry V roused unspeakable enthusiasm fraught with pride and patriotism.'[240] But Benson, although his ascetic features were sometimes aglow with passion, seems to have lost the unequalled 'fire and beauty' which he brought to the part of Henry in his youthful days.[241] And although fire and exuberance would before long become passé, for the moment it was heroics and not a sermon for which audiences clamoured.

Notes

1. *Bookman* 3.18, 193.
2. Thomas Beecham, *A Mingled Chime* (Hutchinson, 1944), p. 177.
3. Findon, *Play Pictorial* 32(91), 17.
4. H. W. Massingham, *Nation* 19.10.18, 74.
5. H. G. Hibbert, *A Playgoer's Memories* (Richards, 1920), p. 220.
6. *Graphic* 16.6.17, 736.
7. *Evening News* 4.4.17, 3; *'Era' Annual 1918*, p. 37.
8. *Era* 25.4.17, 15; *Era* 21.3.17, 1.

9. *New Statesman* 11.4.14, 20; *Era* 2.1.18, 21.
10. *Graphic* 24.3.17, 358.
11. St John Ervine, *The Theatre in My Time* (Rich & Cowan, 1933), p. 114.
12. *The Times* 30.4.17, 11.
13. *Era* 4.4.17, 8; *Era* 7.3.17, 8.
14. *Era* 21.3.17, 1; *The Times* 17.12.19, 12.
15. £2561 for nine performances at Liverpool; and two packed houses at Cardiff's largest hall, with hundreds turned away (*Era* 4.7.17, 8, 10).
16. *Era* 6.6.17, 8. But watch committees at a few places maintained the ban, neither Ibsen's play nor Brieux's being permitted at Bristol (*Era* 12.9.17, 8; *Era* 3.4.18, 8).
17. *Referee* 18.3.17, 3.
18. *Era* 6.3.18, 12; *Era* 13.6.17, 1; *Three Plays by Brieux* (Fifield, 1917), p. 175.
19. *Referee* 5.3.16, 3. Well before this production, the stabbing was criticized by Grein as 'violence without being tragic' (*Sunday Times* 31.1.15, 4).
20. *Era* 15.5.18, 8.
21. *Era* 12.12.17, 8; *Era* 20.2.18, 8.
22. *Era* 20.2.18, 8.
23. 'J. M. Barrie as Dramatist', *Bookman* 55 (December 1918), 103–6 (103).
24. It was for servicemen only, under the direction of Henry Baynton, late Bensonian, who played Laertes in Irving's 1917 *Hamlet* (*Era* 7.8.18, 8).
25. *Sunday Times* 14.4.18, 4. Beaverbrook sacked Grein from his post as drama critic on this paper because of his involvement with the production.
26. Winifred Loraine, *Robert Loraine* (Collins, 1938), p. 247; *New Age* 30.7.14, 291.
27. It was also seen at the Kennington, where Lionel Rignold began a tour of a twice-nightly version shorn of induction and epilogue (*Era* 8.3.16, 10).
28. *Era* 18.11.14, 6; *Era* 25.11.14, 13. In Ireland responsibility lay not with the Lord Chamberlain but with the Lord-Lieutenant, though this power had not been exercised in living memory when in 1909 an attempt was made to ban Shaw's *The Shewing-up of Blanco Posnet* at the Abbey Theatre.
29. *Era* 17.11.15, 15.
30. The Stage Society, which began its career in 1899 with a Shaw play, produced it in December 1920 (Lyric, Hammersmith).
31. Loraine, *Robert Loraine*, pp. 216, 237n. About the same time an Artists' Rifles group mounted a production of *Man and Superman* in a French town hall (*Referee* 1.4.17, 3).
32. *The Times* 17.12.17, 11.
33. *Referee* 16.12.17, 2; *Referee* 17.2.18, 2.

34. *Daily Chronicle* 8.3.17, 2. Cf. William Hill's 'Benn's Guide to Glory and to Shame', *Contemporary Review* X (1916), 755–63, which had a full-page redaction in *Public Opinion* 22.12.16, 581, headed 'The Terrible "Homes of Our Heroes" – What Are We Going to Do about Them?' But doubtless Newton preferred *The Times*'s glib reassurance (10.11.14, 9) that far more 'working-class homes are quite well-to-do ... than people suppose whose knowledge is derived from Labour–Socialist literature'.
35. *Era* 23.1.18, 1.
36. Frank Harris, *Bernard Shaw* (Gollancz, 1931), pp. 301–2, 309.
37. *Ibid.*, p. 306.
38. McCarthy, *Myself and My Friends* (Thornton Butterworth, 1933), pp. 202–4. Evidently it had also been shown to Mrs Patrick Campbell, who was likewise eager to star in it.
39. Quotations follow *The Plays* (Duckworth, 1929).
40. There was also Galsworthy's neat one-acter, *The Little Man*, not done in London till after the war but given at the Birmingham Rep, 15.3.15. Street, in his censor's report, aptly describes it as 'full of his very deep and genuine sympathy with the poor and with the self-sacrificing, and his ironical scorn of almost everybody else' (LC 1915: 5/3230).
41. *Era* 4.7.17, 1.
42. In reality it is 'the ball of a cistern, of such a frank domestic nature as to set some simple cheeks ablush from a sense of exaggerated delicacy' (*Athenæum* 8.17, 395).
43. *Sunday Times* 18.11.84, 19.
44. *Sphere* 11.9.15, 284.
45. *Referee* 5.3.16, 3.
46. *World* 7.9.15, 236.
47. *Era* 22.12.15, 17.
48. Fred Kerr, *Recollections of a Defective Memory* (Thornton Butterworth, 1930), p. 152.
49. Hope, *New Age* 18.11.15, 60.
50. *Referee* 20.6.15, 9.
51. Grein, *Era* 14.2.17, 13.
52. *Era* 12.12.17, 8.
53. Quotations follow A. E. Wilson's edition of *The Plays of J. M. Barrie* (Hodder and Stoughton, 1942).
54. *Era* 3.7.18, 13; *The Times* 29.6.18, 7.
55. *Referee* 28.3.15, 2; C. B., *Cartoon* 8.4.15, 284.
56. *Graphic* 27.3.15, 412.
57. *The Times* 23.3.15, 7.

58. Rachael Low, *The History of the British Film 1914–1918* (Allen & Unwin, 1948), p. 86.
59. *Illustrated London News* 27.3.15, 386.
60. *New Statesman* 2.1.15, 319–20.
61. *Referee* 27.12.14, 2.
62. *Sphere* 2.1.15, 26.
63. J. M. Barrie, *Der Tag* (Hodder and Stoughton, 1915), p. 8.
64. *The Times* 9.4.17, 9.
65. *Graphic* 14.4.17, 444.
66. *Era* 12.12.17, 13.
67. Lena Ashwell, *Modern Troubadours* (Gyldendal, 1922), p.186.
68. Desmond MacCarthy, *Drama* (Putnam, 1940), p. 319.
69. *The Times* 26.12.14, 9.
70. *Bystander* 29.3.16, 582.
71. *Graphic* 15.4.16, 522.
72. *Era* 21.10.14, 8; *The Times* 16.10.14, 11.
73. *Era* 10.1.17, 1; *Referee* 14.1.17, 3.
74. Hamilton Fyfe's words, in *Arthur Wing Pinero: Playwright* (Greening, 1902), p. 51.
75. *Era* 9.9.14, 8; *The Times* 7.9.14, 10.
76. A. B., *Era* 3.10.17, 1; Newton, *Referee* 30.8.17, 3.
77. *The Times* 5.9.17, 9.
78. *Era* 6.9.16, 12.
79. Carroll, *Sunday Times* 28.7.18, 4; *Illustrated London News* 27.7.18, 112; Massingham, *Nation* 10.8.18, 495–6. Stoll declared publicly that over the past decade he had been repeatedly invited to buy a knighthood (£10,000 to £15,000), and a more formal indictment of the honours system came from Lord Loreburn (*Daily Sketch* 14.1.18, 7; *Graphic* 10.11.17, 572).
80. *The Times* 2.11.14, 10.
81. *Referee* 30.5.15, 2; *Referee* 4.7.15, 3; *Referee* 13.6.15, 4.
82. January 1915 (p. p), pp. 74–7.
83. Max Beerbohm (ed.), *Herbert Beerbohm Tree* (Hutchinson, 1920), pp. 48–50. Arthur Roberts, *Fifty Years of Spoof* (Lane, 1927), p. 228, considers 'Roman Catholic opinion in matters of the theatre ... a very potent factor'; and reports by the Lord Chamberlain's staff around this period betray considerable nervousness: in *Her Mother's Crucifix* a nun nursing a wounded RFC pilot kisses him; and in O'Riordan's *His Majesty's Pleasure* it is enough merely to suspect that 'the Angelus has sounded' (LC 1915: 34/3927; LC 1915: 28/3808).
84. *Era* 7.7.15, 8.

85. *Sunday Times* 13.6.15, 4.
86. *World* 15.6.15, 855.
87. Edward Knoblauch, *Round the Room* (Chapman & Hall, 1939), p. 204.
88. Thomas was more noted as actor than playwright, but his one-act farce, *Stopping the Breach*, was thought particularly 'delightful and amusing' (*Era* 10.4.18, 1).
89. *Era* 9.1.18, 1.
90. Quoted in *Era* 12.6.18, 9, amongst other rave notices.
91. *Sunday Times* 18.8.18, 4.
92. The sequel, *The Man Who Went Abroad* (1917), managed only 28 West End performances, whereas the original ran for 586.
93. Lechmere Worrall and J. E. H. Terry, *The Man Who Stayed at Home* (French, 1916), p. 26.
94. Harold Terry, *General Post* (Methuen, 1919), p. 75.
95. *The Church and the War* (Oxford University Press, 1915), p. 15.
96. *Final Report of the Committee on Commercial and Industrial Policy after the War* (HMSO, 1918), p. 60. Germany had seen extensive debate on whether wartime collectivism was effectively fulfilling Marx's catastrophe theory. But Balfour's move was already anticipated by Robert Liefmann, *Politische Flugschriften, Bringt uns der Krieg dem Sozialismus näher?* (Stuttgart/Berlin: Deutsche Verlags-Anstalt, 1915), pp. 14–15.
97. Findon, *Play Pictorial* 30(181), 50.
98. When Wareing's production reached the Kennington, it was noted that until well after 1883 the 'text was sacrosanct' (Newton, *Referee* 20.5.17, 3).
99. *The Times* 3.2.15, 11; Newton, *Referee* 7.2.15, 3.
100. *Era* 23.12.14, 8.
101. *Athenæum* 6.16, 304.
102. *Era* 18.4.17, 8. However, things went more comfortably for Newton (*Referee* 22.4.17, 3) 'after the first coarse word had come like a thud, and nobody had fainted and nobody had laughed'.
103. *Era* 18.4.17, 1.
104. Grein, *Sunday Times* 31.1.15, 4; *Referee* 31.1.15, 3; *Athenæum* 30.1.15, 102.
105. *Referee* 9.4.16, 3. Shirley's *The Sisters* was resurrected at the Birkbeck Theatre by trainee teachers of Graystoke Place College (*Era* 10.7.18, 8).
106. *Era* 2.12.14, 8; Keith Wilson, *Thomas Hardy on Stage* (Macmillan, 1995), p. 98.
107. *New Age* 29.7.15, 308. Webster (p. 241) recalled Dion Boucicault as a martinet, whereas Barker 'allowed a latitude of interpretation to the actor'.
108. *New Age* 10.12.14, 148.
109. *World* 1.12.14, 165.

110. In the words of Thomas Hardy (Wilson, *Thomas Hardy*, p. 90).
111. *Stage* 27.5.15, 18.
112. *Sunday Times* 6.6.15, 4. Cf. *Athenæum* 12.6.15, 535, on Stephens's apparent 'fear lest he should estrange public opinion by admitting the possibility of anything good in our enemies'.
113. *The Times* 2.6.15, 9.
114. Stephen Phillips, *Armageddon* (Lane, 1915), p. 47. Cynthia Asquith had 'swallowed the rather high-faluting platitude that [fallen soldiers] were not to be pitied, but were safe, unassailable, young, and glamorous for ever' (*Diaries 1915–18* (Century, 1968), p. 91), until faced with the death of her brother.
115. *Referee* 6.6.15, 3.
116. *Athenæum* 12.6.15, 535.
117. *Referee* 20.6.15, 5, 11.
118. *Pall Mall Gazette* 16.9.14, 3, noting the military drawback that 'it cannot be fired from an ordinary field gun' but needs one of difficult construction.
119. Huntly Carter, *The New Spirit in the European Theatre 1914–1924* (Benn, 1925), frontispiece.
120. John Martin Harvey, *The Autobiography* (Sampson Low, Marston, 1933), p. 455.
121. *Era* 9.6.15, 11; *Drawing* 1.4 (8.15), 76; *The Times* 2.6.15, 9.
122. At Hull Harvey received word from the Voluntary Aid Committee's secretary that 'every "unstarred" man in the United Kingdom should be made to go and see it' (*Era* 3.11.15, 10).
123. *The Times* 6.11.14, 11.
124. John Masefield, *The Faithful* (Heinemann, 1915), p. 61.
125. *Era* 8.12.15, 9.
126. *Era* 24.5.16, 21.
127. *Referee* 19.11.16, 3. He recalled the prohibition of Tate's version in 1681, but also recognized that it was currently being studied 'for the Local Examinations'.
128. That Morton's play, 'a good deal against Russia', was tactfully set aside in 1915 when it 'might have contributed its mite towards the overthrow' of a hateful system 'calls into question the advisability of tact when it conflicts with the demands of humanity' (*Passing Show* 10.4.15, 18; Farjeon, *Era* 19.9.17, 1).
129. Sybil and Russell Thorndike, *Lilian Baylis* (Chapman & Hale, 1938), p. 57.
130. *Ibid.*, p. 80.
131. *Daily Chronicle* 8.3.17, 2.
132. J. E. A., *Manchester Guardian* 10.12.15, 10.
133. *Era* 14.3.17, 8.

134. *Era* 25.4.17, 13. Cf. *Referee* 7.3.15, 3, on Constance Collier's letter to the Society of Arts about Shakespeare's appeal being stifled by 'scholastic reverence'.
135. *Era* 2.2.16, 7.
136. *Era* 7.2.17, 14; Anderson, *A Few More Memories* (Hutchinson, 1936), p. 153.
137. *Referee* 4.2.17, 3.
138. Cf. *Era* 14.8.18, 10, where Shakespeare's unpopularity is ascribed to his use as schoolbook; without that disadvantage, and boosted in the manner of a revue, a Shakespeare play would run for months.
139. Douglas Reid, 'Popular Theatre in Victorian Birmingham', in David Bradby, Louis James and Bernard Sharratt (eds), *Performance and Politics in Popular Drama*, (Cambridge University Press, 1980), p. 82.
140. *Shakespeare Tercentenary Observance in the Schools* (Tercentenary Committee, 1916), p. 21.
141. Thorndike, *Lilian Baylis*, p. 61.
142. Greet claimed that during his four years at the Vic, 'over 500 performances have been given to an average of well over 1,000 pupils on each occasion' (Winifred F. E. C. Isaac, *Ben Greet and the Old Vic* (p. p. [1964]), p. 166).
143. *Era* 8.11.16, 13.
144. *Era* 3.1.17, 17.
145. A 1914 *Twelfth Night* production in Leipzig included a new prologue claiming that Shakespeare came as refugee to a welcoming Germany (*The Times* 10.11.14, 9). German attempts to adopt Shakespeare were spoofed by Mary Packington, *Shakespeare for Merrie England* (LC 1915: 8/3303), where a German professor seeks to label a garden-bust of Shakespeare 'the Divine Teuton Wilhelm the Third' but ends up with the ass's head of Bottom. Philip Page (*Daily Sketch* 30.9.14, 5) discovered that Reinhardt, despite the outbreak of war, was encouraged to continue his Shakespeare productions, so that he would 'soon become a German classic. He will, I infer, become German by having conquered the German stage. In the same way we may say that General French will shortly become a Prussian soldier.' P. W. Wilson, *The Unmaking of Europe* (Nisbet, 1915), p. 236, retails 'a delightful story that Berlin was permitted to witness *King Henry V* because Shakespeare was a German who had the prevision to write: "And then to Calais; and to England then." ' But H. B. Irving spoke more in sorrow than sarcasm in noting that Berlin could boast three mainstream Shakespeare productions against the West End's none (*Era* 14.3.17, 8).
146. 26.6.18, 13. When Lena Ashwell, 'The Theatre and Ruhleben', *Fortnightly*

Review, vol. 104 (February 1918), pp. 574–9 (p. 575), protested that 'the Ministry of Information has definitely decided not to make use of drama or music in propaganda', Newton (*Referee* 6.10.18, 2) gently pointed out that there was good reason why the authorities, intent on the most effective (undisclosed) propaganda, should not have taken Ashwell into their confidence.

147. Richard Révy, 'Züricher Shakespeare-Aufführungen im Jahre 1916', *Shakespeare Jahrbuch* LIII (1917), 139–58 (158).
148. Isaac, *Ben Greet*, p. 138.
149. *Era* 9.10.18, 8.
150. George Rowell, *The Old Vic Theatre* (Cambridge University Press, 1993), p. 96.
151. *Era* 7.10.14, 12; Newton, *Referee* 11.10.14, 3.
152. Edward J. Dent, *A Theatre for Everybody* (Boardman, 1945), p. 53.
153. *The Times* 30.3.74, 9, extract from Robert Atkins's MS autobiography. John Casson, *Lewis and Sybil* (Collins, 1972), p. 40, mentions Sybil Thorndike earning ten shillings a performance.
154. Isaac, *Ben Greet*, p. 53.
155. *Athenæum* 13.11.15, 354; *Stage* 25.2.15, 23.
156. *Era* 14.6.16, 13.
157. Isaac, *Ben Greet*, p. 132.
158. Thorndike, *Lilian Baylis*, p. 69. Newton (*Referee* 22.4.17, 3) notes that Greet followed the second quarto, omitting 135 lines.
159. *Athenæum* 3.16, 152. Stack, idol of Old Vic audiences, seems to have been 'too mannered' for West End taste, being 'steeped in the Shakespeare tradition' (Henry Kendall, *I Remember Romano's* (Macdonald, 1960), p. 40).
160. *Era* 20.3.18, 8. Its Theatres and Music Halls Committee stated: 'the Council has no statutory powers such as the Lord Chamberlain has, but it can and does make representations to licensees when it is considered that there is anything objectionable in performances, and suggestions made have invariably been complied with' (*Era* 7.3.17, 8). The Vic's first *Cymbeline* was on 4.3.18, 'the bedroom scene (almost a film-thrill in itself)' evidently escaping the gelders (*Era* 6.3.18, 1; Newton, *Referee* 10.3.18, 2).
161. *The Times* 19.1.15, 10.
162. *Daily Telegraph* 10.11.14, 4.
163. Isaac, *Ben Greet*, p. 131; *Sunday Times* 10.10.15, 4.
164. *Athenæum* 3.16, 152. Wilson was clearly good; Grein said that she had 'the feeling and the malice required for the part' of Rosalind in *As You Like It* (*Sunday Times* 10.10.15, 4).

165. *Era* 1.11.16, 21; Richard Findlater, *Lilian Baylis* (Lane, 1975), p. 138.
166. *Era* 8.11.16, 1.
167. *Athenæum* 27.11.15, 394; Grein, *Sunday Times* 28.11.15, 4.
168. *Referee* 21.11.15, 3.
169. *Sunday Times* 7.3.15, 4.
170. *Era* 21.2.17, 22. Anderson made her return to the London stage in the sleep-walking scene at the Vic's Shakespeare tercentenary matinée, her first-ever Lady Macbeth in Britain (Newton, *Referee* 30.4.16, 3).
171. Thorndike, *Lilian Baylis*, pp. 34–5. Sybil's Lady Macbeth was a severer version of Amy Coleridge's at the Coronet, less a 'dread schemer' than 'a misguided woman working for her husband's welfare, regardless of honour, morality, or humanity' (*Era* 10.2.15, 13).
172. *Athenæum* 3.16, 152; *Era* 24.4.18, 8.
173. *Athenæum* 6.11.15, 338.
174. *Era* 2.10.18, 11.
175. *Illustrated London News* 12.10.18, 444.
176. *Sunday Times* 6.10.18, 4.
177. *Era* 14.7.15, 8.
178. Isaac, *Ben Greet*, pp. 70–1; Newton, *Referee* 23.1.16, 3.
179. *Era* 4.10.16, 8.
180. Isaac, *Ben Greet*, p. 128.
181. *Era* 3.10.17, 8; Thorndike, *Lilian Baylis*, p. 78.
182. Thorndike, *Lilian Baylis*, p. 125.
183. *Era* 12.4.16, 9; *Sunday Times* 31.10.15, 4.
184. *Era* 5.5.15, 13; *Era* 18.11.14, 9.
185. *To-day* 24.6.16, 250; *To-day* 15.7.16, 349. Cf. C. K. S., *Sphere* 21.11.14, ii, who writes that Tree would surely have preferred to produce *Henry V*, rather than 'the little-known *Henry IV*, . . . were it not that a play upon the conquest of France would scarcely be acceptable just now'. L. H. Jacobsen, *Stage* 13.8.14, 22, discussing the availability of war plays for revival, points out that in many cases the enemy is inconvenient, and 'even *Henry V*' would need toning down.
186. *The Times* 28.12.14, 3.
187. Given at the Queen's, Slade herself playing Henry 'with fire and spirit' (*Stage* 6.7.16, 18).
188. *Era* 30.12.14, 21.
189. *The Times* 28.12.14, 3; *World* 5.1.15, 270.
190. Reginald Denham, *Stars in My Hair* (Laurie, 1958), p. 66.
191. *Daily Graphic* 12.1.15, 7; *Sunday Times* 17.1.15, 4; Constance Benson, *Mainly Players: Bensonian Memories* (Thornton Butterworth, 1926), p. 281. Benson told an *Era* representative (6.1.15, 8) of a woman who,

confessing 'that for some time she had prevailed upon her son to refrain from joining the Colours, added that since she and her son had seen "Henry the Fifth" the young fellow *would* join, and that she was now proud of the fact'. Benson had already secured 40 volunteers with the play at Stratford (*Referee* 3.1.15, 2).

192. *Daily Graphic* 12.1.15, 7.
193. *Stage* 3.2.16, 20.
194. Profits, like those earned simultaneously by Tree in New York, were devoted to the British Red Cross. The gesture was typical; a month after the war started the prime minister 'cordially accepted [Harvey's] offer to deliver every Sunday evening a public lecture on the war and the country's needs in the theatre of each town' where he was playing (*Era* 9.9.14, 9), and, uniformed as honorary lieutenant in the Legion of Frontiersmen, he kept it up for the duration. The Somme offensive inspired him to urge an enormous audience at New Brighton's Winter Gardens to 'thank God that they had lived to see this war', only for his wife to say in her following speech: 'War was one endless machine for killing.' For a classical actor Harvey had a remarkably tin ear, describing the troops 'rising like locusts in defence of the Motherland', proleptic irony when many of the survivors would return to what, in the biblical phrase, are often termed the locust years of economic depression (*Era* 30.8.16, 11).
195. Harvey, *Autobiography*, p. 462; Newton, *Referee* 14.5.16, 3.
196. M. Willson Disher, *The Last Romantic* (Hutchinson, 1948), p. 226.
197. *The Times* 30.5.16, 9.
198. Arthur Machen (Harvey, *Autobiography*, p. 469).
199. M. Willson Disher, *Clowns and Pantomimes* (Constable, 1925), p. 230.
200. *The Times* 9.5.16, 9; *The Times* 16.5.16, 11; *Era* 17.5.16, 9.
201. *The Times* 23.5.16, 11.
202. Benson, *Mainly Players*, p. 241.
203. Denham, *Stars*, p. 66.
204. *Referee* 28.5.16, 3.
205. Margaret Webster, *The Same Only Different* (Gollancz, 1969), p. 262.
206. *Era* 7.7.15, 13. Waller was just finishing a three-year world tour when war broke out, his re-entry into the London theatre being in *Monsieur Beaucaire* at the Kennington (23.11.14) when he acknowledged repeated calls with his famous rendering of the Agincourt speech. He was very active in recruitment, asking in Hyde Park why, after 11 months of war, 'British soldiers were ... not fighting on German soil', and answering that it was because 'hundreds of thousands of Englishmen had not yet realised' their country's peril. There, too, he wound up with Henry V's stirring speech (*Era* 16.6.15, 7).

207. *Era* 5.8.14, 11.
208. *Referee* 23.8.14, 3.
209. Loraine, *Robert Loraine*, p. 268.
210. *Referee* 20.12.14, 2.
211. *Punch* 25.11.14, 434; *Daily Telegraph* 16.11.14, 3.
212. *Graphic* 21.11.14, 726; Fenton, *World* 10.11.14, 121; *Athenæum* 21.11.14, 540.
213. British Academy lecture (4.7.18), in *England and the War* (Freeport, New York: Books for Libraries, 1967), p. 123.
214. *Referee* 15.11.14, 3.
215. *Era* 18.11.14, 13; *Era* 16.12.14, 13; Matheson Lang, *Mr. Wu Looks Back* (Paul, 1940), p. 121.
216. *Athenæum* 1.16, 47; *Referee* 26.12.15, 3.
217. *Graphic* 5.2.16, 208.
218. *Stage* 3.2.16, 23.
219. *The Times* 31.12.14, 5.
220. *Sphere* 25.12.15, 348.
221. *Referee* 26.12.15, 3.
222. Newton, *Referee* 22.11.14, 3.
223. *Referee* 26.12.15, 3. Benson (*Mainly Players*, p. 283) decided that George's fresh approach to Bottom, played 'as an attractive boy, ... detracted from the rough comedy of the scenes, and was out of harmony with the other clowns'; but H. A. S., *World* 28.12.15, 657, found his performance 'a revelation of real rustic humour that never degenerated into burlesque'.
224. *Era* 29.9.15, 13 (the sequence of events is misremembered in Lang's autobiography).
225. *Referee* 28.11.15, 2; *Referee* 12.12.15, 3; *Era* 8.12.15, 15; Grein, *Sunday Times* 12.12.16, 4; *The Times* 7.12.15, 11.
226. Newton, *Referee* 31.10.15, 3.
227. Newton, *Referee* 16.1.16, 3.
228. Newton, *Referee* 9.6.18, 3. Edward Compton had taken over the proprietorship and management of the theatre on 4.2.18, the first season of the Compton Comedy Company including Shakespeare, Goldsmith, Holcroft and 'a picturesque and well-balanced performance' of Sheridan's *School for Scandal* (*Era* 9.10.18, 8).
229. *Era* 19.6.18, 10.
230. *The Times* 24.4.17, 9; *The Times* 27.4.17, 9.
231. Newton, *Referee* 3.11.18, 2; *Era* 6.11.18, 9; *Illustrated London News* 23.11.18, 686; *Sunday Times* 3.11.18, 4.
232. Newton, *Referee* 20.12.14, 3.
233. *The Times* 3.5.16, 11.

234. *Era* 20.2.18, 14.
235. *Referee* 4.2.17, 3. *Era* 31.1.17, 16, is more diplomatic: 'To a section of the audience on Monday evening the Shakespearean seemed too lofty a standard'; and *Star* 30.1.17, 4, reports him 'well received'.
236. Benson, *Mainly Players*, p. 301.
237. *Graphic* 29.8.14, 340.
238. J. C. Trewin, *Illustrated London News* 12.6.65, 30.
239. *Athenæum* 6.11.15, 338.
240. *Sunday Times* 7.11.15, 4.
241. Ivor Brown's *Observer* obituary (7.1.40). Even so, it was regretted that Benson's subsequent proposal to 'play in a series of short Shakespearean scenes on the variety stage to assist the war aims propaganda should have fallen through; but the ways of Whitehall are past understanding' (*Era* 12.6.18, 8).

7

Fashionable audiences and the opera

Early in Victoria's reign the Royal Italian Opera established itself as the centre of theatrical fashion. Although 'Italian' had disappeared from the title by 1892, its social standing remained until the outbreak of war, when opera was discontinued at Covent Garden, only a handful of performances of any kind taking place there. 'Lancelot' (*Referee* 26 September 1915, p. 5), makes no bones about the reason for this wartime closure. The Opera Syndicate, under Harry Higgins's chairmanship, had preferred a cult following to a popular one, using non-English performers and performances, and the attendant economics, to restrict support to 'a comparatively small number of Londoners'. Clearly wartime conditions rendered this policy inoperable, though a matinée held at the theatre early on provides both an instance of the new fad taken up by its fashionable audience and a hint of the fresh direction to be taken by London opera during the hostilities.

The matinée had Beecham conducting, and the bill included dancers still in Britain following the season of Russian ballet in which he had been involved. But the centrepiece of the show was an operatic version, arranged by T. C. Fairbairn, of Bach's cantata, *Phoebus and Pan*. Phoebus and Timolus were sung respectively by two tenors, Maurice D'Oisly and Frank Mullings, who were to become stalwarts of Beecham's company.[1] A third tenor of note, John Coates, was an amusing Midas; but this was his only London stage appearance during the war and henceforth he would confine himself to the concert platform and to his duties as captain in the Yorkshire Regiment. The piece was only introduced by accident, Beecham's original choice being Rimsky-Korsakoff's *Mozart and Salieri*, an opera again denied to wartime London through the abrupt termination of Rosing's season. But Bach continued to be a Beecham favourite, Searle finding a 1918 performance 'funnier than most revues'.[2]

Fortunately for those who went to the theatre to be seen, charity matinées stayed popular throughout the war, supplying the particular needs of this audience very well. Although at the outset Marie Lloyd had proposed holding matinées (to aid the London Territorials),[3] they were claimed by the fashionable element both in London and the provinces. Besides 'flag days and programme-selling', London stall habitués chattered of the Duchess of Rutland's 'pretty hat', already seen at Drury Lane, or 'Lady Alexander's new creation, ... as sweet as the one she wore at the Aldwych'.[4] They went to be ogled, demonstrating their largesse by paying over the odds: a Russian charity matinée at the Alhambra, attended by royalty, prompted the Grand Duke Michael to buy up the first row of stalls at five guineas a seat.[5] There was anxiety, therefore, in the first month of war, when it was leaked that the King and Queen had contemplated giving up theatre-going for the duration. But a *London Opinion* columnist was confident that their 'extraordinary good sense' would prevail, thereby authorizing society attendance (5 September 1914, p. 380). And the following February a two-horse carriage brought the King and Queen to Covent Garden for a matinée performance of *The School for Scandal.*

The royal box was expressly designed as a counter-attraction to the stage, so it is odd that Maisie Gay should complain about 'the rude habit of training opera glasses on Royalty'.[6] Theatre columnists thought it important to report that the royals had a sense of humour (the queen 'laughed heartily' at a special *Bing Boys* matinée) and a tolerable attention-span: what was described as 'The first Command Performance of a picture-play, ... which lasted for nearly two hours, was followed with the closest attention.'[7] These wartime galas undoubtedly benefited from the alternative spectacle of a royal presence, aid and comfort for the troops being not in itself sufficient inducement: 'The promised visit of the Queen to a Coliseum matinée ... had a splendid effect on the booking', and she was duly accorded a 'hearty ovation from a brilliant audience'.[8] By early 1917 that royal bait had become especially important, fears being expressed for 'the charity goose that lays the golden eggs'.[9] Indeed, the previous year had witnessed hostility within the profession, the great number of matinées held since war began having 'proved how bad they are for the business', deflecting money from theatre proprietors.[10]

Nor was society content merely to parade in front. Its leaders would act 'as chorus girls and chorus men' or even more prominently. The high point of an Ambassadors' matinée in May 1917 was the appearance of the Countess of Cromartie as Katherine in the courtship scene from *Henry V*, the Old Vic's Gwen Lally playing the King.[11] At the St James's, Louis Parker expressly designed a scene in Piccadilly tube station during an air raid to bring the maximum number of stars and 'gorgeously attired society ladies on the stage at the same time'.[12]

That high society had a new plaything was an important factor in the disastrous Russo-French opera season at the London Opera House in 1915. Running from 29 May to 7 June, it constituted 'a record for brevity in the operatic history of London'.[13] *Era*'s 'Post-Mortem' contrasted this with 'Robert Courtneidge's season at the Shaftesbury, the longest on record'. The reasons for this double record are fundamental to the changed conditions of operatic theatre during the war. The Russo-French season was planned to include five operas new to London leavened with several familiar works. Producer-director Vladimir Rosing (1890–1963), who had studied under Jean de Reszke and debuted in *Eugene Onegin* at St Petersburg in 1912, was known to matinée audiences, appearing in one organized by Jean Nouguès (composer of the opera, *Quo Vadis?*) as 'a fatally-wounded soldier' whose fiancée was a colleague from the opera season, Nora D'Argel.[14] Although attempting no further opera productions during the war, he gave a series of London recitals in 1917–18; and thereafter, following an appearance in Carl Rosa's 1921 Covent Garden season, removed permanently to America. As performer he was a modernist, favouring dramatic point over beauty of tone, a fine legato and 'well-shaped, transparent tone' yielding under interpretative pressure to rhythmic distortion and sharp changes of pace or accent.[15]

In 1915 his immediate concern was to restore international opera to London, and he expected a good response to his canvassing of Covent Garden's erstwhile box-holders. But he failed to grasp the nature of the beast. Attendance at Covent Garden may have been the price paid by those who would be *à la mode*, like the woman who expressed a preference for Wagner nights: 'He makes such a lot of noise that one can talk when a Wagner performance is on.'[16] There was no social obligation to attend the London Opera House. Insensitive to such nuances, Rosing was also deficient in business sense. Keeping seat prices relatively low (front stalls half a guinea, gallery a shilling) made sense in a large theatre provided that good houses could be expected. But he coupled this with another gamble, 'opening with a novelty', *Pikovaya Dama*, and thereby alienating a conservative clientele.[17] Tchaikovsky, outside the nationalist school which dominated the outstanding Russian season of the previous year, was virtually unknown to London's operatic audiences, though it was presumably thought that the popularity of his orchestral music would serve to commend an opera with reminiscences of the *Pathétique*.

Rosing handled the high *tessitura* of Herman's 'difficult part' with fine power and restraint. The dramatic coherence of the production is suggested by the two moments singled out for praise in *Era*'s notice (2 June 1915, p. 8). One is the lovely *mezza voce* of Slava Kracsavina's Countess, her 'noble voice' surely toning sadness with dignity as she escaped dreamily into a distant yesterday when she triumphed at the French court. Another moment is the Mozartian Pastorale, apt to seem digressive if its contribution to the love–money opposition is obscured. The opening scene in the park established that pulsing Petrograd life which ceases to exist for the doomed Herman as even love becomes subordinated to his gambling obsession, making him kin to Pinkerton (*Butterfly*) and Gerald (*Lakmé*) in the remaining operas given, the one destroying love by boorishness and the other out of patriotism.[18]

Pinkerton was undertaken by Léon Lafitte, well known in Paris and at the Monnaie, and to Covent Garden audiences since 1906. However, the central attraction was the Butterfly of Tanaki Miura (1884–1946), who had debuted the year before in Tokyo. Curiously, Henry Wood implies that (through his offices) she first sang Butterfly at the New York Met.[19] In fact she never appeared there, though she was singing the part with the revived Boston Opera under Max Rabinoff's management before the end of 1915. Maggie Teyte (Rabinoff's Mimi) found it 'particularly helpful' to study Miura's distinctive Butterfly: 'a good voice – rather small and a little steely in quality, but she knew how to use it.' Europeanizing 'to match Puccini's score', she brought 'a touching purity' through a 'complete lack of sex in the Western sense'.[20] Her combination of Western modes of expression with 'sudden little movements of hands and figure' had already enchanted London reviewers.[21]

Ethnic emphasis, which in *Butterfly* had been furthered by Miura's countryman Yoshino Markino's 'charming scenery',[22] was stronger still in *Lakmé*. The crowded bazaar scene was alive with a mixture of races, including genuine Indian musicians singing to their instruments, while Indian and Persian dancers performed with characteristic 'command of sinuous body movements and of delicate manual gesture'. In particular, Armen Ter-Ohanian's snake dance 'was both a marvellous exhibition of physical flexibility and an object lesson in symbolic expression'.[23] If this jarred somewhat with Delibes's pastiche 'orientalism', it still offered a nice counterpoint to the comic-opera treatment of the British Raj, *The Times*'s critic (3 June 1915, p. 5) drawing an interesting contrast with Covent Garden's 1910 production starring Tetrazzini and McCormack. It was no longer a singers' opera, despite Mignon Nevada's 'easy fluency' in the title-rôle. If her voice was 'rather light for the part', her artistry (she had been trained by her mother, American diva Emma Nevada) triumphed. She discovered dramatic cogency in the 'Bell Song': 'The opening roulades were addressed to the assembled crowd', partly with back to audience. The song itself she 'commenced kneeling',[24] focusing its proleptic and psychological force, its blend of self-revelation and dramatic irony. Lakmé's emotional collapse would seem inevitable when the very means by which she explores the depth of her passion is designed to betray it.

But freshness of approach and an exciting repertory failed to fill the theatre.

Cui's *Mam'selle Fifi*, based on de Maupassant's story of Prussian atrocities, might have turned the trick in this supreme year of atrocity propaganda had it been chosen to launch the season, especially as its composer was now a general in the Russian army.[25] But Rosing missed his chance; and at the benefit performance on 15 July, 'offered as a partial revival of the ill-fated ... season', Rachmaninoff's one-act *Aleko* was chosen, achieving its British première in a mixed programme. Ironically, this was so well received, its 'wonderful gipsy dances' being declared well up to Diaghilev standards, that it received a second performance.[26]

Rosing could have learnt from the recently ended Courtneidge season. Courtneidge played safe, his 11 British principals, mainly veterans of Thomas Quinlan's world tours, being hired on a share basis. He also made a canny choice of operas, beginning with *The Tales of Hoffmann*, which had become extremely popular since Beecham innovated English-language performance in 1910. Nora D'Argel's playing of contrasting rôles was acclaimed in *The Times* (8 February 1915, p. 10), especially her Antonia, 'for her voice has an appealing *timbre* which is apt to intrude into the clockwork music of Olympia'. But for Grein 'her Olympia was as near the mechanical doll with an inner organism of life as can be imagined, and the little fugues, when the machinery clamoured for lubrication and winding up, were delicious'.[27] While casting fell short of the ideal of assigning the multiple rôles to the same soprano and baritone, at least D'Argel's parts and Coppelius/Mirakel were doubled: no other wartime London production went so far.[28] Had William Samuell, adopting an effective 'mystery of manner' as Dappertutto, undertaken the other baritone rôles as he had done before, the resulting unity might have deterred John Harrison's Hoffmann from moving quite so 'blithely' through his several adventures, which hardly suggests the dark entanglement of art and sexual obsession signalled in the *Don Giovanni* framework.[29] Even so, *Hoffmann* achieved an astounding 57 performances, as against the combined total of 44 for *Butterfly* and *Bohème*. But the latter was remarkable enough, recent pro-German remarks by Puccini failing to quench enthusiasm for his operas.[30]

Rosina Buckman, taking up a rôle with which she would be identified throughout her career, was hailed as 'in some respects ... the best Butterfly that has been seen in London'.[31] She was taught by George Breeden at the Birmingham and Midland Institute (as were Mullings and Walter Hyde). Grew describes her as 'an entrancing Madame Butterfly, an exquisitely lyrical Aïda, one of the greater Isoldas of our time, a pathetic Mimi, and a most brilliantly characteristic Mrs. Waters'.[32] He thought her at her finest in *Aïda*, her musical intelligence being never better shown than in the Nile scene in which she caught the 'joy remembered in the midst of grief' where another singer might have inflected it wrongly as a present joy.[33] For another admirer she embodied those qualities which powered vernacular opera; reinforcing the eloquence of the words 'by skilfully contrived crescendos', imparting poignancy without sacrificing 'roundness of tone or … melodic line', and retaining evenness and colour in 'the faintest pianissimo'.[34] Her Butterfly, sung with 'warmth and fullness', caught the right degree of 'artlessness'. And, of prime importance, she and her colleagues were 'intelligible', so that those 'unacquainted with the story would have been in no need of the book of words'.[35] And there would have been many in that situation, with Puccini's operas still fairly novel; the principals at the second Shaftesbury season were new to *Tosca* (London's first in English). So the Buckman factor was properly acknowledged when *Butterfly* had 'at length taken a firm hold upon the fancy of the public'.[36] The version of the opera in use at this time differs significantly from that with which modern audiences are familiar. A sympathetic Pinkerton would be difficult to sustain when he dubs his servants, all looking alike to the untutored occidental eye, (Dog-)muzzle, and is equally contemptuous of the 'nauseating' Nipponese delicacies they will provide. Mosco Carner confuses creator with character in ascribing this to the insensitivity of Puccini and his librettists,[37] but since Italy's colonial ardour had been temporarily quenched at Adowa in 1896, they were comfortably placed to indict imperialist arrogance. It was American rather than Japanese susceptibilities which occasioned tactful editing in later performances, such as the complete recording of 1924.[38] This recording does retain one feature unrevised: it is Kate Pinkerton rather than Sharpless who asks Butterfly to surrender her child, making the entire episode more unbearably painful than usual. However, it is chiefly important for preserving Buckman's Butterfly. There is musical pressure behind her singing even when she drops into *parlando*; and her scene with Sharpless is a mass of fine detail. The tremor in the voice renders her touching as well as incredulous as she repeats the words of Pinkerton's letter, 'Remember me no more?', her vulnerability foreshadowing the final tragedy. And when that tragedy arrives, the sobs and tremors are there but wonderfully controlled, suggesting Butterfly's firmness of resolve. At a 1917 performance it was thought that Buckman's singing had 'never been more appealing and beautiful than it was in poor Butterfly's tender song of pleading, "Love me a little." In fact, the whole of the love scene' seemed unusually ardent.[39] Within two years she and the Pinkerton on that occasion, Maurice D'Oisly, were wed.

D'Oisly, who made modest appearances at Covent Garden both before and after the war, had his best opportunities with Beecham's company and the BNOC into which it was transmuted in the post-war years. He was credited with 'an exceptionally pleasant voice, … midway between the French and the Italian tenor, far sweeter than the former, but lacking to some degree the round fullness of the latter'.[40] The first performance of Courtneidge's *Bohème* found him unexpectedly deputizing as Rudolph, with Samuell as Marcel (*Era* 14 April 1915, p. 11). William Samuell (1885–1916), a Swansea baritone with a fine technique, won favourable notice in all three operas. A suspicion of overacting disappeared when he assumed the title-rôle in *Rigoletto*, a part he had essayed in Australia after joining Quinlan in 1911. In 1914 Henry Russell, director of the Boston Opera Company, gave him a contract; but war saw the demise of both company and singer, Samuell dying suddenly from typhoid in early 1916.[41] His London Rigoletto was as warmly received as that in Australia. *World*'s critic thought the inclusion of this opera a bold experiment, since it was usually thought dependent 'on a strong star cast' (11 May 1915, p. 732). But star opera, foregrounding singer rather than character, was in abeyance during the war, and the result was largely gain. Samuell shaded raw vitality with tenderness, catching the softer side of the character as well as 'the stress and agony of his tortured soul'. In projecting the tragedy of an abused father he excited comparison with the celebrated Battistini by his vibrant singing and 'rare command of tone-colour'.[42] But there was no question of imitation. Frederic King, who had taught Samuell at the Royal Academy of Music, and had the advantage over him of having seen 'the greatest Italian exponents of the part', found the 'old Italian tricks and traditions ... swept aside' in favour of a brilliant display of singing acting.[43] And he had a worthy partner in D'Argel if the duets which she recorded with him are a fair indication.[44] Yet, as so often in the war years, it was the overall merit of the production which told, plot complications being rendered exceptionally intelligible: 'Probably there were a good many in the audience who for the first time in their operatic lives followed the mysteries of the abduction scene.'[45]

A *Graphic* columnist wondered 'that opera in English has not been tried before on really theatre lines; for what Mr. Courtneidge has done is to make the opera into an acting play with a vivid story as well as music'.[46] He appropriated the musical comedy tradition of clear utterance: 'Nothing has done so much to discredit "opera in English" as the inability of many English singers to pronounce their own language so as to be understanded by an audience.'[47] The vogue for opera in English had begun to gather strength just before the war. British singers, accustomed to singing in languages understood by very few amongst their audiences and now confronted with the altogether more difficult task of making themselves intelligible instead of merely gratifying with pleasant sounds, had founded the Society of English Singers, dedicated to promoting appeal 'through words as well as music'.[48] Laziness of delivery could not survive exposure of the myths which helped to sustain it. One was the advantage which the British were said to enjoy over other nations 'in hearing habitually the original text'. Only close familiarity with the language sung will reveal the interpenetration of word and music; otherwise, focus is all on tune and tone, which might make British audiences especially appreciative of melody and tone-quality, but excludes them from 'the dramatic element which ranks first on the Continent'. This is underscored by Major Christopher Stone (of Eton and Oxford), future co-editor, with his brother-in-law Compton Mackenzie, of the *Gramophone*. In Brussels in early 1919, after several years in operaless trenches, he was overjoyed to get a ticket for his 'favourite opera', *Louise*, at La Monnaie. Deciding he had made his usual mistake of arriving for the first act, he relished 'Depuis le jour', then chose to wander about the Brussels streets rather than stay for the last act.[49] Only wartime conditions, with so many of the Stone persuasion otherwise engaged, could have revolutionized taste. Unlike the old-style opera-goer, people were no longer content to admire what was only partially understood. They, and the singers catering for them, were mindful both that 'a clear delivery of the words is conducive to sympathetic change of tone-colour', and 'that English is second only to Italian as a singing tongue'.[50] Clara Butt, 'anxious to see opera in English put on a firm and permanent basis', declared English 'as singable as any language in existence'.[51] Combatted here is another myth, linked to an artistic snobbery supposed to have been extinguished by wartime chauvinism, that English is 'ill-suited to music' (the phrase derives from a centenary tribute to Beecham!).[52]

Once vernacular performance becomes the norm, opera's appeal will broaden beyond a cult following too often leagued with performers in limiting concern to vocal tone and style. (Thus *Athenæum* January 1916, p. 46, which rebuts a still current piety: that a foreign-language production means a higher standard.) Courtneidge had divined this, drawing for the first Shaftesbury season on audiences from musical comedy and variety.[53] It was this matter of audience identification which produced the difference in fortunes between the Courtneidge and Rosing seasons, the former running for 15 weeks. Kate Searle saw how Rosing had fallen between stools: 'The "classes," although Covent Garden's doors were closed against them, did not turn their Rolls Royces Kingswaywards; and the masses, who seem to be strangely and incurably desirous of understanding what all the noise is about, kept away because the operas presented were not only unfamiliar, but were sung in foreign languages.'[54] Hence the outstanding musical success of 1915 had been opera in English. The importance of this to any hope of establishing a truly British opera was widely recognized. Typically, the *Sunday Times* (12 September 1915, p. 15) berated those highbrows who regarded 'Opera in English' with disdain, since this was the only means by which people would come to recognize its 'artistic value': audiences who 'can only glean the outlines of the story that is told from the stage' are shut off from that fundamental consideration, fidelity of music to text. Better an imperfect 'translation that you can hear and understand than a foreign text which you do not understand at all. "Opera in English," moreover, is practically the condition precedent of English opera.'

In the event, it proved easier to produce a native school of singers than of composers. Although the war found Strauss completely ignored, there was no compensating enthusiasm for Ethel Smyth, Britain's foremost opera composer. The war stimulated wide interest in opera, but did nothing to build up a British repertoire. Patriotic desire for a national opera house with a vital repertory comparable to that in Italy or Germany, one which would reveal 'the spirit of the nation to itself', was frustrated.[55] Elsewhere opera was an artistic expression of nationalism just as governments gave it more murderous expression through war. That operatically Britain lagged so far behind was in considerable measure due to that Victorian façade of self-assurance having obviated the need felt elsewhere for searching out a national identity. Now, with confidence strained, Britain sought to telescope two stages: 'the spirit of the nation' had to be discovered simultaneously through opera and war. Searle recognized the changed mood in asserting that 'what is wanted at this psychological moment are music dramas by our own Britishers, otherwise the danger is that the Toscas, the Carmens, the Pagliacci, will get such a hold over us that we shall continue to exist as a musical colony for other nations for a further indefinite period'. It is one thing to absorb foreign influence into a sturdy native growth, quite another to be dominated by that influence so that native growth becomes impossible. And she was practical in pointing to 'the existing choral societies, self-supporting every one of them, and preserved from risk by the fact that each carries with it its own audience', the relatives and friends of its members. Thus 'An important rôle will have to be assigned to the chorus, as important as in oratorio ... . To interest the masses in the national art, to make them part of it, actors in it, is the chief thing.'[56] Indeed her operatic recipe could work even without any flow of new compositions. It was the basis upon which the WNOC came of age during the 1950s, when forgotten works (by foreigners, but given English dress) were revived, invested with new and special meaning for the industrial areas of South Wales. Early Verdi proved a perfect subject for cultural appropriation with its choric *vox populi* and Risorgimento undertones which had their South Welsh analogue. It played to the political and musical strengths of industrial South Wales, the old choral tradition which gave Goossens senior a surprise at Swansea 'in the early 1900s [when] a section of "the gods" in the Grand [joined], with trained voice and perfect knowledge, in the choral passages of the Hall of Song scene in "Tannhäuser" '.[57] The tradition was destroyed with the closure of the coal-pits, but the amateur choirs, based at Cardiff and Swansea, which powered the original WNOC, were abandoned well before Thatcher devastated the South Welsh choral tradition along with its industrial base. Professionalizing the chorus produced obvious advantages, but it also severed the strong national roots and transformed the WNOC into a visiting company which at one point almost re-established itself at Birmingham.

Opera and politics are inextricable, with the native language taking primacy even over native compositions. George Steiner's father, during the World War II occupation of France, reconciled patriotic and artistic needs by confining himself to French-language recordings of his beloved Wagner. But while various national operas were being established on the Continent, the edifice of British opera became a Tower of Babel: Covent Garden renamed the Royal Italian Opera in 1847; dominance of German music and musicians following the arrival of Albert of Saxe-Coburg-Gotha to reinforce a German monarchy; and, as late as 1894, a policy which required native compositions to be given in French or Italian to make them palatable to Covent Garden patrons.[58] Nationalism apart, artistic interests can hardly be to the fore in any measure which restricts communication. But it was left to the German Carl Rosa to form a company for the promotion of opera in English, while it was the Austro-Hungarian Hans Richter who had the faith in British singers and in their language as a singing medium to place before Covent Garden audiences a complete *Ring* in English. (In this *Ring*, says Chamier, 'there was no "star" unless perhaps the conductor';[59] hence Richter supplied the pattern for Beecham.) Wagnerian pressure, so strong in the pre-war years, was towards opera in the vernacular. Richter, like Wagner himself, and more recently Reginald Goodall, saw that Wagner's 'employment of music as a means of expression made it absolutely essential that every word of the text should be intelligible to the auditor'.[60] Now the war, triggering an explosion of national consciousness with a concomitant upsurge of 'interest in music drama among the masses', made national opera a reality. Searle, attempting historical perspective, saw Hanoverian cultivation of opera in exotic form and alien language effectively shutting out the masses in those great new industrial cities, whereas oratorio fitted comfortably into the growing chapel culture. Now, with events stirring people in those same cities to their emotional depths, they found a naturalized opera satisfying their needs.[61]

That such optimism was inspired largely by the Courtneidge seasons suggests that their impact was out of all proportion to their financial success. It is unlikely that Courtneidge's interest in opera for the people was spurred by anything more idealistic than ensuring bums on seats. But he knew how to brighten his shows by means of tricks learnt from long experience of musical comedy. Profits from the spring season, given in conjunction with H. B. Phillips, were restricted by air raids.[62] But although the season closed because of a pre-contract for an *Arcadians* revival, signs were encouraging enough for more opera to be promised for the autumn;[63] by which time he had teamed up with Beecham. Hence the new Courtneidge season also saw the emergence of the most dynamic force in British opera during the war.

But before considering the Beecham phenomenon, it is proper to look briefly at wartime conditions and the activities of other companies, all of them committed to the vernacular and to the cause of British opera. Even Cavaliere F. Castellano's Italian Opera was delivering Balfe and Wallace twice nightly at the Elephant and Castle in the spring of 1915.[64] *Era*'s leader-writer (8 August 1917, p. 11) noted that the autumn of 1917 would 'see at least six "grand" opera companies at work in this country, all giving opera in English or English opera with English-speaking artistes'. Besides the old-established teams this included 'the newly formed Empire Grand Opera Company of over 100 members under the direction of J. Allington Charsley', which toured without a break from June 1917 into 1919.[65] Even this heightened activity left us languishing far behind Italy, with some 360 companies (there was no mention of Germany with perhaps two-thirds of that number).[66] But some comfort was taken from the way that companies continued to flourish despite the effect of call-up on personnel. That male students were 'rare birds' at the London School of Opera resulted in the apologetic choice of *Hansel and Gretel* for performance.[67] With Carl Rosa, too, strong in women singers, tenors were on the list of wartime shortages. Arthur Winckworth recalls: 'In every town we visited, all our men of military age were examined by the military authorities, and we were often in an agony of suspense lest some vital member of the company should be taken at a critical moment.'[68] Hence the considerable propaganda, concerning this and other companies, that their male choruses are 'largely composed of men who have served their time in the trenches'.[69] Harrison Frewin suffered a blow at Northampton when his musical director, David James Corkan, was arrested during rehearsal and 'charged with being an absentee'. Despite having lived 28 of his 29 years in his Irish homeland, he was fined £2 and 'handed over to the military'.[70] Influence enabled Beecham to sidestep much of this. There was common talk that both conductor Julius Harrison and Donald Baylis, Beecham's invaluable business manager, 'had been awarded their commissions and conveniently posted to the R. F. C. depot in Regent's Park as a result of Whitehall string-pulling'.[71] Thirty-year-old Horace Halstead, a C3 man and 'one of the very few oboe players the country possesses', was graded despite Beecham's appeal;[72] but he was more successful with his tenors: Mullings, whose call-up took him out of the Glastonbury production of Boughton's new music drama, *The Round Table*, was back at the Aldwych that autumn (1916).[73] Indeed Beecham himself was liable for service though a question about this in the House was quietly ignored.[74]

Another instance of Beecham clout was his arranging a special railway coach to allow Goossens to rehearse *Boris Godunov* with some of the company on the way to Manchester.[75] Travel was still difficult enough for less well-connected companies, though the first frantic disruptions in rail transport had long subsided. At the outset, touring companies had been crippled by the military's commandeering of everything available, one company being glad to despatch its scenery by fish-truck. So it was perhaps as well that the Moody–Manners heyday of private trains with ten 45-foot trucks of scenery and costumes was over.[76] But there were other difficulties at this early stage. O'Mara and Victor Turner resolved to save their companies by drastic salary cuts. A two-thirds reduction meant that Turner's chorus-members were now drawing £1 13s. 4d. a week. O'Mara temporarily forfeited his own salary 'so as not to throw close on 100 people out of employment'.[77] Unexpected problems became the rule. During the controversy over the army's setting up of camp theatres, Frewin complained indignantly that the house at which he was playing had been placed out of bounds to troops: 'Had I been travelling a "leg-show" I could have understood this action, but as I was giving grand opera, I can only assume that it was done to "freeze me out". Hundreds of my would-be patrons in khaki expressed themselves strongly about this arbitrary proceeding.'[78] Even allowing for the polemics, this is an interesting comment on the catholic taste of soldier audiences. Indeed, the controllers of the camp theatres hired Beecham's erstwhile colleague Fairbairn to mount operas for the troops.[79]

London seasons could be seriously hit by air raids: in 1917 Beecham was eventually losing between £500 and £1000 a week. But Reid is wrong to imply that 1918 was equally dismal:[80] neither Beecham's spring season ('Money turned away has, all through, been the order of the day') nor the summer one ('very strongly supported from first to last') was troubled by bombers.[81] Naturally, even during bad spells, the press gave buoyant reports to demonstrate the inefficacy of German assaults on civilian morale. During a Courtneidge–Beecham *Faust*, Carrie Tubb played Marguerite in her best style, showing remarkable '*sangfroid*' during the West End's first bombardment.[82] Performances of *Cavalleria* and *Pagliacci* during 1917's notorious air-raid week enjoyed 'a lively accompaniment of anti-aircraft guns', 'Tonio's drum and the bangs outside join[ing] in a ding-dong duet'. Indeed 'the inevitable nervous tension seemed to intensify the emotional expression of the singers', Buckman's Santuzza being 'instinct with significance'.[83] Buckman recalled a *Tristan* which had no sooner started when a 'raid began'. For a while executants 'and such audience as had braved the dangers of the streets, were congregated in the concrete-guarded corridors running along behind the stalls'. The danger was real: during 'previous raids the two nearest theatres had been struck with fatal results', and large pieces of shrapnel had been retrieved from the Drury Lane stage. But the performance was resumed at the point of interruption and continued to the end. Of their great duet, 'O Night of Rapture', Mullings 'remarked afterwards that the title seemed strangely incongruous on such a night'.[84] Bombs, of course, don't differentiate between the West End and the suburbs: simultaneously Phillips's company was beginning a fortnight at Stratford with *Rigoletto* in which a cast of 68 entertained an audience of 18. Fortunately the second week, followed by two more at the King's, Hammersmith, compensated with full houses.[85]

The Old Vic anticipated World War II's Windmill by scorning the raids. The Vic's record alone, quite apart from various visits by touring companies, would make nonsense of Rosenthal's claim that 'Such opera as there was in London during the war years was given by the Beecham Opera Company.'[86] Indeed, it was the war period which brought operatic activity at the Vic to fruition. Earlier efforts, beginning in the 1890s, had been hampered since it was licensed as a music hall and not a regular theatre. Even so, by 1906 attendance was averaging between 1600 and 2000 per performance.[87] The *Musical Times* (July 1915, p. 416) reported audiences of 'some 2,000 people, chiefly habitants of the "New Cut" ', though with a sprinkling of more socially elevated music lovers since, 'except for somewhat faded scenery', performances were sometimes of a quality to make Covent Garden look to its laurels. But by now a theatre licence had been obtained and, despite major financial difficulties, the Vic was firmly established as 'the home of Shakespeare and Opera in English' (gallery twopence and orchestra stalls a shilling). It remained a shoestring operation: a volunteer chorus with non-musical occupations during the daytime, and newcomers 'often pitchforked on to the stage without any rehearsal'.[88] Victor Gollancz recalls with pleasure the theatre's proletarian atmosphere, as Charles Corri 'conducted his squeaky orchestra of about thirty, and the stage as well, with an extraordinary presence of mind that could cover up a thousand mishaps'.[89] Corri, one-time cellist with Carl Rosa, may have had fewer players than Gollancz remembers. Dent refers to about 18, with an additional trombone and horns for Wagner. He also emphasizes Corri's musicianship in 're-orchestrating the standard operas for this small assembly, not just cutting out instruments anyhow, but using a composer's imagination to think out how Mozart or Wagner would have scored the operas had they been faced with a small band like this from the very start', thereby ensuring 'proper consistency and balance of tone'.[90]

Inevitably, the Vic's wartime repertoire included what someone had facetiously dubbed 'the English Ring' (*Lily of Killarney*, *Maritana* and *Bohemian Girl*). As usual at this time, interest in Verdi was restricted to that remarkable output of the early 1850s, *Rigoletto*, *Traviata* and *Trovatore*. *Carmen*, *Faust*, and a double bill of *Pagliacci* and *Cavalleria Rusticana* completed the main items. Some of the 1915 performances of *Trovatore* included Alice Esty as Leonora. Esty, American by birth, British by choice, had sung the first Mimi in this country (with Carl Rosa). If her Leonora showed anything like the form demonstrated in excerpts from the opera which she recorded a decade earlier (her remarkable florid singing caught the studio orchestra flat-footed at times) the Vic audiences had a rare treat. It is a common blunder to equate lack of formal education with ignorance: Lord Harewood was once quoted as saying of Cardiff opera audiences, 'They mostly go not to witness the art of the opera, but for the pleasure it provides.'[91] But in those halcyon days when there was no booking for the gods, queue-chatter made it clear that some of Cardiff New Theatre's patrons could have given him a run for his money on the art of the opera. That there was similar understanding amongst Old Vic audiences is firmly attested in the *Musical Times* (July 1915, p. 416) where they are compared very favourably with those at Covent Garden.

There was approval in *The Times* (22 January 1916, p. 11) for the Vic's approaching opera in the same spirit as non-musical theatre: 'We all realize now that the failure of opera in this country has been due to the fashion of treating it as a separate cult, something removed from ordinary stage conditions.' The Baylis team 'has no pedantic scruples about giving an opera as its composer wrote it. The dull parts must go, the play be kept moving with lively-spoken dialogue. In the case of *The Daughter of the Regiment*, Schumann comes in to help Donizetti out at one point, and "The Two Grenadiers," sung by the old sergeant before the singing-lesson scene, was one of the hits of the evening.' One of the grenadiers expires to the sound of 'La Marseillaise', anticipating its use in the Met's 1940 production, soon after the fall of France, as Lily Pons appeared, to wild applause, draped in the *tricoleur*.[92] Indeed, a topical hit was scored in the Met's production of the opera at the Armistice, when Frieda Hempel interpolated 'Keep The Home Fires Burning'.[93] The Vic could field no Hempel, but *The Times* writer was well pleased with Aimée Kemball whose moving and unmannered singing and 'sprightly acting' ranged easily 'from laughter, when Marie claimed her 800 fathers and swore roundly at one of them, to tears, when she sang her farewell to the regiment'.

In this same season *Lucia* also received a couple of performances, but it was not seen again in wartime London since Beecham never brought his production to the metropolis.[94] North of the Thames, says a *Times* columnist, it had been tolerated merely as a vehicle for some showy singer. But for the Vic's habitués it was a drama as involving as Wagner's. And why not? Madame Bovary's empathy with Lucy of Lammermoor is of a kind with the young Hermann Klein's experience of Emma Albani in *Lohengrin*: '*Her* "Dream" seemed to fit in exactly with *my* dream; her excitement, her intense longing to increase my own.'[95] As it happens, *Lohengrin* was the Vic's only Wagner offering during the war, and that for only a couple of performances in 1914. But Germanic opera was represented by Flotow's *Martha*, continually revived, and, if they be allowed in this category, by *Don Giovanni* and *The Marriage of Figaro*. Dent notes that *Don Giovanni* entered the repertory through the kindness of Manners, who had lent scores and parts.[96] That 'Leporello ate spaghetti (as part of his performance) while the stalls sucked oranges' is recalled by Gollancz,[97] presumably as an aspect of that communion between stage and audience which was a distinctive feature of the Vic. Brazen-voiced Sam Harrison, seen there since 1899, 'was incredibly funny as Masetto', enriching the portrayal with a strong Manchester accent 'and a distinct touch of the socialist outlook in his attitude to the Don'.[98] Dent also recalls him in Thomas's *Mignon,* in which 'he sang and acted the venerable harpist Lothario with astonishing dignity and pathos'. Mignon was undertaken by Australian Julia Caroli, 'late prima donna of the Carl Rosa company and a soprano of quite out-of-the-way beauty of voice'.[99]

Besides 'great doings' at the Old Vic in 1915, Searle noted how Carl Rosa, Moody-Manners, O'Mara and Frewin (chorus of 40 and orchestra of 21) had all been touring to 'splendid business'. Opera continued a major attraction in all the big centres throughout the war, encouraging Hugh Marleyn to plan his own company in 1918.[100] The wartime popularity enjoyed by these travelling companies was not, of course, a new phenomenon. But the string of successes recorded during the war period is certainly out of the ordinary: at Plymouth in October 1915, Carl Rosa 'took the astonishing amount of £1,100 for eight performances', but a year on average takings exceeded £1000 per week.[101] And, once into their wartime stride, O'Mara and Turner never looked back.

The start of 1917 had found the seldom-satisfied Beecham 'highly gratified with the response made by the Birmingham public to his great enterprise for giving grand opera a permanent place in the provinces', prompting a second visit in May.[102] Some of those who had been engaged on just such an enterprise for years might have found Beecham's words a trifle presumptuous. The Carl Rosa Company, since its formation in 1875, had given over 20,000 performances, chiefly in the provinces.[103] And even while Beecham spoke, Frewin was doing his bit in providing Liverpool with 16 consecutive weeks of opera, a record for the city; followed by a further fortnight across the Mersey at the Birkenhead Royal.[104] The season included the first British showing of a new short opera by Parelli, *The Lovers' Quarrel,* which 'created a most favourable impression'.[105] The 1918 season, which the shrewd Liverpool manager Kelly extended to an unprecedented 19 weeks, was also innovative. Besides reviving a Puccini rarity, *The Witch Dancers* (*Le Villi*), the company also mounted Welsh composer Addison Price's latest opera, *The Nuns of Ardboe*: its British première, though a French version had already played in France and Belgium.[106] Enthusiasm was such as to prompt speculation about 'a new and elaborate opera house' for the city, while at the same time Beecham was offering to build just such a house in Manchester, on certain conditions. Whether or not the city council would have accepted his conditions became irrelevant since the Beecham family fortune was poised to take a downward turn. But meanwhile *Era*'s editor had a dizzying vision of Beecham setting up a whole series of city opera houses, as if his inheritance had included Fortunatus's purse.[107] What lends interest to this pipe dream is that it could only occur in response to such exciting developments as the war years had witnessed in the operatic sector.

Beecham was naturally aware of the pioneer work upon which he built. At a dinner given at the OP Club in recognition of his service to British opera, he 'said speeches had been made as if Grand Opera were an accomplished fact, and that in some way that result had been brought about owing to his efforts. His efforts had been considerable, but he regretted to say that Grand Opera in English was by no means established.' Two necessary conditions would be the public's belief in their own musicians and an end to press scepticism. Meanwhile, 'An excellent beginning had been made, and since the beginning had been going on for about 50 years, it was high time they saw results.'[108] Here Beecham acknowledges Carl Rosa's approaching jubilee. As well he might: some months earlier an *Era* leader (23 May 1917, p. 13) sensibly suggested some interchange between the two companies as an economy measure; but the Carl Rosa, responding to the growing demand for opera in the big towns, was about to expand from 200 to something like double that number, running two tours of equal strength simultaneously with a regular repertoire of 20 works.[109] In 1917 the company was set for its first visit to Covent Garden and the West End since 1909. However, negotiations to take the theatre for three months at a rental of £250 a week were wrecked when, on 11 January 1917, it was commandeered by the Office of Works. An alternative six-week season at the Garrick proved a sell-out, and was extended by a further month at the Shaftesbury. 74 performances of 18 different operas were given, *Hoffmann* and *Butterfly* being most popular (ten performances each).[110] These included 'perhaps the keenest, live-est' *Cavalleria* ever performed in London. If the music seemed rather high for Ida Carlon, her 'spiritual intensity' was unmatched even by the 'passionate acting' of the Italians.[111] The 'rich-voiced' Phyllis Archibald triumphed as Carmen, 'bursting with vitality', while in *Aïda* (with *Hoffmann*, one of the company's two biggest productions), her Amneris displayed 'the power of a tragic actress'.[112] She showed her sparkling side in Nicolai's *Merry Wives of Windsor*, partnered by Beatrice Miranda, whose lovely voice, 'full of colour, and of fine dramatic quality', helped to make Nicolai's opera one of the delights of the season.[113] Miranda's 'full round tones' were also heard as Giulietta in *Hoffmann*, and her Butterfly, despite her bulk, proved very effective.[114] She had 'plenty of voice' for the *Trovatore* lead, but seemed not 'acquainted with its traditions and the Italian style of the last century'.[115] However, although that 'powerfully dramatic' voice needed scaling down, she made 'a sympathetic Gilda'. She was well paired with Hebden Foster as Rigoletto, whose 'great scene in the Duke's palace ... was very well sung indeed', though more gaiety early on would have heightened his later tragedy. Although in 1918 Shaw was dismayed by the company's scratch *Don Giovanni*, he found merit in this season's *Figaro*, not least the conducting of Henriquez de la Fuente, who 'handled it brilliantly'. There were also Dorothy Robson's sympathetic countess and Clara Simons's 'pretty, pert Susanna'.[116] The next year Simons proved 'the ideal Marguerite, with her young, slim grace and prettiness, her fluttering shyness, and that natural, unstrained power of hers to express the completest crushing grief'. Playing Effie Deans in MacCunn's *Jeanie Deans*, she gave further evidence of a seemingly 'inexhaustible fund of nervous emotional power', causing anxiety that it might affect the voice. In contrast, her Mignon 'is more childish, impulsive, petulant, passionate. It has its pathos, but it is pathos without a hint of underlying tragedy; and it has its saving touches of humour.' *Bohème*, too, benefited from her 'gift of genuine and effortless pathos', while Eva Turner 'in her splendid singing of Musetta's air' reached '"star" magnitude'.[117]

Like all the other companies apart from Beecham's, the Carl Rosa regularly put on the 'English Ring'. Both Glover and O'Mara noted how these operas were appealing to a new generation.[118] But the 1917 London productions were special since the veteran tenor Ben Davies was guesting in two of his old successes. Having been absent from the operatic stage since 1904, he brought back a style, as 'Lancelot' carefully worded it, 'that formerly was widely esteemed and popular'.[119] These appearances were to be Davies's last on the operatic stage,[120] and his partner on that opening night of *Maritana* was a young Eva Turner who, shortly before her death, recalled that Adelina Patti occupied a box.[121] Patti, like Searle, must have relished 'the finished art' of Davies's singing (including an encore of 'Let Me Like A Soldier Fall') and 'the delightful irresponsible humour of his acting'.[122] It was no ordinary occasion when 'Number after number was encored in the old fashion';[123] and *The Bohemian Girl* saw Davies again displaying 'his old fire and ... beauty of tone'. The comedy was played to maximum effect, and 'Archibald gave us another dark-browed flashing portrait from her gallery of gipsies.'[124] *Lily of Killarney*, completing the 'English' trio,[125] featured another old favourite, Canadian E. C. Hedmondt, who had the art to disguise signs that the voice was no longer young.[126]

For its 1918 Shaftesbury season the Carl Rosa mounted two altogether riskier British operas, Hamish MacCunn's *Jeanie Deans* and Stephen Philpot's *Dante and Beatrice*, both of which were performed twice to good houses. It was the first airing of *Dante*, though MacCunn's opera, based on Scott's *The Heart of Midlothian*, dated from 1894, when the company appropriately premièred it at Edinburgh. Its only London performance had been in 1896, though the company's recent Glasgow revival made a gratifying tribute to MacCunn, who had died in August 1916 after many years conducting for the Carl Rosa and Beecham. Unfortunately, his melodious and dramatic music, 'full of "local colour" ', and the best efforts of an excellent Shaftesbury cast, suffered from Joseph Bennett's disjointed book.[127] *Dante and Beatrice*, too, seems to have had more musical than dramatic interest. It was no help that the Dante, newcomer Albert Bond, chosen for 'his "authentic" profile' rather than a voice, was completely outsung by Miranda.[128]

One notable offering at the Garrick in 1917 was Bruneau's *Attack on the Mill*, an episode of the Franco-Prussian War from Zola's *Soirées de Médan*, and adapted for the operatic stage by the author in conjunction with Louis Gallet.[129] When the company gave it at the Royal, Glasgow (23 March 1916), this was the first complete production in English; London had to wait another year, Beecham being at that solitary 1917 Garrick performance.[130] In late 1914–15, singers from the Antwerp and Brussels opera houses toured the halls with the second act of this opera to aid the Belgian Red Cross.[131] 1915, which had seen a translation of Zola's story opportunistically reprinted for Heinemann's Sevenpenny Novels, was the perfect time to trade on Hun brutality. Although the Belgians' excerpt excluded Marcelline, 'in whom is embodied the despair, the useless protest of war's helpless victims', it gave scope for the dramatic soprano Riznini (as Françoise) to show her mettle when aiding her lover to dispose of a Prussian sentry by means of 'the knife she had reserved to herself in case of need'. This is an operatic addition to Zola's story,[132] but accords well with the endless accounts of the fate of Belgian women in atrocity reports. The aptness of the opera was recognized in the Carl Rosa production, where 'Characteristic German frightfulness' was emphasized by having the miller shot dead on stage 'with horribly realistic effect'.[133]

Frewin also underscored the immediate relevance of the piece when he gave it at Liverpool's Shakespeare Theatre, by having the arrogant captain wear a helmet recently retrieved from a Belgian battlefield.[134] Frewin's company came under the management of H. B. Phillips soon afterwards, and towards the end of the war it was acquired by the Carl Rosa. But for the moment the company was thriving independently, and the same year, in response to the 'growing popularity of operatic music in the metropolis', it spent a fortnight at the King's, Hammersmith.[135] Also in 1916, Frewin did his bit for British music, premièring both J. E. Barkworth's full-blown music-drama, *Romeo and Juliet*, and his own one-act comedy, *The Gay Lothario*.[136] This was at Middlesbrough, for as yet the company had no recognized base. That would change as its status changed: whereas in 1915 Liverpool took up a modest fortnight, the company was spending half its time there by 1918, mounting both the prestigious *Lakmé* and a new opera, *Storm Wrack*, by two local men, composer James Lyon and librettist T. H. Barlow. This brief, intense story of adultery in a French fishing village makes no concession to popular taste either with easy melody or set pieces, but Florence Morden, who had left O'Mara the previous year, showed that she could adapt to non-florid music, while Lewys James 'acquitted himself with distinction in the chief rôle of Pierre'.[137]

Premièring a home-grown opera in Liverpool was only the last step in a process of identification with that city, where Frewin had replaced the Moody-Manners Company. Moody and Manners had met while singing leading soprano and bass rôles with Carl Rosa. They married, and formed their own company in 1897. At their peak they had over 50 operas in the repertory and two teams on the road, keeping a company of 175 employed for most of the year, and were noted particularly for a choice chorus. By 1914 they were much depleted, though offering an imaginative programme at the Prince of Wales's when war broke out, including two Wagner items and two by Kienzl. Their autumn tour in the first phase of war began aptly at the Artillery Theatre, Woolwich. By now there were no German items in the programme, but the tour was evidently successful despite the trying conditions, Kelly congratulating them on their 66 packed performances at his Liverpool theatre.[138] They had been averaging a couple of months there each year for some time, and indeed Kelly booked them for ten weeks in 1916, a record, albeit short-lived, for Liverpool or any other city outside London.[139] Despite this success, Manners was not sanguine about the future with both singers and instrumentalists becoming liable to call-up: 'Unlike the modern revue, men were essential in opera, for ladies ... could not be given the parts of Mephistopheles or Valentine.' He declined to sign up with Kelly for 1917, being reluctant to plan beyond a four-month summer tour of the colonies.[140] That November found him advertising for chorus singers ('who must be young'), and declaring that rumours of the company's professional demise were greatly exaggerated;[141] but it had given its last performance, and 1918 saw the stock auctioned off, some of it snapped up by the Vic. As long as he lasted, Manners clung to his policy of 'promoting native talent'. In 1915 he premièred Colin McAlpin's prizewinning *The Vow* at Nottingham, an impassioned one-acter founded on the story of Jephtha's daughter.[142] In 1903 McAlpin had won the £250 prize put up by Manners for a new British opera with *The Cross and the Crescent*, given a single performance in Manners's Covent Garden season with Moody in the soprano lead. Opposite her was Joseph O'Mara, considered by Hurst to be 'the finest English-speaking operatic tenor' of this period, as well as a first-rate actor.[143]

O'Mara formed his own company in 1912 (following reduction in the Moody-Manners operation) and continued to tour until the year before his death in 1927. During the war he was noted not only as the country's most ardent Puccini advocate, but for 'the amazing enthusiasm, cohesion, and vitality of the company', including such little-known but outstanding talents as Lewys James and William Boland, the latter 'worthy of ranking alongside John Coates or Frank Mullings as an heroic tenor'.[144] 1915 was notable for the guest appearance of Zélie de Lussan as Carmen, supported by O'Mara, James and Morden. She had played the rôle for decades (the previous year with Moody-Manners at the Prince of Wales's) appearing opposite 57 Don Josés,[145] including Jean de Reszke at Covent Garden and the Met. But she considered O'Mara the greatest actor of them all. O'Mara himself found 'that often the intensity of de Lussan's acting in the final scene made him thankful it was not a real knife he had to wield for he felt like stabbing her to death in earnest'. This, her last Carmen, had some striking features. To screw up anticipation before her first entry a strong light was angled to cast her shadow 'gradually coming nearer and nearer till at length she appeared'.[146] O'Mara's voice combined power with sweetness. Like Mullings, he could move easily from comic to heroic rôles, a boon during the wartime tenor famine. One of his favourite characterizations was Eléazar in *La Juive*, an opera dating from the year before *Les Huguenots*, and, like Meyerbeer, no longer performed in wartime London. The absence of these operas, key links between *Guillaume Tell* and *Don Carlos*, would have been of scant concern at a time when neither Rossini nor much Verdi was being heard. But O'Mara kept them going in the provinces, playing Eléazar himself at the Gaiety, Manchester, in 1915.[147] The opera was 'magnificently performed' in a new translation by Samuel Langford, and deemed 'well worthy of permanent inclusion in any first-class repertoire. In the pageantry of the stage, in elaborateness of treatment, and in broad and dramatic effect "The Jewess" unquestionably ranks high.'[148]

The most popular of English operas, the Gilbert and Sullivan collaborations, were still absent from central London through the depreciation of Sullivan's work soon after his death. They were occasionally seen out east, production by 1918 being in the capable hands of Henry Winston, director of the Stepney Musical Association, who mounted *Iolanthe* at the Mile End Pavilion.[149] More importantly, the D'Oyly Carte Company throve in the suburbs and provinces: it was caught in Dublin during the Easter rebellion. A month into the war, a season at the Coronet was cautiously embarked on and found quick approval, so that others followed in rapid succession at the Kennington, the Wimbledon and the King's, Hammersmith: 'In strenuous times like these it is a welcome relief to turn for a moment to the lilting melodies and kindly, yet caustic, satire of Gilbert and Sullivan operas.'[150] A year on they returned to the Kennington with the first London performance of *The Sorceror* in 16 years, a personal success for Henry Lytton. He was their outstanding player, said to preserve the best Savoy traditions.[151] He had the key rôle of Ko-ko in *The Mikado,* with Leicester Tonks first rate in the name part, Clara Dow 'charming, coquettish and winsome' as Yum-Yum and 20-stone Fred Billington giving his inimitable impersonation of Pooh Bah with 'massive humour'.[152] This hefty Yorkshireman also scored as Don Alhambra in *The Gondoliers,* and as a sergeant of police in *The Pirates of Penzance,* 'a part he created at the copyright performance'. He had joined the company in 1879, and his sudden death in November 1917 left Lytton as the only link with the early great years.[153] However, the company successfully survived this loss, as well as other wartime setbacks, keeping the male chorus up to strength by 'a liberal inclusion of "silver badgers" '.[154]

It is now time to return to Robert Courtneidge, whose second season marks the beginning of Beecham's wartime operatic activity. Courtneidge was missing no bets and had the outside of the Shaftesbury painted brightly by way of compensating for blackout restrictions, though one reviewer declared that the revival of *Hoffmann* was 'well worth braving the blackout for'.[155] Ordinary theatre prices were charged, and Courtneidge also played the patriotic card. At one Saturday performance, as an *entr'acte* between an intensely felt *Cavalleria* and *Pagliacci,* Elgar conducted his setting of Cammaerts's poem, 'Une Voix dans le Désert'. It was effectively recited and sung by the Belgian Carlo Liten and soprano Olga Lynn, against a background evoking war along the Yser.[156] And his efforts paid off; the partnership, beginning cautiously, demonstrated 'that grand opera artistically produced in English, with a competent but not star cast' could pay in the West End.[157] But the 1915 part of the programme included no British operas, as Hans Richter, now repatriated, noted with regret.[158] He, at any rate, had no doubt that Britain possessed the necessary creative as well as executive talent.

Experiment with British opera had to wait until the second half of the season. Meanwhile, Beecham opened with *Romeo and Juliet,* bringing to it a rhythmic élan which still failed to persuade *Athenæum*'s critic that he could have any real enthusiasm for it.[159] Shakespearean provenance is a serious liability. The insertion of the soldiers' French 'Na poo' into Carl Rosa's 1917 production of *Merry Wives* was deplored as a liberty taken with Shakespeare rather than with Nicolai–Mosenthal.[160] But the unprejudiced could relish Gounod, and 'William Samuell accomplished his usual feat of "bringing down the house" by his brilliant singing of Mercutio's song'.[161] This Queen Mab ballad is the most inventive moment in the score, and Samuell's neat shifts of tone, and a humour as light and fleeting as the passage of Mab herself, have been captured in a recording made the same year. Gounod's lovers were impersonated by Webster Millar and Miriam Licette. Millar's pre-war London appearances had been in musical comedy with George Edwardes. But the earlier Courtneidge season had found him playing Pinkerton and sharing the tenor lead in *Bohème* with D'Oisly. He possessed the fluent ease and suavity required by Gounod's music, and was Beecham's preferred Romeo, gamely singing in the Gounod centenary performance when suffering from that terrible 1918 influenza.[162] Licette's link with Beecham slightly predates this production, since she sang a few solos in the 1915 Albert Hall proms arranged by Beecham and Landon Ronald. It was during these Beecham years that her voice grew in size and capability, a common experience amongst those members of the company unused to such 'encouragement – plus the opportunity for constant exercise'.[163] Licette's voice was still fairly light, but her Juliet displayed 'those lovely high floating head-notes' which were a mark of Marchesi's teaching, and she 'received a big ovation after her first-act waltz aria'.[164] Her singing and acting were especially impressive in the love duets, and she 'even managed with considerable skill that quaint interpolation, her collapse while being led to her marriage with Paris' (the first time this addition had been seen in Britain).[165] But critics were not always so admiring. The next year Licette might sing 'the Waltz song like a young girl bubbling over with the joyful excitement of a first ball', yet was 'still rather placid and collected in the romantic and dramatic scenes. One feels that no happening, however thrilling, would be likely to agitate her Juliet to the point of making her miss a meal.'[166]

The popular French repertory was well represented. *Faust* included the splendid Robert Radford, though as yet his dignified Mephistopheles lacked satanic humour.[167] *Carmen* was better, Doris Woodall adding a touch of 'drollerie' to her exuberant playing of the title-rôle. She had both 'a good deal of temperament' and experience, even 'if her Carmen related more to the Old Kent-road than Seville', and she continued to develop her wild-cat impersonation throughout the war.[168] Beecham's special feeling for French music brought the required grace and delicacy to those performances which he conducted. And while he asserts provocatively 'it is the music alone that matters, and if it be of the right sort, no one troubles about anything else',[169] he well knew that wartime audiences did trouble about other things. Indeed it was in considerable measure work done by his company which made Searle identify one factor in 'the awakening interest in opera shown by "the masses" ' as 'the great care and skill now lavished on the vivid presentation of the drama, apart from the singing'.[170] Repeatedly the principals were praised for clear articulation. While such clarity is no guarantee of a fine performance, wartime operagoers were in no doubt that a fine performance is impossible without it.[171] Beecham himself recalls how, during his mounting of *Figaro,* he went to the very back of the top gallery (this was at Drury Lane, a theatre larger than

Covent Garden), and found that he 'could hear not only every syllable of the songs, but of the ensemble pieces as well, all as clearly enunciated as if it had been spoken instead of sung'.[172] Athough noted for insistence on 'clear enunciation',[173] he would have been preaching to the converted with this company, many of whom belonged to the Society of English Singers and were part of a revolution (so thought a *Times* columnist fresh from his *Figaro* production) likely to extend 'beyond the walls of Drury Lane' (4 August 1917, p. 11).

After the Christmas break, the more adventurous phase of the Shaftesbury season brought into focus some of the prejudices against vernacular performance. It saw the first English-language production in this country of Puccini's *Manon Lescaut* (though the Quinlan company had anticipated while touring Australia). *Era*'s review acknowledged the problems experienced with the original libretto, but saw another kind of snag when it was turned into English: immoralities lose 'the glamour in which a Latin tongue veils them'.[174] Nevertheless, the opera was well received, having the American soprano Jeanne Brola (who had made her London debut just before in *Hoffmann*) in the name part. But the moral aspect was not paramount. What is still the main factor in the prejudice against vernacular opera is the difficulty voiced in *Athenæum* over the première of Ethel Smyth's *Boatswain's Mate*: 'We hear phrases that might have come from the pen of Charpentier or Puccini ... wedded to such sentences as "Am I dreaming? I wish somebody would pinch me!".' (How, one wonders, do Charpentier's countrymen manage?) 'The audience laughed but whether at the sentences themselves or at their association with delicate and euphonious sounds, one could not tell. Romance is certainly stripped from the opera by the use of English; accustomed to French or Italian or German, which we do not always take the trouble to understand, we are startled by the sound – and meaning – of our own tongue.'[175] Incongruous, too, seemed 'the occasional lapse into plain spoken dialogue', and it was hoped that future operas would be based 'on more romantic tales than those of Mr. Jacobs'. *The Times*'s reviewer (29 January 1916, p. 11) enjoyed the 'scene of villagers who have had as much as is good for them and make sunset hideous but entertaining with a fiddle, a banjo, and a concertina'. But this was offset by an incongruity of musical styles: the start 'is full of tunes and happy quips of orchestration. One scarcely knows whether the composer is quoting folk-songs or making up her own tunes. The second part, however, is opened with an orchestral intermezzo in which "Bushes and Briars" is strangely coupled with sombre Wagnerian colouring. Except for little patches of the light-hearted folk-tune manner, such as the amusing play made with "O dear, what can the matter be?" ..., the music becomes more ... grand-operatic as time passes.' Had war not intervened, the opera would have had its first airing at Frankfurt and it is wondered whether 'so much fuss and heaviness' has been laid on to suit the German mentality.

Notably, at the 1918 revival, when Buckman resumed the rôle of country landlady outwitting her admirers which she had created so effectively, there was something of a turn-around in *The Times* (13 July 1918, p. 3), it being observed of the second part that 'a good deal of filigree work ... lightened the texture without sounding thin'. Belatedly recognized were Smyth's continuing 'happy illustrated use of folk-tunes' and equally happy jokes like the intervention of Beethoven's '"Fate, knocking the door" ... when the policeman's tap is heard outside'. These had found praise in *Era*'s searching review of the première (2 February 1916, p. 11), along with the 'power and originality' (eclectic, not imitative) of the music, and the psychological penetration, especially of the character of Mrs Waters. Here was a businesslike exterior hiding sexual ardour; and Baughan was taken with Buckman's singing the proposal to dump the body of a supposed murder-victim 'to a gay dance rhythm', suggesting 'to the Boatswain that she is mad, but to the audience that she can scarcely retain her merriment'.[176] Searle thought both Smyth's opera and Stanford's *The Critic* combined 'British sentiment and British humour so happily that their places in public esteem seem to be assured'.[177] Yet in *Era*'s reappraisal (17 July 1918, p. 11), Smyth, allowed 'humour, directness, vitality, and honest, homely sentiment', is charged with 'Wagnerising her simple English rustics out of all emotional knowledge', leaving *The Critic* 'The only out-and-out British opera the Beecham Company has given us.'

The latter's topicality helped, Sheridan's original having appeared 'four months after Spain had declared war on England ... And as we are again in the midst of war, the burlesque of the Armada, with its grotesque Tilbury Fort and a still more funny battle on curly painted waves (to a faint reminiscence of "The Flying Dutchman"), is excellent.'[178] Less apt was its replacement of eighteenth-century stage affectations with Italian operatic conventions as principal target for mockery. The wind of change blowing across the British operatic stage had made gibes at bombastic tenors and mad scenes in white satin as redundant as those at eighteenth-century rhetorical extravagance. Indeed visually the latter dominated, Goossens, on the podium, impersonating Thomas Linley, Sheridan's father-in-law, who had been Drury Lane's musical director in 1779, when the play was first given. Period stage-boxes were filled with women in towering head-dresses and bewigged men in flowered coats. The curtain rose on Tilbury Fort, 'a blatant red and white structure, planted in the middle background against the seascape of fiercely rampant blue waves'. During the sea fight combatants brought on 'more blue waves' and fought 'in the midst of them' while several galleons rocked 'solemnly past in the middle distance and a couple of opposing frigates' began to jerk ponderously into view at each side of the stage before sticking fast. Amongst a spirited cast, Mullings as Don Whiskerandos showed his rare gift for comedy besides a voice 'of unusual power and quality'.[179] Immediate critical reception was favourable, but Baughan missed that 'humorous inappropriateness between the material and its treatment' required by burlesque. This matches Beecham's summing up, 'an able but pedestrian setting of Sheridan's brilliant text', though he adds that 'Rumbold's scenery and costumes were a triumph of comic art'.[180] For Baughan, Rumbold's work both here and in *Boatswain's Mate* was 'far superior in artistic originality to anything done at international Covent Garden'. In the latter, the exterior setting of the Beehive, 'with steps leading to the actual stage, is very novel, and the setting of the interior of the inn, with its high staircase and tattered ceiling, is as brilliant as anything that might have been done for a long run'.[181] Smyth, however, talks of 'amateurish ineptitudes': 'You cannot pull off what Germans call a "Conversazione-Oper" when the "conversation" ... takes place on a tea-tray in the sky at the extreme back of the stage.'[182]

In the event her *Boatswain's Mate* outlasted *The Critic*, which disappeared from the repertory in 1917. Surprisingly, the 1918 revival of Smyth's 'fresh, jolly work' found *Era*'s leader-writer (31 July 1918, p. 11) proposing it as a model 'to the young British composer', especially with 'a basis of popular music hall melodies'. For Smyth's folk idiom is *passé* and we are 'not ready by a long way' for that other oft-advocated source of inspiration, 'socialist ideals and the labour movement'. Nor do the English have the Russians' 'interest or pride in the history of their race. They have no national heroes, except the dramatically much overworked Nelson and Drake.' Even so, the Drake-centred *Young England* (book by Basil Hood to Clutsam and Bath's music) accords with the feeling that a British school might arrive more readily not through grand opera 'but through more or less serious musical comedy of the "Violette" order'.[183] Despite complaints from some that the new work 'took us back to Gilbert and Sullivan', others thought it went 'far towards showing how all British opera might be written if some day we happened to want such a thing'.[184] It saw Courtneidge back on familiar ground and a long way from Beecham, though Harry Dearth, the basso cantante singing Drake, provided a tenuous connection, having appeared in Beecham's 1910 Covent Garden season. *Young England*'s music was designed to throb with the spirit of Drake and those other 'mighty captains who laid the foundations of England's supremacy at sea'. Although lacking the substance and originality of German's *Merrie England*, it answered wartime needs, its 93 performances at Daly's sandwiched between paying periods in the provinces. At the London opening Henry Ainley, in khaki, forged a prefatory link between those Armada days and the new vitalism:

now ye rouse to a dead Admiral's drum,
And young, fresh England hath stood up awake
To spend her youth by following after Drake!

Hayden Coffin sang stirringly, and those 'thatched and lattice-windowed cottages, old grey churches shaded with yews and chestnuts, and apple trees all in a glory of blossom' represented that spurious old England for which our Tommies were supposedly fighting. The great scene was on board the *Golden Hind* at Deptford, with Elizabeth's courtiers surrounding her (Doris Woodall holidaying from *Carmen*) in a riot of silk and velvet finery.[185]

Young England had not shown the way forward, though it helped to compensate for Beecham's neglect of British opera. *Era*'s leader-writer (10 April 1918, p. 11) regretted that the recent Drury Lane season bought success with continental favourites instead of the promised British works. Apparently Beecham lied about having four new British operas 'in the course of preparation' to discomfit *Observer* music critic G. H. Clutsam.[186] In reality he had no more faith in the native product than in native audiences. At one point he declared 'that the only way to make English opera a successful proposition was to start right away and form a new public out of the rising generation'.[187] But despite this, reinforced by Courtneidge's example, Beecham, under growing financial pressure, chose to woo the conservative old guard to his enterprise, which in the long run proved fatal to it. This policy made it all the more important to turn to the Italian and Russian schools, to Wagner and Mozart, and of course to the French. His achievement with each of these will be considered in turn, beginning with the French repertory which was gradually expanded after his removal to the Aldwych and Drury Lane. It was his mounting of *The Fair Maid of Perth* which brought him into conflict with Clutsam, an episode somewhat hazily recalled in his memoir.[188] Nevada was truly a fair maid 'in her flowing rose-coloured gown, with its hanging sleeves of gossamer stuff and close-framing cap. She sang the joyous Polonaise in the first act – an exceedingly florid aria, all trills and runs and picchettate – with the lightness of a will-of-the-wisp.' There were two fine tenors, Walter Hyde singing with 'virile and effective ease ... as the licentious Duke of Rothesay', and Webster Millar as Hal o' the Wynd neatly matching his refined serenade against Foster Richardson's riotous drinking song in the same scene. The palace room with its oak beams, 'graceful gallery and velvet hangings was both elegant and sumptuous. And the street scene, with its gabled roofs lightly touched with snow, made an effective setting for the revels of the good burghers of Perth .... Beecham conducted with a skill that brought out the fragile beauties of the score.'[189]

Towards the start of the war Saint-Saëns had made a passionate public protest against the performing of Wagner in France.[190] At its end he wrote privately to Klein expressing disappointment that the Entente had not caused French music to displace that of Germany in London.[191] But Beecham, fairly ecumenical, had nevertheless done his bit for French opera, giving Saint-Saëns's own *Samson and Delilah* a prominent place in the repertoire. *Athenæum*'s critic (November 1916, p. 560) missed an inspirational quality in the singing, but found the acting admirable. Indeed the fight between Samson (Blamey) and Abimelech (Richardson) 'was more than good acting; it was a piece of realism and Biblical drama, conveying, as it should, the strength of the hero who could slay with his hands alone'.[192] In his appeal to Israel, Blamey 'was shouting defiance, rather than inspiring with song', but he worked his way into the rôle at that first performance, rising 'to real eloquence' in the declamatory passages at the mill with slaves.[193] Later Hyde and Mullings both sang the part admirably, an indication of the company's strength. Perhaps of the three it was Mullings who could best encompass those changes of mood which make the rôle so taxing. He was not only mighty warrior but forceful leader: 'his voice rang out like a trumpet in the scene of the incitement of the Hebrews.' And he could shift from authority through sensuality to tragedy.[194] Edna Thornton retained the part of Delilah throughout, her 'dramatic grip' strengthening and her singing always 'full-toned, powerful, and luscious in quality'. From the outset she was not only vocally seductive but had the 'allure of person necessary for the part of the temptress Delilah'. She and Blamey 'rose to great heights in the temptation scene', the only quibble being that she was allowed to wave Samson's wig as she ran from the house, in accordance with weary tradition.[195] The importance of the chorus to the opera's success was demonstrated at a 1918 revival, the sopranos marring 'the beautiful first scene' by singing out of tune. The scene was saved by the dancers, reliably lithe and expressive. One graceful soloist gained 'special praise for a sinuous Eastern dance in the Temple scene'. Dagon's temple was spectacular, 'adorned with huge idols and supported by immense pillars', the collapse of which was realistically achieved.[196] But perhaps the most important factor in the success of the production was the conducting of Percy Pitt, who had a special sympathy with the work.

Faust, the old war-horse, underwent refurbishing when Nevada sang Marguerite. When the opera first arrived in London in 1863, separate productions just days apart at Her Majesty's and Covent Garden expressed totally different conceptions of the rôle through the different costumes worn. Now Nevada announced her intentions by dropping what had become the conventional blue dress for her first entry in favour of a pink one designed by the painter Herbert Sidney. She appeared

> not alone, but chatting and smiling with a couple of girl friends, and after the colloquy with Faust ran off confused and trembling, as a girl unversed in the ways of wooers would do. Then, when she began pensively to chant the ballad of the King of Thule, this unconventional Marguerite disappeared into her house to fetch her apron ... and there remained during most of the first verse, letting her voice float out through the open window.

Her phrasing combined elegance with rare 'depth of feeling'. In church 'she prayed, not to an altar "off," but to a figure of Christ raised on a pedestal, an idea both scenically and dramatically effective. Again, at the opening of the prison scene, instead of lying immobile on her bed of straw, this Marguerite passed distraught along the stone walls, now touching them with timid fingers, now folding her arms and smiling down at the pale ghost of her dead child clasped in them.'[197] The unmarried mother issue was a deeply sensitive one at this time. It was a bold measure to strip off layers of tradition from an old favourite so as to lay this bare.

By comparison, Robert Radford's shedding of Mephistopheles's red velvets for a black costume and scarlet cloak would have produced little surprise.[198] Like Samuell, Radford had studied under Frederic King at the Royal Academy, debuting at Covent Garden in 1905 as the Commendatore in Richter's *Don Giovanni*. He had achieved prominence in Ernst Denhof's company, and his association with Beecham began in 1910. His Mephistopheles owed something to Plançon,[199] but Ernest Newman, deeply impressed, drew a different comparison: 'His devil has in it a touch of the "grand Seigneur" that used to make Edouard de Reszke's Mephistofeles at once so sinister and so engaging.'[200] Norman Allin brought to the rôle neither Radford's urbanity (that 'air of being "in the Cabinet," of being sure of the permanence of a well-paid job') nor 'the malignant, humanity-hating fiend' complete with Kaiser-moustache favoured by American Robert Parker. He supplied 'a good bourgeois trader type of devil, honest enough by nature, but momentarily perverted from paths of rectitude by the lure of excess profits in the souls line'.[201] Herbert Langley's 'fine manly Valentine' was over-vehement vocally and dramatically; after the 'writhings and teeth-gnashings' of the death-scene, 'it was a relief when his last convulsion laid him flat'.[202] In view of this it seems a pity that Powell Edwards, who had his first real London opportunity in the part, was not seen in it more often. He brought to it 'a keen sense of character' and a 'voice of beautiful quality' artistically used.[203]

The most important venture into the French repertoire, and also the most risky, was the first English-language production of Charpentier's *Louise*. London critics, having overlooked Quinlan's estimable 1912 production, doubted whether a work so intensely French (its protagonist is really Paris) would work in English. But the Parisian atmosphere was well caught both in the workroom scene, with 'a genuine comedienne in Miss Gertrude Ketchell as the Errand Girl besides a wealth of talent for character-sketches among other representatives of the volatile work girls, ... and the Montmartre scene, with its highly coloured Bohemians of the Latin Quarter, its rag-pickers, its delightful gamins and gamines'.[204] There was apprehension, too, over Beecham's casting Licette, noted for 'singing of cool lyrical beauty' rather than drama, in the name part.[205] When interviewed she emphasized the strenuous nature of the rôle, and the heavy preparation entailed: for several weeks she was 'rehearsing every morning and afternoon and playing most evenings'.[206] But it paid off, and the character came alive through the 'easy naturalness' of everything she did.[207] Edith Clegg, whose 'fretful, scolding Mother sounded the right jarring note in the harmony of the home', had the gift of making such rôles seem 'even more important than the leading parts'.[208] For Searle she made the character 'hard, austere, yet not unsympathetic'.[209] Radford gave a notably sympathetic reading of Louise's father, his favourite part; 'Lancelot' placed him beside the foremost exponents, Gilibert and Marcoux,[210] his 'mellow tones seem[ing] to express the very soul of paternal love and tenderness'. For a time the lovers' 'legitimate, youthful longings', in the face of the mother's 'antagonistic harshness', tip the scales in the other direction. 'And thus one is drawn this way and that all through the performance, by arguments for and against youth's claim for freedom, until at the finish the older generation, left with the last say in the matter, upsets the balance effectually with the father's heart-broken cry of "Louise!".'[211] Parker, in the rôle, had nothing of Radford's 'sympathetic mellowness', though Searle found this 'apparent hardness of character, reflected from the vocal timbre, made it possible to bestow more sympathy on Louise'.[212] Her *Sunday Times* colleague (17 March 1918, p. 4) found his performance inconsistent: at times he was 'the simple-minded French workman, querulously impotent against the force which is dragging his daughter away from him; at others his passion denoted a man who would not have failed to bend her to his will'. But this wavering between strength and weakness is there in the music. Perhaps a non-native production obscured the fact that this has been no straightforward conflict between possessive parent and the urgencies of youth. That darkened Paris at which the father shakes an impotent fist is a living, pulsating organism stretching from the heights of Montmartre; brat of the Third Republic, it has become *fin de siècle* harlot to contest his tradition-directed world with her visceral pull.

Italian opera may not have been Beecham's first love, but it was by no means neglected. *Cavalleria* and *Pagliacci* received cooler reviews (usually because one or the other seemed under-rehearsed) than any other of Beecham's wartime productions. But they aroused enthusiasm when first presented at the Shaftesbury, especially for the tenors. D'Oisly had shed completely that stiffness which sometimes marred his acting: 'His Turiddu is an elemental young animal, strong and cruel, calculating and selfish', his *Siciliana* dripping with sex. Blamey's Canio was 'astonishingly good', 'On With The Motley' the more effective for not reproducing 'the mannerisms of more famous tenors in the part'. Langley made much of Silvio, a rôle which 'so often in the "star" performances which we used to hear in another place was allowed to sink into insignificance'.[213] Later he would make Alfio in *Cavalleria* his most successful rôle, where 'his harshness of voice help[ed] instead of hindering him'.[214] The same year, Parker, playing Tonio 'in a strolling player's velveteens, instead of the traditional clown's get-up', offered a 'powerful study of a creature deformed both in mind and body, and his clown in the play, fortified with fresh comic business, lent just the droll touch needed to heighten the effect of the final tragedy'.[215] And in the following season Nevada brought to her first appearance as Nedda the same fresh thinking that she had bestowed on *Faust*. She told 'fortunes among the country folk', and preferred an authentic Columbine's dress over the customary Pierrot costume. This 'poor little strolling player's longing after love and happiness, alternating with her scorn of Tonio's hideous advances and her fear of her brutal husband, the pathos of her attempts to hide her terror under a mask of laughter, were all depicted with uncommon power'.[216] Her Canio was Mullings, who made the part 'as tearingly elemental as his Othello, and at the same time very tragically weary'. He substituted 'tragic gusto' for Italianate hysteria, sending Nedda 'spinning to the boards'; on one occasion Desirée Ellinger landed in the wings.[217]

The Puccini operas benefited greatly from the Beecham Company's characteristic strength in small rôles.[218] In *Bohème*, 'Colline's farewell to the old coat was perfectly done [by Ranalow], sung intimately into its familiar creases instead of being declaimed to the house.'[219] In *Tosca*, Sydney Russell's Spoletta was singled out, as was 'Foster Richardson's well-sung Sacristan, with his air of scandalised piety'.[220] Both Blamey and D'Oisly were effective Cavaradossis. Blamey, 'thoroughly at ease ..., sang splendidly', his voice ringing 'out with fine effect in the cry of victory'. D'Oisly could render the two big songs with 'lyrical beauty. And in the torture scene his acting was remarkably fine.'[221] On his first London appearance in the part, an admiring *Sunday Times* reviewer (24 October 1915, p. 4) was gratified that he, 'despite his foreign-sounding surname, is one of ourselves and has the distinction of being the only English public school man on the operatic stage'. But for some he evidently displayed an overly stiff upper lip, his lack of ardour providing 'no apparent reason for Tosca's exclamation, "My hair is all dishevelled" '.[222]

He found more 'warmth and passion' for the revival of *Manon Lescaut*, to which Brola also brought 'a lighter, surer touch' than hitherto.[223] She was invaluable in Puccini. In 1917 she was recognized as 'the first Mimi with spirit enough to mingle chaff with her demureness and point the sly dig at the poet, Rudolph, in her racconto'.[224] She sang Tosca throughout the war years, keeping the part 'at its true level of a passionate devotion towards the lover she twice betrays with a voice that soared above Puccini's orchestra'.[225] Searle praised the 'ease and balance' of her singing, while 'her painting of the singer's rapidly flying moods was dramatic and vivid'. She and Austin played the 'knifing' scene with intensity, Austin having had time to grow into the Scarpia rôle and play it 'with uncommon power and finish'. (Like Vanni Marcoux he could inject life and individuality without impairing tone.)[226] But Brola topped off her achievement as Minnie in the new production of *Girl of the Golden West*, a part she had taken at Liverpool with the Quinlan Company in 1911 when the opera was first given in English. She sang throughout with her usual vitality, ease, and fine tone quality. Parker 'wore an expression on his face that translated into physical terms those caustic woodwind phrases that paint the Sheriff's character orchestrally'. But against his melodramatic villain, Hyde's hero was perhaps a little too restrained, though his voice was 'rich and luscious'. Producer George King worked up the situations to great effect: 'Nothing could have been better managed even on the film, than the row over the cards in the bar-scene.' And then there was Norman Allin's song of home, richly rendered 'to melt the sentimental hearts of the "boys" '.[227]

In the wartime seasons at the Aldwych and Drury Lane 88 Puccini performances were given. Most popular were *Butterfly* (35) and *Bohème* (33). Although *Aïda* was given 36 times, the Verdi total was only 60. *Rigoletto* was not resurrected after the Shaftesbury performances, perhaps because there was no one to replace Samuell, or possibly because *Trovatore* was thought a sufficient sampling of 1850s Verdi. The latter was something of an embarrassment: Although 'we all agree that the plot is absurd, the situations artificial to a degree, and that their treatment in some instances comes perilously near the farcical', it stubbornly continued to give pleasure, even if 'regarded mainly as a testpiece for the accomplished vocalist'. Thornton, an Azucena who had become skilled in expressive varying of tone colour, 'adumbrated the roulades that our ancestresses loved sufficiently to suggest that mixture of awe, amusement, and affection with which we regard their crinolines'.[228] Langford stood alone in responding to the 'infusion of intellectual power' which the principals brought to Beecham's 1917 production. Even Shaw, deprecating a lack of seriousness in this revival, undercut the praise he lavished on the opera by declaring it 'absolutely void of intellectual interest'.[229] He disliked the non-traditional costumes and 'strange, fantastic, but entirely beautiful Bakstian scenery'[230] (its designers, the Polunins, had worked for Diaghilev). The chorus was unusually 'slovenly' (Searle's word): 'The soldiers, instead of being more fiercely soldierly than any real soldiers ever were on sea or land, were wholly occupied in demonstrating their unfitness to be combed out' (perhaps advisedly with press gangs plaguing theatres in the hunt for draft dodgers). Worst of all, despite some fine playing, he found 'the humorists of the orchestra were guying what they regarded as the poor old opera quite shamelessly'. While the first-night audience was respectful, suffering 'no applause at the stereotyped places' though breaking 'into full cry at the end of each act',[231] critics remained aloof. Powell Edwards, having another opportunity to make good when it was found that Austin lacked the technique for Luna's music, ran foul of Searle's preconceptions. His 'qualities of sincerity and sensitiveness, valuable in true human drama, become defects in this melodrama. The silly old story will not bear the burden of real emotion.' Although elsewhere his 'soft and melodious voice, so fluently produced', won warm approval, he was dropped in favour of Langley, 'whose tremolo was so persistent that every sustained note of "Il balen" ' (in contrast to Edwards's 'sonorously given' version) 'became a trill'.[232] Only those firm favourites Mullings and Buckman (why should Searle find it 'difficult to forgive her for gilding the Verdian lily with new cadenzas'?) could be allowed to take the piece seriously. Thus Shaw: 'There was no spoof about the singing of Leonora and Manrico; they threw about high Cs like confetti, and really sang their music. I have never heard the music of the prison scene sung as it was by the tenor ... A better Leonora was impossible; there is nothing more in the part than she got out of it.'[233]

Buckman and Mullings also paired splendidly in *Aïda*, and Thornton joined them as another tormented figure, singing Amneris 'with fine power and passion'. Although now and again some tonal flaw would intrude, Mullings could sing 'Celeste Aïda' beautifully. At this time his *forte staccato* was 'like a shot from a gun, and his *mezza voce* ... as delicately expressive as a *cor anglais*'.[234] Indeed on one occasion the Buckman–Mullings teaming was such as to bring 'frequent and fervent "bravi" ' from some Italian cognoscenti in the pit.[235] Beecham's choice of tempi could be erratic. He might so rush things in the scene of triumph as to produce a race between chorus and brass, while in the same performance evoking perfectly the mood of night on the Nile: 'a high, thin note is held in the orchestra, symbol of the eternities of limitless desert sand, of human fears and desires, and of the unwinking gods who take no part in them because they see the whole. Round the note an unseen chorus weaves its song without a lapse of any kind to mar the peace of the scene.'[236]

Beecham's shift to Drury Lane was important practically as well as symbolically: 'the big temple scenery, overwhelming at the Aldwych, made a brave show on old Drury's ample boards, where the frescoed columns could stretch away into the distance against a sapphire sky.'[237] It was at the end of May 1917 that the move took place, one very welcome to Drury Lane's management, which was finding it difficult to maintain the theatre's standards of elaborate spectacle under wartime conditions.[238] It was applauded for quite other reasons by *Era*'s leader-writer (23 May 1917, p. 13), who attached the highest significance both to the move, and to the announcement, 'in Armageddon-time, ... that here at last is National Opera come to stay'. Only the choice of *Otello*, albeit sung in English now, to begin the new era gave pause: 'if only for the sake of sentiment, the first work staged in the National Opera House, and sung by an all-British company should be an all-British work.' To revive *The Boatswain's Mate* or *Critic* for this historic occasion 'would stimulate the public imagination and enormously encourage the native composer'.

But possibly Beecham favoured *Otello* not only for its Shakespearean origins but because it provided a suitably explosive start: 'those tempestuous bars of prelude [were] crashed out by the orchestra ... as though their instruments had been charged with electric fluid',[239] and the excitement was maintained with Mullings's first appearance.[240] Beecham had already conducted *Otello* at the Aldwych, with the indispensable Mullings in the title rôle, the Belgian Auguste Bouilliez as Iago and Nevada as the best Desdemona he had 'seen on any stage', the character's 'gentle helplessness [and] simple pathos [being] rendered with perfect judgment and art'. The 'middle and upper middle registers' of the voice suggested just the right quality of 'tender melancholy', and what it 'lacked in brightness and edge was more than set off by the charm of its subdued and creamy tone'. However, Beecham thought Bouilliez's 'downright delivery and robust deportment ... less suited to the sinuous line of Iago, than to Boris'.[241] He was succeeded by Austin, 'an incarnation of Hunnish hate born of conscious power and thwarted ambition'; though he was also credited with a 'subtle power to mood his voice, even in *piano* singing'.[242] But Mullings, albeit no Zenatello, offered a reading 'instinct with high intelligence'. His rendering of the third act monologue and 'sustained singing in the final scene, were worthy of many tenors with great reputations'.[243] By 1918 he was giving 'a well-balanced performance, not "all out" from the start, as at first, but with something in hand for the big climaxes'. There was 'little fault to find, except now and then a loss of beauty of tone in the more strenuous passages'.[244] His recording of the love duet illustrates the variable quality of his singing, burnished warrior tones leading through rapture into sourness as he misses the sustained A flat at the end of *paradiso* despite an aspirated lunge towards it (he actually sings 'afire'). Beecham recalls holding his 'breath in apprehension of some dire physical disaster' when Mullings 'stormed certain high passages ... But in the centre his voice had ease and uncommon beauty, and his singing of quiet passages had a poetry, spirituality, and intelligence' seldom equalled.[245] He adds that Mullings's Otello 'improved fifty per cent' when Italian language performances gave way to English. Verdi, who wrote to Gailhard, co-director of the Paris Opéra, vehemently opposing the performance of *Otello* there in Italian, would doubtless have been the first to approve the change.[246] In that first Aldwych performance, chorus and principals, Nevada apart, were all accused of pronouncing 'the Italian words like their mother tongue'.[247] The Polunins were thought by one critic to have over-Russianized the Venetian scenery. But another detected Craig's influence in the frescoed hall of Act II: 'The graceful arched screen half-way up stage' opened 'on yew-bordered walks, with the figures of Iago and the tormented Othello in the foreground'. The slender blue columns made 'a charming frame for Cassio's meeting with Desdemona, and later, for the crowd of children, women and sailors who bring greetings to their mistress', forming a picturesque 'semi-circle about the young Desdemona seated in their midst'.[248]

Russian influence, like the Polunins, was inherited from those pre-war Russian seasons when the Beechams brought over productions by Balakirev's protegés never before seen in this country. The result was sensational and gave further stimulus to the idea of a British national opera, similarities between Shakespeare's history plays and this operatic preoccupation with Russian history being instantly recognized. The place which the Russians assigned to the chorus also tied in with this nationalist aspiration, later fostered by the idea of a people's war. Wagner, hitherto the dominant influence, had left audiences unprepared for the way that the chorus might figure as vital dramatic element, even protagonist. While Wagner's impact on Rutland Boughton's Arthurian operas is abundantly clear, the reshaping *of The Immortal Hour* in 1913, with its dramatic use of the chorus, may already owe something to the arrival of the Russians in that year. One reviewer of the 1915 Bournemouth revival commends Boughton's innovation, choral music being seen 'as the legitimate precursor of an English national school'.[249]

It was inevitable, then, that Beecham would add the Russians to his wartime repertoire, especially as the pre-war sets and costumes were still in London, stranded by the war. For the first performance of *Boris* by a British company, Manchester was chosen. This was in May 1916, with Bouilliez in the title rôle. He had appeared at Covent Garden just weeks before the war, in *Pelléas et Mélisande*. He joined Rosing in 1915, and the next year was playing Boris and Iago for Beecham. That was the end of his London career until Beecham rediscovered him in the 1930s and brought him back to Covent Garden to sing in *Louise*. His Boris was 'wonderfully vivid and sympathetic', and 'Radford's scene as Varlaam, the drunken monk, was unexpectedly dramatic'.[250] The 1916 performances were given in French, but thereafter Rosa Newmarch's translation, smoothed out by Paul England (Beecham's texts man) and the principals, enabled every word to be followed by the audience. This made it the more regrettable not to include the scene in Pimen's cell, especially when Edwards's splendid work in the last scene gave an inkling of what had been missed vocally as well as dramatically. The Polish act seemed a poor substitute, and an inexplicable one since, having been omitted by the Russians, new sets and costumes had to be found. However, the garden scene had the charm of a Dulac fairy-tale illustration, 'all bluey-green foliage blurred in a misty moonlight'.[251] And in later performances Thornton unfolded its dramatic purpose, her Marina, 'hard, ambitious, unscrupulous', a Lady Macbeth goading a low-born pretender to dare everything for a throne.[252] By this time, too, Radford, promoted to the title rôle, had taken full emotional measure of the tormented czar. Now the opera was balancing three parties: Boris, Grigori (Hyde 'in fine voice') and the people. Throughout the life of the production the chorus aroused admiration: 'Whether they had their faces or their backs to the conductor, the attack was fearless and the intonation clean, and they behaved like sentient human beings whether they were baiting a noble or trussing a monk or exploiting an idiot ... or being knouted or snowed upon.'[253] Here was no conventional operatic chorus, nor yet an idealized picture of the people. In the way that they projected both suffering and the infliction of suffering they realized Mussorgsky's point about rulers setting the pattern for subordinates.

In 1917, 'rushing, torrential' chorus singing prompted nostalgia for that 'Russian steam-roller' now lost to the Allied cause (mass desertions had rendered the Russian army ineffectual months before the December peace agreement).[254] The Revolution upset Beecham's plans, since it was no longer tactful to mount Glinka's *Life for the Tsar*, which he had already tried out in the concert hall.[255] But good taste and DORA were no longer obstacles to the mounting of Rimsky-Korsakov's *Ivan the Terrible*, complete with those images of a populace drilled by the knout into awe of the tsar which a *Times* reviewer missed from *Boris* (28 September 1917, p. 5). The sensational arrival of Ivan (Parker) on his white charger at the market square, 'a wonder of crimson, vermilion, and blue', was the subject of a full-page illustration in *Sphere* (29 September 1917, p. 259). The sight of men and women kneeling in the street being brutalized by soldiers is so reminiscent of 1915 propaganda images that *The Stage*'s reviewer saw Ivan's Tartar-style ogival helmet as a pickelhaube (27 September 1917, p. 16). He was reminded of Irving rather than Chaliapin by Parker's grippingly histrionic Ivan; though in that final scene of grief over his newly found daughter's corpse he did attain something like Chaliapin's authority. However, when the production returned to London a few months on, extravagance was curbed, and the 'passion-ravaged autocrat' acquired a new 'strength and dignity', even a hint of humour.[256]

The music aroused general enthusiasm: at this time Rimsky-Korsakov was considered 'as richly endowed ... as Wagner himself, perhaps more truly so'.[257] The controversy which had already started on the Continent over his orchestrations of Mussorgsky never impinged on the Beecham productions. Searle was struck by the vivid orchestration: 'The scene of the citizens' rising is tremendous', the harmonic combinations evoking the very spirit of revolt. Again, 'the strings' leaping pizzicato figure' in the storm scene strikes the ear with the distinct force of a downpour.[258] Use of folk-song idiom by both Olga and her lover (Brola and Hyde) and by Olga's girlfriends won favour: 'One could admire the courage of the maidens singing in the presence of the Tsar', and enjoy 'the wild theme of their song in the forest'.[259] Goossens senior exercised firm control over chorus and orchestra. This was the first time he had conducted for Beecham. He had enjoyed a long career with the Carl Rosa, interrupted for a few years conducting for Moody–Manners and others. But Beecham recruited him, entrusting him with this opening performance of the 1917 Drury Lane season.

It is the crumbling of that old world so vividly portrayed in *Boris* and *Ivan* which forms the subject of *Khovanshchina*. Like the other two it was first done in English by Beecham's company in 1917. *The Times* (27 October 1917, p. 9) noted a lack of authenticity about the production. Although the Old Believers dressed the part, they lacked the beards which, amongst other things, they would die to preserve; and why did Norman Allin, as their leader, 'ignore one of their most cherished tenets by giving the blessing with his whole hand?' The movements of the chorus had not the purpose, nor their singing that 'something akin to piety', of the pre-war Russians. *The Stage*, on the other hand, found them quite up to that earlier standard both for 'fullness and volume of tone and vigour in attack, notably in some syncopated passages' (1 November 1917, p. 18). Unfortunately, the example of the Russian season was followed in dropping the second act, thereby creating a dramatic imbalance between the opposing forces and losing in the vacillating Galitsin one of the opera's most fascinating characters. But there was still much to relish. The scenery was 'striking and suggestive, particularly the Red Square, with its gleaming gold cupolas and minarets', through which the Old Believers processed singing their hymns. The hall of Khovansky's country palace spelt reaction, 'built of great trunks of trees, rough hewn and coloured red in barbaric fashion'. It is a fit setting for a despot; and as his women serfs are commanded to sing, amending their sad song to one full of life and gaiety, the old, defeated prince feels a youthful stirring. His Persian slaves must dance: 'And they come stealing down the staircase in their sensuous, filmy, clinging garments of gorgeous orange and yellow' to writhe before him while an assassin lurks to strike. Rimsky-Korsakov's orchestration at this point 'employs the subtle seductiveness of the oboe with telling effect', and Seraphine Astafieva, première danseuse in the 1913 production, arranged the dances brilliantly.[260]

Rimsky-Korsakov's *The Golden Cockerel* was the fourth and last Russian work to be given by Beecham's company. Although not quite on a par with *Sadko*, given by a Russian company at the Coliseum soon afterwards,[261] it was enthusiastically received by a large audience on the first night. Whereas the Russians had relegated the singing to commentary on the dance, this new production had a pantomime flavour. Burlesque won out over satire: King Dodon was thought originally to reflect on Nicholas II, the opera remaining under ban in Russia until after the composer's death. Richardson, who had played old Khovansky, demonstrated versatility with his richly caricatured and finely sung Dodon.[262] He shared the vocal honours with Sylvia Nelis, who sang the seductive queen's music 'with its difficult eastern intervals most beautifully .... The mounting was splendid. Against a background of fantastic Bakstian scenery the brilliant colours and gorgeous silks and stuffs of the Russian and Eastern dresses made a feast for the eye.'[263] The humorous representation of a 'war-breathing army chief' seems to have been received with no sense of irony after four years of carnage.

In 1917, when it was reported that America's entry into the war meant a ban on all German operas at the Met, there was both a smugness that Britain had not been so extreme and a grumble that 'there is still in these Islands too much music by living Huns who have even signed Manifestos of Hate against us'.[264] But at the outset, Britain too had experienced a revulsion against German music, some advocating an 1870 cut-off point, thereby salvaging much of Wagner, while others would have banned it entirely. As the *Graphic* noted (10 July 1915, p. 35), many were glad to see Wagner getting a rest 'not on account of any vindictive war idea that he was necessarily a champion of Teutonic brutality, but because he has been an enormously dominating craze'. Every new reported outrage lent strength to the anti-Wagner camp. O'Mara, asked by a reporter during his 1915 Manchester season 'whether any antipathy was shown by audiences to German operas, ... replied, "Not the least. We are leaving that kind of thing to the enemy. At the same time I want to encourage British opera and British artistes all I can." '[265] But before the end of the season the *Lusitania* was sunk, and the Bryce Report on German outrages had been published, and he told his last night audience that on his next visit there would 'be no German opera in our repertoire'. Declaring that his attitude had changed decisively during the course of the tour as a result of reported atrocities, he was loudly applauded.[266] Later he would relent, performing *Tannhäuser* before a full house on his very first visit to Glasgow.[267] Manners, speaking on the last night of his 1915 Liverpool season, explained how he had purposely avoided 'the heavier operas [because] they were mainly German'; and although Wagner was above nationality, there was the problem of royalties.[268] Protest up north against Wagner's operas being put on led to a plebiscite to find which operas people wanted to see. This resulted in 'an overwhelming majority for Wagner's *Tannhäuser*'.[269] In Liverpool, the wily Kelly adopted a similar method after having numerous requests for Frewin to revive *Tannhäuser*. The result of the ballot was 4632 to 182 in favour, so it was hardly surprising that the new production proved a sell-out.[270]

The melodic freshness and dramatic excitement of *Tannhäuser* made it the most popular of Wagner's operas during the war years. It had a firm place in the Carl Rosa repertoire, though it was not until 1918 that Beecham took up the opera, achieving the biggest house in a season of big houses. Beecham, recognizing that at the time of composition Wagner's reach exceeded his grasp, improved matters with 'judicious and generous application of the pruning knife', and supplied 'spirited and emphatic direction'.[271] He approached it as 'a human story of passions and weaknesses, but somehow transformed by a sort of romantic glow of enthusiasm'. In keeping with this the Venus of Gladys Ancrum, a newcomer to the company though she had sung small parts in Courtneidge's first season, had a warmth which went far to excuse Tannhäuser's dallying with her. This tortured Romantic was impersonated by Mullings, singing with 'reckless virility'. His *mezza voce* was beautiful, but 'in strenuous moments his tone became forced and harsh'.[272] He was 'dramatically unrivalled' as Tannhäuser, says Searle of a later performance, making an interesting point that his best moment vocally was when 'the rejected penitent, bent over his staff, narrates his story. The position is important, because it is when Mr. Mullings throws his head up and back – a characteristic action – that his emission becomes difficult.'[273] Buckman as his good angel, graceful in her pale blue robes, sang with all the bright purity and radiance of tone which the rôle calls for. At the Hall of Song 'her enthusiasm in the song of greeting was infectious', and her defence of Tannhäuser focused the nobility and generosity of the character. The hall made a 'gorgeous if rather gaudy gilt and coloured glass setting for the rich dresses of the Thuringian nobles and their ladies'. A 'lofty cave decked with green-grey stalactite and stalagmite formations' created a suitable atmosphere for Venusberg. The one 'blot on the production' was the backdrop ostensibly representing Venus's palace, but looking more 'like the entrance to a "popular" café – there's no wonder Tannhäuser wanted to get away from it'. But the *Sunday Times* critic (24 March 1918, p. 4), perhaps finding popular cafés congenial, was undistracted by this cloth, registering only 'a scene of great power and beauty'. 'The traditional Covent Garden flat intonation' was avoided in the pilgrims' chorus by quickening the tempo, causing the weary pilgrims to step it out smartly as they crossed the stage. But some of this vitality was lost when Beecham relinquished the baton to Percy Pitt, and a similar slackening of tempo was detected elsewhere. Agnes Nicholls had replaced Buckman as Elizabeth. Her prayer, 'wonderfully pure singing' in those 'silvery ringing tones', was 'taken much too slowly [despite] Pitt's efforts to keep it moving'.[274]

Valkyrie, too, was given for the first time in 1918. Beecham's preference for the lyrical and human over the epic and metaphysical made choice of this portion of *The Ring* inevitable. Whether or not it could be taken 'as an expression of German "Kultur",' noted the *Sunday Times* critic (16 June 1918, p. 2), 'musical London was wonderfully glad to hear it again'. The press at large responded gratefully, though without giving much sense of how it was treated. Possibly the adoption of pre-war Covent Garden sets implies a similarly handed-down production; yet Beecham came to it freshly and effectively, 'each climax being approached by a skilful and perceptive gradation of effect. The singers, too, responded to the inspiriting influence of the conductor'.[275] They easily held their own with the 1914 Covent Garden team, several of them being veterans of Richter's 1908 English *Ring*. In their old parts were Radford (Hunding), Hyde (Siegmund: he had sung the rôle at the Met in 1910) and Thornton, whose 'dramatic delivery of Fricka's wifely rebuke' was one of the highlights.[276] Nicholls had been Sieglinde in 1908, though later playing Brunnhilde on the Quinlan tour. Despite some doubt about whether her voice had the radiance and power to ride the orchestra with Brunnhilde's battle-cry, for Shaw she survived an embarrassingly old-fashioned costume to sing the rôle beautifully.[277] Although Parker's 'articulation was the best in the company, and he put in some fine singing', Shaw thought 'his bright hard voice ... not of the right colour for Wotan'. But another witness thought him 'magnificent in the declamatory passages', and he would be seen retrospectively as 'the best English Wotan'.[278] Another newcomer to her part was Licette, who 'astonished critics and public alike with her highly dramatic Sieglinde (her beautiful low notes being so effective)'.[279] She had the right soft-textured, lyrical voice for the rôle, producing that colour and fullness needed for those great rapturous outbursts. Hyde matched her fervour in their first-act love scene, and his 'rich voice and full-throated ease made a glorious thing of Siegmund's song of spring'. The opera closed the season and Beecham's promise of more novelties next time 'brought shouts of "Lohengrin" and "Parsifal" from the house'. But he 'declared firmly that he was going to give Wagner a rest, and his audiences ought to learn to appreciate other things, instead of hankering after forbidden fruit'.[280]

The company's most important venture into Wagner had already been made at Manchester in 1916 when, 'overlooking the prejudices of war time, [Beecham] roused a big house to a state of enthusiasm' for an English-language

Tristan, making 'a forceful argument for English singing in England'.[281] This, like *Otello*, was only made possible by the availability of Mullings; his first Tristan, with Denhof's company at the Prince of Wales's, Birmingham (September 1913), created a sensation.[282] Beecham's production had been freshly designed by Allinson: 'The curtain went up on a ship with salmon coloured spars which was on the point of being overwhelmed by gigantic waves in chocolate and plum mosaic, with foam like sugar icing on a cake.' Reid adds that later 'the offending backcloth was replaced by a sea in assertive green'.[283] But what was considered 'rather weird' by one critic was found striking by another, especially 'the impressionistic scene of the second act'. The designs, said this *Times* critic, were consistent with 'the attempt to take a fresh view of Wagner's stagecraft'. But the next day the same paper offered a serious qualification: 'daring new scenes contrasted quaintly with conventional dresses ... and old-fashioned properties': even the sofa on which the enraptured lovers had reclined ever since the 1865 première.[284] The singers, however, seemed anxious to get beyond the conventions. Evidently this was not confined to the protagonists, though there was only space to discuss Autran's Brangäne (which she had sung in 1913 at Covent Garden) after a later performance. The special quality she brought lay 'in purely vocal effects – firm, strong notes and sincerity of phrase. In the beautiful passages [during] her lonely watch, there was an other-worldly menace of fate which gave one a shiver.'[285] Still more strikingly, Mullings 'invested the third act with a reality seldom achieved; his sense of the drama of the story enabled him to avoid the effect of weariness too often produced by singers who merely follow the music, and his voice was admirable throughout'. So thought *Athenæum*'s critic (July 1916, p. 349), adding that Beecham's 'sense of the needs of the singers' was not jeopardized for the sake of ravishing orchestral sound. But others thought differently. One found the orchestra 'overpowering, ... causing the soloists in the most strenuous passages, to over-sing themselves in order to be heard'; for another the problem was most acute in the first act, when Tristan has little to do: 'Buckman's singing suffered from too much emphasis, but considering that she had to contend with an exuberant orchestra which rarely distinguished between a *mezzo forte* and a *forte* it was surprising how much she made clear, both of words and music.'[286] Her 'emotional and keenly-sensitive reading' survived sufficiently for Notcutt to rank her in the dramatic passages 'with the greatest Isoldes. She has only one deficiency – namely, lack of *mezza voce*.' But 'Figaro', recalling her Beecham days, emphasizes her exceptional 'command of *mezza voce*';[287] her *Butterfly* recording confirms that, the high B at the end of the lullaby being tapered away in exquisite *mezza voce*.

This production went from strength to strength. When it returned to London later in the year, the protagonists had 'grown in dignity, in emotional power, and in dramatic expressiveness'.[288] With Julius Harrison conducting, Buckman got more out of the first act than most singers, with 'bold use of a resonant voice' and 'great sweeping phrases' in the final duet. Not that Harrison was unduly sparing: the horns were taken aback by his headlong tempo at the start of Act 2, yet the galloping excitement contrasted effectively 'with the passionate intensity of the duet which follows'.[289] This duet was always the overwhelming moment since, differing as their conceptions might be, Buckman and Mullings could match each other in ardour. If hers was 'a more earth-born passion', Mullings brought a quiet, insistent fervour to his rôle, a sense of mystical removal such as Wagner looked for. Above all, the passage was 'not over-sung, but given in a way that all its sweetness came to the palate and all its easefulness fell on the senses'.[290] Cardus reflected that 'nobody has by voice and *presence* made me feel with the intensity of Mullings, the inmost heart and mind of Tristan'. At his first entrance 'he brought with him poignantly tragic foreknowledge; he was the music embodied'. Even his vocal defects somehow carried 'tragic eloquence',[291] and in his closing moments, 'almost too much to be borne',[292] this young giant seemed visibly to waste away.

Before concluding with a look at Beecham's Mozart productions, considered the high-point of his wartime activity, it is worth glancing at contemporary tastes in singing, since changing attitudes to Mozart played a major part in shifting standards. Florid singing was one casualty, *verismo* emerging in reaction to a style which had come to seem at odds with actual human behaviour. The nostalgic, du Maurier's *Trilby* providing a good example, saw *bel canto* as a stylistic *mystery* rather than a mode rooted in the mechanics of voice production and tied historically to a philosophy of performance effectively ousted by the Verdi revolution. It was seen in its decadence as inimical to drama, though du Maurier signals no disapproval in describing some of Trilby's vocal effects: 'It was as if she said: "See! what does the composer count for?".'[293] But this is an indictment of her (or her mentor Svengali's) method. All those trills, roulades and other kinds of *fioritura* must follow a code, must work in harmony with the composer's dramatic design: Jenny Lind was properly chided for decorating Handel in a style more appropriate to Bellini. Nor is this just a matter of musical taste. Another factor to which Trilby (if not du Maurier) seems oblivious is that embellishment is an expressive art, properly taking the audience beyond vocal display to a deepened dramatic or psychological awareness. In the early days it would have been a means towards that favourite theatrical ploy, the prepared surprise. The audience would know something of what to expect in the repeat, but the skilled performer might reach for an unconsidered effect, a moment of keen insight.

Now even the world of Albani and Patti (the latter made a last public appearance in a 1914 wartime matinée, while the former, who had retired in 1911, turned up in another as late as October 1918) was becoming a distant memory. It might seem safe to assume that the new, drab stage world which Beecham perceived as Ibsen's legacy would have little use for the art of gracing.[294] Bourgeois realism displacing the old aristocratic theatre brought performers down from the heights of reflected greatness to a 'flat-land of commonplace existence'. This makes them, laments Beecham's rival Henry Wood, 'afraid of being dramatic, hence they become tame and dull, and unconvincing'.[295] But Wood wrote at a time when various factors had contrived to limit options. The war years accommodated a much greater mixture of styles and far more mannered performances than we are accustomed to nowadays. Thus there was Gwynne Davies, a mid-war Faust at the Vic, whose unabashed *vibrato* (it works very well in his recording of Mascagni's *Siciliana*) would startle a modern audience. More in line with recent tendencies was Hughes Macklin, a leading tenor with the Carl Rosa, of whom Eva Turner had expected 'big things' after he went to Italy.[296] His recordings reveal scant feeling for the Verdian line, but he is far better in French opera. During the 1918 Shaftesbury season his Don José displayed a 'beautiful voice and sympathetic personality', a verdict supported by his recording of the Flower Song. If a touch lacking in ardour, it is pleasingly sung throughout. He rises to the high B, taken smoothly in falsetto, softly as the score requires (it was a fad of British tenors to sing high notes in falsetto).[297] In *Mignon* he proved 'a frank, open-hearted Wilhelm, [supplying] beautiful-toned, free singing'.[298] Again this is borne out by his recording of 'In Her Simplicity'. Since *Mignon*'s staying power has proved far below that of *Carmen*, there is no continuing performance tradition. But Macklin's approach is much more what we should expect from a first-rate tenor of the present day than McCormack's highly mannered version, which does startling things with the tempi to accommodate the most delicate filigree. Which is the better? That McCormack could have reproduced Macklin's style far more readily than Macklin could have managed McCormack's trills and portamenti hardly helps. But style must take account of period and of the composer's known aims. In the present case it seems certain that McCormack comes closer to the 1860s style than Macklin, though the latter follows a score which is already liberal in its options far more literally. But if (or since) the composer reckoned on executants who exercised McCormack-like freedoms, the old problem of the unwritten *appoggiatura* in Mozart's day reappears in another guise.

The fastidiousness of Macklin and Licette coexisted with various kinds of liberty-taking; though even she was subject to mild reproach from Shaw for her handling of 'Dove sono' in a Beecham *Figaro*. He accepts the 'little *liaison* of her own at the reprise', since this helps to mark the emergence from self-pity, though he hopes 'she will creep up to it diatonically instead of chromatically in future'.[299] He knows that this particular trick belongs to Meyerbeer and his followers, not Mozart; but he also knows that the 'existing scores' are not the final Mozartian authority. Shaw would probably have accepted Licette's inclusion of unwritten *appoggiature* in her English-language recording of 'Porgi amor' (1918) as a legitimate way of adding expressiveness to the vocal line. But he is pretty abrasive about Beecham allowing his Susanna (Ellinger) 'not only to transpose passages an octave up, as if he could not stand her quite adequate low notes, but to alter wantonly the end of 'Deh vieni non tardar', a miracle of perfect simplicity and beauty, into what seems by contrast a miracle of artificial commonplace, not to say vulgarity'. Ellinger's offence was probably no more than a conventional cadenza, which would have been the norm during Shaw's days as a regular music critic, and is still to be found in some post-1918 recordings by leading singers (who against the trend regard it, like the *appoggiatura,* as a necessary means towards expressive colour). That apart, he found her not only comfortable above the stave but able to manage that A below evaded by some sopranos. Shaw, of course, was an early campaigner for that purism which had invaded Mozart singing, and Ellinger must have sounded impossibly refractory to his ears. And to others, since the next year she was taken to task for introducing into this same seductive aria 'rallentandos in expected and unexpected places' (this time with the connivance of Percy Pitt). The real issue is whether Ellinger's shifts of tempo were mere self-indulgence or a means of getting at that complexity whereby the deception practised on Figaro is strangely entangled with an intense physical and emotional feeling for him. Since her rendering of the part generally gave satisfaction, there is some ground for assuming the latter.[300] Beecham further offended Shaw by permitting Alfred Heather, in Basilio's aria, 'to perpetrate the most third-class of all operatic tricks, the bawling of the last note an octave up in order to beg a foolish *encore* by a high B flat'. Since Beecham insists on 'getting what his artistic conscience demands, he must really consider that his singers are improving Mozart'.[301] More to the point, Heather had difficulty in getting his song across. This was probably his attempt to impose personality on the abstraction woven (according to Shaw) by Beecham about this song.

Carl Rosa's *Don Giovanni,* awkwardly mixing old and new styles,[302] earned Shaw's displeasure, though he discriminates between a liberty taken by the Don Giovanni (James Pursaill) and one by the Don Ottavio. The former's Serenade is praised for its original treatment and there is no quarrel 'with his unauthorized F sharp at the end, because, for a high baritone with an F sharp which is better than his low D, it is a pardonable flourish, and is not in any case a vulgarity like shouting the last note an octave up, with which Mr. Edward

Davies discredited an otherwise excellent performance of *Il mio tesoro*'.[303] When Jadlowker, in an Odéon recording, borrows the strings' trill in bar 68, he is doing exactly what Rubini had done in 1840; although the detail irritated Wagner,[304] it may well have been one countenanced by the composer himself. It is notable that in a subsequent recording made just before the war, the trill had disappeared, perhaps a victim of the new purism embodied in the radical re-presenting of Mozart at Munich and Vienna. The latter, under Mahler's direction, had seen the elimination of unwritten top notes and cadenzas, though not of such *appoggiature* as seemed to be in the style of the music.[305] But Mahler's more hard-line followers made no such reservations, and they were to influence the performance of Mozart for decades.

The increased attention received by Mozart from the 1890s led inevitably to a concern with authenticity. Beecham himself was caught up in this, though he was far from the new German conservatism.[306] Teyte, for whom he was one of the great interpreters of Mozart, recalls that he 'retained all the traditions', a main cause of Shaw's berating him.[307] He was more in tune with those like Landowska, who believed 'that strict adherence to Mozart's notes was often contrary to his true style'.[308]

This sufficiently positions Beecham in relation to the Mozart controversy. His wartime productions would be judged accordingly, though on the whole they were enthusiastically acclaimed, with *Figaro* outshining 'anything seen on the grand operatic stage in this country within memory'.[309] He had directed an English *Magic Flute* at Leeds in early 1914, shortly before introducing a production in German at Drury Lane. Most of the London principals were German, though Hans Bechstein had also sung Monostatos at Leeds ('less audible in German, as it happened, than he had been in English'), whilst of the Drury Lane Britishers, several were to reappear in the opera seasons of Courtneidge and Beecham. It was regretted that the Leeds production had not been brought to the capital: 'Probably Mr. Beecham thought (with good reason, I admit) that the public would not care to hear opera in English.'[310] But presumably that same public would also have been bored by spoken dialogue in German, so it was replaced by orchestrally accompanied recitative devised by Emil Kreuz, a practice retained even when the opera was given in English. Did Beecham 'flatter himself he knew better than Mozart?', asked Walter Legge years later, strangely echoing Shaw's query at the time, or not so strangely since he had recently discovered Shaw's critique.[311]

Of course in one important respect Beecham clearly knew better than Mozart, the latter being necessarily and completely ignorant of 1914–18 theatrical conditions. And Mozart understood how conditions affect response: had he wanted to present *The Magic Flute* before the Viennese elite, disposal of the spoken dialogue would have been one of several necessary modifications.

By the same token, nineteenth-century German productions of *Figaro* and *Don Giovanni* replaced recitative with spoken dialogue. *Carmen, Faust, Mignon* and *Tales of Hoffmann* are amongst the many operas similarly served, whether by the composer or someone else, but while few people nowadays regret (or even remember) the loss of, say, Gounod's *opéra comique* form, it is another matter for one, as Shaw intones, 'who was not for the XVIII century but for all time'.[312]

The Magic Flute was the first Mozart opera essayed by Beecham's company during the war, and it proved to be the most popular item in the repertoire. That it was given in English was an important factor: 'the audience liked the delicious colloquialisms ... a strong argument in favour of those who would have all their opera sung in the vernacular.' This helped to dispel the 'dire reverence' customarily accorded to a classic, and allowed moments of 'merriment'.[313] On the whole the production was warmly acclaimed, though the striped bathing suits of the three genii were a ludicrous feature retained from the pre-war German version,[314] and the snake was neither phallic nor fearsome, merely comic, 'a sort of pocket edition of Alberic's "Wurm"'.[315] Importantly, the first cast of April 1916 remained largely unchanged over several years, a paradoxical stability produced by the uncertainties of war. Hence a 1918 reviewer could write of the great advance from season to season: 'The secret is, of course, that the players grow in grasp and understanding of their task as time goes on, and so are able to impart more to their audience.'[316] Radford was the perfect Mozart bass, moving easily from the monstrous drolleries of Osmin to the polar opposite of Sarastro, an assumption which transcended vocal means to provide 'a channel for the movement of spiritual and tonal beauty'.[317]

From the outset, 'the old reproach about operatic words being unimportant because always inaudible was swept clean away. Every word, except a few of the hasty and unedifying remarks of Monostatos, was clearly heard, and the most uninitiated had every opportunity of puzzling over the contrast between the high morals of the Queen of Night and her ladies in the first act, and their baseness in the second and third.'[318] Ranalow resumed the rôle of Papageno, perfectly combining 'beautiful tone and clearness of articulation',[319] which he had played in the pre-war Beecham production, but Sylvia Nelis was making her first appearance with Beecham in the testing rôle of Queen of the Night. Although crude lighting caused her to remind one reviewer 'of a Zeppelin being located by searchlight', her voice was 'delightfully round and warm in texture, and the famous F's in alt of the second air were wonderfully pure and true'. But by 1918 she soared rather than climbed to the heights: her execution of the rôle's 'bewildering picchetate was brilliant'.[320] Licette, too, would achieve full power by 1918, though even a year earlier Charpentier's *Louise* had been mounted for her 'as a reward' for the way she played Pamina.[321] Opposite her, D'Oisly was criticized for not marking 'the disconnections of his recitative [with] adequate pauses and points of action. But his Tamino becomes a full-sized heroic figure when facing the great door of horrors at the close.'[322]

Seraglio was introduced in the same season as *The Magic Flute*, the first performance being given in aid of the six children of the Spanish composer Granados, who, with his wife, had been drowned when the *Sussex* was sunk by a U-boat earlier in the year. The evening was anything but sombre, and it is easy to suspect a concealed motive for the event: 'The Spanish colours draped over the circle parapet, rich embroidered hangings falling from the boxes', and the Spanish flavour of the costumes affected by society ladies in the audience and selling programmes all produced 'a gay and gala air'.[323] Spliced together were a brilliant first-night atmosphere and that of a graciously patronized charity matinée, and the resultant haul included four ambassadors, several cabinet ministers and an aristocratic contingent led by the Russian Grand Duke Michael. This is worth pausing over, since it points up the one real difference between Beecham and the other purveyors of wartime opera.

It had been noted in frivolous *Bystander* style (12 January 1916, p. 48) that 'if we didn't have a grand opera season at Covent Garden, that was purely for society; owing to there being no "season," we've got a popular one at the Shaftesbury, more successful than any such thing's ever been in peace-time'. Indeed, when Beecham joined Courtneidge it was seen that, amongst other qualifications, 'His association with the season ... assures it a social backing, without which, for the present at any rate, operatic management is a hazardous occupation.'[324] Beecham had no doubt about opera's need for the support of society. In a speech to the last night audience of the 1916 Manchester season, he expressed disappointment at finding 'that the wealthier portion, upon whose pockets opera must always in the main depend, had been rather neglectful in their support. As an elaborate and costly form of art, opera must have more help from the rich if it is to be established in Manchester on a permanent basis.'[325] When two of his major new productions, *Boris* and *Otello*, were given in French and Italian respectively, the *Musical News* gleefully routed Ernest Newman's weak defence that no worthy translations existed: had it been the available scenery which was inadequate, Beecham would have commissioned new.[326] Although it was thought by some that French was used to accommodate the Belgian Boris, Auguste Bouilliez, *Athenæum*'s music critic (June 1916, p. 300) spotted truer motives: Beecham was offering a quasi-Covent Garden season, as might be judged 'from the fact that there is no exclusive employment of the English language or English singers'.

Beecham himself recognized that 'the aristocrats only really care for opera sung by a bunch of great stars – foreign ones, of course. Give them opera adequately sung by a good cast, a well-staged, well-balanced, artistic production, and they don't care a button about it.'[327] If he could give them few foreign stars, there were foreign languages to feed their 'particular kind of snobbishness'. But when he took over Drury Lane he felt confident enough to abandon the foreign language sop, relying on that taste for scenic design engendered by the Russian seasons to draw in a society audience.[328] That his optimism was justified is an indication of the enormous changes wrought by war. Some years before, when Moody–Manners tried Drury Lane, the season was abandoned through lack of support. Looking back, the *Musical News* (30 June 1917, p. 404) ascribed this to prejudice against a company of proven worth because it played the provinces extensively. So did Beecham, who, although better connected, recognized that the real difference lay in wartime idealism and restriction. It was a happy conjunction of man and moment.

With the move to the Lane there was increasing mention of distinguished patrons. Lloyd George was observed there twice in one week; and gossip columnists could devote paragraphs to 'Picturesque Box-Holders' such as 'the wife of the Spanish Ambassador, in blended sweet-pea hues of chiffon, and Lady Cunard, in emerald satin'.[329] Although Beecham's two-edged attitude towards aristocratic opera-goers suggests a practical rather than ideological motive, what he was engaged in is far removed from the 'opera for all' approach of operators like O'Mara and Moody–Manners. At Liverpool the latter was supplying a popular demand: opera in English at prices ranging from a few pence to a few shillings.[330] Playing at this level for several seasons at the Blackpool Opera House, the O'Mara Company must have felt the draught when in 1918 Beecham booked it for a month at the height of the holiday season. (That Beecham in 1916 had mounted a *Lucia* at Manchester's New Queen's Theatre when O'Mara was giving it at the Gaiety arouses suspicions that he was deliberately seeking to queer the latter's pitch, especially as he never repeated it.) But O'Mara was well cushioned. In 1917, savouring the new opera public appearing 'in the lesser towns', he ascribed growing audiences to the decent wages available for munitions work in the various industrial centres, which gave sections of the working class a fleeting prosperity.[331] Indeed, if Beecham wished to popularize opera in this country he was taking a wrong route, as fellow-musicians as well as theatrical businessmen could have told him. Stanford, confident that national opera 'must come', saw that it needed to be 'kept free from intrigue and commercialism'.[332] From another perspective, the success which Kelly had been enjoying with opera in his Liverpool theatres had taught him: 'If you want to make music popular you must popularise it. The day of high prices is dead and gone. And so grand opera must fall into line. That's why I have been letting it out to the masses at from 4d. to 3s. Now you can go down to the docks and hear the dock labourers humming melodies from grand opera.'[333]

But if the Granados carnival was designed to appeal to socialites rather than dockers, there was nothing meretricious about Beecham's choice of opera. This was his first shot in what was to become a prolonged campaign to win public favour for *Seraglio*, a campaign which he would lose for all the care lavished upon the opera's presentation.[334] This time the *Singspiel* character was retained, the spoken dialogue being embellished with topical reference which displeased those for whom the Stephanie–Mozart combination had become sacrosanct.[335] Again, in the 1917–18 seasons, updated 'gags about dug-outs and the butter shortage', 'coupons', or 'medical boards' were expected to have Mozart 'turning in his grave'.[336] But Pedrillo is as entitled to ad lib as Shakespeare's Porter (or Papageno when the spoken dialogue is retained). As Constance, Nevada produced Mozartian singing which was 'exquisite in finish, beauty of phrasing and purity of tone'; she combined clarity of line with easy mastery of the 'profusion of ornament'. 'The brightness and lightness with which the *ensembles* were handled came from the fact that the singers had made themselves at home with the musical language', and this found visual expression in the luxurious colour and airy fantasy which blended stunningly in the Act II garden scene, 'a thing like Mozart's arias in which one can enjoy a thousand details without being distracted by them'. It was the work of Adrian Allinson, whose 'strong blues, greens, yellows, reds, and mauves, ... and his curious Japanesy sort of perspective, give his stage pictures the flat effect of brilliant mosaics'. The palace interior in the last scene impressed 'with the simple sweeping lines of its arches, the grey decorations on the white walls, and the great orange silk lamp hanging from the roof'.[337] Curiously, by mid-1918 this had been abandoned for a new setting which, though 'it was obviously "modern," and therefore in keeping with the spirit of the whole production', wavered uncertainly between being 'daringly Cubist or merely mildly post-impressionist'.[338] Possibly this was part of an attempt to impress the virtues of the opera on a resistant public, though it implies that the problem of making serious and comic elements cohere had not been solved.

During the war Mozart revaluation was by no means complete: the composer's 'attempts to convey this or that emotion seem quaint to a generation that knows Wagner, modern Italy, and the Russian school – perhaps the greatest of all; crises, whether of temperament or of action, are hardly convincing as represented by the ancient school in vocal gymnastics and airs and graces'. Thus *Athenæum* (August 1916, p. 392) apropos of *Seraglio*. The same idea that 'music rather than meaning' held sway in Mozart's (and Gluck's!) day persists in C. S. Lewis's view that it would be unthinkable to value one of his operas 'chiefly for the plot'.[339] Beecham's company did much to show that it would be far more unthinkable to treat the plot as unimportant, as if it was mere accident that *Figaro* had not been composed for the concert hall. Where disharmonies between Mozart and librettist occur, they reflect that familiar tension between what is being said and what lies behind the words. In this sense the dialectic is as compelling as in any of those other styles alluded to by *Athenæum*'s critic. Arnold Bennett's worry about a lack of drama in the last act of Beecham's *Figaro* ('Musically it is as good as the rest') addresses precisely this point.[340]

Beecham had decided on *Figaro* as the climax of a spectacular summer season to mark the company's removal from the Aldwych to Drury Lane, hiring Nigel Playfair to impart 'the style and gesture of the Théâtre Française'. He shifted from old Spain (a concession to *l'ancien régime* censorship) to the France of Beaumarchais's day,[341] borrowing from the latter, as Mahler had done, [342] to clarify the action. Additions were covered by changing recitative to spoken dialogue, entailing a new translation. The result was 'the most vivacious and yet the most pathos-shaded' *Figaro* that Cardus ever saw; 'finer and lighter [and] closer to the comedic spirit which observes the way of the civilized world and doesn't protest too much'.[343] Even for Shaw, despite complaints to Bennett at one performance,[344] it was 'charming; and very little additional care and understanding would make it great', which is hard to square with his claim that Beecham could not distinguish between Mozart and his 'dead as mutton' contemporaries, reducing 'the dramatic and rhetorical parts' to mere decoration. In such matters the reliability of someone who dropped in half-way through the performance is perhaps open to doubt.[345]

Some caution needs to be exercised too over Reid's claim that, following 'the production's first heady impact, people began to wonder whether Rumbold's designs were not, perhaps, on the exuberant side'.[346] For the next season Searle found 'Hugo's dresses and scenery ... even more astonishing and delightful', though she had seen all along how 'costumes and towering wigs [were] monstrous edifices to the eccentricities and extravagances of l'ancien régime. The paniers worn by the fine dames seem expressly designed effectually to prevent the doing of anything that might be useful to themselves or to others.'[347] (The effect would have been the more striking at a time when the rich had consciously set idleness in abeyance.) She loved the boudoir 'with its Cupid-panelled walls and richly-decked bed in a curtained alcove', painted by Alfred Craven under Rumbold's direction, Beecham politicly announcing at curtain fall on the opening night, 'that the designer of the dresses and scenery "which had found such favour with the audience," was an officer in the Army, wounded, and unable to appear'.

Characteristically, Beecham exaggerates in recalling that the *Figaro* cast 'contained hardly one of the better vocalists of the company'.[348] It contained several, including Licette as the Countess. (Later the part was assigned to Nicholls, cherished by Maggie Teyte as one of the two finest Mozart assumptions that she ever saw.[349]) If to begin with Licette's Countess, coquetting 'prettily with Cherubino', seemed 'not quite to the manner born', she subsequently exhibited 'easier and more unconscious grace', giving her panier 'an undulating, swan-like tilt that is quite captivating'.[350] Lockhart recalled the artistry bestowed on her principal arias: 'Her voice floated through the theatre with supreme beauty and an ease I have never heard equalled.'[351] But not always: one performance found her 'Porgi amor' fogged by the din of an air raid.[352] Austin's Count, 'a red-haired exquisite who certainly "jewelled his corruption with fine manners," as the illuminating programme synopsis had it', gave pleasure from the start with his 'stage deportment and subtlety of acting'.[353] For Cardus, no other impersonator of the Count 'has passed across the closing scene of the opera with half of Austin's grace of bearing and suggestion of courtly cynicism'.[354] Ranalow and Ellinger 'gave Figaro and Susanna just the right air of being quite aware of the ridiculousness and worthlessness of their master and mistress, but of being too well bred to say so, even to each other'.[355] Reference back to Beaumarchais would no doubt have wound up the social tension, but apparently not at the cost of crudifying the Mozartian style of half hint and suggestion. There were no weak links: 'Bessie Tyas, a handsome Cherubino, warbled "Voi Che Sapete," in Italian, very daintily', while Clytie Hyne's Marcellina was 'by no means the decrepit sibyl of Susanna's description, but a magnificently attired lady ladies' maid with an air – and a lofty wig'. It was not worth obscuring glimpses of the pervasive sexual tension by this use of Italian, but Marcellina compensates: the part is frequently spoilt by a too broad approach, rendering unnecessarily absurd the lady's marital designs on Figaro.

As ever, Beecham 'aimed at perfection of ensemble, a thing unattainable' when stars are glorified. His principals played 'with a give-and-take to one another that avoided personal display' and brought out the humanity and emotional seriousness of the comedy. Hence the sense 'that the audience was listening to the work as a whole, not for certain numbers'. Shaw, who had *not* listened to it as a whole, was more patronizing: 'It was pathetic and delightful to see the extraordinary pleasure of the audience, many of whom seemed to be discovering Mozart and going almost silly with the enchantment of it.'[356] But perhaps the most telling comment on audience response to this production is that the opera has been 'restored to its former rank as perhaps the most popular of all operas'.[357]

Yet for all its very substantial achievement, the Beecham enterprise would soon fizzle out. Whether, had he not been distracted by financial entanglements, Beecham could have sustained it into the 1920s and beyond is a moot point. In an appreciation written at the time of Beecham's death, Cardus refers to some character limitation which made him 'unable to create a school or an influence of lasting use tangible enough to be handed down'.[358] Klein had seen the consequence of over-dependence 'upon the social equation', something which would last until opera was 'released from the shackles of the foreign tongue and driven right home to the hearts of the people through the medium of their own good Anglo-Saxon vernacular'.[359] Unfortunately, Beecham declined to grasp wholeheartedly Klein's logic, despite the opportunity which the war provided. *Era*'s leader-writer (16 August 1916, p. 11) found it 'unthinkable' that his wartime principals 'should be excluded in the future from filling the chief rôles in ... Covent Garden itself, in the "grand" season'. Alas, their view that preserving the original words at the expense of the original intelligibility was fallacious made them heretics, and once the old guard had regained its grip on metropolitan opera, both they and their heresies were consigned to the outer darkness of suburbs and provinces. Of the very first post-war season at Covent Garden, Francis Toye complained 'that the operas cannot be understood. There is, apparently, a magic about Italian – often bad Italian sung by English men and women – that enables the management to' escalate seat prices.[360] This returns us to the starting point of the chapter. The BNOC, into which Beecham's singers reconstituted themselves in 1922, was destroyed out of ideological motives by Higgins and his fellow Covent Garden syndics. Beecham would have been the only one with the necessary standing and resources to save the situation. But ironically, even had he been available, his pragmatism made him an unconsidered ally of Higgins. When, in late 1917, his financially disastrous season at Drury Lane was wound up a fortnight before schedule, Beecham was scathing about London's over six million inhabitants, notably the middle classes who were as indifferent to opera as they were ignorant of it. Their mark was the 'pictures or a music-hall'.[361] Perhaps their pockets could better afford these despised media (Shaw complained about how much he had paid to see Beecham's *Trovatore*), neither of which was indifferent to opera, though the 'silent' aspect of the former was a major handicap in the several wartime attempts to capture opera on film.[362] Ironically, during the very year in which Beecham made his remark, Turner's English Opera played at the Golder's Green Hippodrome as part of the house's policy of providing its audience with alternate doses of variety and legitimate theatre. The company was subject to the music hall's twice-nightly system: following up *Rigoletto* with *Trovatore* on the same evening must have been a severe strain.[363] But it shows that the popularizing of opera, even amongst Londoners, was a realizable ambition. Clearly opera could hardly be offered at cinema prices. But the need for state aid was already being urged in 1917, to bring Britain into line with continental practice.[364] It was urged not as a means of buying international prestige but of providing national nourishment. Higgins would have been no more interested in that, with all its missionary implications, than are his present-day counterparts. Increases in Covent Garden's share of the arts budget are not conditional on the automatic television presentation of each new production, any more than the theatre's recent temporary closure resulted in hostages to fortune being given by provincial visits. Availability must be a precondition of popularity. Beecham may have been too inclined to equate cost with quality, reluctant to recognize the way that limited resources will sometimes stimulate artistic adventure, but even after establishing Drury Lane as the headquarters of British opera, his commitment to provincial touring remained total. His visits to the north, says Cardus, set 'the local "Watch Committees" by the ears with a sensuous exoticism of stage production never before witnessed in these places of nonconformist darkness'.[365] But Cardus is scarcely persuasive about Beecham's raised standards spoiling the market for other touring companies in the northern cities. There is scant sign of this happening during the war, when the only real casualty was the Moody–Manners company; but the latter's favourite stopping-place was taken over by Frewin not Beecham, who never visited Liverpool. Indeed Manners, credited with having done 'much of the "spade work"' preceding the wartime boom, had headed no shoestring operation. When his theatrical properties were auctioned in 1918, they included 'full equipment for 60 operas ... and 200 tons of scenery'.[366]

But for various reasons, wartime achievements failed to bring about any long-term reshaping of opera's place in British culture, though they offer much food for reflection. In abeyance was the circuitous notion that opera is expensive, therefore rarefied and not of the same order as other drama, its mystique preserved by playing it in a language not understood by audiences. That last is crucial: the WNOC's Christmas 1998 television presentation of *L'Incoronazione di Poppea* was interestingly conceived as soap opera, but the popularizing intention hopelessly crippled by giving it in Italian. (It is a paradox that insistence on the original language in preference to one understood by audiences shows insensitivity to the importance of language in opera.) Another factor was the unavailability of international stars, though as Callas pointed out, they are no guarantee of quality: 'The temptation is for the artist to arrive in time to sing, collect the money, and rush off – no time for rehearsals, consultations, discussion.'[367] At least their absence disposed of a potential artistic and a certain economic imbalance. It also scotched what has become increasingly an argument in favour of presenting opera in the original language: that the globe-trotting performer will learn no other. It became clear that the latter was not essential, perhaps not even desirable. Attentive and musicianly singers, acting with conviction, could produce memorable performances. In short, it meant a more effective, if only because more accessible, delivery of the drama, and at a more economic rate. In these factors lay the secret of wartime opera's burgeoning success, in itself a devastating reply to the claim that consequential theatre disappeared for the duration.

Notes

1. Mullings's relationship with Beecham began at Sheffield (13.10.13), when he was singing the title rôle of *Tristan* in Beecham's newly acquired Denhof Company. He also sang in Holbrooke's ill-fated *Dylan* during Beecham's 1914 Drury Lane season. Several others in that cast, Frederic Austin, Robert Radford and Doris Woodall, would become Beecham regulars.
2. *World* 27.10.14, 64; *Era* 13.3.18, 1.
3. *Era* 12.8.14, 10.
4. *Manchester Guardian* 17.5.16, 4.
5. *Era* 24.11.15, 15.
6. Maisie Gay, *Laughing through Life* (Hurst & Blackett, 1931), p. 205.
7. *Era* 12.7.16, 14; *Era* 9.8.16, 7.
8. *Era* 24.3.15, 12; *Era* 31.3.15, 12.
9. *Era* 14.2.17, 6.
10. *Era* 2.8.16, 13.
11. *Era* 10.5.16, 21; *Era* 30.5.17, 9.
12. *Era* 31.10.17, 12.
13. *Era* 7.7.15, 13.
14. *Stage* 6.7.16, 18.
15. H. T. Parker, *Eighth Notes* (1922, rept. Freeport, New York: Books for Libraries, 1968), p. 84.
16. George Graves, *Gaieties and Gravities* (Hutchinson, 1931), p. 141. Similarly the protagonist of Ellis's *Little Bit of Fluff* (French, 1922), p. 13, has been to Covent Garden without noticing which opera was being performed: 'no decent person ever does – it's bad form.'
17. 'Lancelot', *Referee* 9.5.15, 5; *Athenæum* 19.6.15, 558.
18. *Athenæum* 5.6.15, 513; *The Times* 31.5.15, 9.
19. Henry Wood, *My Life of Music* (1938, rept. Gollancz, 1948), p. 265.
20. Teyte, sister of gifted popular composer James Tate, scored in the part with the BNOC at Covent Garden in 1921. She was not seen over here during the war apart from a few patriotic appearances (singing 'Your King And Country Want You' at the Empire: *Referee* 13.9.14, 3).
21. *World* 8.6.15, 828; *The Times* 1.6.15, 5.
22. *Graphic* 5.6.15, 738.
23. *Sunday Times* 6.6.15, 4.

24. 'Lancelot', *Referee* 6.6.15, 5.
25. Montagu-Nathan, addressing the Russian Society at the Boudoir Theatre, recognized the possibilities but dismissed them, considering German atrocities no 'fit and proper subject for operatic treatment' (*Era* 7.7.15, 9).
26. *The Times* 16.7.15, 11.
27. *Sunday Times* 7.2.15, 4. D'Argel, an excellent and resourceful soprano, was with the Frewin-Phillips Company 1916–18. In the latter year she sang Lakmé at Liverpool to 'thunders of applause'. She had already sung the rôle successfully abroad, but this was its first production in English (*Era* 13.3.18, 1).
28. A *Times* reviewer (4.5.17, 9) expresses regret that the Carl Rosa Company had found triple assumptions impractical in 1917, but for his 1916 production Beecham appeared strangely indifferent.
29. In the autumn season, Alfred Heather took over Hoffmann without engaging with essentials, 'his futile pursuit of an ideal' (*Sunday Times* 10.10.15, 4).
30. *Era* 17.3.15, 11; though he was temporarily out of favour in Paris (26.1.16, 11).
31. *Era* 17.3.15, 11.
32. Sydney Grew, *Favourite Musical Performers* (Edinburgh/London: Foulis, 1923), p. 98.
33. *Ibid.*, p. 99.
34. *Musical Opinion* (June 1920), 715.
35. *Era* 17.3.15, 11; *World* 16.3.15, 498; *Sunday Times* 14.3.15, 4.
36. *Athenæum* 23.10.15, 301; *Era* 17.5.16, 13.
37. Mosco Carner, *Madam Butterfly: A Guide to the Opera* (Jenkins, 1979), p. 70.
38. Courtneidge–Beecham presumably resisted dilution, 'Lancelot' (*Referee* 10.10.15, 5) noting how Blamey 'accentuated the thoughtless callousness of Pinkerton in the first act'.
39. *Era* 3.10.17, 1.
40. *Athenæum* 3.16, 150. An excellent Puccini tenor, he achieved a fine contrast in *Boris* as the crafty Shuisky and the pathetic idiot.
41. *Era* 23.6.15, 9; *Era* 2.2.16, 11.
42. *Era* 12.5.15, 9.
43. Graham Oakes, 'English Speaking Basses and Baritones, 4', *Record Collector* 37 (1992), 138–40 (139).
44. They did not record the final duet, though the *Sunday Times* critic (2.5.15, 4) hoped it would be included. Divas usually declined 'to be dragged about in a sack', but there would have been less temperamental nonsense at the Shaftesbury, and perhaps too much regard for dramatic effect to risk

Santley's experience in Barcelona, where, playing Rigoletto for the first time, he enthusiastically ripped open the sack and revealed a moustachioed face to the audience (Charles Santley, *Student and Singer* (rept. Arnold, 1893), p. 240). There had been a surprise inclusion at Covent Garden's 1894 international season (G. Bernard Shaw, *The Bodley Head Bernard Shaw: Shaw's Music,* vol. III, ed. Dan H. Laurence (The Bodley Head, 1981), p. 246), but thereafter it disappeared until their full post-war revival in 1924 (Dyneley Hussey, *Verdi* (Dent/Dutton, 1940), p. 77).

45. *World* 11.5.15, 732.
46. *Graphic* 16.10.15, 510. After the experience of several more war years, the same weekly could declare: 'grand opera sung in any language but our own is needless' (8.6.18, 698).
47. *Sunday Times* 31.1.15, 4.
48. *Era* 12.7.16, 13. This move lay behind Raymond Roze's season of opera in English at Covent Garden in the autumn of 1913, though Rosenthal claims that Roze's primary motive was to promote his own pageant-opera, *Joan of Arc* (Harold Rosenthal, *Two Centuries of Opera at Covent Garden* (Putnam, 1958), p. 378). This received a gala performance at the Paris Opéra with Marthe Chenal in aid of the Franco-British Red Cross (*Era* 28.11.17, 1). Earlier (15.3.16, 16) Roze's short opera, *Arabesque,* played at the Coliseum.
49. Christopher Stone, *From Vimy Ridge to the Rhine: The Great War Letters,* ed. G. D. Sheffield and G. I. S. Inglis (Ramsbury, Wilts.: Crowood Press, 1989), p. 153.
50. 'Lancelot', *Referee* 20.6.15, 5.
51. *Choir,* 6.16, 135.
52. Alan Jefferson, *Sir Thomas Beecham* (MacDonald and Jane's, 1979), p. 159.
53. *Era* 7.7.15, 13.
54. *Era* 29.12.15, 14.
55. *Era* 7.7.15, 13.
56. *Era* 29.12.15, 14. Beecham observes that by the end of the nineteenth century Britain boasted nearly 5000 choral societies, the best of them led by people with no academic training but 'a refined sense of vocal tone, an appreciation of the meaning of words, and the potentialities of them as carriers of sound' (*A Mingled Chime* (Hutchinson, 1944), p. 66).
57. *South Wales Evening Post* 3.3.61, 6.
58. Hermann Klein, *Thirty Years of Musical Life in London* (Heinemann, 1903), p. 401. Cowen's *Signa* had been translated into Italian for its Milan première the previous year, and was now given in that language; Emil Bach's *Lady of Longford,* with a book by Augustus Harris himself, was nevertheless turned into French.

59. J. Daniel Chamier, *Percy Pitt of Covent Garden and the B.B.C.* (Arnold, 1938), p. 139.
60. Joanna Kilmartin, 'Space-age Wagner', *Observer* (colour suppt) 29.7.73, 17; W. J. Henderson, *The Art of Singing* (New York: Dial Press, 1938), p. 166.
61. *Era* 22.12.15, 17.
62. Robert Courtneidge, *'I Was an Actor Once'* (Hutchinson, 1930), p. 221.
63. *Referee* 9.5.15, 3.
64. *Stage* 15.4.15, 20. Charles Layne, a principal tenor with Castellano, later introduced *Trovatore* into revue (*Why, Certainly!*), singing 'Home To Our Mountains' with Eva Layne, formerly with Turner's company (*Era* 21.6.16, 14).
65. Liverpool, where the wartime growth in opera appreciation was as marked as anywhere, saw the Charsley company for a fortnight in 1918, under the auspices of W. W. Kelly, in addition to the extensive Turner season; and it was booked there from the following Boxing Day for 16 weeks, succeeded by a similar stint from the Carl Rosa (*Era* 12.6.18, 8; *Era* 16.10.18, 8).
66. According to Charles Manners there had been over 400 English-speaking singers in German companies before the war (*Era* 11.12.18, 8).
67. *Era* 9.1.18, 6.
68. 'The Fascination of Opera', *Music Masterpieces* 3 (12.11.25), 96.
69. *Daily Sketch* 3.5.18, 7. Carl Rosa, like other companies, advertised for dischargees to replace mobilized choristers, serious mutilation notwithstanding, 'so long as they have decent voices' (*Era* 10.7.18, 8).
70. *Era* 13.9.16, 21.
71. Charles Reid, *Thomas Beecham* (Gollancz, 1962), p. 166.
72. *Era* 26.12.17, 6.
73. *Era* 16.8.16, 8.
74. Reid, *Thomas Beecham*, p. 166.
75. Eugene Goossens, 'Remembering Beecham', *Opera* 12 (1961), 238–9/281 (281).
76. *Stage* 13.8.14, 24; Perceval Graves, 'The Moody–Manners Partnership', *Opera* 9 (1958), 558–64.
77. *Era* 26.8.14, 9; *Era* 2.9.14, 8.
78. *Era* 17.10.17, 9.
79. *Era* 23.10.18, 8. Beecham records 'that Wagner was the favourite composer of that section of the audience which was in khaki' (*A Mingled Chime*, p. 161), receiving numerous letters 'from soldiers at the front' in favour of retaining *Tristan* (Reid, *Thomas Beecham*, p. 173).
80. Reid, *Thomas Beecham*, p. 180.

81. *Era* 10.4.18, 11; *Era* 31.7.18, 11.
82. *Musical Times* 1.11.15, 679. Lena Ashwell notes that in 1917 Tubb's 'beautiful voice, joyous manner, splendid vitality, and all-pervading good humour' delighted the troops in France (*Modern Troubadours* (Gyldendal, 1922), p. 135).
83. *Era* 3.10.17, 1; 'Lancelot', *Referee* 30.9.17, 3.
84. 'My Favourite Operatic Part', *Music Masterpieces* 3 (12.11.25) 86; *Stage* 4.10.17, 16; 'Figaro', *Musical Opinion* 6.20, 714.
85. *Era* 10.10.17, 8.
86. Rosenthal, *Two Centuries*, p. 388. This even excels *The Times*'s pretence (16.6.16, 11), in greeting Beecham's *Tristan* as 'First Wagner Opera in London Since War Began', that nothing outside the West End exists. In fact, *Tannhäuser* was given during Turner's annual visit to the Dalston in 1915 (*Stage* 4.3.15, 20). So was Balfe's *Satanelle*, apparently its only wartime appearance in London, both having disappeared from the 1916 repertoire.
87. Edward J. Dent, *A Theatre for Everybody* (Boardman, 1945), p. 32.
88. Dent, *A Theatre for Everybody*, p. 68.
89. Victor Gollancz, *Journey Towards Music* (Gollancz, 1964), p. 92.
90. Dent, *A Theatre for Everybody*, pp. 68–9.
91. Stephen Fay, 'A Night at t'Opera', *Sunday Times* (Magazine) 12.11.78, 73.
92. There was a tradition of such substitute endings from at least 1868 (Santley, *Student and Singer*, p. 285), though the Vic's introduction of current expressions like 'Hitchy koo' earned adverse comment (*Era* 16.10.18, 5). Presumably the Schumann interpolation had been used in the Vic's October 1914 performances, but the idea was borrowed from Arturo Spizzi's *Daughter* with which he opened a five-opera season at Stoll's Middlesex the previous month. Principals included Blamey and Florence Morden, while his Grand Patriotic Chorus (recently at the Coliseum under Leslie Stuart) was now conducted by Frewin (*Referee* 13.9.14, 7).
93. *Era* 4.12.18, 8.
94. It was left to the John Ridding Company to revive *Lucrezia Borgia* (at the Central Pier, Morecambe), prompting *Era*'s reviewer 'to wonder why such music has lain for so long "on the shelf"' (4.9.18, 8).
95. Hermann Klein, *The Golden Age of Opera* (Routledge, 1933), p. 37.
96. Dent, *A Theatre for Everybody*, p. 72.
97. Gollancz, *Journey Towards Music*, p. 97.
98. Dent, *A Theatre for Everybody*, p. 69.
99. *Era* 31.1.17, 11.
100. *Era* 24.4.18, 8. Marleyn, known chiefly on the concert platform, in 1896 (aged 20) had sung Mephistopheles (*Era* 9.10.18, 9).

101. *Era* 22.12.15, 17; *Referee* 17.12.16, 5.
102. *Era* 7.3.17, 8.
103. *Era* 4.7.17, 8.
104. *Era* 11.4.17, 7.
105. *Era* 28.3.17, 8.
106. *Era* 17.4.18, 8; *Era* 8.5.18, 5.
107. *Era* 26.9.17, 8, 11.
108. *Musical News* 15.12.17, 378. Beecham's mercurial temperament made his public utterances a mass of contradictions. In a closing speech to the audience he reasonably claimed that the 36-week Shaftesbury season would make 'a sufficient answer to those who have always maintained that we could never do anything worth while in opera without foreign help ... At any rate, English opera was now an established fact.'
109. *Era* 9.10.18, 9.
110. *Era* 19.9.17, 8; *Era* 11.7.17, 8.
111. Searle, *Era* 16.5.17, 1.
112. *Era* 9.5.17, 1; *Era* 16.5.17, 1.
113. *Era* 4.7.17, 5.
114. *Era* 6.6.17, 9; *Era* 9.5.17, 9.
115. 'Lancelot', *Referee* 20.5.17, 6.
116. Shaw, *Shaw's Music*, vol. III, p. 708; *Era* 13.6.17, 7.
117. *Era* 22.5.18, 10; *Era* 15.5.18, 13.
118. *Era* 9.5.17, 9; *Era* 23.5.17, 8.
119. *Referee* 13.5.17, 3.
120. Apart from an appearance in the Carl Rosa Jubilee Matinée, singing an excerpt from *Carmen* (*Era* 12.6.18, 22).
121. Eva Turner, 'Recollections of a Great Career', *Record Collector* 35 (1990), 243–9.
122. Patti had virtually given up theatre-going for the past four years, though she attended a matinée of *Maid of the Mountains* a few months later (Newton, *Referee* 23.9.17, 3).
123. *Times* 15.5.17, 3.
124. Searle, *Era* 23.5.17, 1.
125. Its composer, Benedict, a native of Stuttgart, only came to Britain when he was 31 but stayed for another 50 years, becoming naturalized.
126. Neville Cardus recalls that Hedmondt (1857–1940), despite 'a voice that held the top notes only by strenuous physical convulsion, was an intense demon-possessed Tannhäuser until the third act, when he achieved a most tragic sense of discharge of evil and of all manly self-reliance' (*Autobiography* (Collins, 1947), p. 246).
127. *Era* 27.3.18, 8; *Era* 15.5.18, 13.

128. *Era* 12.6.18, 5. Philpot's librettist, William Miller, indicated that cutting had impaired cohesion; though he also conceded dramatic shortcomings through his unwillingness to fictionalize (*Era* 19.6.18, 4).
129. Angus Heriot, 'Emile Zola as Librettist', *Opera* 11 (1960), 595–9 (596).
130. *Graphic* 26.5.17, 632.
131. *Era* 25.11.14, 14; *Era* 14.7.15, 8.
132. It develops Françoise's apostrophe to the blade, *L'Attaque du moulin* (Paris: Choudens Fils, 1898), p. 111.
133. Searle, *Era* 23.5.17, 1. For her, Winckworth had done 'nothing better than his powerful study of Merlier, the old miller'.
134. *Era* 17.5.16, 8.
135. *Ibid.*, *Era* 10.10.17, 8.
136. *Era* 19.1.16, 11, 13.
137. W. A. R., *Musical News* 2.3.18, 76. James also gave a dramatic interpretation of the high priest in *Lakmé* (*Era* 13.3.18, 1). In 1915, his intense singing of the Wagner rôles in O'Mara's Manchester season had won high praise from Duncan, *Musical Standard* 8.5.15, 358; *Musical Standard* 15.5.15, 379.
138. *Era* 24.2.15, 10.
139. *Era* 5.1.16, 5. The company included Archibald, Hyde, Agnes Nicholls, and Flintoff Moore, and the prices were held at between 4d. and 3s.
140. *Era* 1.3.16, 10; *Era* 8.3.16, 10.
141. *Era* 14.11.17, 10.
142. *Era* 24.2.15, 10; *Era* 19.5.15, 8.
143. P. G. Hurst, *The Golden Age Recorded* (Lingfield, Surrey: Oakwood Press, 1963), p. 108.
144. *Era* 17.7.18, 8; *Musical Times* 2.15, 107.
145. There were 65 according to the *Musical Times*, which adds that she 'prides herself on having been a different Carmen for each'. During this final tour she exceeded her 2000th performance in the rôle, her 'shrewd witchery quite opposed to the cheap flaunting frivolity of your ordinary Carmens' (Duncan, *Musical Standard* 8.5.15, 358). She also sang Cherubino in the Manchester *Figaro*.
146. Robert Potterton, 'Zelie de Lussan', *Record Collector* 17 (1967–8), 173–7 (174, 176); 'Joseph O'Mara', *Record Collector* 19 (1970–1), 33–41 (39).
147. On his next visit he brought *Huguenots*, with Boland as a fine Raoul (*Manchester Guardian* 13.5.16, 6), and a *Lucia* in which Morden showed herself 'a master of the florid style without being at all the slave of it' (Langford, *Manchester Guardian* 4.5.16, 10). The Allington Charsley company also staged *Huguenots*, and in mounting *The Barber of Seville* seems to have been the only company during the war to essay Rossini (*Era* 16.10.18, 8).

148. *Era* 28.4.15, 8. Duncan, *Musical Standard* 8.5.15, 358, more conventionally complained that it was out of date, 'formal and pedantic'.
149. *Era* 27.3.18, 13.
150. *Era* 16.9.14, 11.
151. 'Lancelot', *Referee* 20.9.14, 7; a view confirmed by Hermann Klein, *Musicians and Mummers* (Cassell, 1925), p. 198.
152. *Era* 16.9.14, 11.
153. *Referee* 27.9.14, 7.
154. *Era* 16.19.18, 8.
155. *Era* 13.10.15, 10.
156. *Stage* 3.2.16, 23.
157. *Era* 6.10.15, 15; *Stage* 6.1.16, 18.
158. In a letter of November 1915 he recalled his attempt, through performance at Covent Garden 'of well-translated masterworks, to induce English talent to create national operas' (Christopher Fifield, *True Artist and True Friend* (Oxford: Clarendon Press, 1993), p. 451).
159. *Athenæum* 9.10.15, 250. But in a fragment of recorded table-talk Beecham declared: 'I have ... sufficiently sensuous a nature to think that the spirit of Shakespeare is greatly enhanced by music such as this' (Reid, *Thomas Beecham*, p. 177).
160. *Era* 15.5.18, 5.
161. *Musical Times* 1.11.15, 679.
162. *Era* 3.7.18, 12.
163. Searle, *'Era' Annual 1917*, p. 41.
164. Rupert Bruce Lockhart, 'Miriam Licette (1885–1969)', *Opera* 20 (1969), 856–8 (856).
165. *The Times* 4.10.15, 11.
166. *Era* 19.7.16, 15.
167. 'Lancelot', *Referee* 17.10.15, 5.
168. 'Lancelot', *Referee* 31.10.15, 5; *Sunday Times* 31.10.15, 4.
169. Beecham, *A Mingled Chime*, p. 134.
170. *Era* 16.5.17, 1.
171. Cf. Frederick Ranalow in *Music of All Nations* 15 (n. d.), 92: 'Vocal tone lends colour and expression to the words, but it can do no more, and it fails in artistry if it obscures intelligibility.' Ranalow's own practice demonstrated 'how greatly clear pronunciation helps towards variety and *appropriate* tone-colour' ('Lancelot', *Referee* 7.10.17, 3).
172. Beecham, *A Mingled Chime*, p. 161. Cf. *Era* 10.7.18, 11: 'practically every word [of *Seraglio*] could be heard all over the house, and consequently the interest of the audience was held throughout.'
173. *Monthly Musical Record* 1.17, 2.

174. *Era* 23.2.16, 17. Lawrence Tibbett, *The Glory Road* (1933), in *Lawrence Tibbett: Singing Actor*, ed. Andrew Farkas (Portland, Oregon: Amadeus, 1989), p. 62, reasonably maintains 'that if an opera is vulgar in English it is vulgar in Italian'.
175. *Athenæum* 2.16, 95. Cf. *Stage* 18.3.15, 20, where a critic at the Shaftesbury *Butterfly* was shocked to hear Sharpless respond to Butterfly's words about '"when the robins nest again", that he is not up in ornithology'. It is concluded that 'operatic books ... generally shine least when they are most understood'.
176. Baughan, 'British Humour and Opera', *Fortnightly Review* 99 (January 1916), 551–8 (557).
177. *'Era' Annual 1917*, p. 41.
178. *Graphic* 22.1.16, 138.
179. *Athenæum* 1.16, 46.
180. Baughan, 'British Humour and Opera', p. 555; Beecham, *A Mingled Chime*, p. 148.
181. Baughan, 'British Humour and Opera', p. 552; *Graphic* 5.2.16, 208.
182. Ethel Smyth, *A Final Burning of Boats* (Longmans, Green, 1928), p. 32.
183. *Era* 17.7.18, 11.
184. *Graphic* 17.2.17, 206; *The Times* 26.12.16, 9.
185. *Era* 22.11.16, 1; *Era* 26.12.16, 9.
186. *Observer* 24.6.17, 10. He challenged Clutsam to discover one new English opera, apart from this mythical quartet, worthy of Drury Lane and he would produce it.
187. *Era* 10.4.18, 11.
188. Beecham, *A Mingled Chime*, p. 61.
189. Searle, *Era* 9.5.17, 5; *Era* 13.6.17, 7.
190. *The Times* 8.10.14, 7.
191. Klein, *Musicians and Mummers*, p. 271.
192. *Era* 18.10.16, 1.
193. *The Times* 16.10.16, 11.
194. Searle, *Era* 6.3.18, 1.
195. *Era* 12.6.18, 5; *Era* 18.10.16, 1.
196. *Era* 20.6.17, 10; *Stage* 4.10.17, 16. The excellent Turner production of 1918 effectively rendered this collapse by the sudden darkening of the stage followed by a revelation of the ruined building (*Era* 20.2.18, 6).
197. *Era* 22.11.16, 8. 'Lancelot' (*Referee* 7.10.17, 3), appreciative of her innovations, remarked that she was the first Marguerite he had ever seen 'who showed the slightest idea of how to spin'.
198. *Sunday Times* 7.10.15, 4.
199. *Athenæum* 16.10.15, 267.

200. Quoted from Radford LP sleeve-note (HMV HLM7054).
201. *Era* 4.7.17, 11; *Era* 10.10.17, 1; *Era* 13.3.18, 1.
202. *Era* 4.7.17, 11; *Era* 13.3.18, 1.
203. *Era* 18.10.16, 1.
204. *Era* 24.1.17, 1.
205. Lockhart, 'Miriam Licette', pp. 856–7.
206. *Star* 22.1.17, 2.
207. *The Times* 3.10.17, 8.
208. *Era* 6.6.17, 9; *Athenæum* 2.17, 91.
209. *Era* 10.10.17, 1.
210. *Referee* 28.2.17, 5.
211. *Era* 12.6.18, 5; *Music of All Nations* 3, 85.
212. *Era* 20.3.18, 1.
213. *Era* 1.12.15, 11; *The Times* 28.12.15, 10.
214. *Era* 3.10.17, 7.
215. Searle, *Era* 13.6.17, 7.
216. *Era* 3.10.17, 1.
217. Sydney Grew, *Favourite Musical Performers* (Edinburgh/London: Foulis, 1923), p. 114; 'Lancelot', *Referee* 17.12.16, 5; Neville Cardus, *Second Innings* (Collins, 1950), p. 141.
218. Cf. Searle, *'Era' Annual 1917*, p. 41: 'The work of the secondary singers and of the chorus was from the first rightly considered as important a part of the whole as that of the principals', the choralists apt to excel even 'the wonderful Russians of the Drury Lane seasons'.
219. Searle, *Era* 10.10.17, 1.
220. Searle, *Era* 27.6.17, 1; *Era* 26.6.18, 1. Searle (*Era* 13.6.17, 7) noted that Ferrando's narration in *Trovatore* is rarely so 'dramatically given' as by Richardson.
221. *Era* 26.7.16, 9; *Era* 27.6.17, 1.
222. *Era* 27.10.15, 13.
223. *Era* 12.7.16, 9.
224. Searle, *Era* 10.10.17, 1.
225. *The Times* 26.6.17, 9.
226. *Era* 27.6.17, 1; *Era* 20.3.18, 1; *Musical Opinion* 10.20, 52.
227. Searle, *Era* 6.6.17, 1.
228. *Era* 12.1.16, 13; *Era* 17.10.17, 12; *The Times* 11.6.17, 11.
229. *Manchester Guardian* 14.5.17, 6; Shaw, *Shaw's Music*, vol. III, p. 689.
230. Searle, *Era* 17.10.17, 12.
231. *The Times* 11.6.17, 11.
232. Searle, *Era* 17.10.17, 12; *Era* 19.6.18, 11; *The Times* 18.10.17, 16. Edwards seems to have had the same bad luck with his Amonasro, being replaced

by Parker, who 'adopted a much simpler coiffure' (Edwards's was fearsomely barbaric, and his playing 'alert and uncompromising as a panther'), and singing 'also simpler, occasionally to roughness' ('Lancelot', *Referee* 26.11.16, 5; *Referee* 3.12.16, 5).

233. Shaw, *Shaw's Music*, vol. III, p. 694.
234. *Musical Herald* 8.17, 232.
235. Searle, *Era* 13.6.17, 7. On one occasion Elsa Stralia took over from Buckman, her only operatic appearance in wartime London: 'Except that the significance of the words was easily grasped owing to the clear enunciation of the singers, the rendering reminded me of brilliant nights at Covent Garden' ('Lancelot', *Referee* 30.9.17, 3).
236. Searle, *Era* 6.3.18, 1; *The Times* 4.3.18, 10.
237. Searle, *Era* 13.6.17, 7.
238. *Era* 28.11.17, 8.
239. Searle, *Era* 6.6.17, 1.
240. At Birmingham the previous month his *Esultate* had thrilled Ernest Newman (J. Fryer and J. B. Richards, 'Frank Mullings', *Record Collector* 7 (1952), 5–16 (p. 11)).
241. Beecham, *A Mingled Chime*, p. 152.
242. Searle, *Era* 6.6.17, 1; *Musical Times* 7.17, 325.
243. Notcutt, *Musical Times* 4.17, 162.
244. *Sunday Times* 9.6.18, 4; *Era* 5.6.18, 11.
245. Beecham, *A Mingled Chime*, p. 153.
246. *Verdi: The Man in His Letters*, ed. F. Werfel and Paul Stefan, tr. Edward Downes (New York: Vienna House, 1973), p. 423.
247. *Era* 21.6.16, 9.
248. *Athenæum* 6.16, 300; *Era* 21.6.16, 9; *Era* 6.6.17, 1.
249. *Musical Times* 2.15, 107. However, Boughton's experiments show in *The Birth of Arthur* (1908–9; premièred 1920); Michael Hurd (*Rutland Boughton and the Glastonbury Festivals* (Oxford: Clarendon, 1993), p. 122), describes the chorus functioning 'as singers, as dancers, and as scenery'. The 'rhythmic evolutions', enhanced by red, blue and yellow lights, smack more of Loïe Fuller than the Russian opera.
250. *The Times* 28.6.16, 11.
251. *Era* 5.7.16, 9.
252. Searle, *Era* 20.3.18, 1.
253. *The Times* 4.6.17, 11.
254. *Stage* 4.10.17, 16.
255. Abbreviated version at Queen's Hall (11.12.16), and complete at Manchester's Free Trade Hall (25.1.17) with Nevada, Blamey and Juliette Autran. Early on Mme Ratmirova, of the Imperial Opera, Petrograd, had

chosen the opera to raise money at the Playhouse for the Grand Duke Michael's front-line comforts fund (*The Times* 4.2.15, 5).

256. Searle, *Era* 26.9.17, 1; *Era* 27.3.18, 1.
257. *Athenæum* 11.9.15, 181.
258. *Era* 27.3.18, 1.
259. *The Times* 24.9.17, 11.
260. Searle, *Era* 31.10.17, 1. Chamier (*Percy Pitt*, p. 190) claims that, entrusted with the 1918 production of *The Golden Cockerel*, Astafieva neglected the non-dancing parts and Beecham himself had to save the situation at the last minute; but she was reported to have been taken on specifically for the ballet sections in that and other works, including *Tannhäuser* (*Era* 12.6.18, 21).
261. *Sunday Times* 3.11.18, 4.
262. Stephen Williams, *In the Opera House* (Hutchinson, 1952), p. 168, considered Richardson (1890–1942) the best he had ever seen in the rôle, his voice having 'a slight roughness, a kind of "burr" on the surface which made the tone all the more ravishing when it rose above the stave or melted to a delicious *pianissimo*'.
263. *Era* 24.7.18, 11.
264. *Era* 7.11.17, 10. Germany had brought culture into the arena when Italy entered the war: the Kaiser's ban on music by any living Italian at the royal theatres being slavishly followed at the other German opera houses (*The Times* 2.6.15, 6).
265. He added that, apart from two members of the orchestra, 'a brave little Belgian and a sturdy Russian', every member of his company was British (*Era* 5.5.15, 8; *Era* 26.8.14, 9). Both *Tannhäuser* and *Lohengrin* were given, Boland impressing in both title-rôles by the 'freedom and passion' of his singing (Duncan, *Musical Standard* 8.5.15, 358; *Musical Standard* 15.5.15, 379. Turner, 'Recollections', p. 243, recalled him as 'a very fine Wagnerian tenor'.
266. *Era* 19.5.15, 8.
267. *Era* 14.11.17, 10.
268. *Era* 24.2.15, 10; *Era* 19.5.15, 8.
269. *Sunday Times* 24.3.18, 4.
270. *Era* 14.3.17, 8; *Era* 21.3.17, 8.
271. *Sunday Times* 24.3.18, 4.
272. Searle, *Era* 27.3.18, 1.
273. *Era* 12.6.18, 5.
274. Searle, *Era* 12.6.18, 5.
275. *Sunday Times* 16.6.18, 2.
276. *Era* 19.6.18, 11.

277. Shaw, *Shaw's Music,* vol. III, p. 712. Hurst (*Golden Age,* p. 79) refers to 'the majestic breadth and sweep of her delivery', and her way of imparting unusual 'sweetness' to the big Wagnerian rôles.
278. *Era* 19.6.18, 11; Neville Cardus, *Talking of Music* (Collins, 1957), p. 172. He had shone when the Quinlan company gave Birmingham its first *Ring* in 1913 (Phyllis Philip Rodway and Lois Rodway Slingsby, *Philip Rodway and a Tale of Two Theatres* (Birmingham: Cornish, 1934), p. 177).
279. Lockhart, 'Miriam Licette', p. 857.
280. *Daily Sketch* 29.7.18, 7.
281. *Era* 31.5.16, 13; *Athenæum* 7.16, 349.
282. Fryer and Richards, 'Frank Mullings', p. 7. However, Boland, singing Tristan for O'Mara, satisfied Sam Langford's exacting standards (*Manchester Guardian* 12.5.17, 8).
283. Reid, *Thomas Beecham,* p. 173.
284. *Athenæum* 7.16, 349; *The Times* 16.6.16, 11; *The Times* 17.6.16, 9.
285. *The Times* 19.10.16, 7.
286. *Era* 21.6.16, 9; *The Times* 16.6.16, 11. Beecham's conducting seems to have varied extremely with mood. On another occasion Langford (*Manchester Guardian* 22.5.16, 10) was impressed that Beecham never allowed 'even the orchestral part of "Tristan" to overwhelm the singers'. Whereas the *Daily Telegraph* 17.4.16, 6, noted at the first *Magic Flute* that Beecham conducted with 'almost more than his usual sympathy for the singers', Ethel Smyth, *Beecham and Pharaoh* (Chapman & Hall, 1935), p. 38, finding him unwilling 'to give singers time to enunciate and drive home their words', decided 'that *quâ* musical instrument he really disliked the *genus* singer'. Cf. Eugene Goossens, *Overture and Beginners* (Methuen, 1951), p. 79, of a 1910 performance of *Elektra*: 'Beecham whipped his hundred players into a lather of such excitement that we were often deafened and lost track of the vocal line quite frequently.'
287. *Musical Standard* 12.8.16, 118; *Musical Opinion* 6.20, 715.
288. *Era* 25.10.16, 13.
289. *The Times* 19.10.16, 7.
290. Langford, *Manchester Guardian* 22.5.16, 10.
291. Cardus, *Second Innings,* pp. 138–9.
292. *Musical Herald* 8.17, 232.
293. George du Maurier, *Trilby* (Osgood, McIlvaine), 1895, p. 310.
294. Beecham, *A Mingled Chime,* p. 62.
295. Wood, *My Life of Music,* p. 182.
296. Turner, 'Recollections', p. 243.
297. Edward Davies sang 'Salut demeure' at a La Scala audition when, following 'the custom of English-speaking tenors, he sang the high C

falsetto. "Haven't you got a top doh?" exclaimed the judges. "Yes, and more if you want it," replied Mr. Davies' (*Era* 31.7.18, 8).

298. *Era* 8.5.18, 13; *Era* 22.5.18, 10.
299. Shaw, *Shaw's Music,* vol. III, p. 699.
300. *Era* 6.3.18, 1.
301. Shaw, *Shaw's Music,* vol. III, pp. 700–1.
302. *Era* 29.5.18, 13.
303. Shaw, *Shaw's Music,* vol. III, p. 711.
304. Julius Kapp (ed.), *Richard Wagners Gesammelte Schriften* (Leipzig: Hesse & Becker, 1918), VII, p.75.
305. Erwin Stein, 'Mahler and the Vienna Opera', in H. Rosenthal (ed.), *The Opera Bedside Book* (Gollancz, 1965), p. 305.
306. Beecham, *A Mingled Chime,* p. 126.
307. Maggie Teyte, *Star on the Door* (Pitman, 1958), p. 108.
308. Wood, *My Life of Music,* p. 141.
309. *Era* 8.8.17, 11.
310. Browne, *New Statesman* 30.5.14, 245.
311. Walter Legge, 'Sir Thomas, Part 3', *Opera* 30 (1979), 650–8 (654).
312. Shaw, *Shaw's Music* vol. III, p. 701.
313. Beecham, *A Mingled Chime,* p. 156; *Daily Telegraph* 17.4.16, 6.
314. Browne, *New Statesman* 30.5.14, 245.
315. *The Times* 15.6.16, 11.
316. *Era* 12.6.18, 5.
317. Grew, *Favourite,* p. 126.
318. *The Times* 17.4.16, 11.
319. 'Lancelot', *Referee* 18.6.16, 8.
320. *The Times* 15.6.16, 11; *Era* 19.4.16, 9; *Era* 12.6.18, 5.
321. Lockhart, 'Miriam Licette', p. 856.
322. Langford, *Manchester Guardian* 25.5.16, 10.
323. *Era* 26.7.16, 8.
324. *Sunday Times* 12.8.15, 15.
325. *Era* 14.6.16, 8.
326. *Musical News,* 5.7.16, 34. 'Lancelot', *Referee* 30.4.16, 8, noting that *Lucia,* too, would be given in Italian, made the same point about this 'backsliding to pre-War anomalies'. However, Newman's *New Witness* review of the Manchester *Boris* clarifies his position: 'I am afraid *Boris Godounov* will never disclose its full secret to the British public until it is sung in English' (Ernest Newman, *Testament of Music: Essays and Papers,* ed. Herbert Van Thal (Putnam, 1962), p. 183).
327. *Era* 9.8.16, 11.
328. Beecham, *A Mingled Chime,* p. 143.

329. *Era* 25.7.17, 8; *Daily Sketch* 29.7.18, 7. Already by October 1916, Arnold Bennett noticed at *Seraglio* 'too-well dressed women in boxes, attended by their courts' (*Journals 1896–1928*, ed. Newman Flower (Cassell, 1932–3), vol. II, p. 175).
330. *Music Student* 4.15, 158.
331. *Era* 9.5.17, 9. Arthur Winckworth, 'The Fascination of Opera', *Music Masterpieces* 3 (12 November 1925), 96, recalls how, during his wartime days with Carl Rosa, 'men and women of the working classes paid for admission to the highest priced seats rather than be disappointed, and even if those were not available they would cheerfully stand for hours'. But Carl Rosa maintained its modest pre-war prices throughout the war, only contemplating an increase in the very last weeks (*Era* 9.10.18, 9).
332. *Graphic* 2.3.18, 282.
333. *Era* 8.5.18, 8.
334. Beecham, *A Mingled Chime*, p. 155. *Era* 10.7.18, 11, notes of a *Seraglio* first night that Drury Lane was 'not quite as full as it might have been'.
335. *Era* agrees that 'the new dialogue ... livened up the book. Even phrases like "Mind the step," "Wait and see" – which brought a roar of laughter – were introduced. But these colloquialisms only emphasised the incongruity of spoken dialogue in "grand" opera.' 'Wait and see' had been Asquith's evasion as information was impatiently sought concerning Lloyd George's controversial budget of 1910. But it came back to haunt him during the war.
336. *Era* 14.11.17, 14; *Era* 17.7.18, 11; *The Times* 4.7.18, 3.
337. *Era* 26.7.16, 8; *The Times* 25.7.16, 9.
338. *The Times* 4.7.18, 3.
339. C. S. Lewis, *English Literature in the Sixteenth Century* (Oxford: Clarendon Press, rept. 1962), p. 327.
340. Arnold Bennett, *Journals 1896–1928*, vol. II, p. 203.
341. *Era* 11.7.17, 8.
342. Stein, 'Mahler', p. 308.
343. Cardus, *Autobiography*, pp. 236, 246.
344. Bennett, *Journals*, vol. II, p. 203.
345. Shaw, *Shaw's Music*, vol. III, pp. 696–704. Shaw's cavalier approach to theatre-going had become habitual; he announces brazenly of *Valkyrie*: 'Fricka I did not hear, because I dined, Bayreuth fashion, between the first and second acts' (p. 712).
346. Reid, *Thomas Beecham*, p. 174.
347. *Era* 6.3.18, 1; *Era* 18.7.17, 1.
348. Beecham, *A Mingled Chime*, p. 160.
349. Teyte, *Star on the Door*, p. 39.

350. Searle, *Era* 19.7.17, 1; *Era* 6.3.18, 1.
351. Lockhart, 'Miriam Licette', p. 857.
352. *Stage* 27.9.17, 16.
353. *Era* 18.7.17, 1; *Musical Times* 8.17, 175.
354. Cardus, *Autobiography*, p. 236.
355. Searle, *Era* 18.7.17, 1.
356. *Monthly Musical Record* 8.17, 175; Shaw, *Shaw's Music*, vol. III, p. 703.
357. *The Times* 4.3.18, 10.
358. *Guardian* 9.3.61, 9. Beecham was said to have 'a positive dislike to committees of more than one member, namely himself' (*Daily Telegraph* 3.6.16, 5).
359. Klein, *Thirty Years*, p. 460.
360. *Nation* 14.6.19, 320.
361. *Daily Express* 26.11.17, 3.
362. For opera 'On the Halls', see Powell Lloyd, *Opera* 20 (1959), 21–7. The *Walpurgisnacht* scene from Beecham's *Faust* migrated to the Palladium (*Era* 5.12.17, 1).
363. *Era* 16.5.17, 14.
364. *Era* 23.5.17, 13.
365. Cardus, *Autobiography*, pp. 247–8.
366. *Era* 28.8.18, 8; *Era* 11.9.18, 8.
367. *Observer* 15.2.70, 25.

8

Conclusion

It is both neat and fitting that this examination of the wartime stage should begin and end with musical theatre. Opera in Britain seemed at last to be moving towards that place in the popular estimation which it had long enjoyed in Italy and Germany, while revue provided the *entrée* for a good deal of advanced continental theory which had hitherto failed to penetrate the commercial theatre. Not the least important aspect of this involved use of music-hall elements to revitalize mainstream theatre. This was the last great phase of music hall; and revue, held to pose as much of a threat to its continuance as the cinema, is perhaps better understood as one of its avatars. Revue undoubtedly cut into the single turn, but the effects were serious for the small-timers, not the stars, who moved freely between revue and variety stages.

For all the counter-effect of the emergent producer, stars were in the ascendancy. In the West End it was only Beecham who represented an alternative, demonstrating the virtues of ensemble at a time when the star system was seen as indispensable to profitability. He belonged to the old actor-manager tradition which was rapidly yielding to the big combines: a familiar pattern whereby ownership narrowed while the market was enjoying unprecedented expansion. Occupying the conductor's podium rather than centre stage only meant that he could reap the benefits of the old tradition while avoiding its more obvious defects. Thomas Burke was one of many to single out the Beecham operatic enterprise as proof that there remained a substantial audience for quality entertainment during the war.[1] Beecham, thought Cardus, 'identified himself in a shabby community of cash values with the great cause of cheering us all up'.[2] The difference between Beecham and West End commercial managers is clear, but Cardus is in danger of implying that the latter had no interest in cheering people up. It must be emphasized that his 'great cause' offered not only a quick route to profit but a neat distraction from any thought that a deeply flawed economic system had been responsible for the very miseries which had to be conjured away for a few hours. Moreover, if Beecham's style of conjuration separated him decisively from the world of the large combines, it was only while the family fortunes remained that he could continue in the old way. Herein lay the problem: Beecham's irascible idealism had not provided any long-term basis for the popular success of serious theatre, operatic or otherwise, in this country. This is one reason why the conception of wartime theatre as a temporary interruption gained considerable ground. With peace restored, Shaw, who before 1914 had looked the most interesting of British dramatists, could emerge from hibernation and present his masterpieces; and in the same way, the urban poetry of O'Casey in the 1920s could be seen as the natural outcome of Synge's pre-war work.

But more compelling arguments than Beecham affords may be mustered for the importance of the war period in the development of British theatre. Revue forms one, as an escape route from naturalism and the tyranny of text. Another is the emergence of the Old Vic as the one permanent London home of both Shakespeare production and opera for the duration. And this circumstance, unlike the Beecham legacy which unhappily petered out with the BNO, developed that Vic–Wells momentum which survives today at the Coliseum. The recent history of the Vic had been as a temperance music hall, and an important aspect of the new venture was that it continued as popular entertainment. Since all forms of entertainment belong to larger patterns of national life, it is important to emphasise the Vic's achievement against that other trajectory in wartime solace from tango craze to shimmy. This is not on any straightforward quality ground; rather that the latter too easily becomes a chilling metaphor for the sameness of outlook characterizing British foreign policy at both ends of the war: from moral posturing in August 1914 over poor little Belgium, to late 1918 proposals for military intervention in the Netherlands in the event of a left-wing electoral victory.[3]

Thus Carter's central claim, when writing *The New Spirit in the European Theatre*, that war had caused the stage to 'become less and less detached from life and of increased social value',[4] only begs the question. Certainly the theatre, not least the operatic stage with its disputes over the playing of German music, demonstrated that it is never 'above the battle'. As for its increased social value, there were many youngsters rotting in French soil who had been taught to thrill to war's panoply and glitter in the wartime theatre. Saturation propaganda customarily works through complicity, belief insinuating itself as a prerequisite for retaining a sense of ordered existence. So, despite a measure of soldier opposition to some forms of stage representation, merely seeing through the distortions of the stage, like those in the newspapers, guaranteed nothing. Not only was rejection a too unsettling alternative for many, but the very conditions of theatre, calling on a certain multi-consciousness, would have furthered acceptance. Besides, wartime theatre was often pretty exciting, inheriting those 'Three Rs' (Ragtime, Revue and Russian ballet) which Disher identified as revolutionizing London entertainment in the years just before the war.[5] By the Armistice, ragtime was already beginning to blur with jazz, and would soon succumb to it. But revue, a form denying form, perfectly caught the pulse of disturbed times. It was the supreme embodiment of the new, unashamed in its eager commercialism, displacing not only variety's single turns but also its rivals in the legitimate theatre. The way in which it dissolved and resolved into khaki realities reminds us that parade-ground drill is rehearsal for both parade and battle. And so to the Big Parade, or what Elsie Janis called *The Big Show*. She was an outstanding revue star, and with the arrival of American troops in France her big show was turning cartwheels on the backs of wagons within range of the heavy guns. Whether this was improvising on those London shows which she had graced or realizing their secret is hard to determine. For West End revue itself, as accompaniment to *Götterdämmerung*, might seem to have out-Dada'd Dada. Janis had her own distorted sense of this in finding post-war theatre intolerably dull.[6]

Notes

1. *Evening News* 26.10.17, 2
2. Neville Cardus, *Autobiography* (Collins, 1947), p. 248.
3. Public Records: FO 371/3254.
4. Huntly Carter, *The New Spirit in the European Theatre, 1914–1924* (Benn, 1925), p. 92.
5. M. Willson Disher, *The Personality of the Alhambra* (Birmingham: Odeon Theatres, 1937), p. 13.
6. Elsie Janis, *So Far, So Good!* (Long, 1933), p. 181.

Select Bibliography

Note: Works are London published except as noted.

Anonymous, *WAAC: The Woman's Story of the War*, Laurie, 1930.

Archer, William, 'The Music-Hall, Past and Future', *Fortnightly Review* 100 (July–December 1916), 253–62.

Asche, Oscar, *Oscar Asche: His Life*, Hurst & Blackett [1929].

Ashwell, Lena, *Modern Troubadours*, Gyldendal, 1922.

Asquith, Cynthia, *Diaries 1915–18*, Century, 1968.

Baker, Richard Anthony, *Marie Lloyd*, Robert Hale, 1990.

Beaumont, Cyril W., *The Diaghilev Ballet in London*, 1940, rept. Putnam, 1945.

Beecham, Thomas, *A Mingled Chime*, Hutchinson, 1944.

Bennett, Arnold, *Journals 1896–1928*, 3 vols, ed. Newman Flower, Cassell, 1932–3.

Benson, Constance, *Mainly Players: Bensonian Memories*, Thornton Butterworth, 1926.

Boardman, W. H., *Vaudeville Days*, ed. David Whitelaw, Jarrolds, 1935.

Bottome, Phyllis, *A Certain Star*, Hodder & Stoughton, 1917.

[Don Brophy and Harold Price], *A Rattle of Pebbles. The First World War Diaries of Two Canadian Airmen*, ed. Brereton Greenhous, Ottawa: Canadian Government Publishing Centre, 1987.

Caine, Hall, *The Prime Minister*, Heinemann [1919].

Cardus, Neville, *Autobiography*, Collins, 1947.

—— *Second Innings*, Collins, 1950.

Carter, Huntly, *The New Spirit in the European Theatre 1914–1924*, Benn, 1925.

Chamier, J. Daniel, *Percy Pitt of Covent Garden and the B.B.C.*, Arnold, 1938.

Coborn, Charles B., *'The Man Who Broke the Bank'*, Hutchinson, 1929.

Cochran, Charles, *The Secrets of a Showman*, 1925, rept. Heinemann, 1929.

—— *I Had Almost Forgotten*, Hutchinson, 1932.

—— *Cock-a-Doodle-Do*, Dent, 1941.
Courtneidge, Robert, *'I Was an Actor Once'*, Hutchinson [1930].
de Courville, Albert, *I Tell You*, Chapman & Hall, 1928.
Denham, Reginald, *Stars in My Hair*, Laurie, 1958.
Dent, Edward J., *A Theatre for Everybody*, Boardman, 1945.
Disher, M. Willson, *Clowns and Pantomimes*, Constable, 1925.
Ellis, Walter W., *A Little Bit of Fluff*, French, 1922.
'The Era' Annual, ed. Alfred Barnard, 'The Era' Office, 1917, 1918.
Ervine, St John, *The Theatre in My Time*, Rich & Cowan, 1933.
Esmond, H. V., *The Law Divine*, French, 1922.
Fergusson, Louis, *Old Time Music Hall Comedians*, p. p., 1949.
Finck, Herman, *My Melodious Memories*, Hutchinson, 1937.
Ford, T. Murray, *Memoirs of a Poor Devil*, Philpot, 1926.
Fryer, J. and J. B. Richards, 'Frank Mullings', *Record Collector* 7 (1952), 5–16.
Gay, Maisie, *Laughing through Life*, Hurst & Blackett, 1931.
Gollancz, Victor, *Journey Towards Music*, Gollancz, 1964.
Graves, Charles, *The Cochran Story*, Allen [1951].
Graves, Robert, *Good-bye to All That*, Cape, 1929.
Grew, Sydney, *Favourite Musical Performers*, Edinburgh/London: Foulis, 1923.
Harvey, John Martin, *The Autobiography*, Sampson Low, Marston [1933].
Hibbert, H. G., *A Playgoer's Memories*, Richards, 1920.
Hicks, Seymour, *Me and My Missus*, Cassell, 1939.
Hurst, P. G., *The Golden Age Recorded*, Lingfield, Surrey: Oakwood Press, 1963.
Isaac, Winifred F. E. C., *Ben Greet and the Old Vic*, p. p. [1964].
Jesse, F. Tennyson and H. M. Harwood, *Billeted*, French, 1920.
Kendall, Henry, *I Remember Romano's*, Macdonald, 1960.
Kerr, Fred, *Recollections of a Defective Memory*, Thornton Butterworth, 1930.
Klein, Hermann, *Thirty Years of Musical Life in London*, Heinemann, 1903.
—— *Musicians and Mummers*, Cassell, 1925.
Knoblock, Edward, *Round the Room*, Chapman & Hall, 1939.
Knowles, R. G., *A Modern Columbus*, Laurie [1916].
Lillie, Beatrice, *Every Other Inch a Lady*, 1972, rept. New York: Dell, 1974.
Loraine, Winifred, *Robert Loraine*, Collins, 1938.
Lupino, Stanley, *From the Stocks to the Stars*, Hutchinson, 1934.
MacCarthy, Desmond, *Drama*, Putnam, 1940.
Macqueen-Pope, W. J., *Gaiety: Theatre of Enchantment*, Allen, 1949.
—— *Ghosts and Greasepaint*, Hale, 1951.
Mair, G. H., 'The Music-Hall', *English Review* 9 (1911), 122–9.
Mayer, David, *Harlequin in His Element: The English Pantomime, 1806–1836*, Cambridge, Mass.: Harvard University Press, 1969.
Miller, Ruby, *Champagne from My Slipper*, Jenkins, 1962.

Mistinguett, *Mistinguett: Queen of the Paris Night*, trans. Lucienne Hill, Elek, 1954.

Nicoll, Allardyce, *English Drama 1900–1930*, Cambridge: Cambridge University Press, 1973.

Oughton, Ann, *Thanks for the Memory*, Edinburgh/Cambridge/Durham: Pentland Press, 1995.

Randall, Harry, *Harry Randall Old Time Comedian*, Sampson Low, Marston [1930].

Reid, Charles, *Thomas Beecham*, Gollancz, 1962.

Robey, George, *Looking Back on Life*, Constable, 1933.

Rodway, Phyllis Philip and Lois Rodway Slingsby, *Philip Rodway and a Tale of Two Theatres*, Birmingham: Cornish, 1934.

Rosenthal, Harold, *Two Centuries of Opera at Covent Garden*, Putnam, 1958.

Russell, Dave, *Popular Music in England, 1840–1914*, Manchester/New York: Manchester University Press, 2nd edn 1997.

Santley, Charles, *Student and Singer*, rept. Arnold, 1893.

Shaw, George Bernard, *The Bodley Head Bernard Shaw: Shaw's Music*, 3 vols, ed. Dan H. Laurence, The Bodley Head, 1981.

Short, Ernest and Arthur Compton-Rickett, *Ring Up the Curtain*, Jenkins, 1938.

'The Stage' Year Book, ed. Lionel Carson, 'The Stage' Offices, 1915, 1916, 1917, 1918, 1919.

Stein, Erwin, 'Mahler and the Vienna Opera', *The Opera Bedside Book*, ed. H. Rosenthal, Gollancz, 1965.

Stone, Christopher, *From Vimy Ridge to the Rhine: The Great War Letters*, ed. G. D. Sheffield and G. I. S. Inglis, Ramsbury, Wilts.: Crowood Press, 1989.

Teyte, Maggie, *Star on the Door*, Pitman, 1958.

Thorndike, Sybil and Russell Thorndike, *Lilian Baylis*, Chapman & Hall, 1938.

Tilley, Vesta, *Recollections*, Hutchinson, 1934.

Turner, Eva, 'Recollections of a Great Career', *Record Collector* 35 (1990), 243–9.

Vanbrugh, Irene, *To Tell My Story*, Hutchinson, 1948.

Webster, Margaret, *The Same Only Different*, Gollancz, 1969.

Wilson, A. E., *Christmas Pantomime*, Allen & Unwin, 1934.

Wilson, Keith, *Thomas Hardy on Stage*, Macmillan, 1995.

Wood, Henry, *My Life of Music*, 1938, rept. Gollancz, 1948.

Index